CRADLES OF EMINENCE

Cradles of Eminence

VICTOR GOERTZEL

and

MILDRED GEORGE GOERTZEL

LITTLE, BROWN AND COMPANY   •   BOSTON   •   TORONTO

LIBRARY OF CONGRESS CATALOG CARD NO. 62-13913

Second Printing

*Published simultaneously in Canada
by Little, Brown & Company (Canada) Limited*

PRINTED IN THE UNITED STATES OF AMERICA

To our sons, Ted, John and Penn

Foreword

> Sit down before fact as a little child, be
> prepared to give up every preconceived
> notion, follow humbly wherever and to what-
> ever abyss nature leads, or you shall learn
> nothing.
>   — T. H. Huxley

CURIOSITY about the training of that most valuable human
resource, the capable child, led us to attempt this survey of
the emotional and intellectual climate in which eminent people
of the twentieth century were reared. Some of these men have
been as eminently wicked as others have been productive of good.
Most of them, however, have devised new social groupings, set
people thinking in a different frame of reference or added to the
sum of human culture. We use the term "eminent" to describe
them because they became important enough to their contemporaries to have books written about them. This is the only basis on
which Hitler and Schweitzer, Dali and Steinmetz can be on the
same list. They are all eminent, in the dictionary sense of "standing high in comparison with others."

To know why people differ as well as why they have common
characteristics, it is necessary to have a large number of subjects
to examine. Do dictators have similar backgrounds? Where do
famous people come from — the country, a village, a city? Do
celebrities grow up in warm, permissive homes? Were they usually
happy as children? Were they usually healthy?

The list of individuals which we compiled (see page 301) may
very well be amusing to the critics and scholars of the year 2062.
Traditionally, the men of any given age have not been clever at
recognizing those of their own contemporaries whom future
scholars are going to value. This list of the eminent is, in a sense,

everybody's list. Into its compilation went the judgment and preferences of countless other persons: all the people who read, write and buy books; the critics, authors, editors, and publishers.

The research plan finally used for the selection of subjects was as follows: "Include each person who has at least two books about him in the biography section of the Montclair, New Jersey, Public Library if he was born in the United States and all persons who have at least one book about them if they were born outside the United States. Include only those who lived into the twentieth century and are described in a standard reference work."

This plan often frustrated us, as it must anyone who has strong likes and dislikes for the outstanding men and women of his times. Ralph Bunche is not included because there is no adult biography written about him. William Cody (Buffalo Bill) is included. Like Einstein, he has five books about him in the biography section of the Montclair Public Library. That is not the fault of the book buyer at the library. It represents the lack of biographical books about scientists in general and it also evidences a public interest in William Cody. Einstein, to be sure, has twenty-one non-biographical books about him in the same card file; Cody, none.

We have been invited on several occasions to speak about our research before neighborhood groups. Men, in general, have treated us well during the question period. They may like being told that there are many fathers who have failed to achieve their own goals but whose sons have not seemingly been harmed thereby. The mothers in our audiences enjoy hearing about the troubles of the O'Neills and the Wolfes and the Chekhovs, then rebel against our recital of woeful facts and assume falsely that we advocate mistreatment of children as a way of stimulating creativity. All we can then do is to reiterate that we are reporting a survey and that we have no intention of becoming ogres at home on the off chance that one of our own three sons may become a playwright or a novelist. It may be currently possible to be both creative and comfortable. We suspect it isn't, but our suspicions are not scientific data. We emphasize that we had nothing to do with the child-rearing practices of parents who lived decades ago.

They did it, *we* didn't. Mothers are more likely than fathers are to apply every statement made by a speaker to their own children regardless of its relevance.

We do not consider all the persons we write about equally eminent and rely on the weight of the published material about the person to decide that for us. Time alone can sort out the truly great, and still people will disagree. This is not a matter of great concern to us. Some of the least well-known people write with the most insight about what went on in their homes and give the best clues as to the things parents and teachers can do to teach and nurture all bright, curious children, regardless of talent. The people who had the most biographical books about them catalogued in the Montclair Public Library are: Franklin D. Roosevelt, 28 books; Mahatma Gandhi, 21; Sir Winston Churchill, 20; Albert Schweitzer, 17; Theodore Roosevelt, 17. The top five in the circulating department of the New York Public Library at Forty-second Street are: Churchill, 27; Franklin D. Roosevelt, 26; Gandhi, 20; Schweitzer, 16; Theodore Roosevelt, 16. Within limitations, most sizable libraries have much the same biographical collections.

We used the Montclair Public Library because it was the nearest adequate library and has a fine collection of thousands of biographies on open shelves. It was, incidentally, the first library in the country to use an IBM system to record its circulation. Montclair is a prosperous suburban residential town of 40,000 with a large percentage of professional and business people.

Once a person was included by virtue of the card catalogue in Montclair, we were free to read about him from books found anywhere. We have used the New York Public Library, the Newark Public Library, the Indianapolis State Public Library, the Toledo Public Library, California public libraries in Santa Barbara, Ventura and Los Angeles, our personal library and our friends' libraries, as well as bookstores and commercial circulating libraries. We usually used *Books in Print* to find out what material is available and also to be sure that no really significant person had been omitted.

Sometimes we regret not extending our coverage to Americans

with only one biography, but a list of "one-book" American celebrities would include dozens of minor politicians, athletes and actors. Biographies of the foreign-born which reach us are less likely to have only topical interest. Therefore, we required only one volume for such individuals. We did, however, exclude persons whose biographies are published because of their inherited positions: kings, queens, princes, and so forth.

"Do you think these famous people are like the children who are called 'gifted' today because they test very high on intelligence tests?" is a question often asked us.

Many of the children of the past who were to become eminent, like the intellectually gifted children of today, tended to possess superior ability in reasoning and in recognizing relationships. They showed intellectual curiosity, had a wide range of interests, did effective work independently. They showed their greatest superiority in reading ability; many read at the age of four. Almost all were early readers of good books. They were original thinkers and had scant patience with drill and routine. They were likely to be rejected by their playmates and had parents who valued learning. The majority of them came from middle-class business and professional homes. Their brothers and sisters were capable. Most of those children who became eminent would probably have tested high on today's intelligence tests.

Admittedly, there are those who question the reliability of the autobiography or biography as a source. We cannot be sure that the authors we have used are telling the truth; we are only reporting what they say. To check the reliability of what a person says about himself or of what his biographer says of him is not part of our self-set task. We can only hope to be accurate in reporting what they say and sensitive in the selection of material chosen to report. But it is not so easy to be untruthful or misleading as may be believed.

Henry M. Stanley, the man who found Livingstone, tried to conceal both his nationality and the fact that he was illegitimate. His true identity became known and the consequences were disastrous for him. He told the true story of his life in his autobiography in his old age. So far as we know, Stanley is the only one of our subjects who ever attempted a major deception. Misrepresentations when they occur are more often the result of omission than of commission.

In pre-Freudian days many felt free to make statements comparable to the one Carnegie made about his mother: "After my father's death she was all my own." Then came a period when stories which might be subject to psychoanalytic interpretation were omitted by wary writers who did not wish to seem naïve or to betray fundamental weaknesses. We are now in an era of self-conscious revelations made in full awareness of the significance in Freudian terms of the behavior described. It is in omission and selectivity that we get the half-truth, which is different from untruth. By taking statements as fact from many sources we hope to approximate reality. When Thomas Mann says, "I loathed school," we record him as one who disliked school, relying on forthright statements such as these.

There is a tendency for biographers to pass on the cliché type of observation, with scant reference to the homely but candid statements by the subject and his relatives. In family accounts the mothers of Clemens, Freud and Churchill emerge with personalities more unconventional and dynamic than the versions of them in biographies by writers who pass on accepted stereotyped images or those which support a preconceived theory of personality development.

When we can, we report from the subject's autobiography, or from accounts written by family members, neighbors or close personal friends, corroborated by detailed descriptions of events and behavior, expressed in simple, colloquial terms.

In the 1950's we wrote a chapter on "The Gifted Child" for a college textbook, *The Clinical Psychology of Exceptional Children*, edited by the late Professor C. M. Louttit. Since that time we have had a heightened interest in the gifted children selected by Lewis M. Terman in the 1920's on the basis of tests of teacher-nominated California school children; the 1500 with intelligence quotients of 140 or over have been studied since that time. These studies appear in the series *Genetic Studies of Genius*; the fifth volume of the series, *The Gifted Group at Mid-Life*, published in 1959, presents these individuals as comfortable, solvent, conservative, well-functioning citizens. Their principal achievements have been in science. Three men have been elected to the National Academy of Sciences. There has been, however, a lack of outstanding accomplishment in esthetic fields.

We have ourselves seen a number of intellectually gifted youngsters grow up and fit themselves competently into suitable and remunerative positions which offer them little intellectual stimulation or deep satisfaction. These same children had financial and emotional security in their childhood homes and received the best of schooling. When we turn to biographies and autobiographies, we find exciting, experimental, creative men and women who in their childhood experienced trauma, deprivations, frustrations and conflicts of the kind commonly thought to predispose one to mental illness or delinquency.

The inexplicable difference between the bright child in the classroom who becomes the competent, unimaginative adult and the academically unsuccessful child who later makes his impact felt on a whole generation continues to challenge our attention with increasing force and persistence.

We thought of studying the life histories of men and women who were more creative than the Terman group. We sought for a group who were more deeply involved in politics or social reform, more likely to be musical or artistic or literary and/or to challenge the usual in our culture. If there are Edisons and Einsteins and Thomas Manns among the younger generation, we want to anticipate their coming and to help accelerate their progress.

Since 1957 we have had occasional reading sprees in the biography section of the library and used the resultant data in lecture rooms where, ironically, graduate students in education were more vulnerable than PTA audiences to the following hoax: We asked several groups to listen to these descriptions of children and to predict the children's future development. In five years, we asked, would they be functioning as gifted, average-normal, psychotic, neurotic, delinquent or mentally deficient persons?

Case 1. Girl, age sixteen, orphaned, willed to custody of grandmother by mother, who was separated from alcoholic husband, now deceased. Mother rejected the homely child, who has been proven to lie and to steal sweets. Swallowed penny to attract attention at five. Father was fond of child. Child lived in fantasy as the mistress of father's household for years. Four young uncles and aunts in household cannot be managed by the grandmother, who is widowed. Young uncle drinks; has left home without telling the grandmother his destination. Aunt, emotional over love affair, locks self in room. Grandmother resolves to be more strict with granddaughter since she fears she has failed with own children. Dresses granddaughter oddly. Refused to let her have playmates, put her in braces to keep back straight. Did not send her to grade school. Aunt on paternal side of family crippled; uncle asthmatic.

Case 2. Boy, senior year secondary school, has obtained certificate from physician stating that nervous breakdown makes it necessary for him to leave school for six months. Boy not a good all-around student; has no friends — teachers find him a problem — spoke late — father ashamed of son's lack of athletic ability — poor adjustment to school. Boy has odd mannerisms, makes up own religion, chants hymns to himself — parents regard him as "different."

Case 3. Boy, age six; head large at birth. Thought to have had brain fever. Three siblings died before his birth. Mother does not agree with relatives and neighbors that child is probably abnormal. Child sent to school — diagnosed as mentally ill by teacher. Mother is angry — withdraws child from school, says she will teach him herself.

When Eleanor Roosevelt, Albert Einstein, and Thomas Edison had been categorized by our audience as delinquent, mentally ill and retarded, respectively, we then spoke of the danger of making snap decisions on superficial, incomplete evidence and emphasized the need for objective examination and adequate case study in making proper judgments.

The audience in turn frequently retaliated by making us confess that we could not account for the high achievement and resilience of these children from troubled homes.

The completion of the survey and the writing of this book were interrupted by other concerns and duties. In the normal course of things, professional research in the Goertzel family is confined to the rehabilitation of mental patients. An opportunity to present a preliminary paper at the annual meeting of the National Association for Gifted Children provided an outlet for our extracurricular interest in the emotional and intellectual climate in the home which produces eminence. The motivation was our own unsatisfied curiosity — and an audience.

Leonard Buder, education writer for the New York *Times*, reported these preliminary findings. The quick public response at home and even abroad persuaded us that there were many other persons who shared our curiosity about the child-rearing practices of parents whose children became famous, so we set to work to complete the survey and to write this book.

We deliberately chose to make this a homework assignment. We wanted to read for several weeks without choosing the specific items to be looked for. We decided that at least one person should read all the material about each of our subjects to get the full flavor of the emotional and intellectual climate in the homes. It was not, for example, until several hundred books had been read that the impact of the recurrent father-failures made itself felt. This item, we feel, would have not been noticed had the task of reading been delegated to a number of readers. This extracurricular, self-initiated project has been in a very real way a labor of love, and a source of real enjoyment.

Consequently the only persons hitherto admitted to the close, two-year closed relationship between us and the Four Hundred have been our patient, prescient editor at Little, Brown, Alan D. Williams, and Anita Kramer, a personal friend, who has taken time from her own family duties to volunteer as typist and research assistant.

In the process of satisfying our curiosity we have found a few answers and raised a whole new series of uncomfortable queries.

Contents

Contents

CRADLES OF EMINENCE

[I]

Homes Which Respected Learning
and Achievement

Einstein continued to work hard at his
physics until the end. The curious thing was,
he worked in complete disagreement with
almost all of his contemporaries.
— C. P. SNOW, *New Statesman*,
March 26, 1960

A STRONG DRIVE toward intellectual or creative achievement is
present in one or both parents of almost all of the four
hundred men and women of the twentieth century who are under
investigation here. The parents of these celebrities are curious,
experimental, restless, seeking. They are physically driving, intellectually striving, they respect learning, love truth and sometimes
beauty.

There is no geographical center for giftedness, no racial or national or cultural monopoly. To find these families we must seek
out the farms, villages, and small towns where most of them live.
They come from the North, South, Midwest, East and West in
the U.S.A. — from Blue Hill, Maine; Diamond Grove, Missouri;
Elwood, Indiana; Fresno, California. They come from places like
Dean's Marsh, Australia; Graves County, Kentucky; from Mün-
chenbuchsee in Switzerland; Oologah, Indian Territory, U.S.A.;
from Pokrovskoye, Siberia; Nagyszentmiklós, Translyvania;
Zapotlán, Mexico; Tienghua, China; Gorcum, Holland; and
Nkroful, Africa — from every continent on the globe. The minority

3

come from the metropolitan centers, and many of the city-dwellers have to be sought in the green fringes at the outskirts. The common ground for these scattered families is the driving need to be doing something, learning something, changing something, or going somewhere to better themselves.

This respect for learning is not to be confused with a love for the classroom. By conventional standards the attitude of the family toward formal schooling is often careless or negative. A few boys and girls never went to school at all. Parents are prone to withdraw the children from school, to teach them themselves, to take them on trips, or to let them go to work. Thomas Edison and Guglielmo Marconi were home-taught boys. Wilbur and Orville Wright tinkered and traded, and never went to college.

The scientist, the doctor, the teacher, the lawyer — all who perform specialized services and must be licensed, do manage to reach the good colleges and are usually happy there, but not without having given their parents many anxious hours.

The parents try hard to make the most of the children they know are capable. Harvey Cushing, eminent brain surgeon, was a very poor speller in his youth — also as an adult, but then it did not matter. His letters home from Yale and Harvard reveal such boners as: *priviledge, definate, sacarafice, pharsical, cronicling,* and *amatures.* When he was in grammar school, his mother, Betsey Maria Williams Cushing, who was never one to let time hang on her hands, drove this youngest of her ten children back to school after his noonday lunch. During the half hour in which the horse ambled and Harvey chafed to play ball, she taught him spelling. When he was in high school, she helped him with his Latin and Greek. This was no more than she had done for her older children or for the half-brothers and sisters she helped to rear — or for anyone else who needed her for any reason whatsoever. When her husband, Dr. Henry Kirke Cushing, told her that he had brought home an aged woman for her to care for, an abandoned woman without any arms, she was immediately sympathetic and rushed out to welcome — a plaster cast of the Venus de Milo her husband had purchased as a household decoration.

Her recreation was to read from a propped-up book while she knitted useful garments for her family. Her son says of her, "Her day was planned to get the most out of it, and often, singing at her tasks, she went at them from early till late with untiring enthusiasm."[1] These are the women who rock the cradles of eminence.

When communication and understanding are good between an adult and a promising child, the relationship is rewarding for both. Mothers achieve this happy state more easily than do the fathers, who are sometimes carried away by overenthusiasm and a desire to be experimental when they have such receptive students right at hand.

William and Henry James and their brothers and sister were always in and out of schools, always traveling here and there with their father, a wealthy Swedenborgian of cosmopolitan interests. His eagerness to have the children know many cultures and countries well had varying consequences — not the least of which were two eminent sons.

Norbert Wiener, mathematician, son of Leo Wiener, professor of Slavic languages at Harvard, was put through a grueling course of study by a father who professed to believe that each pupil is capable of learning more than he is ever taught, and that it is the skill of the teacher alone which determines what is to be learned by the pupil. No boy was ever so rigorously tutored by a father as was Norbert Wiener, but even he cannot bring himself to say that he would like to have had it be otherwise. The advantages of not being bored made up for the disadvantages of being driven.

Woodrow Wilson did not learn his letters until he was nine, or learn to read until he was eleven, because his father read to him. He could not wait for Woodrow to learn to read the books he himself enjoyed and wanted his son to enjoy. The brilliant and verbal minister kept the boy home, read to him, explained the meaning of what he read, then asked for Woodrow's reaction to the ideas of the book.

Another experimental parent was the California rancher and lawyer George Patton III, who believed that ontogeny recapitulates phylogeny, that each boy lives out the history of the human race and must start life as a savage enjoying fire, water, earth, the simple speech rhythms of the native chant and the nursery jingle. He did not believe in teaching children to read until they were adolescent and could read history books for themselves. George Patton III kept George Patton IV home on their isolated ranch and read to him. When father went to work, the mother and an aunt took over the storybook. They read nursery jingles, graduated him to stories of witches, to animals that speak, to goblins, to legends. When George Patton IV went away to boarding school at twelve to be tutored for West Point, he was an authority on epics, he could write script, but he could not read print. To say that he was unhappy at school is an understatement.

In homes which cradle eminence there are strong tendencies to build directly on personal strengths, talents, and aims rather than to assume that there is a large, specific body of knowledge that everyone should possess. A family, or some member of the family, is likely to take off wholeheartedly on a course of investigation or action which sets him aside from his contemporaries.

This nonconformity is not self-conscious or forced. It seems to happen because the individual is not able to do otherwise. When parents permit the child to be different from his playmates, or involve him in an unusual learning situation, they may be acting from what they feel is weakness rather than strength. They are often self-critical, and argue among themselves. They can become guilt-ridden and anxious. Relatives and neighbors contribute to parental ambivalence by being critical. There are letters from relatives who thought it odd that young Woodrow Wilson was so dull and backward, and expressed sorrow for his parents. The fathers and mothers in these Four Hundred homes are not prescient. The road to eminence is not paved with plaudits, or even scholarships. Boys and girls who are to become famous are not often "all-around," competent, conforming students. To parents who love good books and respect learning this is frequently frustrating. There is a personal involvement with ideas in these homes. There are few passive receptors of fact.

That this stress on learning is a part of the pattern of producing eminence is verified by a study done by the psychologist Anne Roe in which she reports, in part, the testing and interviewing of sixty-four outstanding physical, social, and biological scientists in the United States. Because of the very personal nature of these interviews, much of the pertinent data will not be made known to this generation. In the partial findings published, the names of the sixty-four persons are not revealed. Learning was also highly valued in these sixty-four middle-class, low-income, professional homes. Generally the fathers and mothers showed overprotection and also firm control. These boys also pursued their rather independent paths, and followed their own particular interests with more than usual intensity.

Like the Four Hundred men and women under survey, many of these children in the Roe study, from learning-centered homes, had school problems. A few, who were thought retarded, were kept back in school. A famous psychologist had a "hell of a time in kindergarten."[2] A scientist's mother was always at him for reading too much. A physicist led a stink-bomb attack on the faculty. One boy overate because he had no other pleasures. A biologist says he was always lonesome; the other children did not like him, but he never knew why. Another youth was always in flight from two or three overgrown louts who liked to catch him and twist his wrist. "The Work" to which they were individually committed became their chief pleasure and continued to be so in adulthood. They were not good scholarship material in the sense of being good all-around students, leaders, versatile. Many of them had to work their way through college — did not have scholarships.

In 1929 Paul Witty,[3] psychologist from Evanston, Illinois, also found parents of gifted children engrossed in mathematics, music, reading, travel, invention, religious work, sports, politics, dramatics, or lodge work. P. F. Brandwein,[4] in 1955 studied a group of New York high-school students who had won Westinghouse talent awards. They too came from homes which had substantial libraries; they had parents who wanted their children to become professional men and women.

Dael Wolfle,[5] who directed an extensive study of American sources of specialized talent, estimates that about half of each year's gifted high-school graduates come from homes where the parents have no particular interest in schooling or in learning and that this half tends to become wasted. A rule of thumb for predicting success is to know the number of books in the home and the father's occupation. Until we learn to motivate an enthusiasm for learning when it is not found in the home, economically valuable human potential is wasted yearly.

They Had Driving, Striving Parents

Leslie Stephen, father of the English novelist Virginia Woolf, was a champion walker with an enthusiasm for twenty-, thirty-, fifty-mile hikes. He was president of the Alpine Club, was the first man to climb the Schreckhorn, and as the indefatigable editor of the *Dictionary of National Biography*, often worked at his desk until he was exhausted and ill.

Captain Samuel Edison, Jr., who stood six feet and one inch in his stocking feet, could outjump any man in his township at the time he was forced to flee for his life from a spot in Canada to the United States border eighty miles away for two and one half days while the King's men, Indian guides, and bloodhounds followed in hot pursuit. Had he been captured and punished for his part in the abortive Mackenzie uprising, which aimed to effect separation of Canada from England, he might never have lived to be the father of Thomas Edison, whose own physical stamina enabled him to cut his sleeping time to five hours daily.

Leonard Jerome, grandfather of Sir Winston Churchill, was an active, exuberant man, a gambler, diplomat, newspaper editor, and also the first man to drive a team of horses four in hand down the streets of New York City. The father of H. G. Wells was a champion amateur cricket player.

The mothers of many eminent men were not prone to faint or flutter after the manner of the Victorian lady. The eighty-one-year-old mother of Edmund Allenby, military hero, a few hours after an appendectomy, thrust her head out of a window and frightened a laggard gardener with her expostulations. Adelaide Nansen, the mother of the arctic explorer Fridtjof Nansen, was a tall, vigorous woman who went skiing although the other women in her neighborhood thought such activity unwomanly. She dug in her garden like a man, and tailored the suits of her sons and stepsons until they were eighteen. For a hobby Adelaide Nansen read history. Jennie Jerome Chruchill, mother of Sir Winston Churchill, encouraged Englishwomen to wear comfortable outdoor clothing.

An admiring reporter called her the "panther woman" and the Englishwomen ascribed her exuberant energy to her one-eighth Iroquois Indian ancestry.

In the parents of Wendell Willkie, one time candidate for President of the United States and author of *One World*, we have what might be called a representative family among the sample, a driving, striving family, physically vigorous, intellectual, dynamic, bookish. It is typical in that the mother is more driving than the father.

As a small-town lawyer in Elwood, Indiana, Herman Willkie made bitter enemies as a crusader for reform. The town was wide open, with thirty saloons and a red-light district. But this six-foot man could lift an office safe without assistance, and was not someone to be lightly challenged.

His wife, Henrietta Trisch Willkie, was the first woman ever admitted to the bar in the state of Indiana. Her only sister was the first woman doctor to be licensed in the United States. Their mother, an emigrant girl, had fled from the South because she was nearly mobbed when she expressed her views about the sale of Negro children in a public square. Henrietta Trisch Willkie was a big woman with strong features. Each day she went out to work and played a man's role as a lawyer. At home she painted delicate designs on her china plates and cups and saucers or played the piano. The five children were never as close to her as to their father. On her tombstone is written, "A woman driven by an indomitable will."

The children ran about unattended except for the casual supervision of the housekeeper during the day and were combed, and scrubbed, and dressed in proper clothes by their mother when she came home from work. After supper the family gathered in the new library with its 6000 volumes to hear the father read from Dickens or R. L. Stevenson or George Eliot. When the first child dropped off to sleep, Herman Willkie would carry it tenderly upstairs to bed. The father always returned to the library to continue reading to the children until the last sleepy child had been carried to bed. As they listened half-awake from the upstairs bedrooms, the splendid sounds of piano music played by their mother filled the big old rambling frame house that still stands at the end of A Street, half in the country, half in town.

In another striving and driving, middle-class lawyer's family in England, during approximately the same period, small Clement Attlee, one day to be Prime Minister of England, was experiencing another type of bedtime ritual. Both the father and the mother were strongly concerned with the children's academic achievement. Each evening they sang the songs their mother had taught them, while they marched about the room. While the mother played the piano and the children caroled, a nurse took the younger children off to bed, one by one, as each became exhausted. The older children then had dessert with the parents in the dining room and there was conversation with both parents about the happenings of the day. (The children were cautioned to be very kind to a new governess. She was still quite upset over her experiences with her last charge, that incorrigible little Winston Churchill.) Ellen Attlee was not a mother to let any one of her three daughters and five sons be uninstructed in letters or morals. When three-year-old Clem, the youngest, had temper tantrums she was stern about his behavior. As a result, he hid his head in a pillow and called out when he saw her coming, "Clem 'penting" (repenting). His enforced quiet meditation had impressed him deeply. The father took a keen interest in the education of both the sons and daughters, set them writing essays on such subjects as "How To Govern England" and "How To Bring Up A Family On A Fixed Income A Year."

There is frequently a dreadful urgency in the drives of these parents which made them difficult for the children to endure. Langston Hughes, the Negro poet, was rebellious and angered by his father's compulsion to keep busy and to keep everyone else busy. He says in *The Big Sea:*

"Hurry up!" was his favorite expression in Spanish or English. He was always telling the employees under him at the electric light company, the cook at home, or Maximiliano, or me, to hurry up, hurry up and do whatever we were doing — so that we could get through and do something else he always had ready to be done.

His father, impatient with race prejudice directed toward him in the United States, went to Mexico and became successful there as an American businessman and as a rancher. He expressed to his son complete contempt for the slothful and indifferent, and was often out of bed at three in the morning ready for a long, exhausting day. He was reluctant to spend money, but quite willing to give his son money for college expenses.

The father of Karl Flesch, the violinist, was a physician in general practice in the small Austrian town of Wieselburg and regarded his profession as a mission rather than as a means of earning money. He often gave free treatment to the poor, and was reluctant to press any patient for fees. His attitude toward money was one thing; toward work another:

Work was his credo. In no circumstances did he tolerate idleness. His stereotyped question used to be, "What are you doing now?" I owed it to his systematic education that, in later years, I felt an insatiable need for activity, which almost mounted to a vice; "pleasure trips" were not only repulsive to me, but actually resulted in attacks of neurasthenia.[6]

The father's essential loving kindness did not shield the boy from being sent away from home at nine. Karl had no particular love for the violin. It was not he who choose the instrument; he might even have preferred playing the piano, but his two older brothers and sister took piano lessons and it was more convenient for the family for him to play the violin. The piano was always in use from 4:00 to 7:00 by the older children. Karl spared no trouble to shorten his practice hour, cut his strings, put the big clock ahead a quarter of an hour. Despite his indifference, it soon became obvious that the boy had exceptional ability. To the family this indicated he should develop this ability.

Neither the kindly father nor the fiery mother, who was still boxing Karl's ears when he was sixteen, hesitated to send the talented nine-year-old boy to Vienna, where he could have the best of teachers. Aunt Regi, an unloving egotist to whom he was nothing but a source of extra income, took him as a boarder. Unhappy Karl, returning to the city of Vienna after a too brief holiday in rural Wieselburg, often shut himself in the lavatory of the train to cry unnoticed. At eleven, Karl contemplated suicide, stood on a bridge that crossed the Danube, stared into the cold, black water, decided it would not be best to jump. The desire of the family to have the talented son make good use of his musical gift outweighed consideration for his personal happiness.

The mother of Agnes de Mille, the American dancer, was the daughter of Henry George, the wife of the film director William de Mille, and the sister-in-law of Cecil B. De Mille. Anna never permitted herself to waste time, required her daughter to say prayers in French for the dual purpose of communication with the Deity and practice in a foreign language. Anna too had a favorite phrase which her daughter describes:

"Don't just sit there, dearie," she would say coming into a room. "Do something!" To this hour I find it impossible to read a book before sundown unless it has some immediate connection with my work.[7]

The mother's drives were by no means merely physical. Agnes continues:

As the daughter of Henry George, Mother had early settled for herself the causes of war, of economic depression, of unequal distribution of wealth, and so on, and she naturally found it a matter of no great effort to reach definite conclusions on hats, dresses, interior decoration, manners, painting, music, plays, cooking, the rearing of children, and sex.

William de Mille, father of the would-be dancer, was a physically vigorous man. At seventy he could wallop young players on the tennis court. William was considered the intellectual in a learned family. His interests were not confined to his work on the movie lot:

In the tradition of his father, Henry de Mille, Pop was a liberal and a free-trader. He never hesitated to speak out for what he believed in, even buying space in the reactionary Los Angeles *Times* and more reactionary *Examiner*, to argue the case for the people. His political articles were brilliant. . . . Pop's outstanding characteristic was his wit. Language was his delight and tool.

The drudgery of becoming a dancer was faced by the daughter with an attitude appropriate to the household climate:

My well-filled curriculum — classes, homework, tennis, piano, editing — was ordered with just one thought: to make room for the dance practice. I rose at six-thirty and I studied and practiced at breakneck concentration until six in the evening when I was at last free to put on dancing dress and walk — to Mother's bathroom.

All through the lonely, drab exercises beside Mother's tub, without music or beat, proper floor or mirror, I had the joy of looking forward to dinner with Father, to hearing him talk about his scenarios and what was going on at the studio. . . . Sometimes after dinner he sang and I accompanied him. . . . These evenings my cup ran over. I went to bed early planning next day's practice, praying to do better in class. And as I lay waiting for sleep, breathing in the moist garden smells with my fox terrier slowly pressing me from the comfortable center of the bed, I used to dream about dancing on the stage with Pavlova, dancing until I dropped in a faint at her feet so that she would notice me and say, "That girl has talent."

The child who shows musical talent is particularly vulnerable to parental pressure if he is to be a performing artist. A composer, a writer, or an artist may postpone his "practicing" years, but the dancer or musical performer must make good use of the pre-pubescent years if he or she is to develop skills. Since the musician almost invariably shows his talent early, his parents are faced with early decisions. In these families it is usually the parent who urges the child to practice, thereby making it possible for the child to achieve success as an adult. There is probably no family which was so fragmented by one child's unusual talent as that of Pablo Casals, the cellist.

Pablo was born in Vendrell, a little Catalan town about seventy kilometers west of Barcelona, the second in a family of eleven children. His father, the church organist, was a modest man, a remarkable musician, a true artist. It was he who gave his children their initial musical training. When the boy was eleven and a half, the mother insisted that the boy should go to Barcelona to undertake advanced study. "He must go to Barcelona, and I shall take him there."

Take him she did, and until Pablo was twenty-two the home was fragmented, burdened, impoverished by the weight of the mother's consuming drive to see the talent of her son actualized and recognized.

My father thought that all these schemes did not make sense and attributed them to what he called my mother's "folie des grandeurs." They argued with such bitterness that it pained me terribly and I felt very guilty.[8]

When Pablo left the village of Vendrell where he had had a happy, carefree childhood, he had no dreams of becoming a great artist. It was his mother who dreamed for him. He never lost his love for his native village and often returned there as an adult. His mother installed him in Barcelona with relatives. After a year passed his mother joined him, left the father at home with the other children. The family ties of affection were not broken by the mother's decision to divide the family by coming to Barcelona to make a home for Pablo. Pablo's father bought him a full-sized cello, came to Barcelona, rode with him to the hall by tram, when Pablo gave his first concert, reassuring the frightened boy all the way. Pablo was always to love his father, but he appreciated his mother also and credited her with his ultimate success.

As time passed there were no spectacular gains, and Pablo, while going through a period of religious mysticism, had thoughts of suicide which he did not describe to his mother for fear of making her unhappy. When he finished his school at Barcelona and was graduated from the Municipal School of Music, his mother took his two youngest brothers and moved to Madrid with seventeen-year-old Pablo. They rented a garret in a slum dwelling where the hall porter's two mentally defective children were disturbing and the neighbors were noisy and dirty. The Count de Morphy became interested in Pablo, but wanted him to become a composer. Pablo's mother thought differently! The cello must come first. Relations with the Count became strained and the fragment of the Casals family went on to Brussels, where they had prospects of support. Throughout the long, lean years she was supportive, optimistic.

Pablo and his mother went to the Conservatory of Brussels, where he had been offered a scholarship. A sarcastic teacher's first reaction was to ridicule Pablo before the class because the boy said he could play certain selections. When the new student demonstrated his truthfulness, the teacher was abashed and begged the boy's forgiveness, but Pablo would not stay.

The day after this humiliation the family left for Paris, where they lived in a hovel, dieting to save money, until Pablo became ill with enteritis, dysentery, and hemorrhage. The mother cut her hair and sold it to get money; the father sent money until his own savings melted away.

In despair, Pablo and his mother and baby brothers went back to Barcelona, where Pablo's luck changed. He found his first adequately remunerative employment as a teacher in his old school, the Barcelona Municipal School of Music. A former teacher, Garcia, had vacated a post to go to Argentina, and recommended Pablo to fill the post. When Pablo was twenty-two and went again to Paris, his mother stayed home with her husband and the younger children. Her son says of her:

She was an exceptional woman! Just think of what she did in Madrid: she studied foreign languages and more or less did the same lessons as I did, partly because she thought it would help my work, but mostly because the deep feeling we had for each other should not be affected by any difference in our education.[9]

The question of what happens to the other brothers and sisters in such a family is forced upon us by a consideration of the Casals. We were sensitive, throughout our study, to this query, and made notes about the careers of the brothers and sisters in each instance where that information was given.[10] A brother of Pablo's also became a musician and stayed in Spain at the time Pablo left because of his rejection of the Franco government. In general the siblings fall into a category familiar to those who do studies on the brothers and sisters of gifted children. The same striving, driving parents who produce one child of extraordinary ability produce other children who are capable and intelligent.

A family which once lived at 6 Stanhope Gardens in Paddington, England, was perturbed when the sixth son in the family of ten children was considered too academically inept to follow the family tradition of going to Oxford. The father, Professor David Baden-Powell, was an insatiable seeker for knowledge who did not live long enough to know that each of his sons was to be catalogued as distinguished, that each daughter was to marry a man of ability, except the youngest, Agnes, who remained a spinster. She helped her older brother Stephenson to use their father's memory (although they lost him when they were four and three years old) as a model for the ideal "Scoutmaster." There is no other family among the Four Hundred which produced so many sons and daughters who may be found in encyclopedias and other reference books.

Professor Baden-Powell, lecturer in mathematics at Oxford, was such a busy man that he usually managed with five hours' sleep each night. He lectured to his classes and wrote learned articles on the need to liberalize religious thinking, on labor relations, and on natural philosophy. He maintained intimate contact with the learned men of his day: Benjamin Jowett, Dean Stanley, John Ruskin, Robert Browning, and his wife's cousin Charles Kingsley.

The professor found time to take his children on nature hikes, encouraged them to make collections, drew amusing caricatures for them, taught them to make playthings from discarded possessions. They did special experiments and art projects in his study, where he could be on hand to give advice and encouragement. They were paid a penny for each four errors they could find in the articles he was writing. Since he had been teaching at Oxford for thirty years when his sixth son, Stephenson Baden-Powell, was born, his patience was not drawn from a well of youthful strength.

The Royal Geographic Society was founded by Professor David Baden-Powell. He was the first editor of the *Manchester Guardian*. He also found time to lecture before many audiences about health, religion, and education.

His third wife, Henrietta Smyth Baden-Powell, married the professor when his oldest daughter was only eight. Henry was five, and the youngest daughter was three. She bore Professor David Baden-Powell ten more children, of whom seven lived to be adults. She also found time to do volunteer work for hospitals which housed the indigent, and was a member of the Central Committee of the Woman's Education Union, which in 1872 founded the Girls' Public Day School Company. She was an accomplished artist.

When Professor Baden-Powell died, Henrietta's youngest son was one month old and her oldest stepchild was twenty-two. To the best of her ability she continued to rear the children as her husband would have wished. David Baden-Powell had had a horror of learning by rote and rule and believed that children learn best when they learn happily. His wife developed theories about inductive reasoning which she applied to her own home-grown laboratory of boys and girls.

Robert Stephenson Smyth Baden-Powell, the founder of the Boy Scouts, a redheaded, twinkly-eyed lad, did not observe the proper barrier between master and student when he went to Charterhouse. His classmates could not understand this overeager lad who was so ready to assume a father-role, to keep his fellow students amused, to be useful to the teachers. When the school moved from the city to a new location farther out, "Ste," as he was called, was of much help to the school administration. The teachers liked him; the students thought him "odd."

He became a member of all committees, chairman of none. He did impromptu imitations, drew amazing caricatures, reproduced bird calls, imitated animal sounds. He took the comic roles in the school plays. He worked with all his heart to keep his classmates happy after the manner of a father as a four-year-old half-orphan remembered him. At that age he had not been capable of noticing his father's devotion to science and mathematics and philosophy.

When it was time for "Ste" to go to Oxford, he was not accepted by the old friend of the family, Benjamin Jowett, who said the boy was not "quite up to Balliol form." His father had taught there; his older brothers had achieved there. That very year his half brother George Baden-Powell had won the Chancellor's prize. "Ste" was rejected.

Haig Brown, headmaster of Charterhouse, said that his faith was shaken in Jowett's judgment of men, and that mother wit had truly triumphed when Stephenson passed second place for cavalry and fourth for infantry in an army examination taken by 700 candidates.

The brothers of Baden-Powell were to make the kind of adjustments which the majority of the 1500 gifted children studied by Terman made. The brothers were competent to a degree far beyond the average man on the street, but they achieved highly without making an original contribution. They did not lack recognition. The oldest half-brother became a judge. The half-sisters married well. The oldest full brother was knighted for his work as a geologist. George Baden-Powell was knighted for his services as an administrator, was a Member of Parliament. The next living brother became a competent artist and barrister. Another became Astronomer Royal of Scotland. The youngest was knighted as an aeronaut and was an experimental balloonist. A sister was married to a man who was knighted for his services as director of the Natural History Museum. There are many such outstanding siblings in the homes which produce the Four Hundred.

The originality and imaginativeness rather than the intellectual qualities of Stephenson Baden-Powell set him apart, made him eminent. He was always a good-natured, boyish fellow who could not compare his definitive treatise on *Pigsticking* with the scientific and scholarly contributions of his brothers who were better educated than he. Yet it was his drive to perpetuate the child-rearing habits rather than the intellectual interests of his opinionative parents that made him famous.

Most of the parents who so loved learning, created a home climate which produced eminence — and also competence of a high order.

Not all parents are as altruistic and patient and unselfish as was the lovable Professor David Baden-Powell, or the long-suffering father of Pablo Casals. Some of the fathers resent being put in second place in the family by a talented son who absorbs too much of the mother's attention. There are mothers as well as fathers who are too intent on their own careers to do much more than be an example of industriousness. They are too busy to be bothered by the special needs of a son or daughter.

A son can sometimes extend the drive of a father who rejects him. Douglas Fairbanks, Sr., deserted by his own failure-prone but energetic father, had, while a boy, been hyperactive, forever bounding, climbing, leaping, out of pure animal spirits, brilliant, but inattentive in school. When he married and later divorced the mother of Douglas Fairbanks, Jr., he did so without any special regard for the feelings of his fat, unattractive boy. Douglas, Sr., failed as completely to develop paternal feelings as had his own father.

Beth Fairbanks, mother of Douglas, Jr., described the situation:

Senior was perfectly tender and nice, he just did not have the instinct of being a father. All through Douglas' youth he paid no attention to him. He used to come into the house, day in and out, and he wouldn't know the child was there.[11]

The father was frantic with rage and anxiety for his own hard-earned career when the son, whom he had never liked, was, at thirteen, starred in a picture under the direction of a rival producer, Jesse L. Lasky. Douglas Fairbanks, Sr., did not want to be known as the father of a hulking thirteen-year-old boy. He insisted that the boy should prepare for college. Junior's inevitable failure as an actor would surely shame the boy and ruin the father.

The film was a flop, just as the father predicted. Instead of admitting defeat, Douglas Fairbanks, Jr., started at the bottom of the industry and made a new beginning, supporting his improvident mother and her clinging Southern female relatives. Meanwhile he became an assistant cameraman, lugged heavy supplies, spent tedious hours in the cutting room. It was Mary Pickford, the tactful stepmother, who was sympathetic and understanding, who understood the implacable push to create, the need for self-expression through acting, in both son and husband. She helped them to become friends when the son's growing success made him more acceptable to his ambitious father. Douglas, Jr., never did get to college. When he was a success in the John van Druten play *Young Woodley*, his father is quoted as saying, "Have you seen my boy's play? I guess I was wrong. He shouldn't be doing it at seventeen, he should be in college, but pay no attention to me; he's an independent cuss, and by God he's gotten away with it."[12]

It had taken the father fifteen hard years to fight his own way up to stardom. He had not been inclined to let his son, so opposite from him in temperament, threaten his status in the industry. The son, although alienated from his father, extended his drive for achievement.

Isidor Schnabel, wool merchant, was also not inclined to subordinate his career to that of the son in the family. The family business was in the small Austrian town of Bielitz. When the son Artur showed talent beyond the family's ability to subsidize, the mother found patrons for the boy who enabled the family to move to Vienna. The father was to find new customers for the wool business in Vienna, the son was to study there.

The arrangements were satisfactory to everyone except the father.

Business there had not come up to expectations. . . . he must have disliked the family's partial dependence on the patrons of his young son . . . he turned the agency over to an old established Vienna firm. In the following year, the entire family, without Artur, returned to Bielitz.[13]

The arrangement was a fortuitous one since it left the father and son each free to develop his own abilities in his own way. The stormy weekly scenes between mother and son were ended. Ernestine Schnabel was so grimly determined to see him a great artist that his tendency toward laziness exasperated her. She was always eager to display his talent. She infuriated his teacher by arranging a concert for Artur, when he was eleven, in his home town during his holiday period. More than a thousand persons attended, crowding into Bielitz's largest hall. The mother and son both enjoyed the affair, but the crusty teacher considered it premature. The teacher was prone to humiliate Artur to tears in class by demanding more of him than of the adults in the class.

Artur, turned loose in Vienna, commissioned to fulfill his talent by his family on his own, enjoyed himself completely. He chose his own boarding places; when the Nelkens bored him, he moved in with the lively Frau Husserl, a widow with four student sons and a pretty daughter with whom the precocious Artur fell in love. Artur was a popular guest in sophisticated homes where the children of his age were sent to bed while he played for the adult guests and joined in the conversation. At twelve or thirteen he was enjoying all the privileges of an eligible young bachelor in wealthy and cultured circles. His ambitious mother, back in Bielitz, had to be content with the continuing reports of adequate progress. There was, nevertheless, an incomplete satisfaction in this situation for Artur. "Life in this atmosphere was not always pleasant. I was not always happy there." Despite his unhappiness, his need for training kept him away from home and on his own.

THE LOVE FOR LEARNING CAN PERSIST INTO PARENTS' OLD AGE

There is frequently a love for learning and achievement in these aged parents which is commonly associated with impetuous and ebullient youth.

John Butler Yeats, Dublin artist, author, and philosopher, felt so strongly about playing second fiddle to his son, the famous William Butler Yeats, that he became a self-exile in New York at the age of sixty-nine and enjoyed a personal renaissance there. He had no ill-feelings for his children and grandchildren, whom he was never to visit again. His personal relationship with his children was always that of a contemporary. He wrote to them often, and sometimes corresponded with his son William Butler three times in a day. In New York he enjoyed an income and adulation he had never known in Dublin, where he had been sensitive about being introduced to men who had more fame than he, where he had deliberately submerged himself among the failures in the artistic set. In contrast, his paintings sold well in New York; he began to read and to write with vigor and enthusiasm, and his extraordinary conversational ability was valued in literate circles. For thirteen years, until he died at eighty-two, he was the old man who ran away from home and made good.

An old man who stayed home and made good just to show that "if my son can write, anybody can,"[14] was the acrimonious, impossible Dr. William Gilbert, whose arguments with his equally unpredictable son, Sir William Schwenck Gilbert, were good theater. Dr. Gilbert, contemptuous of the praise given his son, set himself to write a number of novels and proved his point to himself, if not to posterity, when Shirley Hall Asylum and Dr. Austin's Guests became best sellers.

The dependence on books and the urge to be creative can survive sickness, penury, disappointments, tragedies, and the infirmities of old age.

To all of these points the Beveridge family can bear witness. The Beveridge children as described by the parents, long before the traits of the gifted were compiled by scholars, show the traits catalogued by contemporary students who select such children by means of standardized tests. The story of the Beveridge family is told by their son, William Beveridge, in his book *India Called Them*. This son, a sociologist and the father of English social security, makes these parents the most intimately known to us of any of the Four Hundred.

Like many other parents of the gifted, they were not in early youth when they bore their children. Annette was a schoolteacher and social reformer whose good intentions for the fourteen young Indian women whom she was teaching to be independent and modern were being lost in a drab battle over spoons, forks, filters, absconding servants and drunken landlords, when she met and married a shy widower, Henry Beveridge, who declared himself on their fifth meeting. Agnostics both, they were married at the Registry. The voluminous love letters they wrote came later, when, because of the needs of the four children they bore, they were often separated. She was thirty-two, he was thirty-eight when they married. He was a colonial administrator in the Indian Service.

The contemporary ideal home is economically stable, emotionally serene, the children grow up in a familiar neighborhood where there is a competent community health department and child welfare clinics. Journeys, if they must be made, are quickly carried out. The Beveridges enjoyed none of these advantages. They were burdened with financial problems, serious illnesses, deaths in the immediate family, disappointments in professional and social life. They were, during the children's first years, constantly moving and traveling.

India was dotted with graves of English children. Every dish of food was prepared under close supervision by Annette, but care did not suffice. Annette had cholera. The youngest child, Herman, was stricken at eight months with a high fever; was thereafter speechless, hyperactive, destructive, out of contact with reality. When the remaining son, Will, almost died with a similar undiagnosed fever, Annette took all four children to England and bought a house there. She was cheated in its purchase; the drains were bad, the cook got typhoid, inept sanitary inspectors dug up the fine old lawn. A dear relative, Aunt Bessie, who came to help, was killed in an accident. The school chosen for

Will turned out to be sham and façade. He was beaten after school by a big boy who resented the new boy's precocity, until Annette challenged this bully and threatened to have him arrested if he ever touched her son again. A knighted physician was no more able to help Herman than the bungling doctors they had seen in India. Henry, who had never won preferment in the colonial service in India because of his views about Indian home rule and other matters, was hard put to keep the divided family going financially. He had other dependents, a sister, and a mother who at seventy-seven was a giddy, helpless woman — it was his father, so prone to bankruptcy, who had been vital and aggressive.

The parents were never distracted from their books by misfortune. The happiest year of their married life was one they spent in an isolated post to which they were sent as a disciplinary measure by a bigoted superior. They enjoyed the opening minds of their growing young children, their books and papers, and each other when they were sent away from the previous area, where they had been deeply involved in the petty intrigue of the station.

The four children they bore were a daily pleasure and excitement to the parents, who, when separated, wrote intimate, tender letters about their dreams for the children. On furlough in Scotland Annette wrote a two-thousand page "Memorandum" about her three oldest children. Although they had flopped on the street in London to peer curiously through gratings and embarrassed her, she was not too weary of them to catalogue their beauties, virtues, and talents. In a document which is a discriminating observation of three gifted children, she parallels studies made years later. Leta S. Hollingworth in *Children Above 180 IQ* describes the gifted children whom she isolated for study by test as being taller, stronger, handsomer than other children. These New York children were sensitive to injustice, emotionally moved by reading about man's inhumanity to man. One child cried when reading about the treatment of the South by the North after the Civil War. They were, like the Beveridge children, likely to be pedantic, painstaking in expression, to impress observers as being quaint, old-fashioned, overly adult children.

In the Beveridge family Annette described, decades before, these same qualities in her own English children. Letty at six was tall, slender, had hair the "color of a chestnut hulk," was an excellent walker, was "bookish." At six she could read both German and English. She cried when Annette read to her about the death of a poor collier's boy. "She cried most naturally and would not be comforted." Letty then made the interesting discovery for herself that it did not move her to tears to read the poem silently and discussed the probable reasons for this reaction with her mother.

Willie at four years and nine months was slim and compact, with fair hair and loving blue eyes. He spent much of his playtime writing series of arithmetical and multiplication statements very neatly. "One of the distinct traits of Willie's character is his accuracy of statement. He speaks deliberately and requires it of others. He allows no one (not even sister Tutu) to lapse into mistake." When his mother mispronounced a German word he corrected her, not in a dictatorial fashion, but as one who had the right to make an observation. He read German better than English, although he loved to be read to in English and spoke it well enough.

Tutu at three and a half was a curly-headed child with a piquant face and rotund figure. She did lessons for about twenty minutes daily, and could read about two pages from a German reading book. Since coming to Scotland she had given up her stately dance in which she "used to don a sari and move slowly before my bedroom fire in Bankipur to the music of Bogmonia's song. She now dances jigs with tremendous energy." Annette makes reference to the children's refusing to talk Hindustani in Scotland. The children were at this age trilingual. Annette and Henry in their letters used as many as four languages easily and learned others for pleasure.

The peregrinating Beveridges were willing travelers. Annette never minded trains, however many children she had with her, and turned journeys into sightseeing tours, purposely taking the long way around to see new sights. Annette triumphed over everything crossing Europe with her retinue. She crossed the sea from Genoa to Bombay, traversed India by train, stopping off at Bankipur, changing at midnight at Allahabad. Once in India, the family delighted in excursions to remote and difficult areas. They went down to the valley of the Runjit River, 5000 feet below Darjeeling, and became giddy on the swinging canebridge across the river.

Annette was quite aware that her children were exceptional in ability. The English relatives often referred to them as prodigies. As time passed, one of them, William, surpassed the others. This too, is usual. They were also typical in that it was Willie who had the problems in school adjustment. Boys more than girls among the gifted are prone to problems. The girls soon made friends when they came to England, but Willie did not, and his mother characteristically met his attacker head-on in argument, then set about seeking friends for her son. Annette was the more aggressive of the two parents — which is also customary.

William Beveridge as a child and as a man was capable of long, self-initiated problem-solving. To a marked degree this was present in both parents, whose love for books and learning persisted to the end of their days. One of the unexpected observations we have been able to make while doing this survey concerns the number of parents who stay intellectually and physically active long past middle life — until they are eighty or even ninety.

Henry retired at forty-six and came home to Annette and the children. "On January 14, 1893, he stepped out of India's service all but unnoticed as quietly as he had stepped into it thirty-five years beforehand, on the night when he heard the jackals howling on the tiger-haunted island of Saugor."

Annette and Henry now had time to read — histories, travel, biographies, novels, philosophy, poetry. Each became absorbed in a task of translation from Persian to English — Henry working on the Abul-Fazl, "The Owl," and Annette on the Gul-Badan. Annette learned Persian after Letty died in adolescence. Henry suggested this activity as a way of keeping his wife from devastating melancholy. She later learned Turki in order to translate the Babur Nama.

Henry finished his translation in 1921. At eighty-four he occupied himself with errata, index and addenda. Annette published her translation of the Babur Nama in four volumes in 1922 when she was almost eighty — despite deafness, operations for cataracts, and a major abdominal operation at seventy-seven. Henry moved down to the country cottage with a servant at eighty-eight, but Annette would not join him except for weekends because she needed to be near the library in order to work on her revisions. They both died in 1929. Annette, the first to go, was working on her books the day before she died.

John Cowper Powys came from a curate's household which produced four novelists and other men and women of distinction. His morbid and melancholy mother, a descendent of John Donne, had a contempt for success and for good health and happiness. God's ways were sad ways. She liked the shade, feared the sun. John remained her favorite son only because his self-depreciating ways kept her from knowing that he was really celebrated. He takes notice of the drive that makes for fame, but gives no credit to the stuff of which the driver is made, when he says of the successful:

The majority of eminently successful men, such as the "vulgar" call great, are successful because they want to be just that above everything else. Mistakes do happen, as when some quiet mathematicians are suddenly hurled, like meteoric projectiles, into notoriety. But as a rule it is those with energy and will and the desire to be at the top who are at the top.[15]

The "bookish" and driving quality of these homes which cradle eminence lasts through the years and has no relation to money, as is evidenced in this statement about his father's will by William Beveridge, who says:

By the time he ended he had parted even from most of his books, except those with a family association. His will was sworn at eighty-two pounds. He went out of the world with almost as few possessions as those with which he entered it.[16]

There are only two of the Four Hundred, both politicians, who flatly say they had no early love for learning. Al Smith professed a scorn for books, said that in his lifetime he had read only one book, a biography of a famous prizefighter. His father, a truck-driver, he does not credit with learning or status or power drives. However, his mother, always a driving woman, blamed the father for not being willing to buy a farm in what was then outskirts, which later sold for fabulous sums as city lots. Al Smith's talent, developed early, was in leadership, a quality not yet measurable by a standardized test. At ten, however, he won a prize for oratory.

Nikita Khrushchev describes his father as a man who had no use for schools or learning. It was not until Nikita left home to live with relatives who were deeply involved in reading and revolutionary activities that he became a hungry reader. The father, a blacksmith, does emerge as a man of physical vitality, a great eater and drinker. There was music, dancing, singing, and physical exuberance in the parental climate. The mother has a shadowy role in the scanty data — a widow driven by necessity. It was relatives who communicated a love for learning to the adolescent boy. The physical driving and striving he seemingly found at home.

Only one parent among the 700-plus is described as a physically lazy woman, but her husband was driving enough for two. This was the mother of the writer Konrad Berkovici.

The Family Value System

It is, then, the family value system which seems to have the strongest impact on the child with ability. If his parents respect ability and have strong intellectual and physical drives, he is evidently more likely to become outstanding among his contemporaries.

A willingness to let a young man or woman leave home to further his achievements is seen as a factor making for achievement by Fred L. Strodbeck, one of a group of four scholars whose four-year study of identification of talent is reported in their volume *Talent and Society*.[17] Among the Four Hundred there are young children sent away from home to seek training the local community does not offer. There are husbands and wives who endured unwelcome separation in the interests of their children's development.

The love for learning is seen as a lifetime trait. It continues despite illness and frustrations, and even after reasonable and satisfying success. It is not particularly associated with a desire for material gain. Along with the drive for knowledge and achievement there is often a physical vitality in both the parent and the child. These intellectually striving, physically driving parents and children are likely to enhance, if not advance, the *status quo*. Only one person in the family may become eminent, but the entire family is likely to be competent and useful.

Over ninety percent of these Four Hundred families show a love for learning and achievement.

[2]

Opinionative Parents

> In those days young people, unless invited
> to speak, were seen and not heard. But as
> soon as father considered us old enough to
> have opinions, we were given full scope to
> express them, no matter how adolescent. . . .
> He hated the slavery of pattern and following
> of examples and believed in the equality of
> the sexes: . . . fought for free libraries, free
> education, free books in the public school . . .
> took single tax in his stride. . . .
> — MARGARET SANGER, *An Autobiography*

RECENT FASHION in parental attitude favors the neutral parent who is warmly supportive, provident, nondirective. Fathers and mothers discipline themselves to patience, especially for the critical adolescent, because they do not want to be responsible for delaying his maturity or stifling his creativity. If, despite their best intentions, they express themselves blatantly and embarrass their child with statements of opinion which run counter to the opinions commonly held by most of the neighbors they are defensive and guilt-ridden. If they persist in any kind of nonconformity, they do so under the deep burden of conscience and are painfully aware of the social problems to which they subject their child.

Most parents today act on the premise that the child has a right to do what others do and to have the things that others have, and to feel a part of the common culture of the neighborhood. The parent tries to stay in the background of the child's life. To this end he relinquishes much that he might like to see established as a family tradition.

The neutral parental attitude was practically unknown to the families in this study. Two hundred and twenty-seven families among them espoused strong political attitudes, held sectarian views about religion, or were religious liberals with equally strong feelings, or were atheists or agnostics, or espoused unpopular causes, or worked in reform movements, or expressed controversial views in print or on the public platform. These parents with strong concerns we chose to call opinionative.

Among them were partisans of Charles Darwin, Henry George, and Robert Ingersoll, parents who rejected the theories of infant damnation and predestination, and parents who believed that science and religion could and should be reconciled. Some worked for the abolition of slavery and for civil liberties, or were involved in civic reform movements in their communities. Better housing, better public health, better schools and hospitals were popular causes. There were few extremists, only one family was a member of a communal community which withdrew from society at large. One father was a Populist, another a Chartist leader. Two mothers were mediums. Four fathers were Swedenborgians. A number were socialists.

Most of the causes to which they committed themselves would raise no eyebrows today. In their own times, however, fathers and, less often, mothers found themselves in conflict with the established order and accepted mores. The contemporary parent who would self-consciously emulate them has an almost insurmountable problem. He must first make a choice among the "far-out" causes of his own day and choose one which, although it is a minority cause today, will make him admired as its exponent decades later. His involvement in this cause must be sincere, altruistic and without regard for possible negative repercussions which will affect the economic welfare or social status of his children or his wife or himself. He must feel that his dedication to principle is a spontaneous reaction to environmental stimulus.

REBELLION IN THE HOMES

The children in these opinionative homes are more likely to emulate the parent than to be rebels. Over one-fourth of the boys and girls adopt the parental attitude and make it the springboard of their own fame, or fulfill a family daydream, or enter the family profession. They are like Charles Darwin, whose grandfather preceded him by writing a poem on evolution.

The brash, critical adolescent who quarrels with his parents or disagrees with them violently about cultural or political matters is not often found in these families. He is more likely to be tagging along after opinionative parents trying to find out what the excitement is all about. He is much more likely to be expelled from school than to run away from home. Patterns in rebellion in adolescence may have changed, however, with the adoption of compulsory education. It is the teacher, in these biographies and autobiographies, who is the butt of hostility. Today's parent, rather than the teacher, being a less retaliatory target, may have accommodated himself to the need of the adolescent to be critical and rebellious. This is a point for speculation.

The boys and girls who rebelled against parents were few — twenty-four — and their rebellions were often short-lived. Jules Verne ran away at eleven to be a cabin boy, but was relieved when his father, a lawyer with a poetic streak, brought him home to his affectionate mother, who was prostrated with anxiety. It was the school, rather than the home, from which he fled. For school he had a definite hostility, and he filled his books with designs for ships and flying machines. He was punished for running away by being put on a bread and water diet and in a repentant mood said to his mother, "After this I shall travel only in my imagination."

Harold Laski, phenomenally brilliant, at eighteen threw his ambitious Orthodox Jewish family into complete confusion by coming home from a summer cultural conference with a twenty-eight-year-old Gentile bride, a highly opinionative young woman interested in genetics and politics, herself a rebel. The couple was immediately separated by his parents, and Harold was sent along to college. The bride went back to Scotland to wait until Harold was out of school. When he was graduated, the marriage was resumed, and the parents became reconciled when a grandchild was born. When their son became well known and it was obvious that his wife had a good influence on his professional career, they lost most of their hostility for her.

Arnold Bennett refused to be a clerk in his father's law office and went off to London to be a writer the year after he was graduated with honors from secondary school. His mother took money budgeted for groceries to finance his rebellion. Henrik Ibsen cut himself off completely from his entire family after he left home at seventeen. He rejected the family's religious fundamentalism and was ashamed of his father's financial failure.

A rebel who is communicative about his rebellions is the psychiatrist Ernest Jones, best known as a biographer of Freud. His father was a Liberal in politics, an agnostic, a self-made man involved in community activities, the school board, the parish and district councils and the like. Ernest was deeply attached to both of his parents and justifiably regarded himself as the bond of the union between them. They were warm and supportive, liberal and opinionative, but his father had difficulty being able to admit he was ever in the wrong. However, Ernest Jones says he never knew his parents to be angry with each other. When he was thirteen, his own sharp tongue and outspoken ways led him into an acrimonious argument about a siphon pump which caused a rift between the father and son for a period and hurt the father's feelings.

Frederick Delius rebelled against entering his father's wool business and fled to Florida on a pretext which left him time for music. Unlike most of the other parents, his father never forgave him for his rebellion.

CHILDREN WHO EXTENDED PARENTAL OPINIONATIVENESS

The number of instances in which the child extends the parent as does the bud on the branch, if described, would of themselves fill many volumes. The clearest examples are those in which the parents are involved in humanitarian or reform movements and the children express similar concerns. It will be noted that children who did not reject their parents' unconventional ideas but used them to advantage in their adult lives were often not conformists at school.

To the Hicksite Quaker father of Jane Addams, no cause which his daughter ever undertook was contrary to his convictions. A close friend of Lincoln, he valued a letter from him inquiring as to the direction in which the Quaker conscience was pointing on a specific issue. He was always concerned about questions of peace and brotherhood and conditions among the poor. His daughter Jane was to win the Nobel Peace Prize in 1910. She was also known for her social work and reforms in labor relations.

Jane used to creep downstairs in the night to ease the fears that came to her so often because of a recurring nightmare. In her recurrent dream, she knew that everyone in the world was dead except herself. Upon her alone rested the responsibility of making the world resume its course again and this mission could not be accomplished unless Jane could make a wagon wheel. She was all alone in a deserted world. The village street looked as it always looked, except for the lack of people. The blacksmith shop was in the usual place with the anvil near the door, but there were no human beings in sight. In her dream Jane always had the over-whelming responsibility of having to start the world moving again, of having to do this before all the lost people could ever come home again.

She was never able to tell her father this particular nightmare. Over and over again in autobiographies, subjects tell of fears and persecutions they endured without ever once telling any adults about them. The inarticulateness of childhood, even of verbally gifted children, is frightening, and places a tremendous responsibility on adults.

The father, a widower, enjoyed these nocturnal visits from his delicate youngest daughter. She asked him about her anxiety that she was not as knowing as were her playmates who completely understood the meaning of "predestination." Jane confessed it was all a puzzle to her.

Her father replied, "You and I do not have the kind of minds that will ever understand foreordination, Jane," he said. "But it really isn't very important. . . . It is very important not to pretend to understand what you don't understand and you must be honest with yourself inside. . . . Mental integrity comes above everything else."[1]

The need these gifted young children have for communication with adults was met (in part) for Jane by her father. She is reticent about her village school except to indicate that it did not meet her needs. Her father gave her his support when she could not accept the emotional evangelism of her boarding school.

Another girl who had school difficulties as a result of being influenced by her own opinionative parents was Pearl Buck. Until she had gone away to Miss Jewell's School in Shanghai at seventeen, Pearl had previously had most of her lessons with her dynamic and imaginative mother at the dining room table. The school did not have much to offer her scholastically, but she liked being assigned to help the girls at the Door of Hope, a rescue home for Chinese girls who had cruel mistresses. Since Pearl spoke colloquial Chinese, they chatted with her freely about having been raped by adolescent boys in the homes of their masters, of being beaten with whips by bad-tempered mistresses or burned with coals from pipes or cigarettes.

Pearl's missionary parents had deliberately chosen to live among the Chinese people and had not restricted themselves to a compound. Pearl had played with her Chinese playmates in the tall pampas grasses or under the verandas where the brown earth was cool and dry. When she went walking and strange children called out, "Little foreign devil," she struck them dumb by replying (in Chinese), "Little turtle!" She knew this meant, "You bastard!" but her parents did not. The children did not resent her yellow hair and blue eyes so much when she could answer them in their own street language.

Her parents did not restrict her from fighting the dogs away from the bones of dead children lying on the hillside. She met lepers on the street and saw starving people during the famine year. Her mother sought Pearl's companionship and assistance in trying to bring comfort and help to their neighbors. Consequently, Pearl found it difficult to be companionable with the students at Miss Jewell's School, since their parents had not allowed them to associate so intimately with the distressed Chinese population.

Because of her parents' views about the level of association with Chinese people, she felt she *was* Chinese, not American.

Her ideas about religion made her an outcast at school. She quoted to the girls in her dormitory from her father's monograph on the similarities between Christianity and Buddhism. He also believed that Jesus and Confucius had both formulated the ideas associated with the Golden Rule. He advanced the theory in a monograph that Jesus himself might have visited the Himalayan Kingdom of Nepal when he was a young man, during the unrecorded years of his life. Her father gained this idea by reading of it in the Vishnu Purana, an ancient Hindu scripture, and had often discussed these theories with Pearl.

The girls relayed Pearl's account of her father's views to Miss Jewell and the shocked headmistress took Pearl out of the dormitory and put her in a little room alone, which did not displease Pearl because she could then read after the lights went out in the other rooms. She did not like school, with its prayer meetings, moans, sighs, grovelings, or the talk of infant damnation about which her mother also felt so negatively.

There were other children whose parents' zeal for good works led them to acquaint their children early with poverty and disease and man's inhumanity to man.

Among these was another humanitarian and writer, Pierre van Paassen, who is sometimes called the non-Jewish Zionist, who describes his childhood in *Days of Our Years.*

This boy, brought up in the small urban town of Gorcum, Holland, had three opinionative persons in his household; his mother, his bachelor uncle Kees, and his father.

His mother was drawn into the relief activities the Protestant community set up for Jewish refugees fleeing from Russian pogroms. At his own dinner table Pierre heard a weeping father tell how his wife had been forced to watch her two children thrown into a burning furnace before she was granted the mercy of a like fate.

Her other interests were in the ill and poorly housed in their own city. She took young Pierre with her to call on families where destitute children lay dying of tuberculosis. On his way home from school he stopped by the slum section where she had organized a cleanup campaign. The street was so narrow that he could stand in the middle of the street and touch the walls of the houses on either side with his outstretched hands. The walls crawled with vermin.

His father took him all the way to Utrecht to hear Oom Paul Kruger talk of the unspeakable horrors of the Boer concentration camps and heard Kruger say, "England told them to shut the door in my face and all of them obeyed." Exiled and intransigent Boers became his heroes and with shivers of horror he heard them tell how Kitchener had said falsely in one of his communiqués that Boer women were totally bereft of the normal maternal instinct, and how these women were subsequently given over to the lust and cruelty of a whiskey-crazed soldiery.

It was Uncle Kees, a bachelor landscape painter, who was his favorite teacher. With him he roamed the countryside searching for landscapes to paint, staying away for weeks, camping, returning home suntanned and weatherbeaten. From Uncle Kees he learned more history than from all the schoolbooks combined. Uncle Kees, who foretold a coming bloody war, declaimed upon the significance of the Franco-Prussian War, the era of Napoleon III and the Commune of Paris. He told Pierre of his personal acquaintance with Vincent van Gogh, Tolstoy, Renan, and Bakunin. As they walked the countryside, he spoke of Irish independence or Macedonian nationalism and Pierre drank in his words as if he had been born in Cork or in the Balkans, such was the spell of his uncle's oratory. Uncle Kees was a liberal and acquainted the boy with Voltaire, Rousseau, Saint-Simon, Proudhon, and Goethe.

The elders in Pierre van Paassen's family, with all their opinionativeness, seem to have closed their eyes to what went on in their son's school. Of his headmaster he says in his autobiography:

his face was a mask of deep wrinkles, his bony fingers tapering off into nails as long as those of a Chinese mandarin, he inspired me with so much more terror than respect that I still see his ghost at times . . . in a blaze of anger, his lips curled in a tigerish leer that revealed his yellow stumps of teeth . . . pounding upon a fellow pupil [of Pierre's], beating the boy until he sank fainting to his knees.[2]

The headmaster had found a sentence in this pupil's copybook which infuriated him. The incident made such an impression upon Pierre van Paassen that he remembered when he was adult the phrase which offended the headmaster, "snowflakes fluttering from a pitilessly gray heavenly roof."

When a younger brother died and the mother's reason was consequently feared for, when the father's business failed, Pierre was happy enough to postpone college, and his surviving brother was willing to forego attendance at a military academy in Holland. The whole family emigrated to Toronto, Canada, where schooling was less rigid. Pierre's first work in Canada was with religious exiles, the Dukhobors and the Hernhutters, and his mother was delighted with this assignment given her son by the dean of theology at Victoria College in Toronto.

CHILDREN WHO ADOPTED RELATED CAUSES

Ernest Bevin, English statesman and labor leader, had a mother who did day work in the kitchens of wealthier people. She was the community midwife. When she received her fee, she always asked the father for a few extra pennies for the Methodist Chapel, and at such a time who could refuse her? She was a strong temperance worker and a fanatic Dissenter. For years she devoted her spare energies to the raising of money for a chapel to be built on the road to Dover. There was only one cemetery in the community, and it was Anglican, which raised a serious consideration among the Anglican authorities when she died. There were those who objected strongly to her being buried in the village graveyard and her coffin was at the church door before the rector and churchwardens gave consent.

Her youngest son Ernest was seven when she died. At three he had passed out hymn books at the chapel. When he was five and his mother lay very ill, he went to church alone then came home and told her what the minister had said in his sermon. At thirteen the orphan boy ran away from the farm of William May, where he had been scaring birds, following the dibble, hoeing and cutting up mangels and turnips for the cows. There were words over the chores. Ernest was whipped, frightened the punishing farmer with a sharp tool, and ran off to Bristol with his clothes and savings. It was at the Methodist Sunday school that he first became interested in learning and in the problems of labor.

Maxim Litvinov (born Meer Wallach), Russian diplomat, had parents who were among the Jewish intellectuals of Belostok. His father, Moses Wallach, a produce merchant, and his mother, Anna Wallach, made of their home a center for book-loving Belostok intelligentsia. Moses was an intelligent man, interested in contemporary literature, especially Turgenev, Dostoevski, and Tolstoy. People were always dropping in to borrow a book and talk over the latest news, and discussions lasted until late at night. Five-year-old Maxim was deeply affected when secret agents came and took away his father and held him incommunicado for six weeks. A rival in the produce business had given false information about the father but the matter was happily resolved. On his release he was welcomed by his townsmen.

Another child reared in a home which was turbulent with opinion who also did not adopt the parental cause but found a tangential cause upon which to expend her energies, was Margaret Sanger. This protagonist of planned parenthood was one of eleven Higgins children, who were used to being called the "children of the devil" because of their father's admiration for Charles Darwin and Robert Ingersoll. Higgins once rented the biggest building in Corning, New York, in order to present Robert Ingersoll to the public. The building happened to belong to the Roman Catholic Church, and when an indignant mob drove the speaker and his audience to a field behind the Higginses' house, his daughter was tagging along. Her quarrels with the Roman Catholic Church were to be over birth control and planned parenthood. She, too, was a school rebel, and expelled herself from her eighth-grade class when the teacher was insulting and sarcastic.

On another family tree, Bertrand Russell, English philosopher, mathematician, teacher, writer, and iconoclast, found a variety of opinionative ancestors. His father, Amberley Russell, willed his sons Bertrand and Frank to the custody of two agnostic friends. The British public was offended and the children became wards of the court, which placed them in the custody of the paternal grandparents instead. Lady Russell, who took over the rearing of the four-year-old Bertrand and the ten-year-old Frank, had been known as the "Deadly Nightshade" by the members of her husband's cabinet during the period he served as Prime Minister. At the time custody of the boys was given to their grandparents, the grandfather, a dynamic reformer in his day, was old and ill, sat in his Bath chair and ignored their noise. Lady Russell was still exceedingly active. At seventy she quit the Presbyterian church, in which she was reared, and became a Unitarian. She openly opposed Imperialist Wars and the government's attitude toward the Irish. Their own father had not done well in politics because he had introduced a bill in Parliament to make the giving of secular lectures and debates legal on Sunday. Bachelor Uncle Rollo, who also lived in the home, read them his poems about "contending atoms." Frank ran away from home, and was subsequently sent to boarding school, but Bertrand was educated for college at home. When he was fourteen, he thought of suicide because of his torments over religion, but once he had resolved that matter by becoming an agnostic like his father, he was relieved of his burden.

The influence that Daniel and Lucy Anthony had on their daughter, Susan B. Anthony, was early, direct, and lasting and turned her toward a desire to be politically effective. As mill owners they exercised a paternal jurisdiction over the young factory girls who worked for them, housing them in model cottages with flower gardens. The men employees were not allowed to have liquor on the premises. Each Sunday all the workers were invited to the owner's house to hear discussions of world affairs. Daniel was an abolitionist, a worker in the temperance society, and as a Quaker he accepted the equality of women. Susan was having difficulties as secretary of the New York Women's Temperance Society because the New York Men's Temperance Society thought it improper for women to organize. The parents attended a meeting and heard Elizabeth Cady Stanton speak. Her father's enthusiastic letter about this woman prompted his daughter to seek her out, the beginning of a long and fruitful association.

The Anthonys were an independent family. Daniel Anthony was not perturbed to have a daughter who wanted to take part in politics. In a Quaker business meeting the weight of the woman's decision is as strong as the man's and if any one person expresses disagreement with the sense of the meeting no action is taken.

Even among Friends, Daniel and Lucy were unique because Lucy was a volatile outsider brought into membership in the quiet meeting by her husband. The meeting was inclined to demur at accepting the vibrant girl with a singing voice that resounded in the hills when she sang outdoors.

Daniel's business failed during a national panic, and Susan was delighted to be withdrawn from her restrictive school. There was almost nothing in her career which was not the natural flowering of the family influence upon her.

FATHER'S BOYS AMONG THE OPINIONATIVE

A statement by George Bernard Shaw to the effect that mother's boys have a "narrow-minded wisdom" and father's boys a "broader humanity" would seem true in many of these families. Father's boys are more likely to be social rebels or revolutionists or philosophers. Mother's boys more often turn to the arts.

A look into some of these father-centered homes which were highly opinionative will show how boys often act out the paternal daydream. Among the Four Hundred, one-fourth extend the parent in vocation or in ideology. Although several of the boys are rebels in the community, they are often heroes to their fathers. David Dubinsky's father did not object when his son went on strike to get higher wages for bakery employees, although the father owned a bakery shop. He bribed a jailer to get his son released from imprisonment as an agitator.

The mother of William Allen White was an abolitionist Republican. She was a Yankee schoolteacher who lost her job because she insisted on admitting Negro children to the white school she was hired to teach in Council Grove, Kansas, a town with a nest of Southern sympathizers. The tall, thin, thirty-year-old spinster attracted the attention of a pudgy, middle-aged storekeeper and sometime physician, a Democrat during the Civil War who was called a Copperhead because he believed in a negotiated peace and thought Lincoln should have insisted on a peace conference even after Sumter. (Robert Frost's father was of the same opinion.) He was not only a Democrat in a town where eighty per cent of the men were in the Union Army, but he was also a free-thinker who was castigated in the press because he cut wood on Sunday.

Their son, who loved them both profoundly, says:

Never had a child more strongly minded parents who were so different in their ways of thinking. . . . I am amazed that they lived together with an approximation of peace and amity for something more than fifteen years.[3]

David Ben Gurion, the first prime minister of Israel, did not disappoint his father when he was arrested for leading a street meeting in Warsaw which extolled Zionism. (Ben Gurion's boyhood name was David Green.)

David was in jail and had to send for his father to get him out. Avigor was not surprised and had quite expected this to happen when David left home and went to Warsaw to matriculate at the University. He arrived, top hat and all, the efficient, practiced lawyer, used to getting clients out of petty scrapes. Since the police-adjunct also had the surname "Green" and felt avuncular toward the boy the formilities were soon over.

"This boy of ours will be known all over the world some day,"[4] Sheindal Green used to say. Only six of her eleven children survived infancy and "Sheindal the Righteous" tended to overprotect David. Under her care he was withdrawn, sickly, and introverted. He sat among the visitors listening to the talk of Zionism that went on about him; he played chess with the men and was spoken to as an adult. After his mother's death, when he was eleven, he became active, strong, and aggressive.

The town of Jiquilpan, where Lázaro Cárdenas, who was to be president of Mexico, was reared, was in the days of his youth an active center of revolutionary thought and activity. Most of the householders of Jiquilpan were engaged in light industry, making scarves or sandals. The young men in the town went away to work in Mexico City and came home periodically to report the new ideas they learned there. Señor Carreón, the most influential man in Jiquilpan, was not only the tax collector, but also the editor of the liberal periodical *La Popular*, published every fifth day.

Domasco Cárdenas, father of the precocious Lázaro, was also a respected civic leader. Domasco had a strong desire to raise the health and the living standards of the town. Since there was no physician or hospital, he read medical books and treated his own and the neighbor's children. None of his eight children died in infancy; this made the family unique. Domasco valued education for all children. When Lázaro and a friend played truant, he whipped both children impartially.

This driving and opinionative man was a freethinker and was responsive to the new ideas about the need to improve the living standards in Mexico. He tried hard to improve his own lot. When his loom was unremunerative and confining, he started a soap factory that failed. His billiard hall was more successful, but his oldest son, Lázaro, disliked the drinking and gambling of the men who frequented it. The father was sympathetic and apprenticed the eleven-year-old, after graduation from the only school the town afforded, to his own close friend, the revolutionary editor of *La Popular*. It was here that Lázaro Cárdenas was really educated. He learned to read Victor Hugo instead of buccaneer fiction and was taught revolutionary techniques.

When President Lázaro Cárdenas raised health and educational standards to a new level in Mexico, when he established federal education, nationalized the oil industry and the railroads and abolished the parochial schools, he was not rebelling against his home training. Sons among the Four Hundred often accomplish what the fathers wish they might have done. In his own personal life Lázaro Cárdenas showed the strong paternal drives of his forthright father. President Cárdenas required his own family to live simply and added eight orphaned children to his household.

In 1815 a wealthy young Unitarian liberal, Richard Potter, married a "strange, introspective, mystic, wayward 'creature,' " whose empathy with the rejected and despised made her identify with them and "be them." She called herself a Jewess and dreamed visions of taking the Jews back to the Holy Land. She also sometimes called herself a gypsy. It is thought that she really was an English girl of Celtic origin. Mary Sedden Potter and Richard Potter's only son married Laurencina Heyworth, the daughter of a Liverpool merchant who was associated with the Anti-Corn Law League and other radical activities in his area. Laurencina, a learned and charming woman, and her husband had nine learned and opinionative daughters each of whom married an outstanding man, four of whom were at one time or another Members of Parliament, each of whom had a specialized talent, almost all of whom were highly opinionative. Two descendants of Mary Sedden and Richard Potter are among our Four Hundred eminent men and women. These two are their granddaughter Beatrice Webb and their great-grandson Sir Stafford Cripps.

Stafford Cripps was a boy who identified strongly with his pacifist father, Charles Alfred Cripps. Stafford had the freedom of action and affection that many pre-politicians enjoy, and was the intellectually superior child in his family. Like most people who are to become involved in politics or in some phase of political science, he found this vocation late in life. His first goal was to be a scientist.

Stafford was nicknamed "Dad" or "Dadialissimus" because of his persistent habit of offering unsolicited information (a frequent habit of the gifted child) and advice to his elders.

"Dad" was the youngest in a family of five children. When Stafford was a year old, his mother, Theresa Potter Cripps, identified this child as the "rising genius" in the family. By the time he was three the rest of the family had to acknowledge that "Dad" had unusual intellectual powers.

Theresa Potter Cripps died when her youngest son was four. As a legacy she left messages to her husband and children, "I should like the children to be brought up as much as possible in the country, and to be educated in much the same style as their father was. I should like their living to be of the simplest, without reference to show or other follies. . . . I implore my children to stand by each other through thick and thin." Her sister, Beatrice Webb, described Theresa Cripps as "a born artist with an intense sensitivity for people and a power to seize the really significant facts about a person or event."[5]

Stafford's early potential was recognized by the whole family. There were many traditions he could follow, but his father, who became the first Baron Parmoor, wished him to be free to make his own choices. Baron Parmoor was the eighth in four generations of his family to be elected to the House of Commons. He served also as Vicar General of the Archdiocese of Canterbury. Three paternal uncles, a grand-uncle and his great-great-grandfather were Members of Parliament.

Stafford's mother's family was equally distinguished. Aunt Kate Potter Courtney was a second mother to Stafford after his mother's death. She was the wife of Leonard Henry Courtney, a political economist, a leader-writer for *The Times*, and a Liberal Parliamentarian. Blind for many years, he was still a great British statesman. He pursued a liberal-pacifist line, as did Baron Parmoor.

Stafford Cripps had an early acquaintance with other highly opinionative relatives and family friends. His aunt, Margaret Hobhouse, another of the nine granddaughters of Mary Sedden, was a Quaker and pacifist, and was the wife of Henry Hobhouse, a member of Parliament and of the Royal Commission on Secondary Education. Stafford's youngest aunt was Beatrice Webb, who, with her husband Sidney Webb, was a leader of the Fabian Socialist group. Stafford's mother before her marriage did volunteer work in improving housing conditions for the indigent under the direction of Canon Barnett of Toynbee Hall.

His life was never entirely bounded by his family, although the family had the most important impact on his thinking. He was also to be influenced by an adult Quaker, William Sturgis, a family friend with whom he spent time on a holiday, and later by his Quaker stepmother, Marian Ellis, and by his principal at Winchester, The Rev. H. M. Burge.

Whatever the family climate of opinion, being treated as an adult is incomparably important to a young child who is intellectually capable. When he receives an audience and can speak and be spoken to, he is emotionally as well as intellectually satisfied by the experience. Other children find him difficult, as is evidenced by the nickname "Dad." Teachers and parents who have the confidence of an exceptionally able child in his formative years have a tremendous and exciting responsibility. At school Stafford Cripps was a scientist, did well, acquired knowledge, was not particularly aware of social or political issues.

There are wide divergencies in this family, but a central tendency toward social concern operates within the wider framework. A cousin, Stephen Hobhouse, refused to inherit his father's property and, while in prison as a conscientious objector, wrote *English Prisons Today*, a valuable sociological document.

Various contemporary members of this opinionative family are presently concerned with freedom for colonial peoples, the furthering of the United Nations and of agricultural advances which will help to feed world citizens in underdeveloped areas, town planning, rural housing, vagrancy, footpaths and national parks. Among the descendents of Mary Sedden Potter are the children of a distinguished African diplomat, Joseph Appiah. A great-great-grandson, Col. Richard Meinertzhagen, who is a military hero as well as a scientist, shows the family strain of individuality by naming as his recreations in the current *Who's Who*: "biology, geography, solitude and space." Eccentric and energetic ancestors, however opinionative, are not to be underestimated. The "neutral" parent who flattens his own affect in order to be the colorless background against which his child can appear with distinction may find that his children are also colorless and mediocre.

As boys and girls, the Four Hundred, as if they were adults, enjoy the intimate companionship of stimulating adults who speak to them. John Galsworthy, whose parents were not congenial, felt that his mother's limited approach to life made such a formidable barrier in their mother-son relationship that he could never enjoy her company. She bored him with her closed mind. No famous man surveyed says that he is sorry he had an opinionative parent, but often says he likes having had parents with something to say who were not afraid to be outspoken. Even when he repudiates the conclusions to which they came or rejects the causes for which they labored he tells anecdotes about them to illustrate something about which he cannot openly boast — his inheritance of intellectual capacity and curiosity and vitality of expression.

Parents Who Suffered Death or Prison or Exile

Certain offspring, however, although they approve of their parents, seem wary about actually extending the parental pattern when the statement of a strong conviction or a rebellious action has caused an ancestor to be exiled, to be imprisoned for an appreciable period, or to meet an untimely death. They turn, perhaps unconsciously, not to the cause for which the parents labored but to artistic expression.

Ignace Jan Paderewski was only three when his father was imprisoned for a year and a month because of anti-Russian activities. The stories he heard of his father's imprisonment affected Ignace deeply. He turned to music, but espoused the cause of Polish freedom in his later years with equal intensity. He had psychological difficulties in both careers, and turned to farming for a period when he was physically unable to play the piano. He was never easy or relaxed in either of his vocational roles. To what extent his father's imprisonment was related to his own problems is not at all clear.

Joseph Conrad, the Polish-born boy who wrote his novels in English, was never to tell a story more tragic and tender than that of his father, Apollo Nalecz Korzeniowski, and his mother, who was born Evelina Bobrowsky. Their marriage was postponed for six years by the bride's family because the handsome fiancé did nothing but sit in the mansion on his father's estate and write poetry and plays which were never published. It was only because Evelina became physically ill with frustration that her brothers consented to the marriage when she was twenty-five and Apollo was thirty-six. They considered themselves among Apollo's best friends but demurred against his marriage to their sister.

To the consternation of the relatives on both sides of the family, Apollo, who had taken a position as an estate manager to please his in-laws, soon lost his own inheritance and also the money which was his wife's dowry. Evelina loved him nonetheless and both became involved in the cause of Polish freedom. When Apollo Korzeniowski was sentenced to exile in Siberia he was fortunate, since it was only because of his distracted relatives that he was spared execution.

Evelina demanded that she be permitted to be considered a political prisoner also. The authorities consented and the delicate wife and four-year-old boy joined the caravan of prisoners on a rugged three-month coach trip to Siberia. No other woman or child was in the group. When she was a maiden in her own home, Evelina had not even dressed herself. Joseph nearly died on the terrible journey; and Evelina, near death when the journey's end was reached, never fully recovered. Conrad watched his parents die lingering, painful deaths; first his mother when he was seven, then his beloved father when the son was twelve.

At seventeen he refused to go to college and his affectionate but puzzled relatives let him have his way. The orphaned boy wanted to find the sea about which he had only read: the warm, faraway South Seas. Secondary school had been an obnoxious experience to him despite his brilliance. During the long Siberian winters Apollo Korzeniowski had been his son's tutor, and no classroom teacher could ever take his place. Joseph Conrad, as he is known to the English-speaking world, never espoused the cause which his parents adopted so passionately. Nature was the enemy which preoccupied him.

Another boy whose father suffered persecution is Konrad Bercovici. In the Bulgarian community in which this Jewish boy was reared, there was only one citizen who treated the gypsies like human beings: Konrad's father. Young Konrad had a gypsy nurse to whom he "belonged." She was so much like a mother to him that she was permitted to take him away from the home with her for long periods of time.

Konrad was not fond of his own mother, who lived in a fantasy world where the novels she read incessantly were more real to her than her husband and children. Konrad Bercovici was his father's boy, and when he found school unbearably dull because it did not challenge him, his father enthusiastically tutored him at home. Both father and son enjoyed the rapid academic progress the son made. They were kindred spirits, volatile and quick of understanding.

This domestic tranquillity was ended when the father was fatally beaten in a pogrom directed against the Jews and gypsies in the community. When the father died, Konrad ran away with the gypsies. He never became a community leader like his father, but he won fame as a writer about gypsy life.

William Cody, better known as Buffalo Bill, always felt that the abolition movement took his father from him. Isaac Cody set up a store near Salt Creek in the Kansas Territory, was a member of the Topeka legislature and an officer for the New England Emigrant Aid Society, which brought in abolitionist settlers.

Isaac was well on his way to achieving both economic security and political status when he was stabbed by pro-slavers; was forced to hide in a cornfield to avoid further attacks; was overworked by the demands of his tent city of emigrants who were bogged down in the mud. His death from a respiratory infection was attributed by his family to his abolitionist activities. Bill Cody, at eleven, took a man's job as a rider for Russell, Majors and Wadell of the Pony Express in order to support his widowed mother and sisters. He was never deeply concerned with politics or reform movements as his father had been.

Clovis Gauguin, father of Paul Gauguin, an ineffectual journalist for the *National*, a liberal Republican paper, fled France when Napoleon III came into power and was en route to Peru when he died of a heart attack.

To Aline Marie, the pretty and flirtatious wife of Clovis Gauguin, her husband's death was merely another calamity in a long series of adverse events. In her childhood she had once been kidnapped from her school by her father, who was later sentenced to twenty years at hard labor because he shot and seriously wounded her mother, the beautiful and dynamic Flora Tristan Chazal. For twenty years, Paul's grandfather grieved because his lovely young wife had left him to go about Europe preaching the doctrines of the Comte de Saint-Simon: socialism, sex equality, and free love of a noble sort. He obtained custody of his son through the courts. For twenty years Chazal loved and desired the woman who had left him to lecture and to write books and pamphlets, each more inflammatory than the last. When he shot her, she was seriously injured and never fully recovered. All France was titillated over the trial.

To young Paul Gauguin, an exiled child in Peru, these family stories were a familiar part of his heritage. He always spoke well of his grandmother when he was an adult, called her a "deuce of a woman, a true blue socialist, a pretty and noble lady."[6]

In his middle years, Paul Gauguin was not to be opinionative like his father and grandmother, but turned to a re-creation of the life he lived in Peru at the time he lost his father.

Claudio Toscanini, father of the Italian conductor Arturo Toscanini, made a vocation out of being a follower of Garibaldi and took part in three campaigns. On one occasion he was sentenced to be shot. He watched his comrades die, was placed against the wall to be executed, teased, taunted, then was reprieved and sentenced to three years' imprisonment.

When he came home to his family, which was in poor financial circumstances, he could not bring himself to work for long in his tailor shop. Instead, he roamed the streets seeking citizens with whom he could argue about politics. When his adolescent son assumed the support of the family, Claudio was not sorry. In his old age he still buttonholed citizens and made them listen to his speeches, but the content was changed. He talked of the incomparable skills and infinite glory of his son Arturo. Arturo Toscanini did not extend his father's interest in politics, but neither did he accept fascism when it came, becoming a voluntary exile and refusing to perform in Nazi Germany.

Status and Opinionativeness

Families with wealth or inherited status for whom there are multiple listings in standard reference works and who also have a representative among the Four Hundred are: Adams, Balfour, Baldwin, Byrd, Cecil, Chamberlain, Churchill, Cooper, Cripps,

James, Kennedy, Nehru, Rau, Roosevelt, Rockefeller, Russell, Sitwell, and Taft. In these families the contribution is commonly in the field of political action. Accumulative opinionativeness in the family, an expectation of achievement, and a habit of speaking out and making definite decisions are inherent in the total family climate of opinion.

Low-income families less often contribute multiple names to fame. When they do so, the honors frequently come for shared achievement. This too speaks for the power of family cohesion, the value of pooling ideas, and the need for support in working out difficult problems. Wilbur and Orville Wright, sons of a strong-minded small-town United Brethern minister, were looked upon with affectionate feeling and were respected for their right to work out their ideas in their own way. They sorely needed the support they gave each other. Disbelieving major newspapers would not report the news of their accomplishment at Kitty Hawk in 1903.

Among the other famous brothers who came from opinionative families with comparatively low incomes are the medical Mayos and Menningers. Those who have known Walter, Victor and Roy Reuther since their young manhood cannot conceive of the contributions of any one of the brothers having been as readily accomplished without the support of the others.

Each Sunday their father, a union official in a Wheeling, West Virginia, brewery, gathered his four boys together in a back bedroom upstairs for a discussion on labor reforms, politics, and woman suffrage. He took them to see Eugene V. Debs in prison. Their grandfather, a German socialist leader, was a family hero.

POLITICS, RELIGION, RACE AND NATIONALITY

Politics and religion, in that order, were the subjects about which parents were most likely to be opinionative. Abolition of slavery, woman suffrage, colonialism, reforms in education, and world peace were topics the children heard discussed at dinner. They were concerned with the reconciliation of science and religion; the single tax; the Boer War; the special problems of India and Ireland; civic reform and education for the masses.

Only twenty-seven of the families were strictly sectarian in religious practices and tried to restrict their children's participation in the larger community of ideas and beliefs. Political views were most frequently described as liberal.

Forty-four parents were partners in interdenominational or international marriages. Winston Churchill, Thomas Mann and William Carlos Williams are among those who speak favorably of having parents who represent two nations. Santayana had the most involved national background. Marcel Proust, Fiorello La Guardia, and Stephen Spender each came from homes where one parent had been reared in a Jewish, the other in a Gentile tradition. Norbert Wiener, Erica and Klaus Mann, and Charles Chaplin had both Jewish and Gentile ancestors. Diego Rivera and Paul Klee had ancestors representing both the dark- and light-skinned races.

There is no evidence that ability or achievement must be confined to any nation or race or mixture of nationalities or races. There is no way of determining to what extent provincialism or prejudice have inhibited expression of talent in the past or present. Terman, in the twenties, found only one family on the West Coast of the United States with more than one intellectually gifted child. This family had four Eurasian children. Leta Hollingworth found only one family in New York City with more than one child who had an intelligence quotient of 180 (Binet) or more. These children had one white and one Negro parent.

Among the newer biographies which are not included in this survey (because in each instance there is only one volume about the person) are indications that children born of interracial marriages are beginning to enter the ranks of the eminent. There are excellent biographies of Harry Belafonte and Katherine Dunham (both born of Negro-white marriages) and of Eugenie Clark, an American-Eurasian ichthyologist married to a physician of Greek ancestry.

Although there is a drift toward more unconventional marriages among the parents of the Four Hundred, most of them married persons of their own race, nationality, and religion. Among the Four Hundred themselves there is an increase in the less conventional marriages. David Daiches, Enrico Fermi, Harold Laski,

Abraham Flexner, Virginia Stephen Woolf, Artur Schnabel, and Bernard Berenson are among those who made Jewish-Gentile marriages. Kwame Nkrumah is married to a young woman from Egypt. Syngman Rhee married a Westerner.

Lafcadio Hearn, the son of an English father and a mother from Malta, married a Japanese girl; and Santha Rama Rau, a writer from India, is married to an American. It can be noted that Samuel Clemens's only granddaughter has a Jewish father.

The plain listing of the religious backgrounds of the children reared in these cradles of eminence might seem to be a simple though tedious detail. In practice it was a complex and frustrating task. In one out of eight families it was not possible to find any description of religious preference; not in accounts of births, marriages, or deaths, nor in the indexes of many books thumbed through, nor in reference material, nor in the thread of personal narrative in an unindexed autobiography. Sectarianism is not a familiar phenomenon.

Naming of religious background is not to be confused with indicating the religious preference of the eminent adult who comes from this family. G. K. Chesterton, reared an Anglican, became a famous protagonist of Roman Catholicism. Alfred Adler, a member of the only Jewish family in his Roman Catholic community, became Protestant. The drift in the families, as well as it can be estimated, is toward nonsectarianism or agnosticism. It is often the work which is the absorbing goal of the famous man or woman. Education and science tend to replace religion as the pathway to what is thought good.

In an age when even to read Darwin was daring there were a significant number of agnostics or freethinkers or avowed atheists among the parents. Among these was the "freethinker" Moses Carver, foster father to the slave boy whom he bought back from the kidnappers who had stolen the child in order to resell him. Moses Carver played an important role in giving the talents of George Washington Carver to the world.* Not holding the con-

*Families where one or both parents were agnostic had the following eminent children: William Beveridge, Konrad Bercovici, Clarence Darrow, Isadora Duncan, Albert Einstein, Bernard Berenson, Anatole France, Ford Madox Ford, Havelock Ellis, Paul Gauguin, Diego Rivera, Charles Lindbergh, ventional attitudes toward established religions of the place and time in which they lived, makes these parents particularly opinionative.

A highly opinionative group at the other end of the ideological scale were the twenty-one ministers,* two rabbis and one Greek Orthodox priest who fathered eminent sons and daughters. Ministers' sons have been observed to be exceptionally competent. In the 1921-1922 volume of *Who's Who in America,* according to Stephen S. Visher,[7] the clergymen of all denominations were represented by one son for each 20 fathers; the professional men by one son for each 46 members; farmers by one son in 690; skilled laborers by one child in 1600; and unskilled laborers by one in 48,000. Among the clergymen, Unitarian ministers, known for their love for learning and opinionativeness, were the most frequently represented, with one son for each seven of the fathers.

It is one thing to be exceptionally competent and another thing to enhance or disturb the status quo sufficiently to become the subject of a biography. There are no sons of Unitarian ministers among the Four Hundred, unless we include Clarence Darrow, whose father left the ministry before his son was old enough to know him in that role. There are, however, sixteen sons of Unitarian laymen among the Four Hundred. David Daiches and Harry Houdini were sons of rabbis; Ivan Pavlov was the son of a Greek Orthodox priest.

Roman Catholic parents, internationally, are not often involved

---

H. L. Mencken, Thomas Alva Edison, Bertrand Russell, Margaret Sanger, George Santayana, Hans Zinsser, George Bernard Shaw, William Allen White, Eugene Debs, Fiorello La Guardia, Benito Mussolini, Alexander Woollcott, George Washington Carver, Sergei Prokofiev, Lázaro Cárdenas, Sigrid Undset, Romain Rolland, Salvador Dali.

*Ministers' sons and daughters noted among the Four Hundred included: Phyllis Bottome, Pearl Buck, Stephen Crane, Grover Cleveland, Reginald Fessenden, Charles Evans Hughes, John Cowper Powys, Henry and William James, Martin Luther King, C. Day Lewis, Field Marshal Montgomery, Cecil Rhodes, Reinhold Neibuhr, Albert Schweitzer, Freidrich Nietzsche, Martin Niemöller, William Saroyan, Olive Schreiner, Woodrow Wilson, William Osler, and Orville and Wilbur Wright. Sean O'Casey was the son of a paid Protestant executive. Lloyd George was reared by a minister uncle. Grenfell's father left teaching to go into missionary work in a hospital. The fathers of Clarence Darrow, Frank Lloyd Wright and Cecil De Mille left the ministry for other occupations.

in controversial social issues and do not often produce scientists or humanitarians. They do become involved in revolutionary or political movements. The nonopinionative families are often engrossed in business or in the arts. Almost none are described as reactionary in politics, few as fundamentalist in religious beliefs. The seven persons* who became eminent as representatives of a specific religious organization had interests which reached far beyond their own sectarianism. They were involved with trying to further peace, or with the problems of displaced persons and migrants, or with furthering cooperation between Christian and Jewish groups, or with the problems arising from race prejudice, hunger, and disease.

It is the non-Catholic families, internationally, which are highly opinionative, and which contribute to the world pool of talent in science, in humanitarian and in reform movements. Knapp and Goodrich,[8] in a study of the origins of American scientists, found that "a disproportionally large number of scientists are produced in the U. S. A. by Protestant middle-class backgrounds and are trained in the small liberal arts colleges that mirror these values." All of the sixty-four eminent scientists studied by Anne Roe[9] were Protestant in childhood background except the six Jewish members of the group. Jewish families are well represented in all major fields of endeavor.

One-half of the Four Hundred come from highly opinionative families. It is these homes which produce most of the scientists, humanitarians and reformers.

---

*Sister Cabrini; the Roman Catholic fathers John LaFarge and Dominique Piré; and John R. Mott, Reinhold Neibuhr, Martin Niemöller and Rufus Jones.

[3]

Failure-Prone Fathers

> The family ruin seems to have been the
> lifting of the dam upon their creative poten-
> tialities. . . . Within two generations they
> gave four names to the National Biography.
> Father's name was the fifth.
> — SIR NIGEL CONAN DOYLE
> (son of Sir Arthur Conan Doyle)

APPROXIMATELY one-half of the fathers in this study turn out
to be failure-prone in the routine of everyday life. Since it
is impossible to know whether they are more or less addicted to
failure than were their male contemporaries in the geographical
area and in the times in which they live, we can only conclude
that bankruptcy or professional failure on the part of the father
does not preclude success on the part of the offspring. A child can
make the most of himself in a home where the economic basis for
subsistence is insecure and variable. Seeing his father try and fail
does not seemingly inhibit the child's striking out into untested
areas of achievement.

An examination of the emotional climate in these homes
affected by father-failure finds that there are two types of fathers
who have difficulties in their professional careers and in their
business ventures. First are the fathers who are given to daydreaming and to scholarly retreat from the mainstream of life. Second
are the fathers who are impractical, grandiose — who leap before
they look. Both groups are inclined to believe that good times
are just around the corner.

55

Erich Fromm says that creativity requires the courage to let go of certainties. Certainties are let go in these families with abandon; often before the new course is charted. Norbert Wiener is an American citizen because his father got stranded in New Orleans on his way to join a communal colony in South America where vegetarianism could be practiced. He ended his career as a professor of languages at Harvard. In a goodly number of these families the father is prone to flights of fancy, is restless and experimental. The father of Richard Nixon was restless by nature, was extroverted, argumentative, and gregarious. He was frequently moved to sample the job opportunities in various places, was a glass worker, potter, grocer, a painter of Pullman cars, a potato farmer, a sheep rancher, a pioneer telephone lineman, motorman, roustabout in the oil fields, carpenter, and a labor agitator who organized the streetcar motormen after he froze his own feet standing in an open vestibule. When he finally settled down to his fruit store and gasoline station in California (where the warmth was kind to his tender feet), his store became a kind of neighborhood club where the proprietor talked politics and his wife soothed the ruffled customers. Had not illness struck the family, however, he would probably have achieved some security in his old age.

Major George Whistler, a onetime army engineer, was the father of the erratic bachelor painter James McNeill Whistler. It was the major who made the decision that the family should go with him to Russia, where he was commissioned to build a railroad from St. Petersburg to Moscow. His wife, always a foreboding woman, did not want to go and never quite recovered from the shock of having a child die in her arms en route. Major Whistler did not find getting employment easy. His work changes in the United States were too frequent; he had little ability in handling his own financial affairs. As an engineer he was apt at cutting roads through difficult terrain; he enjoyed solving technical problems, but his employers were prone to mistrust his judgment. The Tsar was excited by the ebullient American and gave hundreds of reluctant peasants orders to help him build a railroad through four hundred miles of swamp. When cholera broke out in the labor camps, Whistler's father died. The Tsar offered to give the two oldest boys, James and William, positions as pages in his court; but the family, left in straitened circumstances, sought refuge on a Connecticut farm.

Abraham Maslow[1] in observations of "self-actualizing people" uses descriptive terms which are found over and over in characterizations of fathers of eminent sons. But the fathers of the Four Hundred are often not successful, although they are willing to be reasonable adventurers and take calculated risks — qualities necessary in those who do make significant contributions. The inference is that a son with these traits may succeed although the father failed.

Maslow has observed that the famous man often has a "second naivete," that he is frequently childlike in his spontaneity, is unfrightened by the unknown, attracted by the mysterious and the puzzling. He finds that men who have achieved highly can be "comfortably disorderly, sloppy, anarchic, chaotic, vague, doubtful, uncertain, indefinite, approximate, inexact, or inaccurate," which he defines as being desirable qualities at certain moments in science, art or life in general. He finds that great men have less need than other people to be pleasing to other men, that they are commonly indifferent as to what people think of them.

Cursory examination of the adult lives of the Four Hundred would tend to support Maslow's observations. We can certainly cite the frequency with which individuals of this type are the fathers of eminent men. Nor is Dr. Maslow the only scholar who makes the observation that naïveté is a characteristic of the creative. Ernest Jones has observed that great men can be credulous and have characteristically receptive natures. He cites Goethe, Copernicus, Newton and Darwin as his examples. Thomas Mann observes that there can be the union in some human beings of the greatest intellectual gifts with the most amazing naïveté.

Arthur Koestler, while discussing the characteristics of his own father, an ebullient, erratic man who was sometimes a business failure and sometimes very wealthy, says:

The financial heavyweights who have crossed my path, publishers, art-dealers, bankers, movie producers — have been without exception idiosyncratic, eccentric, irrational and basically naïve individuals. . . .

Apparently the shrewd, cold calculating type is mainly to be found in the light and middle-weight categories of business.[2]

Morris Gershwin, father of the composer George Gershwin, a man who specialized in business failures, created a folklore of Gershwinisms based on his spontaneous and childish reactions. His sons once counted twenty-eight flats in which they lived while moving about to be near their father's latest business. Morris tried his hand at restaurants, Russian and Turkish baths, book-making, bakeries, a cigar store, and a pool hall.

Milovan Djilas, Montenegrin-born, a politician, and author of *The New Class,* had an incapable farmer father who set his stone house high on a windy hill where the chimney could be seen for miles around. The family lived on the second floor; the animals were warmer below. His overworked wife cursed the wind and cared little for the view. The father was a tireless worker who built irrigation ditches where no water was ever to flow, planted seeds in barren soil. His children knew their mother was right; the house should have been built in a sheltered valley, but they were always glad to see the house on a hilltop when they returned from afar. "So men are divided. Some are for the useful, some for the beautiful. I placed myself," says the son, Milovan, "on the side for beauty."[3]

Amadeo Modigliani's mother was in labor when the bailiff called to cart off the household goods. Her son was born amid valuables hidden in his mother's bed to save them. Fortunes were made as well as lost in this family. They were never really poor, merely experienced catastrophic reverses.

An engineer, Joseph Ravel, father of Maurice, won no acclaim for the two-cylinder horseless carriage he built and patented in 1866. Instead he was fined for disturbing the peace. Anatole France, whose father rose from peasant to bookseller, only to find that he had more chair-warmers than customers, was torn between his cold, withdrawn father and his weeping, smothering, neurotic mother. François Zola, who died while involved in a scheme to build canals, left his young son Emile and his helpless wife destitute. Sigmund Freud was just plain irked when his gentle father told him he could no longer support a twenty-six-year-old scholar. Dr. Freud was his mother's boy, and had a mild contempt for his father.

An extreme example of compensating the mother for the business failure of the father is Andrew Carnegie. This was not accomplished without trauma, and the influence of the dreaming, idealistic father emerges strongly in the life of the adult financier.

Through no fault of his own, William Carnegie lost his means of livelihood and it was his wife, Margaret, who became the head of the household and made plans for them to sail to America when Andrew was ten and his brother Tom was five.

There was no work for William Carnegie in Dunfermline, Scotland, where as in all Great Britain, the new textile mills replaced the hand-loom weavers. The family might have starved, as 300,000 workers in Ireland had already done, had not the wife opened a shabby grocery store and mended shoes while William unsuccessfully peddled his woven tablecloths from door to door.

When Andrew became rich, he lived with his mother in a succession of hotels. He longed for a home, but she preferred to flit from hotel to hotel. At forty-four he fell in love with a girl of twenty-two, but did not marry her until he was fifty-two and his mother had been dead a year. He never forgot the family's arrival in America, his own employment at twelve as a bobbin boy, his promise to his mother never to marry and to make her rich. When his gentle father died, Andrew had mother all to himself. She used to say, "No woman is good enough for my Andra."

William Carnegie had never been a terribly good provider when there was a steady market for his work so the family had no resources for an emergency. William was an incorrigible dreamer, an idealist, a man unconcerned about money unless an acute need for it threatened his wife and children. He turned to Swedenborgianism, but his wife confided to her oldest son that she preferred the old-fashioned Scotch Presbyterianism in which they had been reared.

Andrew's "Uncle Tammie" Morrison, the Chartist organizer, was known from one end of Scotland to the other. Uncle Tammie, his mother's brother, tramped from one village to another carrying a huge cudgel, whiskers flying in the wind. He was a forceful speaker, was even in jail for a week. Andrew had planned to be a Chartist like his own father. Once when William was speaking to a big crowd, Andrew tried to push through to the front to hear his father. The undersized boy was lifted to the shoulders of a strong man in the audience and sat there trembling with pride to hear his father speak while other men listened.

Boys who dislike their fathers, who have poor peer relationships and have mothers who are self-centered and socially withdrawn, are often hostile and unfriendly adults, but Carnegie had a gentle affection for his father. Andrew Carnegie became a generous and kindly man to those he met in person. He responded to begging letters, had a long list of pensioners, and immensely enjoyed returning to Dunfermline as a rich man. In business, however, Carnegie could be ruthless if not completely thick-skinned: the Homestead strikes upset him and he went to Europe until they were over.

He required his wife to sign a marriage agreement promising not to be his heiress although he endowed her generously so that she would never fear want or dependency. His gifts to libraries, research projects, and world peace totaled $330,000,000. His booklet outlining the social responsibilities of rich men became a bestseller in the United States and in Europe for a brief period. The personal debt he felt he owed his mother was paid in full; most of his personal wealth he gave away. He was always to be torn between his father's idealism and his mother's materialism.

Tom Carnegie, his younger brother, was never burdened by a compulsion to "make it up to mother." He married a young woman of his own age, had a houseful of children and always worked for his brother, who took a paternal attitude toward him. As Andrew Carnegie grew richer and older, the sight and touch of the money he earned offended him. He could not carry money on his person, was once put off a London tram because he had no coins in his pocket. Henry Ford and Charlie Chaplin, other poor boys who became rich, also had a distaste for the actual handling of money.

Another boy whose father experienced spectacular ups and downs was John D. Rockefeller, who was born on a farm near

Richford, New York. The father, William Avery Rockefeller, was a traveling vendor of quack medicines. Big Bill, when he came home, was a flamboyant, good-looking giant, racing sleek horses, with never less than a thousand dollars in his pocket. He doled out five-dollar gold pieces to his children. During the long intervals when he was not at home they had lean living; on one occasion James and William could not have their pictures taken with the class at school because their clothes were shabby. John D. used to sit by the road waiting month after dreary month for his father to come home. "Big Bill" was a charlatan who sold a cancer elixir by the bottle and offered treatments for twenty-five dollars each. The signs he posted outside the village hotels promised to cure all cases of cancer, unless they were too far gone — even then they could be greatly benefited.

Big Bill cheated his own sons whenever he could, just to teach them to be clever in handling money. He gave them early responsibilities, sent John D. to buy cordwood for the family when he was ten, and a little while later commissioned him to build a house. The boy employed an architect, let out the contracts, saw that the house was built. The father-failure in this instance was that of periodic, drastic nonsupport. The ups and downs of life are harder on the children than poverty which is unrelieved by riches. Unless there is actual hunger, children like Alben Barkley, whose father was a sharecropper on many poor Kentucky farms before he could buy his own small farm, are not affected by the consistently low standard of living experienced by the family.

Even when a family is actually very wealthy, the children can experience strong anxieties about money if the father frets about business matters. Diana Cooper, daughter of an English lord, a girl who lived in a castle with parents who were wealthy, developed real fears about poverty because of her father's way of speaking about taxes. John D. Rockefeller's daughter Bessie, during a period when her father was under public censure, lay physically stricken in France, and was also deeply disturbed, sure she would die penniless.

When John D. Rockefeller's wife, Cettie, died, her body could not be taken home to Cleveland for burial because Cleveland tax assessors said John D. owed the city money and were waiting to serve him with papers if he brought his wife to the family plot. Being rich does not mean the children have no experience with failure, which can be based on other than financial factors. The succeeding Rockefellers have been concerned at times with the failure of their ancestors to win universal public acclaim and respect. John D.'s brother Frank disinterred his two dead children from the family burial plot as a protest against his brother's business practices.

John D. Rockefeller, Jr., was never permitted to feel rich, as a matter of parental principle. His own children had only one tricycle so that they could learn to share. A penny was the fine for coming late to prayers. Away at school, John D. Rockefeller, Jr., pressed his own pants under music books.

When John D. Rockefeller, Jr.'s family went on a trip each child had a job and a salary. Each child had an allowance and his books were closely scrutinized. The children helped with baggage, cleaned shoes, hung up clothes. When they were home they swatted flies, weeded gardens, shined shoes, raised rabbits and sold them to a laboratory. When Nelson and Laurance spent a summer with a Grenfell group in the northern wilds, and the cook became ill, the two boys were able to take over the sick man's work and do it better than he.

According to William Manchester, author of *A Rockefeller Family Portrait*, the tradition of simple living and sticking to a budget persists:

When a Rockefeller allowance is gone, it's gone. Nelson was talking to a visitor in his Seal Harbor home not long ago when one of his sons came in. "Dad, I've got five dollars left," the boy said. "If I just had five more I could go to the dance." Nelson looked sympathetic. "Gee, that's too bad," he murmured, and went on talking.

The energy and imaginativeness of the picturesque old medicine man who told amusing stories, and lived to be a spry one hundred has not been dissipated in his great-grandsons. Nelson Rockefeller has an impulsiveness and physical energy which has been known to send him mountain climbing in the evening after he has exhausted his fellow workers during the day. Manchester says, "Nelson's talent is for action, for plunging ahead. . . .[His] brothers lack his impulsiveness, but they all have something of his physical energy."

Caitlin Thomas, in her book *Leftover Life to Kill,* says of her father-in-law:

. . . that most unhappy of all men I have ever met; who did all the spade work of casting off the humble beginnings, bettering himself, assiduously cultivating the arts; and finished up a miserable finicky failure; while passing on to Dylan, on a heaped up plate, the fruits of all the years of unrewarding labor.

To F. Scott Fitzgerald, the failure of his father to make an adequate living for the family as a wholesale grocery salesman was the catastrophe that turned him into a boy who was alternately crawling in front of kitchen maids and insulting the great. When he was sent to a school for wealthy Roman Catholic boys by his aunt, it was not only his feminine prettiness but also his habit of debating with and contradicting the boys who had more money than he which made him a social failure. He was always a "poor relation" among the rich.

A boy can be ashamed of his father's failure and try to conceal the family's low status. Henrik Ibsen never forgave his father for the sudden failure which impoverished the family, moved them from the well-to-do section of town to the impoverished outskirts, and required his son to be an apothecary's assistant rather than a college student. Albert Berenson, the immigrant peddler, was once greeted in the kitchen of a customer for whom he was displaying his wares with the news that a certain young man, the important Bernard Berenson, a scholar and critic, was in the house as a guest.[4] The abashed father hastily gathered his wares and left before his own close connection with the honored guest could be known. Albert Berenson was modest and unsuccessful. His relatives did very well in the liquor business and his wife and children resented being poor relations. He could talk beautifully about French history, philosophy, Voltaire and Rousseau, but his "dreadful laugh" annoyed his son; they did not get on well together. No one talked much to the father, not even his wife, who placed her hopes on her son; so the lonely old fellow went about speaking to himself.

Paul Ehrlich, famous bacteriologist, had such a father, an innkeeper in the small town of Strehlen in Upper Silesia, a kindly, eccentric man who sat talking to himself while his wife ran the tavern. Two expedients are common in homes where the father is not a good provider: keeping a boarding house or tavern, or keeping a private school.

One of the families which made a good adjustment to an early catastrophic experience was that of Dwight David Eisenhower. His parents, before they had finished their freshman year, quit college to marry. Within two years they lost the $2000 and 160 acres of Kansas farm land near Abilene which David Eisenhower had been given as a wedding present by his well-to-do and thrifty father, an important dignitary in the local Church of the Brethern congregation. David had not wanted to be a farmer, had intended to be an engineer. His dynamic young wife, Ida, an orphan girl who had been overworked on a farm owned by inconsiderate relatives, had spent her own small inheritance on her schooling and a fine piano. She was a music student.

The young husband and wife mortgaged their land to David's older sister Amanda and bought a small general store at Hope, Kansas. An absconding partner robbed the till and left the country. Bills he had said were already paid were presented for payment. Customers who were given credit could not pay what they owed because of a drought and a drop in the price of wheat. The distracted young husband put his affairs in the hands of a lawyer who also cheated him and kept the remaining money. A move to Denison, Texas, was also a mistake and disappointment. The relatives coaxed them to come home.

When the family was reestablished, with David as foreman of the Belle Springs Creamery in Abilene, Kansas, there were no scenes, no recriminations. To Ida, their early misadventures were as much her responsibility as his. She once bought law books to try to find out how they might get some returns from the lawyer who cheated them, but soon gave up the lost cause. The children never heard their parents quarrel, and it was always David who was deferred to as the head of the household — but it was Ida who was the more dynamic and could make a decision a minute. She never worked outside the home, even when times were bad, and spent her spare energies on her embroidery and on her music. She made the boys do their chores over and over until they did their work right; she supervised the selling of vegetables from the three-acre garden tract upon which their home was situated in the "wrong" part of town. The children were busy, but never poverty-stricken. Their neighbors were not more wealthy than they.

David was a dreamer and seeker. Religion was his hobby; he read all books on religion that came his way and once occupied himself trying to correlate Bible history with the building of the pyramids, drew diagrams, made computations. Ida Stover Eisenhower was a Lutheran, and when they were first married, they attended the Lutheran church. Later, for a time, they went to Methodist services. Mostly, they attended the Church of the Brethren, the denomination in which David had been reared. Eventually he broke from the River Brethren church and met, in his own home and in the homes of others, with a group that called themselves Bible students. He had an inquiring mind, never found an answer to his religious doubts, and left this last organization because he could not go along with the dogma. The sting of his early failure kept him from accepting the law as an honest profession. For soldiers or lawyers he had little admiration. He felt even more sorrow over having a lawyer son than a soldier son. The "doctor" son he wished for he never had. To David Eisenhower the physician was always the most admirable of professional men.

THE ALCOHOLIC FATHERS

The alcoholic, failure-prone fathers of the Four Hundred present some unusual findings which are corroborated in part by sociological studies. A convincing relationship between subsistence anxiety and insobriety was found by D. Horton,[5] who analyzed fifty-six primitive societies and found that the greater the anxiety concerning the drought or flood or crop failure, the greater is the consumption rate of the available alcohol. He sees alcohol as a means of reducing anxiety. The amount of alcoholism in a culture also depends on the degree to which the culture operates to bring about acute needs for adjustment, or inner tensions in its members; the set of attitudes toward drinking which the culture produces in its members and the degree to which the culture provides suitable substitute means of satisfaction.

A great many of the alcoholic, failure-prone parents in the Four Hundred are caught in anxiety-producing situations. An unexpected and provocative observation not previously noted is that twenty-one alcoholic fathers in this survey produced fourteen children who are actors or singers or writers with an exceptional sense of humor.

George Bernard Shaw's reasoning as to this relationship between a drinking father and a clowning son is as follows: "If you cannot get rid of the family skeleton, make it dance."[6] He explains that a boy who has seen his father, with an imperfectly wrapped goose under one arm and an equally unwrapped ham under the other, butt at the garden wall with his tall hat and crush it into a concertina will not become a boy who makes tragedies of trifles instead of trifles of tragedies.

His own father, George Carr Shaw, was a failure as a clerk and as a government civil servant, and made a bad investment when he bought a corn mill which was always near bankruptcy. Impending failure set George Shaw giggling; funerals drove him to helpless laughter. His own tippling shamed him, however, since he did not believe in drinking. He gave talks to that effect which his son sincerely believed — only to find out with consternation that the father was a secret drinker.

When his wife left him and went to London with a fellow music teacher, the older Shaw drank less, and started calling on old friends. He reformed almost completely as to drunkenness but never gained in competence as a business man. It was a need for income and revulsion for her husband's drunkenness, not love, which prompted Mrs. Shaw to go away with Vandaleur Lee, an older man who had shared a house with the Shaws in Dublin so that both Lucinda Elizabeth Gurly Shaw and he could have an impressive studio for their pupils. Her son always described the separation of his parents in terms of financial straits, not passion.

He said that anyone who could have seduced his mother could have seduced the Virgin at Nuremburg, that she could have boarded and lodged the Three Musketeers and D'Artagnan and would have taken no notice of their sex — unless they smoked in the living room.

Shaw could jest of his boyhood, but his descriptions are essentially tragic. Pearson describes the house as cold with penury and rejection. Lucinda Elizabeth never liked her son, who may have reminded her of her husband. To her daughters she was somewhat less rejecting. She worked hard at her music and the ill-paid servants were "unfit to take charge of three cats, let alone three children." The meals were of stewed beef and badly cooked potatoes. The tea was left on the hob until it was pure tannin. When Mrs. Shaw went to London with her daughters she left the boy with his father and for six years she did not write to him. There was no picture made of him. No one valued his personality or his abilities or planned for his future. He disliked himself and felt that he was correctly regarded as a disagreeable "little beast." For his father he had such contempt that he would not volunteer his help when his father struggled for hours over accounts which the son could have done quickly. The father was too proud to ask the boy to assist him. "The way we were brought up, or rather not brought up, doesn't bear thinking of," Shaw said when he was eighty-six. He was more neglected than ill-treated, which gave him a dreadful self-sufficiency but delayed his emotional development. He says, "It left me a treacherous brute in matters of pure affection." At his own mother's interment he entertained himself and his one companion with a witty monologue as to the dead woman's probable reaction to the scene she was missing.

Joshua Cobb, father of the American humorist Irvin S. Cobb, was a little bantam of a man who injured his eyes while he was a Confederate soldier. While leaning over a campfire to light a cigar, he ineptly let fall a pistol cartridge from his belt. The explosion injured his tear ducts so that he was forever tearful and his lower eyelids were inflamed and painful.

As a tobacco merchant, and as a steamboater, he was a failure. He was a proud little man who wore the finest of starched shirts;

his tiny feet were shod in expensive handmade boots; he smoked the very best cigars. He loved the sound of children's laughter and bought their respect and affection by gifts. When the circus came to town, he took not only his own children, but the neighbors' children as well, and brought them home at nightfall stuffed with red popcorn and parched goobers. A whole week's salary was not too much for him to spend on an outing for the children.

The red-eyed little man was the poor son of a rich father whom the Civil War ruined financially. Joshua Cobb was a failure as an in-law. When he married into the Saunders family, he had no chance to prove excellence in that distinguished circle. His father-in-law, Dr. Reuben Saunders, who supported him and his family during frequent periods of financial crisis, was known internationally for his discovery of the effectiveness of atropine in treating cholera. The Cobbs were always "poor relations" and the situation was both irksome and humiliating. Joshua Cobb had not finished college when he was invalided out of the Confederate army and could not go back to school because of his eyes.

His oldest daughter, Reubie, named for her grandfather, took his wife's time and most of her affection. They could have left Paducah and gone where job opportunities were better had it not been for neurotic Reubie, a pocket-sized Cinderella whose niece described her as a female Jonathan Swift. She was the spoiled first daughter. Her grandfather bought her a diamond ring for Christmas the same year he bought the tone-deaf Irvin a violin. When she was disappointed — about what no one ever knew — she became a young recluse, pulled the shades of the windows and would not go outdoors. She dressed carefully each day, tripped from window to window in her size one shoes, peered out at passers-by and made clever and caustic comments about them. Her mother was completely absorbed in Reubie and her problems. Her son Irvin always felt rejected by his mother although he loved her.

Joshua lost his job with the steamboat company when it changed hands. His sizable insurance policy had a suicide clause so he set himself, his son later felt sure, to drink himself to death deliberately. Joshua was a strong, healthy man except for his sore eyes and it took him four painful years to die. Irvin Cobb says in his autobiography: "They were a hard four years on my mother, too. The memory of them is still like a scar burnt on my brain."

Irvin Cobb married an out-of-town girl and went off to New York to be a newspaperman and a humorist; Reubie eventually came out of retirement. She was gay and competent in her old age, took tender care of her mother and had a charming, important man of Paducah as a steady suitor. Each evening for forty years he came to dinner. Each evening they went for a drive. Three days after the mother died, Reubie married her sweetheart. Both were dead within the year.

Stephen Leacock, the Canadian humorist, came from a troubled home, with an alcoholic father who was also failure-prone. Like the senior Eisenhowers, the Leacocks married very young. Peter Leacock was a handsome, likely lad, born to wealth and a good family in England. He led a casual life, sailed his boat, attended school irregularly. At the age of eighteen he courted and secretly married a poor girl, Agnes Emma Butler. Since Peter was a Roman Catholic, her Protestant family would not have him in the house.

The immature husband and wife were sent to South Africa to farm. The locusts ate their crops, so they were sent to Kansas to farm, where grasshoppers ate their crops. They moved to Canada and lost a third farm; but Grandfather Leacock sent money for a special tutor for the children when he was told about the poor schools.

As Peter Leacock grew older, he became abusive to his wife and children. The two oldest boys left home, and it was seventeen-year-old Stephen Leacock who took his father to the railway station, brandished a whip, and threatened to use it unless his father left home and never came back. For fifty years Peter Leacock lived in Nova Scotia under the name of Captain Lewis and never came home. His wife, assisted by two faithful Yorkshire retainers, lived in perpetual indebtedness until the younger children were old enough to help her. Stephen was the one among the eleven children who resented his father most, and was also the family member who was to win fame as a humorist. The Leacocks were never actually indigent, because they were helped by wealthy relatives.

A whimsical writer whose father became alcoholic and deserted the family when his wife died was Kenneth Grahame, who was the oldest child in the family. The children were turned over to the indifferent care of the maternal grandmother, who had no affection for them and considered them an intolerable burden.

Maurice Chevalier was glad when his father, a housepainter, deserted his wife and three boys, because his father was abusive when he drank — which was often. Maurice tried to help support his mother as soon as he left school at fourteen, but when he hurt his finger while laboring in a tack factory, he spent his unexpected "time-out" getting his first professional job as a singer. When Maurice was a famous man, his father came to see him in his dressing room, but Maurice sent the old man away in anger. Remembering the sadness in the eyes of the hesitant, shabby fellow, he was somewhat sorry, but he never saw him again. His mother was always the most important person in Maurice Chevalier's life. "There was a quiet and a sweetness about Mama and the beauty of simplicity. . . . Her smile when it came was like a light. . . . She seems always close to me now, just as [when] she was alive."[7]

The father of Charlie Chaplin died of alcoholism. Charlie's parents taught him to jig and sing as soon as he could toddle. His mother soon began to develop symptoms of mental illness which were never to leave her; she withdrew from reality, sometimes did not recognize her own sons. Charlie spent his years from five to seven in an orphanage where there was never enough to eat, where the children were treated like criminals, were flogged and put into solitary confinement. At ten, through the management of his thirteen-year-old half-brother, Sidney, who acted as his agent, Charlie was playing a good role at the London Hippodrome. He toured the provinces in an appropriate role of boy hero in a rags-to-riches play, became quite the successful young actor, enjoyed his success, dressed well, sported a cane. Charles and Sidney were soon able to take their mother from sordid surroundings and put her in a good nursing home. It was Charlie's alcoholic father who gave him his stage premiere by pushing him on the stage when he was five to sing a coster song, "Jack Jones," as a substitute for his mother, who had suddenly become ill.

Charlie Chaplin's father, who was his wife's third husband, was a popular singer of sentimental ballads in England and also in the United States, and his wife was a successful singer and dancer who sometimes played in Gilbert and Sullivan shows. It was she who taught Charles to mimic and to note bodily posture — she had an intuitive knack of knowing a stranger's personal problems by observing his posture. Two sons by a former husband stayed with their own father. Sidney, an infant, she kept with her, and Charles was born to the third marriage. The Chaplins had drifted apart before the husband died of alcoholism.

The tragic stories of humorists with alcoholic fathers is not complete without the story of Alexander Woollcott, whose life story has been so candidly told by Samuel Hopkins Adams, who knew and loved him well. Alexander Woollcott was brought up in the Phalanx, a socialist-communal colony in New Jersey. It was made up of Unitarians, Universalists, Congregationalists, Jews, Presbyterians, Quakers, Swedenborgians, and a leavening of agnostics who found a common denominator in a lofty Fourierist thesis. Frances Bucklin, daughter of the founder of the Phalanx, against the advice of her elders married a visiting Englishman, Walter Woollcott, whose alcoholism and erratic ways made him an extremely poor provider. The destitute wife and children spent so much time at the Phalanx and so little time with the husband and father that some of the Bucklin relatives caustically remarked that Walter's function was for "breeding purposes only."

Alexander Woollcott rejected his father severely, although the unhappy man was essentially kind and never abused the boy. Walter Woollcott became very rich at one time — when he struck up a friendship with a stock market plunger named Gibbs. The whole family moved into a mansion for less than a year. When failure struck hard, Walter Woollcott said that he was very tired and took to his bed for two years. Alexander Woollcott described himself as the son of a crazy father and a doting mother. When Walter Woollcott dropped dead on the streets of New York, his son Alexander interrupted his card game for an hour to arrange for a cremation and returned to the card game.

The part which rejection of the alcoholic and failure-prone father played in Alexander Woollcott's difficulty in sexual adjustment is probably considerable, however. His sister Julie and her best friend aided by making a pet of the youngest boy in the family, who was so delicate and precocious. They sheltered him from rough contacts with other boys, dressed him as Puck in a neighborhood tableau. When he went fishing, Alexander took a hat along to trim. Another feminine influence was his first public school teacher, Sophie Rosenberger, who made him a devotee of Louisa May Alcott and her works. In his early teens he loved to dress up and pass himself off as a girl and had a girl's name, Alecia, which he used while doing his female impersonations. A case of mumps in his early adulthood is thought to have almost neutralized his sexual capacity. He was never described as a homosexual and a friend who knew him in early manhood attested to his "private life which even the straitest-laced Puritan would have admitted was blameless. The more honor to him." However, he was not able to have a husband and wife as guests, although he could entertain either if the other were not present. All of the Woollcott children adored their mother, and all of them except Alexander liked their father whom they regarded as "an amusing, if somewhat irresponsible crony." In this family it is the boy who felt the greatest antagonism to the alcoholic, failure-prone father who made the family skeleton dance in the most effective fashion with his wit and caustic wisdom.

No humorist, actor, or actress has a serene happy life with well-adjusted parents, but not all of the parents of humorists or actors are alcoholic. Samuel Clemens, Harry Lauder, Eddie Cantor, and Ring Lardner had failure-prone but non-alcoholic fathers.

Stalin's mother is described as being pleased when her abusive alcoholic husband died. Had he lived her son would have been expected to be a shoemaker. When he died, she was able to plan for her son to be a priest. Both Tito and the early-orphaned Rasputin lived in the squalor of rural slums made the more untenable by their fathers' frequent drunkenness. Tito's father was amiable and the boy's school adjustment was superior. The hypnotist and scheming charlatan Rasputin had an abusive father and lost his mother, sister, and brother when he was young. There was no friendliness in his home community for him or his family, no teacher who recognized his ability and his drive to rise above his station.*

Terman noted that the teacher is ordinarily a proper, middle-class individual with middle-class mores. The child from the "good family," the child who is clean, proper and well brought up, is bound to have, in the thinking of most teachers, more possibilities for achievement than is the neglected son of the town drunk. Children from broken homes or homes where the parents are immoral or alcoholic or eccentric are likely to be downgraded in the minds of the community and school and are expected to be problem children. A Yale University sociologist, A. B. Hollingshead, tells of this attitude in *Elmtown's Youth*, an excellent study of a typical Midwestern small town.

This denigrating attitude faced Sherwood Anderson in the small town of Camden, Ohio, where he was reared. Sherwood was late thirty-two times one semester, but the school authorities did not notify his mother because of the unusual home circumstances. Everyone in Camden knew that Sherwood Anderson, or "Jobby," as he was commonly called, was a hard worker, was always on the search for a new job — hence the nickname. There was nothing honest he would not do. He sold innumerable copies of the Cincinnati *Enquirer*; he helped his mother by gathering her customers' dirty wash and bringing it home to her and by delivering the clean laundry.

Sherwood always had a book in his hand. When he went fishing he took a book, and while acting as manager of the baseball team he read between innings. He showed no special talent as did his

---

*The eminent men and women in our study whose fathers were alcoholic were: Fred Allen, Sherwood Anderson, Louis Armstrong, John Barrymore, Ethel Barrymore, Lionel Barrymore, Enrico Caruso, Charles Chaplin, Maurice Chevalier, Irvin S. Cobb, Kahlil Gibran, Kenneth Grahame, A. E. Housman, Laurence Housman, James Joyce, Gertrude Lawrence, Stephen Leacock, G. E. Rasputin, Eleanor Roosevelt, George Bernard Shaw, Joseph Stalin, Joseph Broz Tito, Thomas Wolfe, and Alexander Woollcott.

sister Stella, who recited verses nicely, or his brother Karl, who drew well.

Jobby's industry was in contrast to his father's inactivity. After his harness business failed, his wife had to take in washings. He drank and was unfaithful to his wife. Jobby knew all this and was defensive of his mother.

The school authorities did not consider him a potential scholar and decided that it was permissible for him to stay out of school to help his mother.

Elliott Roosevelt, father of Eleanor Roosevelt, was a child of "sun and fortune." When he married, he was tall, aristocratic, tanned — and the heir to $200,000. He had just returned from a tiger hunt in Africa. To Anna Hall, the lovely, spoiled oldest daughter in a well-to-do family, he was a romantic figure, just the playboy husband she needed to join her in her amateur dramatic club and to accompany her in a fatiguing round of social activities to which she was committed. The marriage began to break up when he decided to work in New York like any other man and began commuting from their home in Long Island each day. When she wanted to have fun, he wanted to rest. When they had a homely little girl, the father was enchanted with his little daughter and preferred to play with her in the dirt of the back yard rather than to accompany his wife to social functions. Anna Hall Roosevelt related well to her two sons, born subsequently, but she could never bear to have her homely daughter touch her. She called the child "Granny," and ridiculed her before guests for her quaint, old-fashioned ways.

When Eleanor was five, Elliott Roosevelt broke his leg, and began to drink to alleviate the pain. He became alcoholic and the family went with him to a sanitarium in Italy. Eleanor was put in a boarding school nearby where she was very unhappy. She swallowed a penny to gain the sympathy of the nuns, and was shamed by everyone but her father for her behavior. By this time she had developed habits which made her mother think her an impossible child. During this same period, however, she came back walking instead of riding from a pony ride. The boy who had been hired to lead the pony had sore and bleeding feet, so Eleanor insisted that he should ride and that she should walk. Her parents separated while her father was still in the sanitarium in Italy, and the mother and children went back to New York.

Anna Roosevelt died of diphtheria and the youngest child, "Ellie," whom his mother had never reproved and who was so beautiful, did not long survive her. Eleanor and her brother Hall were left in the care of their maternal grandmother, to whom Anna willed them because she did not want their father to have their legal custody.

Some time after Anna Hall Roosevelt died, Elliott came to speak to Eleanor and took her for a long drive. He promised her that some day she could come to live with him, to be the mistress of his household. He went away and she was left to live with him in a dream world where she was the heroine and he the hero. In her autobiography she says, "Into this world I retired as soon as I went to bed, and as soon as I woke in the morning, and all the time I was walking, and when anyone bored me."[8]

Having failed to gain control over her own four adolescent children, Grandmother Hall determined to be really strict with her grandchildren, especially with Eleanor, who was "a Roosevelt."

She was never permitted to have much to do with the Roosevelts of whom her grandmother disapproved, not even kind Great-aunt Gracie, whom even her mother had loved. Aunt Gracie had taken Eleanor to the wax-works, told her stories, gone with her to the dentist, but Grandmother Hall said that the father's family was a bad influence. There were no more trips to see the crippled children in the special hospital set up for them by her Grandfather Roosevelt, whose life was filled with charitable activities.

Grandmother Hall never said "Yes" when she could say "No." Eleanor was invited to go see the Old West, but her grandmother refused and gave no reason. When she was not reading, Eleanor daydreamed of her father. She remembered how he took her to help serve a Thanksgiving dinner in a newsboy's clubhouse which his father, Theodore Roosevelt, Sr., had started. Elliott explained that all the ragged little boys had no homes, lived in wooden shanties or vacant lots or slept in vestibules of houses or public buildings. Elliott was always thoughtful of poor children and when he was only seven had given his good coat away to a shivering child. Eleanor knew too that he gave dolls to poor children and told them about his little girl whom he saw so seldom.

When she was ten and was told that her father was dead, she cried bitterly, then went on living with her father in daydreams even more than when he was alive.

Her relatives were not happy with her. She lied, she stole sweets, she was poor in spelling and in arithmetic and in grammar. She bit her nails; she had a great fear of burglars and the dark; she was shy and awkward. She was dressed in short skirts when other girls her age had their dresses down to the ankles, and wore heavy flannels from November 1 to April 1 regardless of the weather.

A neighbor, Mrs. Henry Parish, who was friendly to the Roosevelt family, was kind to Eleanor and let the lonely girl play with her own small children. The washerwoman, Mrs. Overhalse, was a cheerful woman and Eleanor spent many hours with her. Governesses, French maids, German maids Eleanor walked off their feet. As she walked she daydreamed, always of her father.

The only time she ever saw boys was when she was permitted, at Christmastime, to go to a party at her Aunt Corinne's home. Aunt Corinne was her father's sister and had nursed him during his last illness with great devotion. The girls at these parties were not kind to gawky Eleanor in her odd clothes. Her ankles were weak and she fell down when she tried to skate with the others. It was there that she met a handsome boy, also a Roosevelt, a fifth cousin named Franklin, who was kind to her. Her own father had been this boy's godfather.

Grandmother Hall said there was too much gaiety in her own home for a girl going on fifteen, and she feared that Eleanor might get as unmanageable as were her young aunts and uncles. When she was sent to the Allenswood School at South Fields, near London, she took with her the memories of her father. When he died, the Abingdon, Virginia, papers described him in an editorial as a young man whose name was a byword among the needy for his abundant and unostentatious charities. In this family the alcoholic father, whose acquaintance with his daughter was brief and infrequent after she was five, surely played a positive and definite role in channeling her sympathies and in the selection of her future concerns.

Louis Armstrong, deserted by his alcoholic father and neglected by his mother, who was usually "out on the town," was lucky when he was picked up for firing a pistol on the streets and was sent to a home for colored waifs. He learned music there and appreciated the food and comfort of the humble institution.

Thomas Wolfe, who turned the story of his own childhood into literature, had teachers, Mr. and Mrs. J. M. Roberts, who recognized his talents and helped him. His brothers and sisters used to tease him at the family table about his love for Shakespeare. From his mother he inherited an indomitable will and a dogged persistence. This odd-looking boy with his little head on his big body used to spit in people's faces when he stammered. He had two roofs and no home, for his mother ran a boarding house, while his alcoholic, book-loving artistic father lived in the family homestead with his daughter as housekeeper.

John Stanislaus Joyce, father of James Joyce, ran through a modest fortune while becoming the father of either sixteen or seventeen children in eighteen years. The drama of life and death played itself out so frequently that count was lost. Yet the family always maintained an address in the right part of town. John Stanislaus Joyce was a man who diddled his life away with song and story and gay companionship. As long as he had the money which he inherited, he was popular in the bars and restaurants and racecourses. He lost his fortune by investing it unwisely. John Stanislaus had many positions, none of which he filled well, but was at one time secretary to the National Liberal Club in Dublin. He never felt like a poor man, but thought of himself as a rich man experiencing bad luck. His children and his wife, however, often felt very poor and James Joyce disliked his father intensely.

CONTRIBUTIONS OF THE FAILURE-PRONE FATHER

A willingness to take risks is a distinguishing characteristic of fathers of many of the Four Hundred. Lillian Smith, born in the small town of Jasper, Florida, had a father who was opinionative, learning-centered, and also experimental. The daughter was willing, as an adult, to "burn bridges behind her" by discarding the race prejudices of her family and Southern community. She says in *Killers of the Dream:*

We knew we were a respected and important family of this small town but beyond this knowledge we gave little thought to status. Our father made money in lumber and naval stores for the excitement of making and losing it — not for what money can buy nor the security which it sometimes gives. I do not remember at any time wanting "to be rich" nor do I remember that thrift and saving were ideals which our parents considered important enough to urge upon us. Always in the family there was an acceptance of risk, a mild delight even in burning bridges, an expectant "what will happen now"! We were not irresponsible; living according to the pleasure principle was by no means our way of life. On the contrary we were trained to think that each of us should do something that would be of genuine usefulness to the world, and the family thought it right to make sacrifices if necessary, to give each child adequate preparation for this life's work. We were also trained to think learning important, and books, but "bad" books our mother burned. We valued music and art and craftsmanship but it was people and their welfare and religion that were the foci around which our lives seemed naturally to move.

Bill Mauldin, son of a daydreaming, improvident farmer, also had childhood experiences which made it easier for him to risk personal failure by expressing himself uniquely as a cartoonist. Mauldin describes his irrepressible "Pop" and his many projects in his *A Sort of a Saga:*

When he talked about a new scheme he went on for hours, painting a glorious picture and giving all the objections and then batting them down, as if six or seven people were discussing the matter instead of one. Sid [brother] and I never got over being entranced when Pop sold himself on something new. But as time went on my mother's eyes became less and less starry. . . .

Van Wyck Brooks says that it was his father's failure to fit into the business world which made him seek another kind of expression for himself, made him critical and observant of the social scene. His father was a scholarly man who owned a nickel mine in Nevada, but the nickel was too far down to be easily worked and the mine was too far from the railroad. Worry over his investment destroyed the father's gaiety and wit. In *Scenes and Portraits* he says:

The irony of it is that he had once owned a world famous mine and traded it for this chimera in the Nevada mountains. . . . I felt my father never should have been a business man. I was melodramatic, no doubt, in my view of the case. I hated business and saw it as a Moloch that devoured whatever was best in the American mind.

Among the Four Hundred, the end result of having a father who experiences failure is not the child's withdrawal from action or conservatism but his release from fear of innovation.

The wife of the husband who does not do well may turn for comfort to a son, who frequently tries to make her happy by his own success. In most instances, however, he does not achieve fame by a conservative, cautious approach to problems, but puts his imaginative, creative qualities to better use than did his father.

The men and women who are able to produce a novel product or add to the knowledge or pleasure of mankind seem almost to depend for their creativity upon their fathers' childish eagerness for new experiences, their naïveté, even their inefficiency.

[4]

Dominating Mothers,
But Few Dominating Fathers

> When she herself [the poet's mother] was
> unable to fulfill her desires for personal ac-
> complishment, she transferred her ambitions
> to her children. That she loved her children
> goes, perhaps without saying. But that an un-
> compromising stubbornness toward an ideal
> preceded that love is nearer to the truth.
> There was little softness in her. . . . That
> long purpose, outside of herself, made her a
> difficult person to live with. . . . The excuse
> for domination seems valid.
> — WILLIAM CARLOS WILLIAMS,
> *Yes, Mrs. Williams*

AMONG THE PARENTS of the Four Hundred, the dominating mothers are those who would today probably be career women. Today they might be leaving their sons to the casual companionship of the television set and be completely engrossed in adult education or community betterment activities. Mothers of the Four Hundred often found that the best outlet for their own drives and abilities was through capable sons. The pendulum in child nurture today has swung through a wide arc, and devotion to a son's career is not now so frequently a mother's principal source of satisfaction.

If the dominating mothers keep within reasonable bounds their tendencies for decision-making and for planning ahead, they may ultimately be honored by famous sons and receive credit for their sons' successes. Annette Beveridge and Ida Eisenhower were such women. Many aggressive women who dominate their households have philosophical husbands. This has been observed to be a common pattern in Jewish homes, which are known to be excellent cradles of eminence. Dominating mothers are apt to keep a close eye on the larder, on new branches on the family tree, and on the inscription of the family name in some hall of fame.

The dominating mother who oversteps reasonable boundaries, however, makes it hard for her captive son to rebel, since she is the focus of both love and authority. If he does not progress, she can withdraw affection. If she has a husband who is failure-prone, as ninety per cent of the dominating mothers do, the son often resolves to make her so proud of him that she will forget her disappointment in her husband.

The boy who rebels against domination makes an easier adjustment in courtship and marriage than does the boy who is sorry for his mother and identifies with her. The man who was a "mother's boy" is frequently uneasy with his male contemporaries. He is apt to quarrel with professional colleagues; and, if a soldier, he is likely to consider human life expendable. He is wary of democratic procedures and may become dictatorial, mistrusts mankind, thinks he (and mother) know best. He needs to have women around him who approve of him; and he gets along best with older women, with children, with animals. He may marry only after his mother dies, or remain a bachelor. If he marries, he expects his wife to play a secondary role to his mother, or to re-enact her supportive role. If the mother bears down too heavily on him and he tries to rebel, he may become highly introverted and creative but is seldom happy in his personal relationships.

At least eighteen of these dominating women were the young wives of men old enough to be their fathers. Others seemed deliberately to choose husbands whose only function would be to father sons and leave their wives free to guide their sons.

The dominating father, despite the place given to him in the novels of the Victorian days, is comparatively rare. When he does overwhelm his family, he is critical, irritable, driven by compulsions he cannot resist. He seldom has grandiose plans for a son and is more likely to retard than to block his son's ambitions.

Sometimes he wants the son to repeat his own career by staying in the family business or profession. It is the mother whose daydreams are more often infinite.

The parental daydreams do not so often encompass the daughter, and the family may actually be disturbed by the daughter who wants to be a career woman. Certain groups such as the Quakers and Unitarians were more likely to accept the woman who wanted to work, but even they accepted her more easily in the role of a social reformer. When a girl did become eminent, she most often did so out of a deep personal concern for the ills of mankind, or out of a need to use a talent. Two only daughters, Maude Adams and Marie Montessori, experienced mother domination but it is ordinarily male children who are driven to succeed by the intense desires of the mother.

Some Homes Are Matriarchal

Some of the homes are not only mother-dominated but tend to be matriarchal in composition. A Nobel prize-winning microbiologist, Selman A. Waksman, born in the bleak town of Novaia-Priluka in the Russian Ukraine, lived in what was essentially a matriarchal society. His mother, at twenty-one already a dynamic businesswoman, was urged into marriage by female relatives who feared she was likely to be an old maid.

Soon after the wedding ceremony, the husband, a coppersmith, left for the army and did not return for five years. When he came home to his bride, he found that she had made a home for her mother and for those of her seven sisters and her nieces and nephews as needed a roof. She and her widowed mother had been very successful with their thriving dry-goods business. She was more than a businesswoman; she arranged for dowries for poor girls; she loaned money without interest; she was interested in every citizen of the village who had a problem.

The death of his small sister turned their son to thoughts of medical research. The household was a friendly one, but the middle-aged father played only an incidental role in the boy's life. His mother's interests were so scattered that he escaped being overwhelmed by her. When she died while he was in late adolescence, he was helped by people who had been helped by her.

Edwin Jones, the father of the Quaker educator Rufus Jones, a poor farmer from near North China, Maine, wore his overcoat the year round; in winter to keep the heat in, in the summer to keep the heat out. He was prone to moods, neglected his work, then finished it quickly in a burst of energy. He kept no hired hand, worked alone. His own youth was disturbed by seizures. In Friends' Meeting his message seldom varied in content and had to do with "making a little heaven on the way to Heaven." He was a kind man, silent and self-effacing.

When his wife, the energetic, nineteen-year-old, redheaded Mary Hoxie, moved into the already woman-dominated home, she became the new mistress of the household in fact as well as name. Her energy, her humor, her tact and understanding made her a good hostess to the stream of guests who visited the household — often one or two a week, each of whom brought news of the outside world and spoke dynamically of world concerns.

Already in the household was Edwin Jones's mother, Susie Jones, a rugged pioneer woman who smoked her pipe three times a day, was an elder in Meeting, a competent cook, dairymaid, weaver, tailor, gardener, soapmaker, and nurse — and a woman with great breadth of mind and depth of heart. A maiden aunt, Peace Jones, a mystic and woman of remarkable culture, lived in the household. She had a fanatic faith in her nephew's potentialities.

On the periphery of the household was Sibyl, the wife of Eli Jones, the much older brother of the inarticulate Edwin.

It was because of Aunt Sibyl and Uncle Eli that the little town of North China, Maine, was well known to Quakers all over the world, and due to them that the small rural meeting had so many international visitors. Aunt Sibyl had a voice like the wind in the pine trees and had spoken in Nova Scotia, in England, Liberia, Sierre Leone, Europe, Greece and the Holy Land.

His mother's will, Kwame Nkrumah says, was not to be disregarded. He was the only son of one of the several wives of a man who lived in what was then the Gold Coast — now, largely through the efforts of Kwame Nkrumah, the independent country of Ghana. All of the mothers were responsive to the needs of all the children. These women did not quarrel among themselves, and his older half-brothers tended to spoil Kwame Nkrumah, as did his mother. She used to coax him to eat by wrapping food in plantain leaves and hiding it under his pillow. It was she who persuaded his father to educate her only son.

When she became a widow, and Kwame's uncle became his guardian, her drive to see her boy educated was not lessened. When he returned to her after his college years in the United States, she did not know him because of his maturity — and also because of dental work he had had done. No man in her experience had ever come home with a gap in his front teeth miraculously filled in, and she was bewildered by the inexplicable change in his appearance. Since she was illiterate, communication with her had been through letters read to her by a friend of her son who sometimes journeyed to her village. Kwame Nkrumah delayed marriage until after the death of his mother. He had always professed to believe that wives impeded the progress of men bent on achievement.

Children with Special Talents

It is, however, the child with a special talent who brings out the most dominating traits in the mother, who may disregard other family members in her zeal for him, as did the mother of Pablo Casals.

Another performer who owes his career to his mother is Noel Coward. It was his mother who guided him in his career, who read an advertisement in the *Daily Mirror* asking for the services of a talented boy of twelve in an all-children's play. During his second engagement, Noel and his mother had real problems with a magistrate who passed on the applications of children of school age who wished to work at the theater. The judge was inclined to believe that the parents wished to profit by the two pounds a week the boy was to earn. Noel's mother dramatically described the emotional breakdown the boy was sure to suffer if he were deprived of the pleasure of acting; she would herself, to avoid that catastrophe, bring the judge four pounds a week if he would let the boy act instead of going to school. The courtroom spectators were amused; the judge hastily dismissed the case and let the boy and his mother have their way.

When he was sent to school during periods when he was not acting, Noel used to be truant and wander about the city "acting." He pretended to be a poor waif with an alcoholic, brutal father. In reality his father was a kind and gentle man, but even in fun Noel did not tell tales about his mother.

Payne's Piano Company failed, and his father had no employment. The mother took over a boarding house in London. Mrs. Coward cooked the meals, rushed up and down stairs, dealt sternly with tradesmen. Noel's father made model yachts to sail in Clapham Common pond, beautiful, delicate boats, exquisitely made in every detail. When his youngest son Eric was home, he played with his father at the pond. Eric was his father's boy; Noel, his mother's.

Had Mrs. Coward been willing to enlist the aid of her husband, she might never have had the near collapse she was to suffer as the mistress of the boarding house. Noel went with his mother for a holiday at the seashore while the much more sociable Mr. Coward ran the boarding house quite successfully. He had a grand time chatting with the boarders and went "hopping in and out of rooms with breakfast trays." Noel did not marry and continued to center his life around his mother when he was an adult.

Some mothers planned careers for sons not yet born. The mother of Frank Lloyd Wright believed in prenatal influence. Even before her son was born she decided that he should be an architect. She framed ten full-page wood engravings of old English cathedrals and hung them in the room that was to be her son's. She never doubted that her child was to be a boy and also an architect.

When the rural schoolteacher Anna Lloyd Jones was twenty-nine, she had married a forty-six-year-old itinerant music teacher who visited her community. She knew that he had already given up medicine because it was not a true science and also law because he became disillusioned with its practice. He then turned to the teaching of music and to the Baptist ministry. Since he was seventeen years older than she, the dynamic teacher with the long free stride was not able to change his life patterns appreciably — although she tried hard; she did influence him to turn from the Baptist ministry to Unitarianism, which cost him employment. At the time when she told him gently but firmly that he might leave the household, her son was eighteen, she was ill, and the household was poverty-stricken. The irritable, unhappy husband had not turned to alcohol in this instance, but to the learning of Sanskrit and the reading aloud of "The Raven" while pacing the floor of his study. Anna Wright did not expect William Cary Wright to leave her when she told him he might go since he was of no use to the family; but he went, and for fifteen years, until he died, she expected him home again.

Louis Bromfield, the novelist, also had his career chosen for him by his mother. Her husband, Charlie Bromfield, was always in easy touch if a friend was broke; his humble farmhouse was always full of indigent or ill relatives. If he earned a little extra cash, some "wild, romantic scheme would siphon it off almost as soon as it had appeared." What he had to give his children was his love of land, for animals and his endless enjoyment of friendly contact with his fellow man.

Annette Bromfield decided that her first-born son was to be a writer. Shelves were stocked with the classics, and Louis was made to read for a definite number of hours each day while his sister Marie practiced at the piano. Her mother had wanted to be a musician when she was young, but there was no money for lessons. During her married life she collected responsibilities as a sheep collects burrs. After she married, she had to go back to her old home twice each week to cook and clean for her father, a widower. She also nursed various ailing relatives who came to visit and to die. All of her personal ambitions had to be extended through the lives of her children.

Had Louis Bromfield not loved reading, her domination might have irked him to rebellion as it did her second son Charles, who became a businessman and a professed nonintellectual. Marie died before she could fulfill her talent. Annette Bromfield's drives did not lessen with age. At eighty she was still determined to dominate her sons, and there were stormy scenes when she came to live at Malabar Farm with her novelist son Louis. All her days she sought to possess her children by a pathetic pursuit of them.

The Dominating Mother Is an International Phenomenon

The tendency to dominate is not racial, national, or cultural. Wealthy mothers and poor mothers apply their will with identical intensity. The child who is talented in musical performance is the most vulnerable, since his talent is evidenced early. Pablo Casals is not the only musician with a dominating mother, although few of them are as determined as the mother of the nineteenth-century composer Anton Bruckner, whose mother stopped on the way home from his father's funeral to enroll him in music school.

The mother of Yehudi Menuhin did not expect to be the mother of musicians, but when her son showed exceptional talent she isolated him from his contemporaries and included her daughters in the edict, presumably so all the children could share their isolation together. She was quick to withdraw her affection if any one of them deviated from her exacting ideas of good behavior. Her daughter Hepzibah says of the way in which they were reared, "It made awful fools of us all when we faced our first life situations."[1]

When Giacomo Puccini's father died, his mother looked among her children for a boy to carry on the family tradition. A Puccini had been the village organist in Lucca for four generations. She needed the older boys to help earn a living for the big family, so the six-year-old Giacomo was her arbitrary choice. He did not want to be an organist. His father had been a kindly man, but the uncle who assumed the unwelcome task of teaching the recalcitrant pupil was abusive and kicked his student in the shins when the young musician made an error. Giacomo Puccini developed a muscular tic which made him jerk his leg whenever he heard a wrong note being played.

The dominating qualities of Sara Delano Roosevelt have been documented in numerous volumes written by the family and by the many biographers of her son, Franklin D. Roosevelt. She extended her rule for two generations. Of this grandmother, James Roosevelt says:

This [Hyde Park] was Granny's home and we all knew it. She laid down the rules, and all of us — even Father and Mother — accepted them. We "chicks" quickly learned that the best way to circumvent "Pa and Mummy" when we wanted something they would not give us was to appeal to Granny.[2]

When Franklin D. Roosevelt was adult, he paid no attention to his mother's comments on public affairs, but he was always vulnerable in terms of his personal and family life — because it was Sara Delano Roosevelt who held the purse strings, and she was niggardly. James says that his father rarely exploded, but that he seethed under the drip-drip of maternal advice and never ceased resisting his mother's attempts to tell him what to do and what not to do, how to insure the regularity of his digestive tract, and how to manage her grandchildren, whom the family agrees she spoiled woefully.

Sara Delano Roosevelt used to say, "My son Franklin is a Delano, not a Roosevelt at all!" Sara Delano was twenty-six when she married the fifty-two-year-old James Roosevelt, whose son by a first wife, James Roosevelt Roosevelt, was exactly her own age. Young "Rosy," as he was called, was one of the flamboyant playboys of his age. Her stepgrandson was already at Groton when she sent her son Franklin to school there.

Sara's father, the adventurous Warren Delano II, had given his daughter acquaintance with financial insecurity and world adventure by the time she was ten. Warren Delano lost his wealth in the crash of 1857 and he sailed for China to recoup his fortunes by engaging in the opium trade, a legitimate enterprise aimed at supplying medical needs. The whole family joined him there; the mother, servants, and six small children made a 125-day journey halfway around the world on the square-rigged clipper *Surprise*. The sea adventure was so successful that Sara eventually inherited $1,338,000 from the father she admired and whom her only son was to resemble. She was niggardly with her money, would never touch the principal, resolved to hand it on intact to her son at her death. She doled out money to him, was slow to pay bills.

Sara's father had objected to the marriage because of the age of the bridegroom, but the imperious Sara had her way. Opinionative James Roosevelt, her elderly husband, in his own youth served for two months with Garibaldi and went on a walking tour through Italy with a mendicant priest. Three times in his business career he gambled for high stakes in money and power, and all three times he lost. He was voted out of control of a company which took heavy losses in the 1873 panic. He failed when he tried unsuccessfully to get control of a railroad in the South. He also helped form a company which attempted to dig a canal across Nicaragua, raised six million dollars, then had to give up the project when the depression of 1893 dried up his funds.

The husband was not dominated by his wife, by all accounts, but Franklin was not so fortunate. Franklin admired the father, who controlled the mother, who in turn controlled the boy. James Roosevelt taught his son many skills — hunting, fishing and boating. Until he was fourteen Franklin studied at home and his education was supervised by his mother. The family went to Europe each year after Franklin was three years old, taking with them tutors with whom the mother often quarreled. Among the governesses was a liberal and discerning Swiss woman, Mlle. Jeanne Sandoz, who taught the boy to be aware of such human factors in history as the plight of the Egyptian workers sacrificed to the Pharaohs, who built the Pyramids. Mlle. Sandoz corresponded with her pupil when he was an adult in public life, advised and admired him.

From the beginning Sara Delano Roosevelt was confident that her only child was to be a great man. She saved every scrap of paper upon which he wrote school exercises and bundled and labeled his baby clothes for the reference of future historians. His indifferent career at Groton and equally undistinguished career at Harvard did not shake her aplomb as to Franklin's superiorities. There is no record of her feeling a need to lecture him when he failed in Greek or made C's in his major subjects.

In this attitude she was probably justified; as John Gunther says of the boys who were Franklin D. Roosevelt's classmates at Groton:

The boys who were the best "Grotties" usually turned out to be nonentities later; the boys who hated Groton did much better. . . . The boys who became successes were not conformists, hence they were apt to be excluded from the compact group that made the core of each class.[3]

Gunther quotes Sumner Welles to corroborate the observation. When Welles was asked once if he had had a good time at Groton, he replied, "Oh Lord, no, I was a worm."

Franklin D. Roosevelt went unnoticed at Groton. He was not liked or disliked. He was called "Uncle Frank" because his nephew "Rosy" was in the form above him. He was not "boxed" (shoved into a locker too small to hold a boy in comfort) or "pumped" (taken to the lavatory and half-drowned by basins of water poured over his head) as were the boys who were really "odd." Franklin was hazed by being made to stand in a corner and dance while other boys struck at his ankles with hockey sticks.

He debated; and in his last year he developed an interest in lessening social discrimination against Jews and Negroes, of whom Groton then admitted none. This represented a rebellion against the mother, who was, according to Phyllis Bottome, not inclined to accept Jews as social equals. This did not mean that he was not to love her deeply, or fail to write her frequent letters which began, "My Dearest Mummie." His father died during Franklin's freshman year at Harvard and Sara Delano Roosevelt moved to Boston to be near her son.

Once a boy among the Four Hundred has known the unshakable faith and admiration of a mother he needs the continuation of that homage from other women. James Roosevelt says of this trait in his father:

Father was a man who enjoyed feminine companionship. He was at his sparkling best as a conversationalist when his audience included a few admiring and attractive ladies; this was an entirely natural circumstance, for Father was a great show-man who enjoyed being the center of attention.[4]

His wife was not always able to give him the uncritical adulation to which his mother had accustomed him. Eleanor Roosevelt says:

He might have been happier with a wife who was completely uncritical. That I was never able to be, and he had to find it in other people. Nevertheless, I think I sometimes acted as a spur, even though the spurring was not always welcome. I was one of those who served his purpose.[5]

The Roosevelts frequently speak frankly about themselves and each other. James closes his lengthy comments on his grandmother as an authoratative figure by saying:

Eventually, Granny lost out when Mother began to grow in other directions — and to build for herself a life larger than the one bounded by "Ma-ma" the "chicks," the sewing circle and social obligations. Mother became a personage in her own right, not to be dominated by anyone, not even by Father.[6]

THE ROLE OF WIVES

These complicated individuals sometimes make significant personality changes as adults. It is not possible in this survery to go beyond the childhood period in a discussion of all the Four Hundred persons and it is only with the most eminent that it becomes expedient to note the possible effects of childhood experiences upon adult attitudes. It is also not possible to discuss the contributions that wives or other adults have on the development of the eminent men. Lewis M. Terman found that the gifted young men in his group were more likely to succeed when they married women who were themselves interested in learning.

Had it not been for the role played by Eleanor Roosevelt after her husband's polio attack, he would probably not have tried to continue his career. Other wives have played definite roles in their husband's careers and we have noted some of them; the wives of Salvador Dali, Edward Elgar, and Anton Dvoràk come to mind. These are mentioned to indicate that recognition needs to be paid to the ability of the intelligent, sophisticated adult if he is to continue to mature and to be positively or negatively influenced by others when he is past his childhood.

In 1898 General Arthur MacArthur was ordered to the Philippines. His wife went to Milwaukee instead, took an apartment there, and hired a tutor to coach her young son, Douglas MacArthur, for the West Point examinations. A doctor was set to work to treat a slight curvature of the boy's spine which might conceivably stand in the way of his proposed Army career.

In June of the same year, the young man passed his tests with the highest score ever received by an applicant, a score of 99. His nearest competitor scored 77.9. His mother had been his only teacher until he was thirteen. A goal desired by both parents was achieved.

Until she died at the age of eighty-two, Mary MacArthur lived for her gifted son. Like Sara Roosevelt, she outlived her husband for many years, and like Sara Roosevelt, she stayed on to be near her son while he was at school.

A classmate reported that young MacArthur was "arrogant from the age of eight." Fellow plebes at West Point were not inclined to be gentle with the young man whose mother lived so close and so obviously regarded her son as a child of destiny. The upperclassmen made young Douglas do knee bends until he passed out.

The cadets at West Point had only a brief period during the day when they could be completely free, the half hour between dinner and the call to quarters. When the weather was fine, the mother and son strolled along Flirtation Walk. If he ever walked with a girl there, the incident is not recorded. On stormy days, he talked with his mother at the hotel, told her of his day's adventures, received contraband fruit as a gift. He sometimes overstayed his limits and on one occasion had to be sneaked out through the coal chute when the Commandant of Cadets came to call on his mother.

In 1935, when President Roosevelt asked General Douglas MacArthur to go out to the Philippines to build up the native defenses, the general debated as to whether he should go, because his mother did not seem well enough to make the trip with him. Knowing that he wanted to go, she accompanied him despite her dislike of the sea and a progressing cerebral thrombosis. By the time they reached Manila she was very ill, and she died before medicines flown out to her could be of any use.

General Douglas MacArthur, in his middle years, married a young woman whom his mother met on shipboard, recognized as the perfect wife for her son, and introduced to him.

A mother who used her beauty, her ill-health and femineity to dominate was Isabel Mackenzie King, whose son became Prime Minister of Canada. As a child she suffered hardships and humiliations as the daughter of the exiled rebel William Lyon Mackenzie.

She decided early in the life of her most promising child that he should reestablish the family's fame and fortune. Her husband, a gentle and scholarly man, was not capable in the sense that her son, Mackenzie King, was recognized to be by all the family. It was she who kept the family accounts, made decisions, and used her feminine wiles to direct the destiny of her son.

Isabel King was a vivacious and lovely woman who romped with her four children during their early years and was a companion rather than a parent. All of the children deferred to her. When there was not enough money for new dresses for all of the women in the family, the mother had the new dress, the daughters did without.

Away at school, Mackenzie King kept five photographs of his mother in his room and read Barrie's *Margaret Ogilvie* aloud with his mother's picture in his hand. The whole family was patient with the episodes of nervous indigestion which followed her top-speed activities. Her husband joined in the adulation and wrote to his son describing her as being as pretty as a picture in her new dress and lovely little bonnet.

When Mackenzie King was doing his work toward his degree in Chicago and fell in love with a nurse, his mother pled her age and grief and begged him not to marry — at least until she was dead — and if he must marry, please, not to a nurse — a woman beneath his station in life. He wrote 21,000 words of apology to his mother for his unfortunate romance and never married. In his old age he turned to spiritualism to keep in touch with his dead mother and also with other persons from whom he solicited advice, including the deceased Franklin D. Roosevelt. In his isolated study stood a huge oil portrait of his mother. He lived aloof from society in his latter years.

A mother-dominated girl was delightful little Maude Kiskaddin of Salt Lake City, who became better known as the actress Maude Adams. James Kiskaddin was not happy when his wife and daughter left home to become actresses, but there was not much he could do about their activities except to ask that the daughter not use the family name. He worked in a bank in Virginia City and eked out his small salary traveling with mule trains between Denver and Pueblo. James was non-Mormon, but his wife, Annie, was a Mormon who had been reared in Brigham Young's household. Had the first children, twin boys, not died, the family might not have scattered.

At four little Maudie was singing "Somebody's Coming When the Dewdrops Fall" to San Francisco audiences. She played the mining camps with her mother's troupe, was Little Eva in *Uncle Tom's Cabin*, Little Paul in *The Octoroon*, and Alice Redding in *Kit, the Arkansas Traveler*.

Periodically, the mother and daughter returned to James Kiskaddin, who welcomed them. James was a dashing horseman; he was lovable, lighthearted and never let work get in the way of a good time. He stormed a bit when his wife and daughter made a wild goose chase trip to New York only to be stranded when the star of their show ran off with the box-office receipts. He died when his daughter was twelve, and the schoolteachers begged Maude's mother to let their favorite student stay in school, advised that she be trained to be an elocution teacher, but both mother and daughter preferred the stage. In her old age Maudie's mother was very smug about her spinster daughter's lifelong indifference to men. It was a mother-dominated girl from Salt Lake City and a mother-smothered boy from Kirriemuir, Scotland, named James Barrie who delighted a generation of theatergoers with *Peter Pan*, a play about the little boy who never grew up. Neither did the author or the star.

Ludwig Lewisohn speaks of the "unrelenting mother dominance" in the life of Theodor Herzl, Zionist leader. The family was self-sufficient and "lived in a state of hot and brooding intensity." Jacob Herzl, the father, a clothier in Budapest, had his financial ups and downs, lost one fortune, gained another. When the daughter, Pauline, died in late adolescence, it was the one remaining child, Theodor, who was left to compensate and to reward his mother, Jeannette Diamant Herzl. A shattering relationship with the mother was to ruin the son's marriage, according to Dr. Alex Bein.

FATHERS WHO DOMINATE

The father who is dominating is not often concerned with the talents of the son or daughter. He is more concerned with his own potential than with his son's, struggles to maintain his position as head of the family, or to assure his own comfort and well-being. His goals are more immediate than are the mother's long-term dreams of fulfillment through her children and grandchildren. He frequently wants his son to be like him, but not necessarily better than he. He is too proud to live only for his son's success.

Quick-tempered, impatient parents are not necessarily dominating and do not always interfere with a son's choice of career or censor his ideas or choice of friends. Of his father, who was loving and permissive where major matters were concerned, Jawaharlal Nehru says in his autobiography, "His temper was indeed an awful thing, and even in after years I do not think I ever came across anything to match it."

Sir William Eden, father of the English statesman Sir Anthony Eden, was an overwhelming and overwhelmed man. He could be overcome by the sight of red flowers in a garden, the yelping of a dog, or the smell of whiskey or tobacco. His son describes him as being in a state of perpetual internal combustion. Sir William had a sharp and critical tongue, and his son learned early to avoid his father and to believe that any show of strong emotion was undesirable. The father made life somewhat easier for his family by leaving home during the children's school holidays to seek a spot where he could enjoy doing delicate water-color landscapes without distraction. He was not discriminating in his emotional outbursts, including children, servants, and friends in his storms of temper. Only his wife, Lady Sybil, a woman whose rare beauty had attracted him, seems to have been exempt from his rages. Randolph Churchill says of Lady Sybil, "His [Anthony Eden's] mother like many great beauties, was a spoiled women." He says it is a family belief that Eden's resentment over his mother's indifference motivated him to try to succeed. Eden seems to have been more rejected than dominated. His reaction was to withdraw. At Oxford even his tutor was not close to him.

In his autobiography, J. Middleton Murry, the English critic, said of his dominating father, "My manifest purpose in life was to be what he wanted me to be. The idea that a small human being might have needs of its own would have been confusing to his simple soul: therefore it gained no lodgment in it." John Murry, the father, worked from eight in the morning until twelve at night and saw no reason why the son should not study at his lessons with the same persistence. It was the only way for the son to escape from the squalor and futility of the poor working-class family group from which the father and mother came. John Murry had taught himself all he knew, and was a clerk at a hotel by day and a cashier in a Penny Bank at night. His wife kept lodgers. She was ten years younger than her driving husband and was at times also rebellious. She was a warm, gay young girl who once admitted to her son that she daydreamed of running away to join a gypsy caravan.

The family had Sundays together, and on Sunday afternoons the boy was set to doing interminable sums with his father. If any were wrong it was a calamity, since it upset the father, and the whole household was perpetually mobilized to keep the father from being upset. J. Middleton Murry read well at two, and at two and a half could do his tables to 12×12, at seven did quadratic equations; and was a prodigy at remembering dates. He was subject to recurring nightmares which he tried to evade by taking a knotted towel to bed with him. In the nightmare there were great circles of light which bore down on him, circles swifter than light which narrowed and grew intense as they came.

The father of Konrad Adenauer, who gave up an army career to marry a pretty little woman who sang all day at her work, never fulfilled his own ambitions and was a minor civil servant. He taught his children to read before they attended school, and was once in a rage when one of his sons left his homework to run after the firemen who passed the house en route to a fire. Konrad Adenauer became a "lone wolf" at school, was perpetually engrossed in his studies, kept much to himself.

"You made me lose all possible self-confidence and exchange a boundless guilt for it," says Franz Kafka, son of a wealthy merchant of Prague whom the writer detested as much as he loved his exotic, eccentric mother. Two brothers, who were born after Franz, died; and there were three much younger sisters. Kafka's complaints are bitter but nonspecific, and we have no family accounts to give the father's point of view.

Lieutenant Colonel H. H. Kitchener did not believe in blankets although the family lived in a dark, damp house in a famine-stricken corner of Ireland where he was an administrator. He taught his children that they were of a master race and must not accept the Irish children about them as equals. His wife, a delicate, sickly woman twenty years younger than he, objected to being covered by newspapers sewn together, so he tacked them to a frame set about the bed to keep out drafts. She tried, while she lived, to protect her delicate, withdrawn son. When she died, her successor, the music teacher Emma Green, did not stay married long to the eccentric martinet.

Rules for the children were stringent. They lived by a code which required them to punish each other sadistically for minor infractions of an unintentional sort. No real naughtiness was permitted. Horatio Herbert Kitchener, the son who was to be eminent as a military leader, was once found spread-eagled on the lawn, flat on his back in the hot sun, pinned to the ground by his arms and legs which were roped to croquet hoops. Herbert was a timid, silent boy who never defended himself and once crawled under a bed and hid like a sick animal when he hurt himself badly.

As an adult, according to Brigadier C. R. Ballard, "Kitchener could not unbend. If he cared anything for personal popularity he certainly never stooped to court it." He discouraged advice, avoided discussion; it was his "driving power which crowned his plans with success." His men did what was considered impossible when he drove them hard enough. He was displeased if a man on his staff married; never was he known to be interested in a woman.

Henry Louis Mencken, a rebel in adolescence and a rebel in adulthood, is one of the fifteen boys among the Four Hundred eminent persons who had a strong conflict with his father over the matter of the choice of a vocation.

H. L. Mencken commences his autobiography, *Newspaper Days*, by saying:

My father died on Friday, January 13, 1899, and was buried on the ensuing Sunday. On the Monday evening immediately following, having shaved with care and put on my best suit of clothes, I presented myself in the city room of the old Baltimore Morning Herald.

The animus which evidences itself in the first words of the autobiography is pathetic, in view of what seems to have been the headstrong father's good intentions. August Mencken was a hard-headed businessman, the owner with his brother of a thriving tobacco business. He was a pronounced agnostic, a loyal Shriner, an expansive, genial practical joker, a strikebreaker, an opportunist, a man tolerant of corruption as long as "corruption was harmonious with his self-interest," according to his son's biographer, William Manchester.

According to his lights he was a permissive and devoted father to his two sons and daughter. He played active romping games with his children, set up a photographic darkroom for Henry; took the children on trips, bought them a pony, devised endless adventures and entertainments for them. He gave them piano lessons, bought Henry a printing press, sent him to the YMCA for special setting-up exercises to straighten his shoulders — rounded by poring over the books he read so omnivorously. August Mencken rewarded Henry with a hundred-dollar purse when he stayed at the top of his class at the Polytechnic Institute. He hired a tutor to teach the boy good Spanish so he could be of more use in the tobacco business. When he forced the boy to spend two and a half years in the tobacco business, only bitterness toward the father seems to have remained. Henry would not accept the alternative of being sent to Johns Hopkins to be trained as a lawyer. The widowed mother consented to Henry's plans to sell the family business and made no objections to his becoming a journalist.

"There were two parties in my family," Mao Tse-Tung, Chinese Communist leader, told Edgar Snow. "One was my father, the Ruling Power. The Opposition was made up of myself, my mother, my brother, and sometimes even the laborer."[7]

The family lived in a simple cottage although the father was a successful rice trader. One day when there were guests, the thirteen-year-old Mao quarreled violently with his father, cursed him and left the house. The mother ran after the boy and begged him to come back while the father followed hard on the boy's heels, also shouting and cursing. At the edge of the pond Mao threatened to jump into the water if his father came one step nearer. After demands and counter-demands there was a compromise. Young Mao promised to make his father one knee bend if his father would promise not to beat him.

His mother is described as a warm, generous woman whose husband scolded her for giving rice away to the poor. Mao once ran away for three days and wandered in the woods because his father had punished his mother for her generosity. He returned only because he thought his mother might need him. He was a Buddhist when he was young because his mother was Buddhist, and at eight he contemplated burning the temple of Confucius because his father was a follower of Confucius. The mother wanted the boy to be a teacher; the father wanted Mao to keep the family books because the family had lost money using the abacus. Mao could read three times as fast as any other student in his class and was accelerated in all his subjects.

Those close to him say that they cannot remember a time when Mao was not writing martial poetry. He wrote verses as a boy; he wrote verses all during the Revolution. At conferences he "doodles" poems and his followers often pick them up from the floor to save as mementos.

Like seven others who loved mother and hated father, Mao combined a military career or a fascination with violence with an interest in martial poetry. How overprotective his mother was and how much of his father's ire was justifiable are difficult to determine. In his old age the father had mellowed and did not evidence an authoritarian attitude.

There are one hundred and nine mothers who can be readily categorized as dominating but only twenty-one fathers who meet this description. The most common adjectives used to describe these traits in the men and women are: dominating, overwhelming, adamant, strong-willed and determined. In old age the mothers become more domineering and the fathers much less so. The fathers "mellow" and often become quite charming and companionable to their adult children as did the dominating father of Pearl Buck, whose aggressive middle years she describes in *The Fighting Angel*. When he was eighty, the daughter and father enjoyed each other. The mothers tend to be right at the gifted son's elbow until the day they die, as was the mother of Luther Burbank, a persistently dominating woman. Dominating mothers are more likely to have sons who never marry, or who have marital problems if they do, than are dominating fathers.

Sons rebel at being father-dominated, but are often lifelong victims of mother-domination. There seems to be a glandular basis for the "masculine, dominating old woman" and the "higher-voiced, gentler old man." In old age women's voices deepen, old men's voices lighten. Luther Burbanks' mother is a typical example, "Mother was of a very intense nature," says her daughter, "walking with a firm step and speaking with a falling accent." Mrs. Burbank had sparkling hair and black eyes at sixty-four, and was at her son's elbow until she was ninety-seven, encouraging him in all that he did. Like many other such mothers, Mrs. Burbank was much younger than her husband, who was fifty-four years old when his son was born. She fought bitterly with Luther Burbank's first wife and was happy when the marriage ended in divorce.

The love for learning and achievement, the physical vigor in the parents, plus the dominating qualities in a parent often pay off in eminence, if not in personal satisfactions.

Fred L. Strodtbeck in *Talent and Society* reports a four-year study of home situations which make for the efficient use of ability, and finds that the combination of a father who relinquishes power, either through weakness or as a matter of principle, and a mother who has strong ideas about achievement is favorable to the son's development of talent. If the father is a strong, dominating man who believes he can control his own destiny, the son is frequently convinced that there are forces beyond his control and acts accordingly. He is fearful of leaving home and is overdependent on his father's guidance.

Both the mother and son are better able to express their own talents in a family climate where the father is not overpowering. *Talent and Society* also reports that the mother who has high, but realistic, expectations from young children in regard to such matters as being sent to the store alone, taking care of their own personal needs, dressing themselves, and so forth has children whose sense of values is high and who do better at work and at school than do children of mothers who expect less from them. The mother's high expectations and performance are presumably not seen as competition by the son; but the son of the very capable father is often less sure of himself than is his father.

These reactions from a large group of families in ordinary neighborhoods would seem to indicate that the dominating mother, although sometimes overwhelming at close range, plays a positive role in developing talent in her children. If she overplays her role, the child is not the less creative but may have serious problems in his interpersonal relationships, especially in courtship and marriage.

[5]

"Smothering" Mothers

I didn't know until I was fifteen that there
was anything in the world except me.
— F. Scott Fitzgerald

THE SMOTHERING MOTHER, as opposed to the dominating
mother and her ambitions for her son, draws a circle about
herself and lets no one inside except her son. He is the center of
her universe, and both the mother and son act on the premise
that the world revolves about the boy. The mother and son see
the whole of society as a force to be manipulated to give happiness
and honor to the son.

Such a boy tends to become precious. He is frequently frail and
sickly and the mother fears he will not live to be an adult. She
has a profound admiration for him and for everything he does;
but, unlike the dominating mother, she is not constantly driving
him toward a goal of her own choosing. He fulfills her by his very
existence, which to her is a daily miracle.

Boys of the lad's own age find it hard to accept his mother's
evaluation of him; hence, he finds peer relations difficult as a
boy and as a man. He is often, although not always, restricted to
easy relationships with pets, with children, and with women of his
mother's generation. If the mother is basically a kindly woman,
he too is kindly. However, he seldom loses his feeling of being
invulnerable, and finds democratic processes irritating although
he may give lip service to them. A "smothering" or overpossessive
attitude in the mother by no means precludes her son's becoming

a creative or capable person, but it seldom increases his chances for personal happiness.

To the degree that the mother is hostile, or is fearful, or feels perpetually abused, the son is likely to be inhumane or fearful. The sons of women who dislike their husbands tend to have few friends and also to have problems in sexual relationships. They sometimes enjoy the excitement of battle, feel invulnerable in the midst of carnage, are moved by martial music and war poetry. They like the rhythm of marching feet and the waving of flags. Presumably they are always proving to Mother and to themselves that they can whip the boy down the street who would not play with them.

A need to bolster a dubious masculinity is suggested in a study by Terman and Miles[1] in which city firemen and policemen unexpectedly rated with the lowest in masculinity among the occupational groups studied. The researchers, believing that an error had been made, sought a second group of policemen and repeated the test. The results were similar, leading them to conclude that these occupations may attract men who need the security of the civil service appointment and the authority of the uniform to strengthen their confidence in themselves as aggressive males. On this same test, engineers, bankers and lawyers scored highest in masculinity.

A need to prove maleness and a clinging to the mother's world and her sense of values are persistent traits of "mother-smothered" sons. The "smothering" mother tries to delay the maturation of her son, and unless he is strongly rebellious she may make him effeminate. Anatole France says of his own mother, "She would have prefered that I should not grow, so as to be able to press me to her bosom. . . . Everything that brought me a little independence and a little liberty offended her."

Gabriele D'Annunzio, dictator, poet and military man, illustrates the pattern of behavior which tends to repeat itself among the mother-smothered boys who dislike their fathers and turn to war or to poetry, or to both. The father, who was mayor of Pescara, was physically repulsive to his son, who described him as a corpulent, full-blooded, fiery-eyed man with a huge neck which bulged over his collar. The father was notoriously unfaithful to his wife, is said to have made mistresses of the daughters of his concubines. He avoided his son, left the boy to his doting mother, and did not attempt to discipline him. He was generous with his money and paid for the publication of a book of poems written by the talented adolescent. His wife, no matter what her son did, found no fault with Gabriele as a child or as an adult. She was the one woman in Gabriele D'Annunzio's life whom he ever truly and profoundly loved. Tom Antongini, who was his biographer and male secretary, quotes him as saying:

I am yours, I am the blood of your blood. I have remained united to you by a strong tie which still emanates from the center of my being. You go on feeding me. . . . I still feel myself palpitating in you as when I was about to be born.

He was unable to feel sincere affection for women of his own generation. At thirteen D'Annunzio was as sophisticated sexually as are most men of sixty. Antongini knew as well, or perhaps better, the identities of the various mistresses: D'Annunzio often became confused in this respect.

The poet's physical relationships with a series of women apparently meant nothing to him emotionally. It was only the mother to whom he expressed devotion in letters and conversation all of his life. D'Annunzio married a rich woman who was useful to him in the early days of his career, but he left her soon after their third child was born. He ignored the sons born of the union. Women's tears meant nothing to him. Eleonora Duse, the actress, left the stage and went into retirement when he described her in *Fuoco* as his aged, discarded mistress.

He had poor relationships with male contemporaries, but he liked animals. So reluctant was he to admit men of his own generation to his intimacy that he was unable to write if a man were in his room, although a woman sitting at his feet did not bother him. The personalities of several of ninety-one pets are affectionately, minutely described.

His mistresses were called "brother" or "sister." This did not reflect affection for his own brothers and sisters, with whom he had unsatisfactory relationships. Pet names given to his mistresses were so indiscriminately allocated that a telegram announcing the imminent arrival of a woman who described herself with one of these diminutives left the sender unidentified and caused confusion in the household.

Like other mother-smothered boys, he felt invulnerable from threat by other males. World War I gave the famous poet an opportunity for eminence as a warrior. The women of Italy, who had been remunerating his barber for clippings of hair from the almost bald head of the poet, found it exciting when the great lover became a great military hero at the age of fifty. "Spilling blood," he wrote, "is just like spilling sperm."[2] He had no personal fear of injury on the battlefield.

Life is a dreadful bore without the fever of war. . . . I fly [military plane] and I wander about beneath the shrapnel, but *I am invulnerable*. . . . Life is for me only a game to be put off from one day to the next and delicious in consequence. I frequently fly over the enemy three or four times in twenty-four hours.[3]

He looked forward with dismay to the day when the conflict might end. "What shall I do? Another war? I'm always ready to fight."

Mother's boys are often sickly, and Gabriele was no exception. His seeming eagerness to risk himself among the shrapnel did not lessen his lifelong hypochondria. Even in battle he was concerned about his baths, his foods, his appearance. He once made himself ill by overdosing himself with patent medicines. He took them all, even when he did not have the symptoms they professed to cure. He often sent for Doctor Dusé, his personal physician, but the doctor injected him with harmless drugs — which had the effect of morphine because D'Annunzio thought he was receiving morphine.

Despite his fears for his health his principal ailment was the common cold. He hated to have to blow his nose, thought it sad to see the brains of a genius blown away on a handkerchief. The "mother's boy" often regards his body as his mother's and is guilt-stricken if he does not care for it properly.

He kept his house stifling hot, sprayed himself with perfume day and night, surrounded himself with symbolic objects which represented "black magic" to him and could ward off evil. After his mother's death, his preoccupation with his own survival and doubts as to his invulnerability grew to psychopathic proportions. His neurotic traits did not preclude literary productivity. He died with his pen in his hand; he worked hard to the end of his days.

The relationship between eighteen-year-old Adolf Hitler and his mother was so close that family friends felt intrusive in their household, where Klara Hitler lay dying while her only son attended her. "Never," says August Kubizek, author of *The Young Hitler I Knew* and Adolf's constant companion during adolescence, "have I come across this same peculiar spiritual harmony between mother and son."

At the time when Klara Hitler was stricken with breast cancer her son had just returned from Vienna, where he had failed to be admitted either to art school or to architectural school. Adolf said nothing of this disappointment to his boyhood friend. Instead, Kubizek says, he lost himself in the nursing of his mother.

His unbounded love for his mother enabled him to carry out this unaccustomed domestic work so efficiently that she could not praize him enough for it. I found him kneeling on the floor . . . wearing a blue apron . . . scrubbing. . . . The kitchen cupboard had been moved into the living room and in its place was a couch on which Adolph slept so that he could be near her at night as well. The little sister slept in the living room.

The spiritual harmony between the mother and son was not so complete that Klara did not find an occasion to speak in secret to August Kubizek. She confided in him her fears for Adolf's future and begged August to influence Adolf to learn a trade or to train himself to become a civil servant as his father would have wished. She also spoke to the young man of her own marriage: "What I had hoped for and dreamed of as a young girl was not fulfilled in marriage, but does such a thing ever happen?"

It is true that her marriage did not have an auspicious beginning. Klara was already pregnant when she became the third wife of her cousin, a surly customs official twenty-three years older than she. She must have been familiar with his marital history when she became his wife. Franzeska, his second wife, a hotel cook who was also young enough to have been his daughter, had already borne him a child when his first wife, who was fourteen years older than he, died without issue.

Vocationally, Alois Hitler had done well enough. For the illegitimate son of a working-class girl to become a customs officer was a satisfactory adjustment and he was proud of his status. At work, however, he often antagonized the other men by his dogmatic statement of his liberal views, and he was said to be a touchy man who flared up over trifles. His regular drinking companions found him difficult. At home he was apt to give his adolescent son a good hiding when he thought the boy needed punishment. Their quarrels were frequent and bitter.

It was not until he was fifteen that Adolf Hitler found a constant companion in a boy of his own age in Kubizek, the sixteen-year-old son of an upholsterer, whom he met at a concert which each had attended alone. For four years the boys were often together. Both of them were smothered by mothers who had seen their other sons die; both boys were frail, socially isolated, and were attracted to cultural pursuits. August wanted to be a musician, but his mother wanted him near her and his father needed him as an apprentice in his upholstery shop. Both boys had made poor marks in school. Adolf was the talker, August the listener.

August was attracted to the pale Adolf, who was so meticulously dressed, who carried his black ebony cane with a flair, who talked and gesticulated like a volcano in eruption as he strode about the town of Prinz planning its architectural revision, speculating about the proper use of this and that vacant lot. August appreciated Adolf's interest in his own desire to be a musician, especially when Adolf was able to convince August's father and mother that they should let their son study music seriously.

Adolf had no interest in ordinary recreational pursuits. It was not because of parental pressure that Adolf did not smoke or drink or use tobacco. He had no interest in games or sports but instead talked, drew pictures, and wrote poems.

The mother-smothered boys whose mothers dislike their husbands resent ordinary boys of their own age. Adolf and August were strolling down the Landstrasse when a well-dressed, friendly young fellow recognized Adolf as a former classmate at the school from which Adolf had been withdrawn because of failing marks. The youth took Adolf familiarly by the arm and asked him in the friendliest fashion how he was getting on. Young Hitler exploded in rage, pushed the young man aside and strode off down the street complaining that he had once had to sit in class with such fellows, all of whom were surely going to turn out to be "civil servants." He castigated the students for laziness and said that school was a place where teachers taught students to be idle. Yet he had himself been idle and failed — despite which, he was angry with his friend for having made poor marks in school. He examined the school exercise books of his little sister Paula and led her to her sick mother's bed to make her swear that she would always be a good pupil in school and do her work well.

He also had an unusual reaction to a girl of his own generation. As the boys walked about the city, Adolf orated to August about Stephanie, a charming and proper girl a few years older than Adolf. Stephanie was not especially aware of his distant adoration. She did not know that he wrote poems about her in the little black notebook he always carried in his pocket as other boys carried tools.

When Stephanie did not smile at Adolf as he passed, he contemplated suicide, and planned that Stephanie should be made to jump from the bridge into the river with him. He demanded, in seeming seriousness, that August engage the mother in conversation so he could kidnap Stephanie, but August was not cooperative.

"Our friendship endured because I was a patient listener," says Kubizek. "He too had no other friends besides me." Adolf was jealous of August's attention, scolded if his friend was late to an appointment, once accompanied him to the funeral of August's deceased teacher rather than be left alone; in short, he was extremely possessive.

As a little boy Adolf had had scant opportunity to form friendships with other children. Although he stayed on the same job, Alois Hitler found it difficult to live in the same house very long. Adolf attended five different elementary schools, in all of which he was lost and unnoticed. His teachers remembered him only as a quiet, good boy and a passable scholar. His mother did not form attachments to the women in her neighborhood. She was withdrawn from everyone except her son. Although the mothers of August and Adolf both approved of the intimacy of their sons, they themselves did not become close friends. Klara was difficult to know, and was not close to her daughter.

On the day of Klara Hitler's funeral her son was not too lost in grief to watch for a flutter of the curtain as he passed Stephanie's house. To him a slight movement meant that Stephanie was watching him as he passed and was grieving with him. August was noncommittal, but unbelieving, as he listened to the wishful thinking of his friend. After the funeral, Adolf was bitter, distracted, and melancholy. He quarreled with his guardian and his brother-in-law, who tried to apprentice him to a trade. Nor would he be a "civil servant." He soon went back to Vienna, alone and without much money. He terminated his adolescent friendship with August Kubizek abruptly. There were no letters, no return visits. When they met as adults, they differed in their political attitudes.

"If my mother had not died," says Antonio Salazar, dictator of Portugal, "I would not have become even a Minister. She could not have lived without me. I couldn't have worked, knowing she was troubled."

His sister Martha, one of two spinster sisters, describes her brother's relationship with his mother; "Our mother . . . was called Mariado Resgate Salazar. She was exceptionally intelligent. I told you she was particularly fond of our brother. He was always absolutely devoted to her. When he was a student at Coimbra, he did some tutoring on the side so he could afford the trip home to see her each Sunday."[4]

He was restricted and uneasy with the boys at school. When he was a student, he could not bring himself to enjoy the easy familiarities of school life. When he was asked to enjoy delicacies sent from home to another boy, he ceremoniously asked the permission of the school authorities before he could enjoy the treat. Even then he stood in the doorway to eat, not wishing to disobey the school rules about entering another student's room. He now is said to enjoy children and older women; he is stiff and formal with other adults.

In speeches he extols the virtues of family life but has never married or been known to be attracted by a woman. He lives with his two adopted daughters and a housekeeper. Like Hitler, he nursed his mother through a long illness. He followed her coffin to the grave on feet so swollen he could scarcely stand.

Another boy who adored his mother is the Arab leader Gamal Abdel Nasser, who also hated his father.*

His father, a postmaster, is described as "stubborn, proud, fatalistic." It was his mother, so curious and so romantic and affectionate, whom the boy loved.

He was also, as a boy, prone to emotional disturbance. At the age of six he attempted suicide because he wished to escape going to hell. If he died before he was twelve, he reasoned, he would be safe, since he would not have reached the age of accountability. He failed at school and was in one elementary grade three years. When he was sent away to live with a bachelor uncle, his homesick letters to his mother brought no response. He returned after a year's absence and found she had long since been buried. He refused to accept a stepmother but was very unhappy with his uncle, who lived in a Jewish section of the city. Gamal Abdel was the only Arab boy in the neighborhood. A foster son of his uncle's accepted the Jewish neighbors very well; but the younger boy refused to make friends and also continued to dislike his father. In secondary school he became a fearless leader of a group of students who were in rebellion against English domination. It was poetry and drama which appealed to him at the school, where teachers gave him grades in order to appease the rebel, who was known to have a strong following among other students.

George Seldes says of Benito Mussolini in *Sawdust Caesar*:

*Alfred Nobel, who left his fortune to promote world peace, was also an excessively mother-smothered boy who hated his father intensely for no apparent reason. Both father and son were manufacturers and inventors of munitions. Nobel wrote a long poem justifying parricide. He was never able to introduce his mistress to his mother. When she bore a child, he paid another man to marry her.

"He was whipped and bullied by his father, pampered and kissed too much by his mother. . . . He never loved deeply, never had a true friend."

At sixteen he had a venereal disease; at eighteen he stabbed his mistress in the thigh. At the same time, he was afraid to walk in the dark alone. He loved poetry about the days of chivalry, and at seventeen declaimed martial poems while standing alone on a hilltop.

When a woman loses other children, remaining children must often bear the brunt of a mother's overpossessiveness. Soon after three sisters died of scarlet fever, Vachel Lindsay's mother nursed him through an illness which was nearly fatal. She carried him about on a pillow for more than a year and "breathed life into him."

During his childhood he was kept apart from other children who might be rowdy or dirty. His curls were uncut, he wore immaculate while piqué suits, and played with two sisters who had also survived their childhood illnesses. His mother wrote a children's play in which Vachel was cast in the role of Cupid.

As a twenty-year-old college student, Vachel complained of being treated as if he were a "premature, brilliant, inspired baby" by his mother, who responded by reminding him of the time in his infancy during which she had willed him to live.

Vachel Lindsay disliked his physician father, whom he described as a man with a queer, baffling savage streak, a man with restless energy who would rather kick open a barn door than push it. The poet pictures his father as an unconquered Ishmaelite who took disabolical delight in driving at three o'clock in the morning at top speed down a muddy road in pelting rain, whipping his frantic horse straight into the thunder and lightning.

Despite the husband's virility, it was the wife who ruled in this household. She dominated her circle of acquaintances, threw herself into church and public affairs with ardor, and organized and taught a class in the principles and achievements of Christian civilization. She was a mystic, given to moments of insight and to hearing voices. She had room in her life for other concerns than her only son. He was desolate when she died, however, and found nothing worth while without her to report to. Three years after she died, when Vachel was forty-six, he married a young woman of twenty-three. In a paranoiac episode shortly before he poisoned himself with cleaning fluid, he talked himself into a fury, recalling the days when the other boys at school would not play with him. He also accused his wife of having taken his most precious possession — his virginity. He adopted his mother's sympathy for mankind, but his relationships with the men and women of his own generation were difficult and painful.

When Oscar Wilde was convicted of homosexuality and was separated from his wife and two sons, his wife used to say to them, "Try not to feel harshly about your father. All his troubles arose from the hatred of a son for his father."

Oscar Wilde hated his father, the physician Sir William Wilde, who was publicly pilloried in a sensational trial for his unfaithfulness to his wife. He also had a smothering mother, who grieved deeply when her daughter Isola Francesca died at the age of ten. Since the time of her birth, Isola Francesca had been the pivot around which the family's affection revolved. Jane Francesca Wilde, the mother, then turned to her fat little boy and tried to substitute him for his sister, even dressing him in girl's clothing.

As a girl Jane had embraced the cause of Irish freedom and written inflammatory articles under the name of "Speranza." When Gavan Duffy was tried for sedition, she rose dramatically in court and took the blame for a seditious action ascribed to the prisoner at the bar. She became a tragedy queen in her old age and lived in semidarkness, a terrifying, severe woman. Her son Oscar was in Reading Gaol when she died.

David M. Levy[5] in a study of maternal overprotection found that husbands of these overwhelming mothers were often passive or were unable to intervene in the relationships which develop between the mother and the child. Such fathers are frequent in the homes of the mother-smothered among the Four Hundred.

A pint of champagne and a mutton chop was the unheeded prescription made by a prominent doctor on behalf of his small son, Duff Cooper. The boy was chronically delicate and debilitated, had no pleasure in the outdoors, sat by the fire, read poetry, and looked at picture books. He memorized much of Macaulay's *Lays of Ancient Rome*, recited Poe's *The Raven* and whole sections of Aytoun's *Lays of the Scottish Cavaliers*. At school he began to lose his fragility, but not his aloofness.

When Duff was called home from Eton because his father was dying, he was not moved by the parent's illness. Although he had never been spoken to crossly by the physician, he never felt close to him. Yet his father had not neglected him; each week Duff had received from Dr. Cooper a letter which described the week's events and gave the family news. It was, however, impossible for Duff to speak to his father about his deepest thoughts. When Duff had a poem published in the *Saturday Review*, his father looked into *Whitaker's Almanac* to discover the salary of a poet laureate and said dryly, "The appointment's not worth the having."[6]

Duff's mother was a solitary woman who had few friends and did not care to make more. It was she whom Duff adored. She ran away from a first husband because she wanted to be with a man she really loved. When her second husband died, she married Duff's father, who had loved her in vain since she was a young girl. Her family always thought the doctor was their social inferior.

Duff enjoyed debating but found no foeman worthy of his steel, and Eton did not permit debate on controversial subjects such as religion or politics. He had few close friends and was eager to be done with Eton, because he felt he had outgrown the society of boys.

Had his father lived, Duff Cooper might have become a poet in rebellion. Instead he went from Oxford to the foreign office, to the Brigade of Guards, to the War Office and on to the Admiralty.

In the Rilke family the father was unable to communicate with his son. Sophia Rilke, the mother of the poet Rainer Maria Rilke, was a foolish, emotional woman, full of whims and flights of fancy, for whom Rainer replaced a sister who died before he was born. His mother pretended he was a girl, let his hair grow long, kept him in girl's house frocks, taught him to dust and clean, called him "Sophie." His playmates were charming little girls with whom he shared his dolls, and for whom he left nosegays under garden seats. He lived in an emotional climate of piety; his mother prayed, he said, as other people took a cup of coffee.

Both parents were fearful lest the delicate boy catch cold and coddled him through innumerable illnesses. Josef Rilke was a soldier who never won the preferment he desired. Even so, he considered leaving Prague and taking a less desirable post so his son could have a better climate. The parents were not congenial, and they separated. Josef could never accept his effeminate son as a poet. Since the family had a military tradition, he insisted his son be sent to military school to be away from the influence of his mother.

At eleven the boy was taken from his mother and put in uniform; his hair was cut short. There were five hundred boys, fifty to a dormitory, at the Military College at St. Pölten. Brutality was the order of the day. Rilke was teased and beaten. He found no place to be alone, except the school infirmary, where he spent a substantial portion of his five years of schooling at the college.

Another father who failed to make his son an out-of-doors boy was an eccentric French count. On the flyleaf of a book on falconry, Count Toulouse-Lautrec wrote to his son:

Remember that an outdoor life under the light of the sun is the only healthy life. Everything deprived of freedom deteriorates and dies quickly. This little book will help you to enjoy the open-air life. If, later on, you happen to taste life's bitterness you will find faithful companions in dogs, falcons and above all in horses who will help you to forget a little.[7]

The marriage which was to produce the painter Henri-Marie Raymond de Toulouse-Lautrec was not a love match and never became so. It was arranged for two cousins to marry so the family fortune could be preserved. Their second child, a beautiful, normal, healthy boy, died suddenly and mysteriously when he was a year old. Their older child was frail, thick-lipped, exceedingly homely, and tiny.

The mother, a dogged, unimaginative woman, set herself to protecting the unfortunate first son from unpleasant experiences and physical danger. He was frequently ill. The only two reasonably healthy years he enjoyed were years when he was away at school. Although he was undersized and homely, he had good friends there and at home he enjoyed his father's company and that of dogs and horses and ponies.

Two falls, which broke his fragile legs, also checked his growth and made his appearance even more grotesque. Children on the street thought him a circus freak and ran after him in ghoulish excitement. His mother moved closer and closer to the boy but made no protest when he enjoyed himself at bars and brothels.

His father had long since escaped into the world of his own eccentricities. He often wore doublet and hose and carried a falcon or rode a white mare, milked her and drank the milk, while strollers in the park watched in snickering fascination. The unconventional Count once lived in a tent on the Cathedral grounds, or shut himself in a tower of his own estate and pulled his food to his quarters by means of a pulley.

Henri's mother was with him when alcohol and syphilis given him by attractive Rosa la Rouge combined to ruin the health of the talented painter. His mind was affected. He saw microbes everywhere. He flooded the floor of his bedroom with kerosene to destroy insects that were never there, while his distracted mother feared that he would burn himself alive. He died at the age of thirty-seven.

Count Toulouse-Lautrec wanted his son to enjoy horses and falcons and dogs, while Thomas Church, an English mail-sorter, held out for the benefits of bicycling. In two autobiographies, *The Golden Sovereign* and *Over the Bridge*, Richard Church, poet, novelist and literary critic, chronicles the life of a mother-smothered boy with sensitivity and a literary finesse which make the two volumes valuable to the clinician who is interested in this area of relationship between mother and son.

Young Richard's universe was centered on his mother's fragrant person. As she took off her garments, her apron, her handkerchief, he would touch them with rapture. The farther he was removed from his mother physically, the darker were his days and nights. His vitality lessened, his confidence in the strength of his own flesh and blood ebbed.

His parents were simple people; his mother was a schoolteacher and his father a postman. Richard's relationship with his musically gifted brother Jack was excellent. He never heard his parents quarrel until the day when the father, who believed in the therapeutic effects of fresh air and exercise, led the family on an exhausting bicycle excursion. Through two autobiographical volumes Richard Church cannot forgive his father for an interest in bicycles and cars. In this instance the father completely failed to enter into the charmed mother-son circle. (It was not broken until the mother's death from bronchial asthma, a sickness through which her adolescent son, Richard, nursed her devotedly.)

When he was nine, Richard was hospitalized as a result of an undiagnosed, debilitating illness. Richard was sent to the Yarrow Convalescent Home at Broadstairs and stayed there for six months. His stomach was distended, his limbs thin. When the wind was in the north his limbs felt numb, his belly full of lead, his vision askew. He was a slave to rhythm; moving objects hypnotized him. Every sound, every color overstimulated the boy, who fainted with excitement when he first glimpsed the evening sky through glasses which corrected his extreme myopia.

Richard had never been able to separate his identity from that of his mother. He was very homesick at the hospital for a few days, but soon relaxed in the warm, comfortable, friendly place. He was left to his own devices and spent hours, while the others went off to town or to the beach, just lying on the couch by the open window surrounded by his favorite dog-eared books. He was now able to think of his mother as someone apart from himself, to feel all around her personality, to observe her with detachment, with the humor and sympathy he used when he looked at his brother or his father.

"All of his life Syngman Rhee has been more influenced by women than by men," says his biographer, Robert T. Oliver.[8] His mother, Kim-Hai Kimsio Rhee, was his closest companion during childhood. A period of blindness caused by the aftermath of smallpox made the child, born to the mother in her fortieth year, even closer to his doting, worshiping mother. A previous son, who had been "sickly" since birth, died soon after Syngman Rhee was born. He was her first healthy son. His elderly father, absorbed in a study of genealogy, in which his son was uninterested, was inclined to leave the boy to his mother's care and supervision.

WIDOWS ARE OFTEN OVERPOSSESSIVE

A third of the fifty widows in the homes which produced eminence can clearly be called "smothering." The least likely to be overprotective are the widows who are left in straitened circumstances. Aneurin Bevan, Ernest Bevin, Al Smith, Abraham Flexner, Marian Anderson, and George W. Norris, children of such women, experienced no coddling, maternal anxiety for their survival, or restriction of normal behavior. There is apparently a considerable advantage in being the child of a poor but respectable widow; but well-to-do widows' children are sometimes subject to an all-encompassing maternal concern.

Although Friedrich Nietzsche was the son of a deceased minister, there was enough money in the family to free his mother and grandmother and two maiden aunts to spend their full time overprotecting, caressing, and overruling the docile boy, who was a model of propriety until he was eighteen and began drinking. His sister also shared in the adulation of the gifted boy. It was they who invented the imaginary world of the Kingdom of King Squirrel in which miniature toys played a part.*

---

*Textbooks describing gifted children often speak of their tendency to create fantasy worlds and to have imaginary playmates. Leo and Gertrude Stein had a secret world and a secret language. Vera Brittain and her brother Edward invented a community called "The Dicks." From the ages of six to eleven, Vera kept the story alive and the characters involved were very real to both the teller and the listener. Betty MacDonald, American humorist, kept alive for "years and years" the exciting tale of Nancy and Plum, who escaped from an orphanage, were kidnapped by bank robbers, captured by gypsies, and who finally adopted a baby who turned out to be a prince. She used these characters in published material. The Tolstoy children had a secret world initiated by the oldest brother Stephen which involved pretending to be Moravian brothers who were creating a perfect world. In this imaginary

Professor Paul Gide, who died when his only son was eleven, was a well-to-do lawyer who made a practice of never accepting a client of whose innocence he was not convinced. Young André was not only mother-smothered, he was women-smothered. The three excessively proper women who brought him up hovered over him and were shocked if he betrayed himself by any expression of boyish spirits. The wealthy, precious boy was moved about from place to place, to the Riviera, to Montpellier. If he trampled on a playmate's sand castle, or was obstinately aggressive, or bit a girl playmate's bare shoulder, he was speedily removed from temptation by a change of scene. Occasional male tutors taught him little except the intimate details of their personal lives — which André found both edifying and stimulating.

A poor widow who centered her life about her son was the mother of Joseph Stalin, the fourth child of Ekaterina and Vissarion Djugashvili of Gori, a little Georgian village in Russia. Ekaterina was only fifteen when she married. Her first three children died soon after they were born. The fourth, a wiry, strong-willed boy, almost died of smallpox. He suffered an infection which left his arm twisted. His toes were webbed. He attended the ecclesiastical school at Gori because his mother wanted her boy to succeed although his father had failed. Vissarion Djugashvili closed his shop when it did not pay, but he became irritable when he went to work in the Anelkhanov shoe factory.

The father died when "Soso" was eleven, and Ekaterina immediately made plans to have the boy trained for the priesthood. At fifteen he entered the theological seminary of Tiflis. There are two versions of his leaving school before graduation. His mother says[9] she withdrew him because he was sickly from overwork and

---

world, no man could have any misfortune. Quarreling was taboo among the "brothers." They huddled together under chairs, hid themselves under cloth tents, cuddled in the dark, practicing "love one another." Leo always thought they were being "ant-brothers," because the Russian words for "Moravian" and "ant" are similar. Sheila Kaye-Smithe, who had a rich fantasy life, imagined long novels long before she wrote one. She was an only child and had an imaginary playmate, who never washed or went to bed and wore dresses made of gold or flower petals.

she feared he might come down with tuberculosis. His official biographers say that he was reading revolutionary literature.

An English widow's son, Arthur Balfour, was fortunate in his mother's choice of a preparatory school. The Rev. C. J. Chittenden, housemaster at a school in Hoddesdon in Hertfordshire, discovered that the only way to teach him the subjects necessary for Eton was to help him constantly to see the general principle in everything and not try to get him to remember isolated facts beyond what was absolutely necessary.

His biographer, Blanche Dugdale, quotes from a reminiscence written by the Rev. C. J. Chittenden: "He had an uncommon power for a boy, of taking in the purport of a number of connected facts and seeing quickly any apparent inconsistency between them."[10]

Teaching eleven-year-old Arthur Balfour was difficult because of his lack of vital energy. The school doctor advised that the boy lie down in the afternoon when he felt tired and try to sleep. He enjoyed this activity if someone played the piano softly in the hall below. He walked with his headmaster while the other boys played at cricket and conversed with the intellectual ability of a boy of at least eighteen.

Arthur's father, James Maitland Balfour, had died of tuberculosis when Arthur, his oldest son, was seven. He could never remember his father well, had only a vague notion of his personality.

Lady Blanche Balfour was a woman with a very powerful personality. When her husband died, she forsook society and concentrated her dominating personality and powerful mind upon her children. In the days of Arthur's grandfather, the drawing room was hung with yellow damask and filled with French furniture and Sèvres china, and the house was filled with guests. When Lady Balfour became a widow, the dust covers were never removed from the furniture; the nurseries and the schoolroom became the heart of the house.

A friend of Lady Balfour wrote of her in the early days of her husband's illness: "To know her slightly — you would never suspect the intense funds of feeling, dashing and flashing and bursting and melting and tearing her at times to pieces."

At Oxford Arthur collected china, spent hours resting in his rooms and was called "Pretty Fanny" by his classmates. In later years Winston Churchill described him as an implacable politician who was fearless in the internecine battles of politics, who looked blandly through his pince-nez at battlefield carnage when he was taken on a tour during World War I.

Churchill says in *Great Contemporaries* that there was no way of getting at Balfour. When he was threatened physically by an irate fellow politician in Parliament, he looked upon the disturbed man as if upon the contortions of a rare and provoked insect. Churchill believes that had Balfour lived during the French Revolution he could have consigned an erring colleague to the guillotine with complacency, but in a thoroughly polite and completely impersonal manner.

This bachelor first Earl of Balfour lived in an aura of nieces. His political friends found it hard to break through the closed feminine family circle in order to communicate with him.

A minister's widow in Newark, New Jersey, was not so wise in her choice of schools for her talented child as was Lady Blanche Balfour. Stephen Crane's mother was a woman of strong principles. When a young girl in the community was bearing a baby out of wedlock, it was Mrs. Crane who took the girl into her home, housed and defended her. Stephen published his first book at twenty-one, soon after his mother's death, and entitled it *Maggie, Girl of the Streets*. He married a woman ten years older than he who was the proprietor of a hotel of dubious reputation. He turned to poetry, to the excitement of being a war correspondent, and to a prose outpouring concerning the fascination of the horror and the fear of spilling blood. Crane annoyed his friend Joseph Conrad by making the assumption that he knew better than Conrad about the language and desires of the Conrad children. Stephen Crane was an affectionate and devoted uncle, but he could never relate warmly to his male peers. With older women, children and dogs he was quite comfortable. In a perverse way he was always his mother's boy and moved in her generation rather than his own, even when he defied her and her smothering, dominating ways in personal habits. For his father he had contempt but never hatred.

Crane's mother was the daughter, widow and sister of clergymen. "You might as well argue with a wave as mother,"[11] said Stephen. Her voice was deep and strong as Ellen Terry's. She spoke slowly as the clock ticks. She wrote articles for Methodist papers and church news for the New York *Tribune* and the Philadelphia *Press*. "It isn't that I dislike books," Stephen protested when she spoke with him about his grades. "It is the cut and dried curriculum which does not appeal to me."

Mrs. Crane tried to rear her youngest son properly. Since she had lost five babies before he was born, and he was so delicate and frail, Stephen was not sent to school until he was eight. When he learned to read, she took his paperback Westerns away from him, but she let him pore for hours over Harper's picture history of the War of the Rebellion. He occupied himself for hours playing at the strategy of war with buttons from her mending box.

War was his favorite game. He almost smothered a playmate by covering him completely with sand while playing at burying dead soldiers. Stephen was spanked soundly by the child's aunt for this misdemeanor.

He liked the Methodist military school he attended and made good marks there except in algebra. It was at the Hudson River Institute that he lost a tooth in a fight because he called Tennyson's writings "swill." He was at his best conducting battalion drill, leading his company in a blue silk sash, shouting "Ho, Hell!" He was an excellent baseball player and was "giftedly profane." However, he had no real intimacy with other boys and had a distinct lack of respect for human beings in the mass and a certain coldness. No teacher ever liked him.

His father was a gentle man who wrote little tracts mildly reproving intemperance, card playing and theater going. He loved animals and never drove his horses over two miles an hour even if a member of his congregation was dying. He turned Methodist when he could no longer abide the Presbyterian doctrine of predestination. Stephen, his fourteenth child, was eight when his father died.

THE FATHER-SMOTHERED

Fathers and whole families may be "smothering" also. It is the youngest child, particularly the youngest girl, who is most vulnerable to inappropriate overprotectiveness. If she is tiny and precocious, delicate and beautiful, and if she is much younger than her siblings, the whole family sometimes develops an over-protective attitude during her "baby-girl" years. The older Crane children had displayed some of this feeling toward Stephen, although it was his older brothers who insisted that his curls be cut.

In other families there is more "family smothering" of the youngest. Clara Barton was family-smothered; but especially by her father.

Her father, who could not forget the days when he was an Indian fighter with Mad Anthony Wayne, taught her to plot battles and to understand military strategy. She would have liked more than anything else to be a boy and to go to war, but her father explained that she was living in days of peace and that war would never come again. He held her on his knee for hours, delighting in her responsiveness.

Clara had her schooling at home with her five teachers, her father, two brothers and two sisters. Dorothy Barton taught Clara to read when the child was three, and Sally Barton taught her geography and spelling. From the age of six Clara wrote reams of doggerel. Stephen Barton taught her arithmetic and how to drive nails. Both sisters and her oldest brother were employed as teachers in the community. The quick-tempered mother taught Clara household skills.

At eight Clara was sent away to boarding school where the curriculum was on a secondary level. The principal, Richard Stone, an old friend of the family, tried to help the child adjust to the older children in his classes, but they laughed at the eight-year-old girl who cried when she missed an answer but knew more than most of them would ever know. A conference with the parents, doctor and school authorities resulted in Clara's being sent home to her parents' farm.

From her eighth to her eleventh year Clara Barton had her "time-out" period. Very little was expected of her since she was already far advanced and no school could be found to meet her academic needs. She moved with her parents to the farm of a widowed relative who needed help and for the first time she had young playmates, five of them, who ranged in age from three to thirteen. She became physically active, rode logs down the river, helped paper the house. There was no repetition of the kind of hysteria she displayed at four when she believed that thunderclouds were angry rams descending to harm her. She remained, however, a father's girl. Her principal pride during this period was her muscular development, which she believed was more masculine than feminine.

An older brother and sister married and found their interests in their own homes, but Dorothy, the spinster schoolteacher, became an "invalid." The mother, always quick-tempered, had little time for Clara. David suffered a fall during a housewarming, and from the ages of eleven to thirteen, the tiny girl who grew up so quickly in some respects assumed adult responsibilities. She nursed David assiduously for two years, applied leeches frequently, and made him completely dependent upon her. She responded to his neurotic weakness and permitted him to make selfish demands on her. It was a doctor who broke up this relationship, got the boy out of the house and up on his feet, and dismissed the small nurse, who had not grown physically during the period and who had become extremely shy and introverted.

In early adolescence she had decided never to have a romance, but animals could be loved without reservation or shyness. There was Buttons, her dog. Later there was to be her Arabian horse, Baba, and her Maltese cat, Tommy. She wrote of army mules as if they were human beings and wrote of the Czars' black horses as if they were kings. Like D'Annunzio, she was sentimental about animals and about war. Dawn on the battlefield could set her writing doggerel. The little woman, never more than sixty inches tall, had an indomitable, unquenchable drive. This father's girl had many of the neurotic qualities of the mother's boys, and her life was to be complicated by emotional disturbances.

Clara Barton first lost her voice in 1854 when she was denied the superintendency of a free public school whose enrollment she had built up from four pupils to six hundred. The school board chose a man to replace her in authority, and she was literally speechless with rage. She had constant conflicts with her contemporaries, both male and female, and her many later nervous collapses were heralded by a lack of speech.

In 1875 she was treated in a sanatorium in Dansville, New York. By 1878 she was much improved and set out to persuade the American government to mitigate the cruelties of war by signing the Geneva treaty and joining the International Red Cross. In 1881 she succeeded in this goal, but she continued to have conflicts with various persons including President Theodore Roosevelt. Susan B. Anthony and Carrie Chapman Catt defended her and probably kept her from a second breakdown. At one time she had her trunks packed, ready to go to Mexico or China — any place where there was no Red Cross.

She maintained her energy in her old age, studied Esperanto at eighty-eight, and learned to use the typewriter at ninety. Like some of the mother's boys — Mackenzie King, Harry Houdini, Conan Doyle, Hamlin Garland — she became engrossed in spiritualism in her old age.

Another sickly, family-smothered girl was Mary Baker Eddy, who was given to a strange sickness marked by physical debilitation, attacks of temper and hysteria, and acute pains in the spinal area. When the child had these attacks, the family physician, Dr. Nathaniel G. Ladd, could always be depended upon to bring her out of them, although the distracted family expected the child to die during each seizure. In these episodes Mary would fling herself upon the floor, pound with her heels, and pass into a state of unconsciousness. It was found easier to let her stay at home and amuse herself than to send her to school. She frequently heard voices calling her which were interpreted by the mother and child as "divine" voices.

The especially attractive child was like a pretty doll to her older sisters, who used to take her to school with them during her preschool years, set her on a table and invite her to tell their playmates what she was going to do when she was grown. She always replied, "I'm going to write a book." Her maternal grandmother had aroused these ambitions in Mary by showing her a scrapbook in the attic filled with the poetic productions of some bygone ancestor. Mary often wrote sentimental doggerel, when she was home from school alone. Within her neighborhood she became known as the young girl poetess; pretty, affected, arrogant and vain.

There were three older brothers, Samuel, Albert and George; and two sisters, Abigail and Martha. The father, Mark Baker, was a harsh, quick-tempered man, a hard-working farmer who was easily embroiled in factional disputes in the Congregational Church at Tilton, where he belabored backsliders.

The older brothers, especially gifted Albert, taught the little sister at home from their own schoolbooks. There was a period in late adolescence when Mary was content to forget her own drives for eminence and look forward to acting as the mistress of Albert's home. Albert was a talented boy who had gone to Dartmouth, who read law in the office of Franklin Pierce, was admitted to the bar, but died just after he had been nominated to Congress in a district where nomination was tantamount to election. Albert's death was a great blow to the nineteen-year-old girl, since she had identified herself completely with him and expected to share the bachelor brother's home and eminence.

The quick-tempered father, rather than the compliant and defeated mother, assumed much of the burden of Mary's care when she became more ill as she grew older. When her attacks of hysteria grew increasingly terrible, he had the local road authorities cover the highway before the house with tanbark to stop the convulsive shudders the girl suffered when she heard horses' hoofs passing by. He rocked her in his arms like a baby when everything else failed. A cradle was built from an old sofa with a rail and the "Lang boy" was hired to rock Mary. Abigail Tilton, her married sister, also provided a home and a haven for Mary in her times of trouble. When Mary was unable to care for a child born to her first marriage, he was cared for by his grandmother until she died. At four, he was given by the family to a nurse who was fond of him. It was only in the later years, when the family repudiated Mary's religious beliefs, that the family's overprotectiveness of their "baby-girl" stopped.

Her father had begun to have some insight as to Mary's seizures before she left his care. The neighbors persuaded him that it would be best to ignore her symptoms. He did so and the experiment was successful, according to the description of her biographer, Edwin Franden Dakin.[12] When his daughter threw herself violently to the floor after he had challenged her in an argument, he walked away and left her lying alone. An hour later, when he returned, Mary had retired to her room; and when supper was called, she came down in the calmest of moods. She was vexed with these recurring episodes of muscular spasm and rigidity all of her life. In her old age her faithful followers assumed the role of the protective family, kept a twenty-four-hour watch about her to ward off the "animal magnetism" of the enemies who were seeking to destroy her. Her son instituted an unsuccessful suit against her to have her declared mentally ill.

Among the Four Hundred families there are eight fathers who might be designated as "smothering," as seeking to withdraw the child unnecessarily from the mainstream of life, as being overly anxious about the child's health or diet, or commanding an inappropriate share of the child's affection.

C. Day Lewis was the son of a clergyman whose wife died when their only child was four. He worried about the boy's weak chest and coaxed him to eat by encouraging the lad to crawl around the table pretending to be a hungry bear. The poet says in his autobiography, "Relying solely on my father for that spiritual infusion which a child can accept only from a parent, and receiving from him the full force of a love which had nowhere else now to turn [since his wife's death] created between us a bond of abnormal tension."

Life in the home of the poet Stephen Spender was played against a background of calamity; there was always a sense of catastrophe in the house. Of his father, an overpossessive, anxious widower, Spender says, "The feeling that the death of my father was arranged at a time when his life had become intolerable to us [the children] did not leave me. I went home at once, prepared to live a newer and freer life." When Stephen recovered from the illness which was the "epilogue to my relationship with him," the adolescent boy began to enjoy perfect health. Unfortunately, the grandmother, previously jolly and sensible, took over the anxious role the deceased father had played and on a holiday trip never let him and his brothers and sisters out of her sight for a minute.

A soldier and amateur poet, George S. Patton, was spared the tedium of the classroom, the competition with his peers and the usual tasks of childhood until he was twelve. The only other child resident of the 1800-acre ranch was his small sister Nita. He was given no frustrating learning tasks to do and when his father, a semi-retired lawyer, tired of reading aloud to his son, an aunt took over the task. George's mother, an athletic, active woman, seems to have left the planning of the reading sessions to the opinionative father. At twelve George could not read for himself.

The boy experienced extreme peer rejection in preparatory school. At West Point he was dubbed a "quilloid" — a boy ready to curry favor by "skinning" other cadets. He gained favor with his instructors by a punctilious keeping to the rules. He was stiff-necked, arrogant, and boastful. He never learned to read well, although his memory was extraordinary. He got through West Point by memorizing whole lectures and texts and parroting them verbatim.

At fifteen he met a pretty little girl of his own age who had been as sheltered and overprotected as he. Beatrice Banning Ayer was the daughter of well-to-do friends of the Patton family. Her interests were literary and artistic. At fifteen she still played with dolls and wore her hair in Alice in Wonderland fashion. Neither ever had another sweetheart, and the families were delighted with the romance. They married soon after George's graduation, had a happy marriage and introduced their children to the Patton family habit of reciting poetry. Kipling was the general's favorite poet, according to his wife.

James Weiland, Patton's biographer, says that his slapping a sick soldier and soon after weeping at the bedside of another is evidence of a dichotomy in his nature. He feels that there was a "soft side" of Patton's nature that he went to great lengths to conceal.

Weiland quotes from a poem entitled "God of Battles" published in *Woman's Home Companion* in which Patton speaks of a great God, who through the ages has "braced the blood stained hand." (Both General Patton and General Montgomery used prayer on the battlefield.)

The military hero whose nickname was "Blood and Guts," whose speech to his soldiers going into battle was a montage of obscenity and profanity, could also coin such phrases as: "He who has heard all day the battle hymn, sung on all sides by a thousand throats of fire."

Patton is another of the overprotected boys who enjoyed battle. "War," he said, "is the supreme test of a man." He had a zest for killing and felt lost and useless when there was no battle to fight. His biographer says of him, "So he gained the generalship, the medals and the glory, but he was never to make many friends."

When the mother-dominated and mother-smothered are considered as one unit, they are seen to include sixty-four per cent of the military men, adventurers and dictators. And the smothering mothers (or smothering fathers) and the dominating mothers rear fifty-four per cent of the poets. The eight persons who find battle exhilarating and also like to read or recite martial poetry come from these homes.

The smothering parents and dominating parents can be considered as one unit because both devote unusually concentrated attention to their children. These children described their parents variously as adamant, bossy, strong-willed, overanxious, overprotective, overpossessive, interfering, and especially as dominating. The dominating parents are those who concentrate on their children's careers; smothering parents demand their children's affection and demonstrate their own love for the child by caresses and sacrifices.

When the sixty-four smothering mothers are considered apart from the dominating mothers we find it is they who rear most of the dictators and also the four whose sexual inversion is discussed by their biographers. It may also be significant that the sixty-four smothering mothers reared twenty-four of the fifty-seven bachelors among the Four Hundred. If the mother is kindly, if she admires her husband, or if there is a family opinionativeness that favors a humanitarian point of view, the "mother-smothered" boy may love freedom and equality as well as beauty. Some of the most able of the eminent are "mothers' boys." However, there is considerable evidence to indicate that the least desirable home in which potentially eminent sons were reared was the home in which a "smothering mother" disliked her husband.

[6]

Troubled Homes

I must make it known that I do not believe
it is required of art, science, religion, philosophy or family to assure every man born into
this life a secure childhood, in which a child
knows only love and harmony. If such a
childhood happens to come to pass for a
child, excellent. If the child, as a result of
such a childhood, becomes a truly pleasant
or excellent adult who functions in a satisfying manner . . . again excellent. The supplying of such a childhood to a child, however,
appears to be impossible. It may not even be
desirable. It may just create a nonentity. . . .
I think it is inevitable and in order for the
human creature to be unhappy in childhood.
I think it is impossible, at the same time, for
almost any new human being to be entirely
unhappy at any time. . . . I was bitterly unhappy as a small child.

— WILLIAM SAROYAN,
The Bicycle Rider in Beverly Hills

IN THE HOMES which cradle eminence, creativity and contentment are not congenial. Both parents and children are often
irritable, explosive, changeable, experimental. They are prone to
depression and exaltation. They make terrible mistakes and win
wonderful victories.

The "normal man," as measured by personality inventory tests,
is not a likely candidate for the Hall of Fame. Dr. Jules Golden,
of the department of psychiatry at the Albany Medical College;
Dr. Nathan Mandel, research sociologist in the Minnesota State

Department of Correction; and Dr. Bernard C. Glueck, Jr., director of research at the Institute of Living, conducted surveys of seventy-three men of twenty-six years of age who were problem-free at fourteen. The Minnesota Multiphasic Personality Inventory, a self-descriptive questionnaire, had been given to a group of 1953 schoolboys. These seventy-three represented the most problem-free among them.[1]

The efficiency of the test was proved by the follow-up on these boys. They remained stable and untroubled. There was consistency and conformity in the life patterns of the group. Follow-up was not too expensive or difficult, since most of them had remained in the same metropolitan area in which they had been tested. Fifty of the seventy-three were still available in the same large city for the follow-up study. They had all completed high school; most of them held average white-collar jobs. Only one made more than $10,000 annually, and only one made less than $3000.

They were found to be living comfortable, well-adjusted lives and were untroubled by traumatic marital discords: no separations, no divorces. They had few job dissatisfactions, few particularly high aspirations. They led contented, home-centered lives, showed little imagination, and had limited interests in social activities. They had low aspirations for themselves and for their children. They rated highest in "contentment and compatibility with spouse" and lowest in "richness of personality and breadth of interest."

The data led the researchers to conclude that "normality," as evidenced by a lack of intrapsychic tension, adequate social, economic and familial adaptation and harmonious integration with other individuals at all levels, implies a lack of creativity, imagination and spontaneity. The comfortable and contented do not ordinarily become creative.

This conclusion is adequately borne out by the survey of the family backgrounds of the Four Hundred, of whom only fifty-eight can be said to have experienced what is the stereotyped picture of the supportive, warm, relatively untroubled home. Even these fifty-eight fit that picture awkwardly in significant respects, or are so inadequately described that there is reason to suspect omission of pertinent facts which might change the picture if additional evidence were forthcoming.

Within the framework of turbulence and contention there are group differences. Children who are to make contributions to the theater or to literature have the most intrapsychic tension to report. The dramas enacted in the family theater are often more complex and fantastic than those that the child in the home grows up to invent. Actors and actresses come from stormy homes. The homes of the reformers and humanitarians are the most explosive with ideas and argument. The illegitimate have their special problems, as do the very poor and the very rich. Poor parents are sometimes exploitive; rich parents, eccentric or neglectful.

Children in these turbulent and explosive homes do not always enjoy life. They suffer intensely at times, and they are deeply capable of suffering, since they are sensitive and aware individuals. The Four Hundred had problems and achieved eminence. There is no way of estimating how many equally capable and imaginative children lived in similar homes and became neurotic or psychotic or delinquent or indifferent to such a degree that they were unproductive. A few of the Four Hundred came from warm, supportive, cohesive homes, and these will be described in the next chapter. But our immediate task is to report that contentment and creativity do not ordinarily go hand in hand in the homes which cradle eminence.

In the prime of his life, Pavel Chekhov, father of the novelist and playwright Anton Chekhov, was a vain and selfish man. His wife, in a letter to her son Michael (who became his brother Anton's biographer), described him as a man possessed of "an inborn and inveterate spite." His pleasure was in ritual, uniforms, music, painting and self-display. He took an active part in local elections (opinionative), missed no public dinners or civic or church celebrations in his home town of Taganrog, Russia.

With money given him by his own father, a serf who had freed himself and his whole family by his hard work and ingenuity, Pavel bought a small shop where he sold alcoholic drinks, patent medicines and groceries. Anton was left to do much of the work in the shop because he was the quickest of the children at making change and keeping inventory. Pavel was seldom in his store because of his preoccupation with music, painting, and public affairs.

Anton's father had also been given enough money to buy a plot of land upon which to build a home for his wife and five children. Since he did not want to be cheated, he told the builder that he would pay him a certain sum of money for each thousand bricks used. He would not pay a lump sum for the whole job and be cheated. The builder responded to Pavel's lack of faith in him by building the walls twice the usual thickness. The distracted Pavel borrowed from moneylenders to pay for the piles of bricks, only to find he could pay neither principal nor interest on the loan. In order to escape debtor's prison he left town for the next stop down the line from Taganrog and took the train to Moscow, where his oldest sons, Alexander and Nicholas, were supporting and educating themselves, Alexander at the University of Moscow, Nicholas at art school. They were not happy to see him.

He left his nagging wife, Eugenie Chekhov, to salvage what she could from the estate. The genuinely put-upon woman was cheated as badly as her husband had been and soon followed him to Moscow with the younger children, Mary and Michael. Ivan and Anton, then adolescents, were left behind to complete their secondary education. They would have to earn their own board and keep however they could.

Anton was happy to be left in Taganrog without any family except his brother. His father had beaten him often, overworked him in the store, and had forced him to become a member of the children's choir, which Pavel directed. He had been dragged out of bed at two or three in the morning for special rehearsals and performances. He found it easy to earn his living by acting as a tutor to a wealthy boy, and he enjoyed his freedom.

Despite his cleverness, Anton was a poor student. He could not bring himself to study either Latin or Greek. Ivan, who was younger than he, finished his work and went to Moscow to rejoin the family. Anton failed his examinations twice. Not all of his time was spent in study. He had his first sex experiences at thirteen and found that girls were responsive to his love-making. He loved parties, trips to the estates of his friends, dancing and singing.

His failures at school bothered him so much that he had nightmares in which he saw huge slippery boulders which bordered a deep river he must cross but could not. In the river were tiny tugs hauling enormous barges. When he tried to run away from the river he stumbled upon crumbling cemetery gates, funeral processions and schoolteachers. All his life he was to be haunted by dreams of teachers trying to "catch him out."

After the third try he was graduated, but he did not want to go to Moscow to join his family. He had responded to his mother's whining letters by capturing goldfinches to sell as pets and sending her a little money. His older brothers, his mother said, had taken to drink, women and other follies. The family was sleeping on the floor with coats as covers and there was inadequate food. Ivan was too timid to find work. Pavel had beaten Ivan until the neighbors intervened and the landlord threatened to evict them. The father had pinned a schedule of duties on the dingy wall of the slum room and driven his family to do his will. They had already moved eleven times. The mother feared that when Anton came to the wicked big city he too would turn to drink and desert his family as his older brothers had done. But Aunt Feodossia, who was sick and alone and had moved in with them, was sure that Anton would be able to become the savior of the family if he would only come to Moscow.

Anton thought of striking out on his own, of abandoning his family and going to medical school, but when the time came, he was unable to cut his familial ties. He wrote to his well-to-do cousin Michael in Moscow and asked him to give Pavel a job in a warehouse so far from the apartment that Pavel could not come home except for infrequent weekends. He had no intention of going home if his father was to be there. The cousin was cooperative. Anton then coaxed two of his school friends to come with him to Moscow to board with the family. This would mean extra money for groceries. He would enroll in medical school and find work to support himself, his mother, and his young brother and sister. He would help Ivan find a job.

The prostitutes in the neighborhood hung out of the windows to see the three fresh-faced country boys arrive in Moscow. Anton and his two schoolfellows were welcomed with enthusiasm by the desperate family. Young Michael, outside on the street, did not recognize his brother, who had grown from adolescence to manhood since the family had fled to Moscow.

When Anton came home, the two older brothers returned to the family roof. Alexander had been doing some writing for humor magazines and found similar work for Anton, who wrote clever quips and long pot-boilers for inconsequential magazines, in the midst of confusion and squalor. Nicholas drew cartoons for the humor magazines. Michael found work copying lectures for other students at a fee. Ivan was employed as an elementary-school teacher. Mother, Mary, and Aunt Feodossia kept house, and Mary trained as a teacher. Anton managed his classes and his writings and attended a great many parties among the intellectuals of Moscow. Pavel came home for an occasional weekend and added to the confusion in the three crowded rooms by reading aloud to his wife. Anton's nights were plagued by nightmares. After a hard day's work at the university, he fell into a deep sleep, from which he was suddenly awakened by a real terror. A strange force seemed to throw him out of bed, to tear him up by the roots, and he found it difficult to fall asleep again.

Alexander, the oldest son, talented and creative, was a severe alcoholic. Nicholas became rather well known as a painter. Ivan, who passed his secondary examinations easily and was not as driving as his brothers, was a steady, uninspired (possibly very happy) schoolteacher. Mary, the only girl in the family, was a schoolmistress and artist. Michael, the youngest, who escaped the full force of his father's hostilities, was a writer of children's stories and his brother's biographer. Anton, who strongly resisted studies in which he had no interest, had a great zest for life and was chosen as the child most capable of keeping his father's store. He was the family member most adequate to become the head of the family, and also used his potential most effectively. Within the family the person who is to achieve eminence is usually recognized by his family as being exceptionally capable and original.

The Chekhov family, which produced a great writer, did so despite the cruelty and poor judgment of the father. It also produced four other children who had the drive for learning which distinguished the father. During his middle age, Pavel was hated and despised by his family because of his temper and financial failures but in old age he became docile and kindly and was proud of his son, who had long since died of tuberculosis. Pavel died (appropriately enough as a father of a literary genius) on the operating table, after having suffered a rupture from lifting a box of books.

It sometimes happens that a schoolteacher or a librarian discovers a child who is eager for intellectual companionship which the home does not provide. Theodore Dreiser had this experience, but he was unable to fit himself into the rigidity of the curriculum at Indiana University, to which his elderly female teacher would have sent him for more than one year had he desired to attend. While at college he read widely and talked with people who interested him, but the classroom irked and bored him. It was from the hot, murky context of the family emotional climate that he drew the content material for his best writing.

There seems to have been no love for learning in the Dreiser family, although Theodore became a writer and Paul became a writer of popular songs. It is possible that Theodore Dreiser, even in his lengthy autobiography, did not give a fair picture of his father. He does not explain the impetus which led his father to leave Germany and come to the United States. Nothing is known of the father's education or of his family. Theodore did not know his own father in the days of his success, but only as an old man and a failure. The extremely mother-centered writer may have owed more to his father in the way of intellectual endowment than he conveys in his writing about his family.

When Theodore Dreiser wrote *Sister Carrie* and *An American Tragedy*, he was writing of a world he had known in childhood.

His mother, at sixteen, had run away from her Mennonite farm home to marry a strange young German immigrant who was a Roman Catholic. Her family disowned her. She was an illiterate, warm, amoral woman, with a great faith in her children which survived many tests. Her son Theodore was a "mother's boy." His first memories were of stroking her feet, of weeping over her torn shoes, of crying because of her poverty and of being comforted on her warm breasts. In his autobiography he writes pages in praise of his "happy, hopeful, animal mother with the desire to live, and not much constructive ability to make real her dreams." She was the only person who ever wanted him enough.

His father was a thin, dour bitter man who was out of work for the first seven years of Theodore's life. He had once been successful, even affluent, but his mill had burned and he was cheated. He brooded; he blamed his wife for his children's delinquencies.

As the quiet boy grew, he read hungrily and hated the parochial school to which his father made him go. There was anger and shame and destitution in the home. The oldest son, Paul, was arrested three times, once for forgery, and was living in a fine house in Evansville, Indiana, where he was "kept" by Anna Brace, madam of a house of prostitution. When Theodore visited there as a boy, he was impressed by the luxury of the establishment and by the glimpses of the lovely girls in appealing disarray. It was only the bounty of Anna Brace which kept the Dreiser family above the subsistence level for two years. When Anna quarreled with Paul, the Dreisers were destitute again and began moving from place to place, each home being more squalid than the last. It was Paul who composed the music for the popular song "On the Banks of the Wabash," for which Theodore wrote the lyrics. "Rome," next to Paul in age among the brothers, was a gambler, drunkard and wanderer.

Theodore's older sisters, Mame, Emma, Teresa and Sylvia, came home with presents they received from men. Two of them bore "love children." Sarah Dreiser admired the pretty gifts the girls received from their gentlemen friends. If their father could not buy them pretty things, she said, he should not complain if other men did. The father stormed and no one heard him; he sulked and nobody noticed.

There is no boy among the Four Hundred whose life was so complicated with sordid complications as was the life of Alexei Peshkov. Through 616 pages of autobiography the recital of tension and terror never stops. Yet his heavy-handed grandfather, who beat him insensible, taught Alexei at home so well that the school inspector noticed him and praised him and chided him for wasting his talents by being disruptive in the classroom. In this patriarchal home it was the quarreling grandparents who made the family emotional climate in which the boy was reared.

Alexei Peshkov, when he was four, crouched behind a trunk in his parents' bedroom staring at the white-robed, stiff, twisted figure of his father, who had just died of cholera. In another corner his hunchbacked little grandmother was hopping about the figure of his mother, who was rolling about in agony while giving birth to her second son, Sascha. The dead father, Maxim Peshkov, as a boy had been hunted with dogs and flogged when he tried to run away from his father, an army officer who was finally exiled to Siberia for cruelty to his men. Varya Kashirin, daughter of a brutal dyemaker, had loved her dead husband dearly because he was kind, affectionate and educated. Her bestial brothers, Mike and Jake, disliked their gentle brother-in-law and broke a hole in the ice and tossed him into the water as a welcome to the establishment of his in-laws.

The Kashirin household was shunned by the neighbors. The very house shook with the angers of the big men. Mike and Jake Kashirin beat their wives and beat their children. Servants were teased and tortured. Alexei made a flower garden and his relatives turned the pigs into it to destroy it.

The patriarch of the household, old Vassili Kashirin, beat his wife from noon until dark on Easter Sunday and gave her no food while she lay half-dying. He beat his grandson unconscious when the boy dyed a white tablecloth blue.

Alexei's mother, Varya, was a tall and magnificant woman, but she could not protect her son from her father or her brothers. When she married again, and her second husband beat her, Alexei nearly killed the fellow by knifing him. The boy, well taught at home by the same maternal grandfather who had beaten him, found school dull. When he took a ruble from his stepfather's purse to buy sausages for his classmates and a copy of *Robinson Crusoe* for himself, he quit school rather than be shamed about his theft by his classmates.

When he left home at the age of ten to find work there was only his beloved grandmother to miss him. His grandfather, who had lost his business, made the boy leave. He loved his grandmother fully and uncritically and she gave him the same complete devotion. She was illiterate, but she had an endless store of folk-lore and folk wisdom and an unshakable faith in humanity's essential goodness. He became an errand boy in a shoe store, a dish-washer, a draftsman's apprentice, an icon-painter's apprentice, a birdcatcher. In the homes of his successive masters the family life was not much better than in his own. He went to the country but found the people there even less sensitive than the people in the city. He thought the habit the country boys had of captur-ing young girls, tying their skirts above their heads, and leaving the girls to run themselves exhausted, bare-bottomed and in screaming confusion, was both crude and cruel. He found the peasants antagonistic to learning and to the learned, and uncon-cerned about their own destinies.

He made no close friends, so that when he received a letter saying his grandmother had died, the world was cold and empty. He had no one to speak to about his sorrow, not even a horse or dog that was his own to share his grief. At nineteen he was so weary with the world and the people in it that he decided to kill himself and shot himself in the left side. After a long con-valescence, he recovered. He later gave himself a new name and became Maxim Gorky — "Man of Bitterness."

Sam Clemens, unlike Gorky, was not one to write of psycho-logical conflicts of the kind he saw at home.

When Orion Clemens was approached by an editor who wanted to describe the Clemens family as Orion saw it, Sam was furious and forbade his brother to give any information. This is unfortunate, since Sam Clemens was also a "mother's boy" whose accounts of his mother omit some of the interesting details given by word of mouth to later descendants.

It is Samuel Charles Webster, son of Anne Moffett Webster and grandson of the Pamela Clemens Moffett who was Sam Clemens's sister and eight years older than he, who is our prin-cipal informant about Sam Clemens and his family. Samuel Charles Webster painstakingly collected the family legends while his own mother was still alive.

Jane Lampton Clemens put stepmothers in the same category

as Yankees. It was her eagerness to get away from home which hurried her into a marriage with John Marshall Clemens which was not a love-match; the man and woman, so different in personality, were never congenial.

Pamela was her father's child; Sam, his mother's boy. The only time Sam ever saw one member of the family kiss another was when his father called Pamela to his deathbed to bid her good-by. John Marshall Clemens was especially fond of his daughter and had cautioned her to learn to be a good housekeeper, to see that her husband was comfortable, advised her, "Don't have too many cats in the house." His wife, Jane, was never able to resist a stray cat; she sometimes kept as many as thirty-eight about the untidy place.

Anne Moffett Webster, Pamela's daughter, in her own old age recalled the feelings of her mother about John Marshall Clemens:

My grandfather died long before I was born. Uncle Sam thought his father was very strict, but my mother was fond of him. From my mother I gained a picture of a man of great dignity, a keen sense of humor, and the highest degree of neatness and fastidiousness. He was always called "Squire" by his neighbors. Once on the street someone slapped him on the back, and the family was horrified. He was a scholarly type and had studied to be a lawyer. It must have been hard for a man of this character to have such a haphazard, happy-go-lucky wife.[2]

It was natural that Samuel Clemens should have been his mother's favorite. Her son Orion was born in 1825, her daughter Pamela in 1827. She lost her next three children, Pleasants Hannibal, Margaret and Benjamin. It was Samuel, a seven-month baby who stayed sickly until he was six years old, who had to replace these lost children for her. To make Sam strong Jane Clemens used the water cure, treating his frequent colds by dousing him in cold water.

Jane was as outgoing and dramatic as her husband was dignified and retiring. Like her son Sam the truth never stopped her when she had a good story to tell. She once told a comparative stranger about her dear little daughter Pamela who had been taken away by the Indians and never returned. At fourteen, Sam Clemens had been left in charge, for a week, of the paper where he worked. He tells a delightful, detailed, apologetic story in his autobiography about driving a rival editor out of town by publishing an account of how the lovesick man had pretended to commit suicide by drowning. The truth, as attested by old copies of the newspaper of that date, is that he published a drawing of the editor, with a dog's head, pretending to drown himself because he was overly fearful of dogs during a rabies scare in the community.

Jane Lampton Clemens showed the same indifference to disaster and calamity. She showed no anxiety during a cholera epidemic even when people to whom she had talked in the morning were dead by evening. A neighbor was killed because a calf had run in front of the horse on which he rode. Jane's first reaction was: "What happened to the calf?" When accused of liking cats better than babies she replied blithely, "When you're tired of a cat, you can put it down."

She was never drawn to religion except for the drama of the ceremony. She went to various churches and to a Jewish synagogue — to see the sights and rituals, not out of interest in theology.

My grandmother has been represented in recent years as a Puritan, but nothing could be further from the truth. She loved any kind of excitement. She seemed to be always going to a parade, a circus or a funeral. . . . She was a great beauty, a fine dancer, and very witty. She kept her beauty to the last, as well as her love of color and dancing. . . . Grandma's room was always a perfect riot of red: carpets, chairs, ornaments, were all red. She would have worn red, too, if she had not been restrained. She was modern in her ideas and insisted on wearing her skirts shorter than was conventional. Once when she was having an especially nice dress made, the family gave secret orders to the dressmaker to make it longer than she had said. When Grandma tried it on she said nothing, but promptly sat down and ran a tuck in it.[3]

Jane Lampton Clemens was another of the mothers of eminent men who was energetic and outgoing in personality until her death. At eighty-one she danced for her sons Samuel and Orion as lightly as a girl. Although Samuel was her favorite, it was Orion, for whom neither his mother nor Samuel ever had a word of praise, who took over the care of his difficult mother in her extreme old age. Jane Lampton Clemens used to complain of Orion's pious ways. She saw no reason why he should let his love for various religions interfere with his success in life. She said that Orion had a "jugful of religion," but that she could make do with a "dipperful."

Biographers who confuse her with the more conventional and pious Aunt Polly would seem to be at fault. Nor does she seem to have worried about Sam's quitting school when he was eleven. It was his father, not his mother, who had a regard for disciplined learning. She had a fine disregard for spelling and exactness of expression. She once wrote to her son Samuel, "Kill Susy," (her granddaughter) instead of "Kiss Susy" and did not bother to change the wording. "He'll know what I mean," she said. Her son wrote back an amusing and gory letter in which he pretended to have carried out her whim, and she chortled with glee. He knew how to please her. She always had a great love for the dramatic and macabre and sensational, for mesmerism, spiritualism, strange creeds and exciting events. She lived for the excitement the day brought.

Sam was eleven when Judge Clemens (Justice of the Peace) died, leaving the family in serious economic difficulties. Financial reverses had already caused them to give up their home and move into rooms above the father's office. Before the Judge died, he was hopeful of appointment to the clerkship of the Surrogate Court, a position which would have paid better than that of Justice of the Peace, which he had held for many years. All that the Judge left his family was 75,000 acres of virgin Tennessee timber, which he had bought for $400 a decade before as an investment. He figured the land would be worth a fortune to his descendants. The Judge wrote a fine Spencerian hand, was fussy and hard-working, and once wrote 13,000 words on a case that paid him only thirteen dollars because he thought a matter of civil liberties was involved.

Orion, the oldest boy, was too temperamental to be reliable. Every day Orion awakened with a new idea, which absorbed him all day but died with the night. One day he was practicing to be an orator; the next day he was studying French. He joined first one church, then another.

Sam Clemens was always very critical of Orion, but he was as unable to handle money as were his brother and father. The family lands were frittered away after much quarreling between Orion and Sam. Investment in a typesetting machine that never worked bankrupted the writer. Any romantic views of Sam Clemen's early days on the river are dispelled by a description by DeLancey Ferguson of a recurrent nightmare which plagued Sam as an adult. There are also traces of what may have been boyhood anxieties over money in his dream.

There is never a month passes that I do not dream of being in reduced circumstances, and obliged to go back to the river to earn a living. It is never a pleasant dream either. I love to think about those days; but there is always something sickening about the thought that I have been obliged to go back to them; and usually in my dream I am just about to start into a black shadow without being able to tell whether it is Selma Bluff, or Hat Island, or only a black wall of night.[4]

The Virginia novelist Ellen Glasgow night after night lay awake listening to her mother's voice as the unhappy woman walked the floor in anguish, "to and fro, back and forth, driven by a thought or vision from which she tried in vain to escape." When the mother was happy and played games with her children, the whole house was merry. When she plummeted suddenly into recurrent deep depressions, the younger children in the household of ten ate the "bread of helplessness with the mother."

"My father was," Ellen Glasgow says in her autobiography, "one of the last men on earth she [mother] should have married." The wife could not bear the husband's callousness about animals, for which she had a quivering tenderness. During the week the wealthy ironmonger was away on business. When Saturday came, the beds of Ellen and her sister Rebe were moved from the mother's room to an adjacent room. The family dogs, sensing it was Saturday, looked apprehensively at the whip in the hall.

His daughter describes him as an entirely unselfish man, who respected learning, whose word was as good as gold, a man of "complete integrity." He enjoyed weeping over sentimental stories of the return of prodigal daughters; he was a patient, tireless, efficient nurse in the sickroom when his children were ill, as they often were during childhood.

But he never understood his wife, "not for a single minute," says her daughter. He had no sense of beauty, and he never knowingly "committed an act of pleasure." He tried to censor his daughter's reading when she was an adolescent.

Ellen herself was said to have been born "without a skin," screamed frequently during her first three weeks for no known reason and was carried about on a pillow. No one expected her to live.

When she was seven, she was sent to a school which was intolerable to her. Another girl ate Ellen's lunch when she could not bring herself to eat in strange surroundings. The teachers were kind, but did not protect her from the other children who called her a "White Rabbit" when she vomited and became ill with nervous headaches. Her mother was always waiting at the door for her Ellen's return and greeted her with embraces and expressions of sympathy, and she convinced their family doctor that the frail child might slip out of their hands if they sent her to school. So Ellen was permitted to stay home with the mother, who was the "sun of her universe" and an "innocent soul suffering an undeserved tragedy." The release from the classroom was accepted gratefully by Ellen, who found school so distasteful that "death from exposure would have been a simple escape."

Ellen's brother Frank, who tried to be loyal to both parents, drowned himself. In divided homes the sibling relationship is poor between the children who do not agree as to which parent is the aggrieved party in the conflict. The children who empathized with the mother were more creative but less happy than the "father's children" who married, reared families and withdrew from the household drama. Ellen herself was twice engaged, but never married.

UNFAITHFUL WIVES AND HUSBANDS

Extramarital love affairs are not common among the parents of the Four Hundred. Ellen Terry, actress mother of the stage designer Gordon Craig, had many lovers. The father of Lafcadio Hearn renewed his love affair with an ex-sweetheart after he brought a wife home from the Ionian Islands. Several fathers are said to have been physically unfaithful to their wives but not emotionally involved with the woman concerned.

Among the truly philandering husbands was Count Nicholas Tolstoi, to whom his son Leo Tolstoi credits two passions: cards and women. In his *Memoirs* Tolstoi says of his father, "God knows if he had any moral convictions." The tall, stately man with the bald spot and the lisp grieved to realize that the companions of his youth had risen to high official positions while he was only a retired lieutenant of the guards.

The complications of Nicholas Tolstoi's life are not surpassed by the plots and subplots in the novels his son wrote. A liaison was arranged for Nicholas (for good health's sake) when he was sixteen with a young servant who bore him a son named Mishenka. It later embarrassed his legal sons to be asked for charity by this man, who looked more like their father than they did.

The old countess, Leo's grandmother, was a foolish, vain, rather stupid woman who had been spoiled by her husband and father and expected to be spoiled the rest of her life by her son. Nicholas fell in love with the orphan she reared to be her companion and handmaiden, the pretty Tatyana Yergolski with the sturdy brown body, coarse black braids, agate eyes and strong will. When Tatyana and Nicholas, who were the same age, were twenty-seven, they had not yet married. His mother did not approve: Tatyana was an orphan, a distant relative, and poor, and was not a suitable bride for her only son.

Tatyana waited and made herself indispensable. When Nicholas had to sell the country estate that was his inheritance, she moved with him and his demanding mother into a five-room apartment in Moscow. Tatyana could take punishment without flinching. When she was a girl, she proved her courage by putting a white-hot piece of iron on her bare arm. She did not flinch, not even when her skin ripped and stuck to the bar. Her masochism was to find plenty of outlets during her lifetime.

Nicholas took a regular job in the government office for war orphans. He walked the floor; he refused to see his friends. He sat by his mother's bedside and held her hand while she sympathized with him for having to work. Tatyana and his mother were not his only dependents; he also had a sister and a niece to care for in the small apartment.

His sister Alexandra had made a very bad marriage. When she was pregnant her husband had gone mad and beaten her. Her daughter was stillborn, but Nicholas and the woman tricked Alexandra by substituting the cook's newest daughter, Pashenka, for the dead child. The husband was institutionalized and she and her daughter moved into the Tolstoi home. Tatyana agreed with him that he must marry an heiress. Marya Volkonskaya, the woman he chose, was the heiress to an estate of 2500 acres and 800 serfs. She was five years older than Nicholas and Tatyana, and was both ugly and shy. Romance had passed her by long before.

Her father, a scholar as well as a very rich man, had spent years educating his only daughter and had taught her French, German, English and Italian. He took her sightseeing through Europe, made her study mathematics, physics, geometry and geography, employed a piano teacher for her, and trained her to administer the estate. He was a stern teacher. Marya could never verbally express anger or distaste; instead her face grew scarlet and she cried.

Nicholas brought her home with him to the apartment where his mother and his childhood sweetheart, Tatyana, waited for her. The old countess was never much more than polite, but Tatyana was honest and soon admitted that Marya was a good wife. When she also became a mother, the whole household moved to the wife's estate, the beautiful Yasnaya Polyana (Plain Field) where things had not gone well without the mistress.

"I think my mother was not in love with my father," Tolstoi wrote, "but loved him as a husband and chiefly as the father of her children." There were to be five of them.

Count Nicholas resumed his life as a gay and genial young man with no specific interests or talents. He was not interested in politics; his reading from his large library was desultory. Yet he never whipped one of the eight hundred serfs, among whom was his natural son Mishenka.

The old countess had her own quarters and her luxuries. She

kept a blind minstrel to amuse her and insisted that a grandchild sleep with her in her big bed each night.

Aunt Alexandra had her own quarters and collected a motley of hangers-on, eccentrics, pilgrims, monks, nuns. Her favorite among them was a half-witted pilgrim named Marie who went about in male dress.

Marya occupied herself with her five children. The oldest boy, Nicholas, was especially brilliant and receptive. She used Rousseau's *Emile* as her nineteenth-century equivalent of Dr. Spock. It was Nicholas who told the other children that he had a secret which could make all men happy if it became generally known, the secret of brotherly love.

Turgenev used to say, "Nicholas lacked only a few essential faults to be as great a writer as was his brother." Leo Tolstoi agreed, but Nicholas had no vanity and was unable to criticize others.

Marya was happy with her brilliant children. Her father had had only one child to teach; she had five. The happy days ended abruptly when she had been married nine years. Marya, the only daughter, was then five months old. Leo, the ugly littlest boy, who looked like his mother's father, was almost two.

Her granddaughter Alexandra Tolstoi says of Marya's sudden demise:

The cause of her death was not exactly known. It occurred some months after the birth of her only daughter. Some said that it was caused by fever and others claimed that it was inflammation of the brain. Her aged maid said that it was the result of a blow.

Marya had loved to swing and the servant girls pushed her as high as they could. A swingboard somehow struck her sharply on the head. For a time she was unable to speak. When she could talk, she reassured the maids and promised them not to cause them to be punished by telling what they had done.

Tolstoi in his *Memoirs* does not mention the swingboard incident. His mother, he says, had a sudden chill, then fever. She heard a noise in her ears and found herself suddenly unable to count consecutively. During a recovery period she wrote a long letter to her husband, who was away. He was not to apologize for having taken money from the estate to pay his gambling debts, but: "Your unhappy passion for gambling deprives me of a portion of your tender attachment." She could not permit him to spend so much money that the children's inheritance would be threatened. The estate must be kept intact. Nor would she consent to send the children away to school. She wrote him that she expected to die soon, that something dreadful was wrong, and she could not get well.

"Mama," Tolstoi says in his *Memoirs*, "died in terrible agony."

When Leo was nine, his father died on the streets of a distant city where he had gone on business with two serfs to accompany him. When he was found, his money and papers were gone. The papers were returned later by a beggar woman who said she found them on the steps of a church. The servants were suspected, but there was no proof — or investigation. The assassination of masters was not uncommon in those times.

Tatyana continued to care for the children. Eccentric Aunt Alexandra was the legal guardian after the old countess died of grief and old age soon after her son's death.

Leo was growing up. His educational problems began. A French tutor locked Leo in a dark closet; commanded the boy to kneel before him, twisted his back when he would not. The happy days in the nursery with his mother or Tatyana had ended.

At thirteen he temporarily lost Tatyana, who had never given him anything but complete and uncritical love. He had been fond of Aunt Alexandra, with whom he associated the acrid smell of the unbathed. She had been dirty as a matter of principle. She had waited on her servants and would not permit them to wait on her. But when she died, another aunt came from Kazan and took the children home with her. Tatyana could not go with them because she had once had a proposal from that aunt's husband and he still spoke of the sturdy, black-eyed woman with affection and respect. Tatyana stayed on the estate with the eight hundred serfs.

Adolescence was hard for Leo Tolstoi. A university teacher who was hired to tutor the three younger boys said, "Sergei can and will study: Dmitri will and cannot; Lev [Leo] neither will nor can." His lessons never went well; he was sexually precocious; his social life was involved. He was failed unjustly in history and German in his second year at college because the professor had quarreled with the family. Leo then dropped his major in Oriental languages and transferred to the law school at the University of Moscow. It was there that a certain Professor Meyer took such an interest in the gifted nonachiever that he resolved to stimulate him to love learning. He succeeded so well that Leo quit school to pursue his interest in philosophy without being bothered by adherence to the school's curriculum.

He became the nineteenth-century equivalent of a beatnik, and his sister Marya was amused. "He probably considers himself a Diogenes, or else is under the influence of Rousseau." Obsessed by the idea of leading a simple, primitive life, he startled guests by appearing barefoot in a sailcloth costume he had devised for himself. He took to the deep woods where he lay staring at the sky with his head pillowed on volumes of Voltaire, Rousseau and Hegel.

Back in Yasnaya Polyana, Tatyana was helping to keep the estate in good order for him. It is quite difficult to convey briefly the complexity of the emotional and intellectual climate in which Leo Tolstoi was reared. Many individuals acted out the drama of their lives before the eyes of this small and ugly boy who was so self-conscious about his appearance. There were many servants he knew as well as his relatives.

The dramas continued to play themselves out before him. His older brothers acted out the simple life he only wrote about. Sergei gave up both wealth and social status to marry his gypsy mistress. Nicholas and Dmitri both lived in intentional poverty.

In the homes of the children who are to be eminent in the arts and literature there continue to be the especially intricate social and interpersonal relationships. There are plots, subplots and counterplots in the homes of the playwrights and novelists. It may be that we are establishing the fact that children who are to be writers are especially sensitive to the relationships between the adults in their families. This is, however, somewhat belied by the greater number of divorces and separations in these families.*

* Writers who came from broken homes were: Edna St. Vincent Millay, Richard Wright, William Gilbert, George Santayana, Ouida, Lafcadio Hearn, Hart Crane, Alexander Woollcott, Ilka Chase, Maria Rilke.

Two of the humanitarians, John La Farge and Eleanor Roosevelt, came from broken homes where the parents were drawn to creative expression. The elder John La Farge was a famous artist, and the mother of Eleanor Roosevelt was absorbed in her amateur theater group. Charles Lindbergh, who came from a divided home, had a father who wanted to be a poet but turned to law.

The elder John La Farge was such a sensitive artist that he could not endure the confusion of home life and lived apart from his family. His youngest son John, born when the mother was forty-five and the father fifty-six, seldom saw his eminent father, the muralist and noted creator of stained-glass windows. When the elder La Farge did come home, he was completely indifferent to the feelings of the proper Newport neighbors and went to the beach in a Japanese kimono in which he felt quite comfortable but which embarrassed his children. It was only natural that his wife, whom he neglected, should turn to her youngest son for comfort and companionship.

Gifted children dislike broken homes and quarreling parents as do other children. Although they are made miserable by the conflict or deprivation in their homes, unpleasantness does not destroy their capacity for achievement, and in some instances obviously motivates it. The child in the broken family is often eager to give happiness to a mother who has had few satisfac-

---

Actors whose parents were divorced or separated were: Maude Adams, Charles Chaplin, John, Ethel and Lionel Barrymore, Maurice Chevalier, Douglas Fairbanks, Sr., and Douglas Fairbanks, Jr. The dancers Nijinsky, Agnes de Mille, and Isadora Duncan came from broken homes.

Among musicians and those who sought artistic expression, those from broken homes were: Eisenstein, Toulouse-Lautrec, Prokofiev, Rachmaninoff, Maria Callas, Arshile Gorki, Frank Lloyd Wright and Bill Mauldin. Louis Armstrong, jazz artist, and Jackie Robinson, athlete, came from broken homes.

Politicans and scientists are the least likely to have parents who live apart. The thirty-two homes which are broken by divorce or separation are very few when compared with the one in four divorced homes of today. In the time in which these families lived, to be divorced was to risk social ostracism. There was, in the homes of the Four Hundred, more constant quarreling and estrangement than separation or divorce. What is of moment is that the unconventional homes produced the children who chose unconventional occupations.

tions. Anger and frustration make contentment impossible and seem to whet constructive activity in some of these families.

Many of the children who came from troubled homes would probably have scored poorly on the Minnesota Multiphasic Personality Inventory. This test is a good diagnostic tool. It found the students with few problems; they still had few problems ten years later. It is the interpretation and use of the test that can be harmful. It should not be used, for example, to keep a gifted child out of an enrichment program or a special class. In a recent national educational meeting the principal of a public school for gifted children said that she did not accept students who have personality problems. A girl who cried easily, for example, would not be accepted. The rationale behind such statements is that the school community cannot afford to give special attention to children who may not make a good vocational adjustment because of personality problems. This may be true in the areas of competency where conformity is needed to cherish and maintain our inheritance and to pass it on.

The invaluable contribution, however, is likely to be made by the creative child who is not problem-free and who is not a "good all-around student." He may very well come from a home where the parents are problems both to themselves and to the child whom they frequently frustrate and annoy. This is not the way life should be, but this is the way it has been in the past. There is reason to suspect the pattern still persists.

How to change procedures in order to enable the creative to be comfortable and serene is the contemporary challenge.

To be creative is good. To be serene is good. To rear a child who is both serene and creative is presumably an admirable goal. The parents of the Four Hundred did not often achieve serenity for themselves or for their children although they were frequently creative and intelligent.* To make the assumption that creativity

---

*Homes which produced the 400 were checked for constantly quarreling, rejecting, dominating, and overpossessive parents; for anxiety about money; for the death of one or both parents; for physically handicapped children; for broken homes; for parents who were dissatisfied with the child's school progress or choice of profession. On this basis the percentage of troubled homes in descending order is as follows: Actors, 100%; Authoritarian Politicians, 95%; Novelists and Playwrights, 89%; Composers and Musicians,

plus serenity is the more or less automatic consequence of a parental display of endless patience and the providing of economic security and a bottomless outpouring of affection is naïve. It also puts a burden of guilt on the parents, who are bound to fail in the task they set themselves of being the child's constant bulwark against frustration and pain.

To swing to the other extreme and plan frustrations or purposely incite feelings of insecurity or "let oneself go" in interesting displays of emotion in order to release latent talents in a child is not only naïve but dangerous. The end result may be an incapacitating emotional disturbance for the child or the parent or for both. Most parents manage to make their children unhappy often enough without any intention of doing so; they do not need to fear that their child is being sated with contentment.

Facing the hard fact that serenity and creativity have not been compatible in the homes which have cradled eminence is in itself a frustrating experience, but frustration is a necessary prelude to insight.

86%; Military Leaders, 86%; Poets, 83%; Artists, 70%; Explorers, Adventurers and Athletes, 67%; Humanitarians and Reformers, 62%; Singers, 62%; Psychologists, Philosophers, and Religious Leaders, 61%; Non-Fiction Writers and Educators, 59%; Non-Authoritarian Politicians, 56%; Lawyers, Doctors, and Scientists, 53%; Financiers, 25%; Inventors, 20%. [There are too few financiers and inventors among the Four Hundred to make the percentages reliable.]

[7]

Not-so-troubled Homes

> He had a happy and orderly family background, and an orderly family life is something in the importance of which he has always believed.
> — ALEXANDER WERTH, *Mendes France*

THERE ARE AT MOST fifty-eight homes among the Four Hundred which were relatively trouble-free. These families, and a few others, will be measured against the yardstick of a mythical mid-twentieth-century family which represents the cultural norm for an ideal family.

John and Mary Smith have a comfortable, well-kept, attractive home. After several years of marriage they are still devoted to each other. They enjoy their children, who are attractive, affectionate and co-operative. The family is free of serious illness. The children consistently bring home good report cards. The teachers assure the parents that the children are well liked at school. There is adherence to the family code of right and wrong by all of its members. John and Mary are active participants in community affairs and enjoy the respect of their neighbors.

To what extent this mythical family exists outside the pages of the women's magazines we do not know. It is possible that a survey of the emotional and intellectual climate in the homes of four hundred PTA presidents might find them far from problem-free. This we do not know, but it is possible to observe that even these fifty-eight families are not completely free of tension or trouble.

153

Contemporary homes have one tremendous advantage over those which existed several decades ago. Medical science has removed many of the terrible anxieties which used to beset parents. There is no longer as much tuberculosis or diphtheria, and no longer as much chronic undiagnosed invalidism.

The pre- and post-Freudian subjects who report family happiness sometimes differ in the examples they offer as proof of felicity. Fitting these obstreperous, imaginative families into a conventional pattern is often a futile or frustrating experience.

"My parents loved each other when they were young and when they were old," says Constantine Alexeev, the Russian actor and director who originated the Stanislavski method. The wealthy parents cared little for society and spent their days enjoying their children. They were all fond of practical joking and once made a hairy monster with which to scare guests. "Stanislavski," as proof of the family tradition of devotion, says that his father slept with his own father until the day of his marriage!

This is what is meant by saying that it is difficult to make these cradles of eminence fit the conventional Mary-John Smith picture. Another deviation from the norm in this particular family was the unattractiveness of the small Constantine. He was chagrined when he heard guests talking of his ugliness.

Another boy who fits into the pattern of the trouble-free family somewhat awkwardly is Charles de Gaulle. His father, Henri de Gaulle, married his cousin, Jeanne Maillott, and together they reared five children in a big, high-ceilinged apartment in the old Paris of the Left Bank. The father was both tender and stern with his children. He was a professor of philosophy, mathematics and literature at a Jesuit college, and his children were thus brought up in an intellectual atmosphere. They had family arguments about Jules Verne, or talked about the philosophy of Nietzsche. They read the English and German classics in French translations. Mme. de Gaulle was a pious and patriotic woman. She and her husband lived peacefully in a home which was both pleasant and stimulating.

Although the father could be very stern, he was always eager to encourage any imaginative project the children devised for themselves. The summer Charles was thirteen, his father made it possible for him to organize a group of farm boys who lived near the family summer home into a mock army. They spent the summer on a camping trip which took the form of an imaginary military campaign.

There were three ways in which Charles de Gaulle was something less than the ideal son. He was physically unattractive, his secondary school grades were mediocre and he was not particularly popular. In his teens he loved to play practical jokes and laughed uproariously when someone fell into his booby traps. His nickname at school was the "Long Asparagus." At military school he was cold and withdrawn. He had, however, always a few close and special friends. His photographic memory helped to keep him in the upper third of his class in military school. He met his appearance problem head-on by memorizing and reciting Cyrano de Bergerac's famous nose speech.

A boy among the Four Hundred who comes very close to being the ideal boy from the ideal home is Thomas Edmund Dewey, onetime governor of the state of New York, and Republican candidate for the Presidency. His father, George Martin Dewey, Jr., was the editor of the Owosso (Michigan) *Times*. George Dewey was a genial man for whom his son had both admiration and respect. However, he always left the job of spanking his two sons to his wife, a woman of wit and good nature. They were congenial parents.

The boy had the run of the newspaper office and knew almost everyone in the small town. At eleven he was selling the *Saturday Evening Post* and the Detroit *News*. By the time he was thirteen he had ten other boys working as his assistants. When he was ready to enter the University of Michigan, he had already saved eight hundred dollars.

Work did not interfere with his school or recreational activities. He took part in school plays, debated, was director of the school yearbook, and lieutenant in the cadet corps. He sang, played chess and bridge. Summer vacations meant healthful farm work for pay. His grades were good; he was very handsome. He was popular with his peers and related well to his brother and his parents.

His family had prestige in the town. His paternal grandfather had been a Republican party leader. His mother was also descended from a family of good repute. Her father, a merchant, had been a pillar of the community of Owosso. He belonged to the Episcopal church, and had the best garden in town. Tom himself says he never once heard his parents quarrel.

Young Tom continued his success as a student and as an adult at Michigan. Although no one doubted his sincerity and strong sense of justice, the fellow Republicans closest to the candidate did not deny that he often merited the criticism of being stand-offiish and cold in manner. He lost the national election on two occasions to a rival candidate, Franklin D. Roosevelt, who had been dubbed a mama's boy at Choate, had been a mediocre student at Harvard and had suffered a severe case of polio in his early manhood. Being trouble-free obviously does not always correlate with the greatest success as a politician.

Another small-town boy with the same family name, John Dewey, the American philosopher and educator, was the son of a Burlington, Vermont, storekeeper who joked with his customers and stammered when he had to ask people to pay their bills. He labeled his wheelbarrow: "Stolen from A. S. Dewey." He liked to tell how he had married the young daughter of Squire Rich of Richville, and how Squire Rich was not rich although his neighbors had sent him to Congress.

A. S. Dewey and his wife had no serious problems with their son. Their daily lives were relatively uneventful. They permitted John to read dime novels and play marbles for keeps, but not dance or play cards. Mrs. Dewey had been brought up a Universalist, but the family attended the White Street Congregational Church. His report cards were rather ordinary until his junior year at the University of Vermont, but that did not bother his parents, who had no notion that their only son was to become a remarkable man. In his junior year in college he read a book by Thomas H. Huxley and was swept off his feet by the rapture of scientific knowledge. From that time on he read far into the night; he soon led his class and had the highest mark on record in philosophy.

Placing the emphasis on the "cradle" of creativity does not give proper tribute to the influence of wives in the lives of eminent men. John Dewey is one of those persons who might never have been able to reach a wide audience had he not been helped by his wife. Alice Chapman Dewey, a highly opinionative woman, "strong minded, descended from a family of radicals, and free-thinkers," was the woman who made a success of the late-blooming student. He was content just to think; it was she who grabbed his ideas, appreciated them, and insisted that something be done about them.

John Dewey would have been content with fewer honors. He was always at his best with a child climbing up his pants leg or fishing in his inkwell. These boys and girls who come from the trouble-free families are almost certain to be good heads of families. Unlike the mother-dominated, or the mother-smothered, they marry at appropriate ages and remain happily married. In this instance the dominating wife supplied the "push" the home had lacked.

Martin Luther King, Negro Baptist minister, who has adapted the Gandhian technique of nonviolence to the problem of race prejudice in the United States, came from a family whose emotional and intellectual climate fits almost perfectly the current concept of the ideal home. The parents were devoted to each other and shared a common philosophy and interests. They had status in the community; they were both scholarly. They provided a warm, cohesive home for their three children.

Martin Luther King, who was sent to nursery school, is the only individual among the Four Hundred who mentions having had this experience. From the very beginning he had good peer relationships. Martin was a gifted child, skipped three grades and was ready for college at fifteen. At the same time he belonged to a close group of boys and girls who represented the "best" families in the Negro community and with them he swam, double-dated (often with his sister and her boy friend), played games. He belonged to the debate club, and was popular with his teachers. He attended Morehouse, the college which his grandfather and father had attended before him. When he and his sister and brother were all in school, his strong and vital mother went back to college and finished her degree, which had been postponed by an early marriage to a young theological student. She did some substitute teaching after her children were old enough not to need her constant care. Martin was a handsome, healthy boy who was a joy and pride to his parents.

He started making money very early. At four he was given pennies by family friends who coaxed him to sing for them. At seven he and his sister put up a cold drink stand on the sidewalk outside the house and went into business but drank too freely from their stock to make a profit. At eight he began selling weekly newspapers to earn pocket money. At thirteen he had his own paper route, and a few years later had worked himself up to be an assistant manager in charge of thirty other boys.

He was not overprotected. He was knocked from his bicycle by automobiles on two occasions. He was hit in the head by a baseball bat, but "bounced up" and went on playing. He made kites and flew model airplanes and played with "anybody and everybody" who came along. His parents made no restrictions upon him, other than to ask him to avoid boys with bad reputations.

The father of the family, Martin King, Sr., pastor of the Ebenezer Baptist church and a man of power and prominence in the big Negro community, was not one to take race prejudice lightly. He gave his children the best life he could within the Negro community and sheltered them from being cast in racially subservient roles during childhood. He did not permit them to work for white families nor did he buy goods which required that collections he made by white agents.

When he shopped in stores, he paid cash and insisted on being treated with courtesy. When a shoe clerk asked him to move to the rear of the store to sit in segregated seats, he did not buy shoes for the six-year-old Martin in that store. The family was sometimes fearful that the father's independence would get him into trouble. When a policeman called the elder King "Uncle" or "Boy," he refused to accept the condescending appellation. When a white policeman was rude to the young people at the church, Martin's father arranged for the policeman to be moved to another beat. Once in court he talked back to the judge in defense of a member of the Negro community. A considerable part of his time was spent in "straightening out the white folks" and no harm was ever done to him. The family did not use the segregated buses in Atlanta because of the constant cursing and arguing over proper seating that went on in the buses.

During his childhood young Martin Luther King moved with assurance within the large Negro community and was seldom touched by the fringe of prejudice that surrounded him. At the Laboratory High School of the University of Atlanta, the contacts he had with white teachers were likely to be friendly. Miss Beatrice Boley, his biology teacher, a strict disciplinarian, was thorough in her counseling of the brilliant boy. She made a detailed study of his scholastic strengths and weaknesses and recommended certain remedial practices aimed at improving his study habits.

It was to his mother and his maternal grandmother that the boy looked for a depth of warmth and affection. The grandparents were very much a part of the children's lives. The children called their mother "Mother Dear." Grandmother, a woman of good health and fine spirits, was "Mamma." "Granddaddy" was the person they looked to as the patriarch although he was gentle and permissive in his role as a grandfather. He was a powerful man in the Negro community and was involved in business as well as religious affairs.

Alberta Williams King, Martin's mother, was a strong and amiable woman, tall, dark and deliberate. She had roomed with her husband's sister when she was in the high school at Spelman Seminary and it was through this sister, Woodie Clara King, that she met her future husband. Her parents encouraged the romance with the orphan boy and welcomed their only daughter and her husband into the twelve-room house which was the church parsonage. The temporary arrangement was so satisfactory that it was never changed. Christine and Martin Luther were born, and Alfred Daniel was on the way, before their father completed divinity school. The children were congenial companions. When their father was graduated, he became his father-in-law's assistant.

It was out of this secure, warm, exceptionally cohesive home that the dynamic social rebel, Martin Luther King, Jr., came. The father's opinionativeness would seem to be an important factor in the boy's subsequent development.

It is Martin Luther, the son who extended the parental occupation and his father's independent attitude toward segregation, who has become eminent. The rebel in the family, Alfred Daniel, who resented his father, quit school and married very young, did not have an opportunity to use his talents so well. The father, son of a sharecropper who beat his wife, felt strongly about the family's need to rise in social and intellectual status. He required academic accomplishment and drive for success from his sons.

An immigrant husband and wife in the United States, one of forty-six immigrant families among the Four Hundred, retained their sense of a world culture and also had an intense pleasure in their children.

When Louis Brandeis was graduated from his grade school in St. Louis, he won a gold medal for scholarship. His Jewish immigrant family was well accepted in that frontier town. They had had dreams of being farmers in the new country; when that idea proved impractical they had sought the hinterlands. They avoided the cities where there were established Jewish communities. Their home was an impromptu intellectual center, a mecca for scholarly residents and visitors to the growing city. The whole family was thought remarkable for its learning and culture. Both of the parents spoke three languages.

When a business depression struck the United States, Mr. Brandeis sold his business and the whole family went for a junket to Europe until times were better. Louis was to remember that period as the golden time of his life, although Amy, his sister, became ill with typhoid in Milan, and his mother and his other sister, Fanny, stayed in a hotel to nurse her. The father and the two boys, Alfred and Louis, went mountain climbing in Switzerland together. They made a point of searching for the sources of rivers until Louis exploded, "I don't see why I should have to find the source of every damned river in Europe." He was then, and continued to be, rather easily tired by physical activity.

When the mountain climbing was done, Louis tried to enter the Gymnasium in Vienna and was not accepted by the school authorities; so he traveled to Dresden and searched out the Annen-Realschule. For a time he walked about it like a moth around a lantern.

The rector dismissed his request for admission. Louis had come without a birth certificate, without proof of his vaccination; he had not passed the entrance examination. The implication was that no boy brought up in the wilds of Western United States could ever accomplish such a feat.

The boy rolled up his sleeve and showed the rector his vaccination. "Now look at me," he said, "and observe that I am born." The amused rector accepted him without the formality of an examination.

His parents were delighted with his initiative, and were not surprised that he was in the top section of his class in his studies.

Louis Koren, Detroit psychiatrist, once observed that the chief need of children is to be enjoyed. Fredericka Brandeis was a woman whose principal joy was her children. She marveled at the comradeship between her sons and noted their tenderness to their sick sister. Both parents had faith and admiration for Louis. When his eyesight was poor during his Harvard years, they were sympathetic and supportive, but not overprotective, and their attitude helped him to overcome the handicap.

When the children questioned their parents as to their reasons for not belonging to a synagogue or church, even though they admired the ethical qualities of all religions, Fredericka wrote for them the following statement, which they treasured and saved:

I do not believe that sins can be expiated by going to divine services and observing this or that formula. Love, truth, and virtue are the foundation upon which the education of the child must be based. . . . I wanted to give them something that neither can be argued away, or given up as untenable, namely, a pure spirit and the highest ideals as to morals and love. God has blessed my endeavors.[1]

A wealthy family which also took time to enjoy its nine children was the Kennedy family. It also gave them physical and intellectual freedom. The Kennedy sons, Joe and Jack, used to go sailing alone when they were so small that the sailboats looked empty from the shore because the tops of the boys' heads did not show. The nine children were given both freedom and responsibility, and were pitted against each other by their father in both sports and scholastic achievement. There were high expectations for all of the children.

Among the statesmen there are no instances of divorce or separation among the parents. A number of the men elected to office are orphans or half-orphans but are reared in warm, supportive homes. It is among the statesmen and men and women whose special interests are peace or international good will and among the lawyers and scientists that the most excellent examples of the warm and cohesive homes are found.

Adlai Stevenson was brought up in an explosive but essentially affectionate family. Both his father, Lewis Stevenson, and his mother, Helen Davis Stevenson, were given to repartee and to storytelling and were dynamic and vigorous individuals. The mother believed in spending money on education, travel, and furnishing a home; the father was extravagantly generous and often outraged his wife's Quaker sense of thrift. Since the family was well-to-do and never suffered want because of these differences, this divergence in temperament was not crucial.

Both parents, and also the grandparents, enjoyed the two children: quiet, peacemaking Adlai and his bouncing, aggressive older sister Elizabeth, known as "Buffie." The family traveled so much with the children that Adlai had little formal schooling until he was nine. Adlai's sister, now Mrs. Ernest L. Ives, says that the classics never had for them the "bitter medicinal taste of compulsory education." Their mother read to them from Hawthorne's *Wonder Book*, from Hugo's *Les Miserables*, from Scott's *Waverley Novels* and from Cooper's *Last of the Mohicans*. She read well and had a flair for dramatics.

Within the family, Adlai Stevenson was nicknamed "The Brute" because he was so gentle, well-behaved and excessively conscientious. When his hands were slapped for pulling glasses and silver off the table accidentally, he crept off to sleep in the dog kennel and was found there hours afterwards by contrite and frantic parents.

Although his parents were argumentative and extremely outspoken, Adlai was quiet and amiable. At school he was marked "excellent" in behavior. His grades were low, partly because he was absent so often. In second grade he attended school for ten days during the first semester and the teacher graded him low in reading and spelling and only fair in writing.

Among his peers he was neither submissive or overly aggressive. He had the usual number of fights, overturned privies on Halloween, hoisted wagon wheels to the roof, and put a black kitten into his sister's bed and frightened her into hysterics.

The children went on long nature observation walks with their mother and were taught to observe the specimens and to draw pictures of their findings. They improvised stories at the dinner table. One parent would start a story, the other would embroider it. They tossed the narrative back and forth until everyone was shouting with laughter. Adlai says of his father, "He was one of the funniest men I've ever known."

Since their father was the manager of forty-nine farms, owned by a widowed aunt, he was the first man to be listed as a "farmer" in *Who's Who*, and his children knew the price of corn per bushel before they could spell. The adults shared their own interests with the children.

The formal classroom had little attraction for the children whose home life was so rewarding. Adlai limited his formal studies to the barely acceptable minimum. The teachers complained that his interests were too wide, too varied. They interpreted his boredom as lack of concentration. It was not until he was at Princeton that he became an adequate student.

His Grandfather W. O. Davis was one of the individuals with whom he often spoke. It was from this grandfather that he heard long, detailed accounts of an ancestor, Jesse Fell, a Quaker who was a peace-loving man, a man of large vision and great capability. Jesse Fell became Adlai's hero, the man he wished most to emulate.

A biographer, Kenneth Davis, says, "Of all the boy's ancestral influences Jesse Fell's was the most important. Fell's influence might even be said to have become a central strand of meaning around which was woven the fabric of the boy's education."

Grandfather Stevenson was also important to Adlai. He learned history from the stories of his ancestors. History on this side of the family started with "Little Gabriel," a pious and loud-voiced great-great-great-grandfather who once prayed the devil out of a melancholy preacher sunk into silent gloom.

Grandfather Adlai Ewing Stevenson, once Vice-President, used to coax the children into the library with milk and cookies, then read to them there while they enjoyed their refreshments. When Adlai was six, his grandfather read to him from *Hamlet* and from Robert Ingersoll's funeral oration for his brother. And this same grandfather so aroused Adlai's interest in history that he read all thirteen volumes of Markham's *The Real American Romance* before he was thirteen. Their Grandfather Davis read to them from Burns with a fine Scotch accent.

P. M. Sheldon,[2] who has studied families of highly gifted children, has suggested that more attention be given to the influence of grandparents as it is transmitted to the grandchildren through the parents. He has suggested studying the transmission of pressures from grandparents and implied that the internalization of these pressures by the parents may produce a blooming of abilities in the next generation.

Adlai's mother tended to be overprotective, but he resisted this attitude stoutly and would not permit himself to be made a hypochondriac. He was active, had good peer relationships. He broke his nose twice. In adolescence he was tragically involved in the accidental shooting of a young girl cousin. He was in no way to blame for the "gun that wasn't loaded." The tragic interruption of a holiday dinner, however, affected the boy deeply. His guilt feelings always burdened him.

Adlai Stevenson's sister says of the home, "Underneath and all the time there was so much love."

Thirty American high school students, Westinghouse Award winners who were interviewed and studied by P. F. Brandwein in 1954-55, were quiet, reflective, and inward-looking. They liked to hike, read serious books and magazines and listen to classical rather than popular music. They often chose to do social work or read to the blind and were involved in church work. A vast majority bought books for their own use. They did not smoke until the senior year in high school, or did not smoke at all. They almost never found themselves in difficulties in school although they often disagreed with teachers over the interpretation of schoolwork. They were conservative in dress and spent considerable time in self-initiated projects such as stamp collecting and ham radio. They were seldom elected to school offices; were not the popular type. They came from homes with substantial libraries, and most of the parents had ambitions for a professional life for the children. Twenty-four of the thirty were first children; sixteen of these were only children.

Like the Westinghouse Award winners, neither parents nor children in homes which produce scientists in this sample are disposed to get involved in traumatic interpersonal relationships. There are no homes broken by divorce or desertion or separation among the parents of scientists, unless Selman Waksman's father's long absence in the Army is interpreted as such.

Observation of these homes which produce scientists and physicians uncovers some differences among them which correlate with the emotional atmosphere in the home. Doctors who are also writers of fiction or plays often come from turbulent, unhappy homes and must be omitted from this chapter: Dr. Somerset Maugham, an unhappy orphan; Dr. A. J. Cronin, who describes the tension in his family over his father's death and the differences in religion within his family in his semiautobiographical novels; Dr. Anton Chekhov, who came from a very disturbed home; Dr. Conan Doyle, whose father was the unsuccessful member of an achieving family, and whose mother resented that fact.

Making collections is a favored hobby among the physicians, and their parents are encouraging and tolerant of this activity. They are especially fond of physieal freedom, of roaming far and wide over the countryside.

Hans Zinsser, the physician-bacteriologist, took a great pleasure in his popular book, *Rats, Lice and History*. His autobiography, *As I Remember Him*, tells of his warm and cohesive home, and of the mother who lived only two weeks after his father died. "She seemed to die of his death," the son said. Zinsser was a much-over-protected youngest son who was kept home with his mother until he was eleven.

He had the love of mischief which characterizes so many of the pre-physicians. He dawdled through a preparatory school carefully chosen by his liberal and opinionative father and made a fair adjustment at Columbia, where he studied comparative literature. He intended to be a writer but became a scientist because of a prank. An impulse moved him to throw a snowball at a professor emerging from the Natural Science building. His aim was good and the professor's hat flew off. In order to show the offended man that he had no personal animus for him he enrolled in his class the next semester. Suddenly, Zinsser was cut loose from the department of comparative literature. The science department became to him a world of wonders and revelations.

Becoming engrossed in science did not cure his urge for practical jokes. He pretended to have a fit of hydrophobia in order to frighten a pedantic classmate. In the fracas the laboratory equipment was knocked over. A professor doused Zinsser with a bucketful of sea urchins to make him quit biting his classmate's leg.

William Osler, Canadian surgeon of renown, had extremely permissive parents. He ran home shouting with glee when he got himself expelled for shouting insults at his master through a keyhole. The clergyman and his wife obligingly found another school for their ingenious son, where he distinguished himself by fumigating a matron with sulphur. Since Osler had involved many other students in the practical joke, no one was expelled. The matron sued the boys and was awarded costs and a dollar paid by each offender. The eight other children of the clergyman were not so difficult.

When the boy came under the influence of a teacher who stimulated him, he abandoned some of his mischief. This man's conception of knowledge did not lie in the greatest number of facts which could be drilled into boys, but in the ideas which radiated from them under given stimuli. They were taken on all-day fossil hunts. William learned to make slides for the teacher's microscope to show the other boys.

His biographer is the cantankerous and eminent physician Harvey Cushing, whose explosive manners in the operating room have been the subject for comment by another medical writer, Dr. William Sharpe.

Sir Wilfred Grenfell, doctor, humanitarian, writer and adventurer, had a mother who looked like Queen Victoria and a daydreaming clergyman-teacher father. The dominating mother ran the boarding school which was the source of the family income; the father was the beloved teacher who seemed as childlike as his students.

The parents gave their children almost complete freedom. When they closed the school for the summer, the boys were left unchaperoned. As soon as their parents left, the brothers invited adolescent guests to make merry with them. They once sent their cousins a telegram advising them to come quickly; the coast was clear; parents were gone. The parents thought it a great joke when the telegram came while they were visiting in the home to which the telegram was sent.

Dr. William Carlos Williams, the poet and uninhibited writer of autobiography from Rutherford, New Jersey, came from a home that was warm, but explosive and turbulent. His engineer father was away much of the time. His parents were congenial but there were erratic guests who came and stayed for months, an uncle who went mad and tried to murder them, a grandmother who fought physically with his mother. He and his brother Ed, however, grew up as one person, were constantly together for twenty years, loved each other completely. Their escapades caused their devoted mother real distress.

Poor mother, sometimes she'd whale hell out of us with anything she could lay her hands on. It was a piece of cord wood once. She laid it on good, too, and later took me upstairs to bathe the place with witch hazel.[3]

There was no time or inclination for writing in the Mayo family, where there was more actual working together at the family business than occurs in most families. There was the freedom, the direct contact with earth and sweat and blood that was to stand the boys in good stead when they grew to be men.

Physicians tell more about their parents and childhood experiences than do scientists. Dr. Charles Mayo once said, "The biggest thing Will and I ever did was to pick the father and mother we had." Dr. William Mayo said of their mother, "She accepted what good there was in folks and did not criticize the bad. I never knew her to say a hateful word about anyone."[4]

From the very beginning the brothers Charles and William were always together. "We were known as 'The Mayo Boys.' Anyone that picked on one of us had to contend with the other." Willie was the older, Charlie, the rather sickly, small brother. They had the freedom of the countryside, shot marbles, went fishing, bagged wild pigeons, rode horseback. Will was the reader, Charles the mechanic. Charlie was always fixing something, a churn, a pump, a stove. He contrived a steam engine to do the family wash, to cut wood, to pump water. At fourteen he studied articles about the telephone, and constructed one which led from his father's office to the house. The telephone company claimed an infringement of its patent and the telephone had to be replaced by a conventional instrument.

The father was a country physician, and the whole family assisted him as a matter of course. Mrs. Mayo helped to set limbs and coaxed medicine into sick babies. The boys dressed wounds, prepared microscope slides, went with their father on trips to the country and talked with him about diagnosis and prognosis as they rode behind the horses the father drove at top speed. Will attended autopsies when he was so young that he could not see the body on the table. His father plunked him on the table near the corpse's head, and the child clutched the corpse's hair to steady himself as he watched the proceedings. Charlie took over the anesthetist's job when the man fainted during an especially gory operation and continued to help his father in this fashion even though some of the patients were fearful to see a boy in this role. They went to medical meetings with their father and read the books and papers he published. Dr. Mayo was an original and imaginative researcher as well as a country doctor, and he never waited for the patient to pay before he treated him. He believed that any man with unusual abilities owed his services to the public in proportion to his own strength. There were always plenty of patients, and the countryside was plagued with drought, debt, bad crops, low prices and homes lost because of mortgage foreclosures. Sometimes, however, tensions between the husband and wife kept them from speaking freely to each other for long periods of time.

In a home in Topeka, Kansas, another physician, Dr. Charles Menninger, was bringing up two sons who were to become eminent for the establishment of a diagnostic private hospital for mental patients. Flora Knisely Menninger is one of four mothers of the Four Hundred who write their own books about how they brought up their children. (The others are the mothers of Franklin D. Roosevelt and Robert A. Taft and the stepmother of Gertrude Bell.) She says in her book, *Story of My Days:*

Daddy has always been a devoted husband and a loving father to his boys. I could ask no greater gift than that they might be like him in spirit and purpose toward those they love. My dream was for a husband who was tall and slender and intelligent and interesting. I hoped we would like the same things. My dreams have been fulfilled beyond anything I could have desired.

Dr. Charles Menninger and his wife enjoyed their children. There was no thought of taking a vacation apart from them. Dr. Charles Menninger enjoyed his garden in the back yard; when the boys grew older and needed the space for their Boy Scout activities, he rented three lots close by and fenced the peony garden, which became a community attraction. He was also a member of the National Council of Boy Scouts during the formative years of that organization.

Flora Knisely Menninger began teaching a Bible class in her Presbyterian Sunday School when the youngest of her children was three weeks old. In 1919 she was supervising a total enrollment of four hundred persons. By 1923 the classes were incorporated with the YWCA and five hundred men and women participated. The classes were interracial, and fourteen teachers were needed to teach the groups. To a lesser extent she occupied herself with art classes. The children did not receive her undivided, "smothering" attention.

Walker Winslow, author of *The Menninger Story*, is of the opinion that Flora Menninger was overextended in her community activities and that her early experiences as a poor orphan girl on the farm kept her from filling her function as the wife of a well-to-do doctor with grace and aplomb; but he also indicates that her husband never showed the slightest awareness of this lack in his wife.

Karl Menninger had difficulties as a child. His first-grade teacher thought him dull, and it was not until he was "double-promoted" that his real abilities evidenced themselves. It was he who became a popular writer as well as an eminent psychiatrist.

A survey of four hundred families can indicate trends, discover the major likenesses and major differences between families. It cannot dig deeply into the reasons for personality differences between brothers brought up in the same home. It can indicate that there is some relationship between the severity of the problems the premedical man has in his childhood home and the probability of his also becoming a writer as an adult.

The famous people who are public servants come from comparatively serene homes, but writers of imaginative literature frequently come from troubled, fragmented, turbulent homes. A reexamination of the eighty-seven writers finds a scant handful of homes which have warmth and cohesion. Some of these homes are described here to demonstrate that a writer of prose or poetry sometimes can be reared in home which fits the Mary-John Smith pattern comfortably.

Of his schoolmaster father, A. A. Milne says, "He was the best man I have ever known." His mother, whom he felt he never really knew, was "simple, unemotional and common-sensible." The three Milne brothers never ceased to quarrel but never ceased to feel the need of each other. "We were," A. A. Milne said, "given much more freedom than most children." They spent whole days wandering about London together when they were quite small. They were always well-behaved. They collected everything, including minerals and caterpillars, were read aloud to, went visiting, had pets. There was laughter in the house. They were poor and never knew they were poor. The father made learning fun. "In Papa's house it was natural to be interested, it was easy to be clever."

A poet from an immigrant family describes his mother thus: "The mother however couldn't help saying nice things when we did well at anything. Whether it was schoolwork, or learning the catechism or hanging out sheets and shirts on a cold winter day, she would speak thanks or say I was a good boy." So says Carl Sandburg in his autobiography, a documentary of a happy family. Of his parents' marriage he says, "Mama's wedding ring was never lost — it was a sign and seal of something that ran deep and held fast between the two of them." His father was a strong man who could hold up his end on a piece of work, who could come home after a ten-hour day with his shirt soaked with sweat and have no word or murmur, although he looked fagged and worn.

Another country boy with poor parents, Jesse Stuart, makes his affection for his parents and his appreciation of his childhood home in Kentucky repeatedly known in his autobiographical volumes. Havelock Ellis was the son of a sea captain who was absent each year for nine months, so he and his wife enjoyed a three month honeymoon each year. Their son enjoyed both parents. E. Phillips Oppenheim was the son of a leather merchant who loved both his wife and only son. The father raised funds to pay for the publication of the young man's first book, which a publisher had rejected.

There is no home more exciting, or more admirable for easy affection, understanding and warmth, than the home of Lincoln Steffens, the muckraking journalist who plunged into the problem of the corruption of cities.

Within a given family there is not always agreement as to the merits of the family life experienced by the siblings. Mary Ellen

Chase, who writes with warming felicity about her childhood, says in her autobiography, *White Gate:* "I have never felt a trace of resentment toward my early upbringing, which still seems to me just, if stern and unyielding."

She is quick to add that two of her sisters who have families of their own contend that their parents needlessly controlled and repressed their children and have in consequence used different methods with their own children.

Unmarried myself and, therefore, with no urgent personal stake in this matter, I have, nevertheless, been interested through the years in trying to discover what improvements either in methods or in off-spring they have been able to achieve, given their own time and place.

Her parents were always ready to use a slipper or a whittled shingle as a paddle when a child was disobedient or rude, neglected his chores, or lied. When children became too difficult, the mother deftly attached them with roller towels to the door-knobs and left them swinging with their toes barely touching the floor. As a less stringent discipline, a child might be fastened by a roller towel to the top shelf of the secretary in the corner of the kitchen to read and watch while the mother made apple pies rich with cinnamon or baked ginger snaps in the oven.

Each child was taught to read at home before he was five, and every evening after the dishes were done the children gathered about the table for homework. Even the littlest child had to sit fifteen minutes with the others at the homework table. The lawyer father set them to work measuring the woodpile to determine its volume in cubic feet. "Your father," the mother might say, "is planning to question you soon on the Roman Emperors."

When the fifty-eight homes chosen as most nearly trouble-free were studied, certain common behaviors were observed: the parents and children often enjoy each other; they work together and play together. When the parents like each other, so do the children. The children have considerable intellectual and physical freedom. There is an absence of anxiety about their safety and health.

There is more fun and humor in these families, more tolerance for minor misdemeanors.

There is no absence of firm control, and usually there is a definite family code of ethics. Expectations are high, but not as high as in other homes where a parent is dominating.

The most impressive difference to be observed is the dearth of trouble-free homes among the actors, the few trouble-free homes among the writers, artists, and musicians, and the higher incidence of family solidarity in the homes of scientists, physicians, and some statesmen.

[8]

Children Who Had Handicaps

*Or are these highly productive people more
like the oyster that requires a grain of sand
to make the pearl? — Research on the
Academically Talented Student.
— KENNETH E. ANDERSEN, Ed.*

CHILDREN classified today as "gifted" are ordinarily superior in all areas, physically and emotionally as well as intellectually. They have a high tolerance for frustration, are commonly free from nervous disorders, are attractive, healthy, taller and stronger than are most children.

This is by no means true of all of the Four Hundred, who may show intellectual and creative ability of the highest order, yet be blind, crippled, small of stature, homely, overweight or physically debilitated. A need to compensate for a handicap in physique is described by many of these persons as the reason for their urgent need to achieve.

In many biographies, and especially in autobiographies, there is frequent direct and strong reference to the spur to achievement that adverse circumstances in childhood gives to these individuals who achieve distinction.

THE BLIND AND POOR OF SIGHT

Helen Keller and Ved Mehta are the totally blind among the persons surveyed. Seriously handicapping eye disorders were suffered by Rudyard Kipling, Aldous Huxley, Sean O'Casey, and

Syngman Rhee. Children less drastically affected by their poor eyesight were Harry Truman, Lafcadio Hearn, Reginald Fessenden, Louis Brandeis, Emile Zola, James Joyce, Carl Sandburg and William James.

At five Helen Keller was a willful, wild animal with no way of communicating her thoughts. Her teacher Anne Sullivan, a poor orphan who was also handicapped by poor vision, was responsible for Helen Keller's graduation from Radcliffe, summa cum laude. Helen was quite capable of comparing the philosophies of Kant and Emerson and speculated about war and peace. She read French, German, Latin, Greek and English. She rode, swam, bicycled. Had her mother permitted she would have married.

Meningitis took Ved Mehta's sight when he was an infant. He has no memory of sightedness. His well-to-do father, an Indian public health officer, realized that his first son would remain blind and must learn to live with his blindness. Blindness in India is often a curse and the blind are shunned. It is often interpreted as a punishment for a sin of the parents. Ved's mother had this feeling and turned frantically to native miracle workers, who put bitter drops in the boy's eyes which hurt and frightened him. The parents were not compatible.

At five the boy was sent away to a school for blind children. "You are now a man," the father told the boy as he left home. At fifteen Ved Mehta was hitchhiking alone across the Western United States on his way from Arkansas to Los Angeles.

A man from Dublin who became a playwright also had eye problems. When Sean O'Casey was five, small, shiny, pearly specks appeared on his eyeballs. He began to dread the light, to keep his eyes closed, to sit and moan restlessly in the darkest places he could find.

Sean was his mother's last child, born after two other sons of the same name had died in infancy. One died while she sat pleading for help from callous nurses and doctors who said she must be quiet and wait her turn. They lingered over other patients who were not seriously ill while the child strangled to death from a respiratory infection.

If Sean O'Casey's father had not been so opinionative, the family would have had more financial security. Michael O'Casey's strong convictions about Protestantism led him to accept a poorly paid job as a clerk in an Irish church mission. When he died suddenly at forty-nine, he left his wife and six children no inheritance except his library and his love for learning. The family was thrown into extreme poverty. The O'Caseys are the only family in this sample of the eminent who experienced both cold and hunger repeatedly.

Mrs. O'Casey was a fierce and partisan mother when her children were threatened, but warm and encouraging at home. Sean's eye problems meant endless trips to the hospital for drops, ointments, bandages, hot and cold water soakings.

At the Protestant school he attended, the rector was not sympathetic. "Doctors differ and patients die. . . . If we all carried out the doctor's strict injunctions, none of us would hardly move from the fire. What will the doctor do for him in after years when he has to make his way in life, unable to read or write?"[1]

His mother withdrew Sean from the school after his sadistic master beat him unmercifully, then required him to kneel and beg forgiveness for having kicked the master's shins during the beating episode. Sean's three years of intermittent schooling were over.

Sean learned most from his older brother, Archie, who was active in amateur theatricals. The ten-year-old Sean, who could not read or write, learned scenes from Shakespeare and Boucicault. At fifteen he made his own debut as an actor.

At thirteen, when his eyes had somewhat improved, he set himself an ambitious program of self-education, holding the page close to his nose in order to read. He read Shakespeare, Dickens, Scott, Balzac, Byron, Shelley, Keats, and Goldsmith. When his pay was docked two shillings in an office where he worked for scanty wages, he was so upset that he stole a copy of Milton from a neighboring bookstall. His older sister Isabella tried to teach him grammar, but he resisted. His escape from formal schooling, he feels, was fortuitous, and he believes it was his bad eyes which made him a playwright.

John Lockwood Kipling, a professor of sculpture in an art

school in Bombay, India, and his wife, Alice MacDonald Kipling, lost their third baby soon after it was born. This experience sent them to England to search for a boarding home where they might leave their son Rudyard, aged five and one-half, and Beatrice (Trix), who was not yet two. Through a newspaper advertisement they found a couple who made a business of boarding English children whose parents were Indian civil servants. Once the children were placed, John and Alice Kipling slipped away to avoid tearful farewells. Rudyard was eleven years old when his mother came to take him away.

But in this tidy and proper-appearing household Rudyard was to be driven to near-blindness and to near-madness. From the beginning, the boy from India annoyed his "Aunt Rosa," as he was told to call her, and her rather stupid and sadistic son, who was a few years older than Rudyard. The Old Sea Captain, who was the head of the family, treated the boarded-out boy well enough but soon died.

"Aunt Rosa" did not like the table manners which Rudyard had learned from Indian servants. He sprawled over the furniture as he had sprawled over the studio furnishings in Bombay, where no one had minded his careless ways. His continual conversation, his searching questions, and his lack of response to any demonstration of sentiment repelled his foster aunt. Trix, the charming and obedient infant, was always liked by "Aunt Rosa."

Myself, I was regularly beaten. The Woman had an only son of twelve or thirteen as religious as she. I was a real joy to him, for when his mother finished with me for the day he (we slept in the same room) took me on and roasted the other side.[2]

She introduced him to hell and its terrors for the good of his soul. An unexplained smile (which she probably correctly saw as a smirk) could be cause for punishment. The Kipling children had two grandmothers and a great number of young, celebrated, well-to-do uncles and aunts with young children of their own who all lived in England. The Burne-Joneses, the Poynters, and the Baldwins took a very casual attitude toward Mary MacDonald Kipling's children. The MacDonald grandmother and two aunts made one duty call. They noted that the children were well fed, clean and adequately clothed and left satisfied. "Aunt Rosa" was a pious and proper woman.

Aunt Georgiana Burne-Jones was the most considerate of the aunts. When Kipling was grown, he asked for the bell rope from that house and transferred it to his own so that other children might have the pleasure of feeling happy when they rang it. Each year in December he was invited to visit at the Burne-Jones home for a whole month. The guests represented the most imaginative of the new intellectuals. The furniture was of the latest design. William Morris himself was one of the courtesy "uncles" he knew well there. The Rossettis and Ford Madox Ford and Swinburne had attended the wedding of the parents whom Rudyard dimly remembered. The only crotchety visitor was an old man they all called "Browning," who was annoyed by the swarm of children in the entry hall.

Rudyard liked best to lean over the banisters on the top landing to listen to the rise and fall of the deep voices of men talking at the table about politics and art and literature. There was nothing like this at the dull house in Southsea.

"Aunt Rosa," when she found out that Rudyard liked to read, restricted the pastime. He learned to read secretly in semi-darkness. His eyes began to bother him. His schoolwork suffered, and when he pretended not to have received a poor report card, he was sent to school with "Liar" placarded on his back.

This episode precipitated an emotional disturbance. He saw shadows that were not there and objects which did not exist. "Aunt Rosa" isolated him as if he were a leper. Trix, who had defended him faithfully during the miserable six years, was not permitted to be near him. His Aunt Georgiana appeared suddenly; then a strange doctor, and finally his mother, from whom he shrank, expecting a blow when she bent over to kiss him.

When he had been fitted with thick-lensed new glasses (unusual for a boy to wear at that time), Alice Kipling took Trix and Rudyard and Stanley Baldwin, her nephew, to a little farm near the edge of Epping Forest for a few months. She let the children run free; the only requirement was that they wash before meals. Stanley and Rudyard annoyed the farmer host, who questioned whether they were good for each other.

The mother did not know what to do with her stranger-son. In the fall she moved into lodgings in London. She bought Rudyard and Trix season tickets to the old South Kensington Museum, which was across the road. This gave their "sorely tired" mother a rest. The children invaded the museum, went into the places marked "Private" and divided small treasures they found there. There is nothing to indicate that Alice Kipling was ever an accepting mother who enjoyed her children.

At night Rudyard roamed the boarding house because he could not sleep. It was the beginning of his recurrent insomnia. Soon his mother went back to India, and Rudyard was left with three "dear old ladies" who were cultured and kind and vague. From there he went to the United Services College, whose head was one of the courtesy "uncles" he had known during his holidays at the Burne-Jones home.

The precocious, youthfully mature, "cheeky" boy with the mustache and the new thick-lensed glasses was not popular at school. He looked, Beresford says, something like a small cave man. It was not until he was fourteen and could defend himself against any other boy in school that he had some relief from bullying. During that first year and a half he had made friends with two other boys who were, like himself, "different."

John Lockwood Kipling was less successful than were his wife Alice's brothers-in-law and did not like to ask for special attention for his children. At the end of his first horrible term at school Rudyard had to spend the holiday on the school premises. He went back to "Aunt Rosa's" rather frequently — because his sister Trix was still there — despite the ill treatment Rudyard had experienced in this home. A pale, dark-haired girl two years older than he had taken his place as a boarding child. He fell madly in love with her. They became engaged when he was still fourteen and were still engaged when he went to India after he was graduated at seventeen. Time and distance broke the tie.

Rudyard Kipling is typical of the gifted child with problems. Teachers of children selected for special intellectual ability find them well-behaved except for their inability to wait their turn to talk. They are prone to annoy adults with their verbosity, hairsplitting opinionativeness, and persistence in pursuing their own goals. If they become impudent, they are efficiently so. To a person of limited capacities such a child can be especially infuriating, and the tension between the adult and child can mushroom to alarming proportions. The emotionally disturbed bright boy may seem less like a child than like a needling, hateful adult who happens to be inhabiting a child's body. He has none of the appeal of the innocent and unaware.

Kipling's seemingly neglectful English aunts and uncles can be absolved to some extent. He was not always a good house guest. On one occasion he arrived at the MacDonald household in a rage because he had been slapped by a railroad porter for his impudence. He rolled with rage on the nursery floor, then jumped up and announced his intention of going straight back to the station to "cheek that porter again." He was a little older than most of his cousins and experienced pubescence early. Having him as a guest may have worried and wearied his aunts, since his cousins are said to have found him exciting.

His eye problems, thick glasses, and odd appearance made his social adjustments difficult.

When he was graduated, he spent his last few days with the Burne-Joneses at their cottage in Rottingdean. His Aunt Georgiana often asked him why he had not told how he was mistreated by "Aunt Rosa." "Children," Kipling says in his autobiography, "tell little more than animals, for what comes to them they accept as eternally established. Also, badly treated children have a clear notion of what they are likely to get if they betray the secrets of a prison-house before they are clear of it."

He attributed certain traits that stood him in good stead to his sorry experiences between five and twelve. He learned to notice discrepancies between speech and action; he was always suspicious of sudden favors, was wary and observant, noticing moods and tempers in others.

Syngman Rhee's "smothering" mother sobbed as she took her blind son to the Protestant doctor-missionary who cured him.

To her it was like taking him to the devil. The cure was successful, but she lost her Buddhist son to the new faith, and subsequently to politics.

Aldous Huxley contracted a painful eye disease while at Eton and was thereby saved from becoming just another "public school gentleman." He had intended to be a doctor. His eye infection turned him to journalism as an occupation. He feels that the harshness of Providence is sometimes kindness.

When Louis Brandeis was advised by the first oculist he consulted to quit law school because of repeated attacks of severe eyestrain, he went to another physician, who told him to "read less, and think more." Brandeis took his advice and soon had a reputation for erudition. He also asked his classmates to read to him. One of his readers, son of a wealthy paper manufacturer, asked Brandeis to join him in his own law office after they were graduated. This relationship accelerated his career.

Reginald Fessenden, the Canadian-born scientist, had a serious eye operation when he was seventeen. Not until he was middle-aged did he find complete relief. When doing close work, he removed his glasses and focused his microscopic eyes on the object under scrutiny.

"The other boy made it to Annapolis. I failed it because of poor eyesight," says Harry Truman,[3] who had been coached for the examination by his history teacher.

He was disappointed, since he had always been a good student. When he was in the second grade, he had diphtheria and was so paralyzed for a time that his mother pushed him about in a baby carriage. He went to summer school to make up for lost time, then skipped the third grade, which he missed because of illness. In high school he was a good student and helped establish the school paper. His slight frame and glasses predisposed him to business rather than farming.

Lafcadio Hearn felt like a gargoyle because a playground injury to one of his eyes made it appear small and his other eye looked correspondingly large. A rejecting father, rejecting aunts, and a mentally ill mother were other burdens. James Joyce had lifetime problems with sore and painful eyes. Emile Zola was a sickly boy with deformed features, myopic eyes, and a lisp.

TO BE A SMALL OR SLIGHT BOY IS A HANDICAP

To be smaller than other boys can often make adjustment difficult. Some slight youths become belligerent; others withdraw. Fiorello LaGuardia, the dynamic and controversial mayor of New York City, was not only very short, he was a member of two minority groups as the son of an Italian father and a Jewish mother. He was also not very handsome.

In Prescott, Arizona, the family was accepted as being Italian, although the agnostic ex-Catholic father and the only nominally Jewish mother sent the boy to Episcopal Sunday school. However, when an organ grinder came to town with a monkey, the other boys turned to Fiorello with: "A Dago with a monkey! Hey, Fiorello, you're a Dago, too! Where's your monkey?"[4]

When Fiorello was a grown man, he was barely five feet tall. As a boy he was exceedingly tiny and fought his way through grade school. Once when he could not reach an opponent's face with his fists, he ran sobbing to the schoolhouse and lugged out a chair. One of his classmates, Joe Bauer, boasted that he licked Fiorello every day. Fiorello was, according to his biographer, Arthur Mann, pugnacious, loquacious, competitive and blunt.

Arthur Koestler, at sixteen, was changing his clothes in a bathing cabin at the beach when he heard two women talking. One had made a fondly apologetic remark about her own child's rapid growth. The other had responded, "That's no reason for worry. The terrible thing would be if he were as short as that Koestler boy."[5]

A few years later a Comintern agent was to refer to Koestler's inferiority complex not as a complex but as a cathedral. His shortness was only one factor in the development of this attitude.

He turned to the classroom for real satisfactions. He liked the Realschule, where he studied modern languages and science. In his early teens he spoke Hungarian, German, French and

English. He read Darwin, Spencer, Kepler, Newton, Edison, Herz, and Marconi. He made mechanical toys. At fourteen he felt that aside from the paradox of infinity and eternity, he had solved all the riddles of the universe.

At sixteen his knowledge did not shield him from fear of embarrassment. He refused to go to dancing parties for fear he might be shorter than his partners. If he was asked to a party and was told that a "tall, beautiful blonde would be included among the guests," he pleaded illness and stayed home.

"I cursed my littleness," said T. E. Lawrence, who called himself "a pocket Hercules." Thomas Hardy, J. M. Barrie, Henry Ford, Hamlin Garland, Joseph Goebbels, Maurice Ravel, Adolf Hitler and Mohandas Gandhi were other small boys.

In twenty-three of the Four Hundred, being small was seen as a deeply significant factor in their development. This does not mean that there were not other slight or short youths who were also self-conscious in this respect.

In the Gandhi household, the undersized, ailing youngest child was left to the care of his mother, Putlibai. He was a timid, homely boy who preferred his books to any companions. When he was first sent to school, he ran home quickly to his mother, so that no one could poke fun at him en route. His mother, abstemious as to food, was not particularly concerned about his slightness. Putlibai's piety impressed all her children deeply. For four months of the year (during a kind of Hindu Lent), she ate only a single meal a day. Although her fasts were always begun during the rainy season, she once vowed not to eat until she saw sunshine. The tradition of patient fasting was in the climate of Gandhi's home.

His father, Karamchand Gandhi, a fiery, impatient, emotional man of strong principles, was once arrested and held for a few hours because he defended a native ruler against the unjust criticism of a British political agent. He did believe in laying up vast sums of money for his children to inherit and his son Mohandas, in his autobiography, described him as "a lover of his clan, truthful, brave and generous, but short-tempered."

The insignificant Mohandas was the fourth and last child of his father's fourth marriage. His brothers, Laxmidas and Karsandas, more handsome, more aggressive and much better students than their droll, ugly little brother, paid him little attention. No one expected much of this last child. He was fearful of serpents, ghosts and darkness, and clung to his mother for support and affection. His mother loved him, but did not exclude others from her affection or dislike his father.

Despite his shyness, Mohandas refused to cheat when he was urged to do so by a teacher who wanted the students to perform well before the visiting inspector. He was inconsolable when a teacher accused him wrongly of having given a false excuse for a school absence. As he grew older, he began to play on the street with the boys, became involved in various delinquencies with a friend, ate forbidden meat, smoked, and visited a brothel, where he was cursed and chased away by an indignant woman whom he insulted by merely sitting shyly on the edge of her bed.

At thirteen he was a sexually aggressive husband but developed guilt feelings about enjoying his marital relationship after his father died while Mohandas was making love to his wife. At eighteen, twice a father, he was obstinate about his decision to go to London to study law. When he promised never to touch wine or women or meat, his mother reluctantly consented. He broke the mother-son circle gradually but definitely during his adolescent years. Boys who admire their fathers usually escape their overly possessive mothers when they become adult.

As a family man Mohandas Gandhi had the self-centeredness characteristic of the small, sickly, mother-smothered boy. His wife and children were given no choice as to behavior even when it was based on his convictions and not their own. He denied his sons schooling and refused to receive his son's bride when Harilal married without his consent. In his battle for the political freedom of one-fifth of the human race the tiny little man in a loincloth was indomitable. In gaining that freedom he was often heavily dependent on women followers: Annie Besant, Olive Schreiner, Millie Polak, Sonya Schlesin, Sarojini Naidu and Madeleine Slade, and upon the love and loyalty of his wife, Kasturbai Gandhi, which grew and deepened with the years.

His smallness and being a mother's boy may have been factors in his lifelong attention to diet and his preoccupation with health foods and unorthdox methods of healing. At one time he became prejudiced against milk and forbade his children and followers to drink it because he thought it excited the lower passions of man's nature.

THE CRIPPLED CHILDREN

If there is any common trait among the crippled children, it is the extremely close relationship which most of them have with one or both of their parents. When a child cannot move freely, he is of necessity often about the house. It is difficult to foresee a day when he is not going to be an extension of the parents; it is easy to make a puppet of the child who is dependent. Compassion for his handicap makes for a tenderness and leniency which if carried to extremes can be in itself a handicap. The most handicapping situation is a maternal inability to accept the reality of the situation. Since the child becomes very close to the parent, it seems especially important that the parent of the handicapped child be sound of character, firm and forward-looking as well as sympathetic. To give quarter to indolence or supineness is especially easy for the parents of the crippled. Guilt feelings which divide the parents of the abnormally formed child also do inexorable damage to the child's chance for happiness, although the division in the home may not interfere with creativeness.

Jane Addams, who had a spinal deformity, was exceptionally close to her Hicksite Quaker father, who was honest and uncompromising in his idealism. Like her father, she accepted the burden of troubled mankind as her own. Charles Proteus Steinmetz had a father who was misshapen. The widowed grandmother and the father were so compassionate toward the extremely malformed motherless child that they gave him the complete freedom of the house, let him burn the rug and damage the furniture — but always in the cause of his scientific curiosity, not in wanton destructiveness. This was the critical difference. When he rebelled against school, they helped him and his teachers work out the problems their overpermissiveness had caused and did not defend the boy for his tantrums and early defiance against an authority which was just and kind.

Charles Steinmetz was not only a great electrical engineer. He worked as a member of the Board of Education in Rochester to set up special programs for retarded children. He was eager to be helpful to all young people, to the bright and eager as well as the retarded. The warmth and compassion of his childhood home reached many individuals, including Dave Garroway, television personality, who once lived in Steinmetz's home. Despite cruel discrimination against Charles because of his grotesque body, he was never bitter or socially isolated.

Some boys are more forcible than are others in breaking through the overprotective smothering of a mother whose judgment is overridden by her anxieties. The mother of William O. Douglas, Justice of the Supreme Court, writer and nature lover, had two catastrophic blows. Her husband, whom she loved deeply, died suddenly while he was still a young and active man. One day he was present and the next day he was gone forever. His small son missed him also. In *Of Men and Mountains*, Douglas says, "The step in the hallway, the laugh, the jingle of coins in the pocket — these were gone as silently as the water of the great Columbia." It was years before the young wife and mother could keep from showing how crushed and alone she felt.

Infantile paralysis then struck her only son. The doctor, once the crisis was past, explained that William could not be expected to live past forty. He advised bathing the helpless limbs of the boy in salt water, and a fifteen-minute massage every two hours until there was evidence of recovery.

Day after day, night after night, the impoverished widow carried out the doctor's instructions. William learned to walk, and the frailty the disease had left seemed to pass. The widow believed that everything the doctor had said was true and that William was doomed to die before he was forty. She tried to restrict his activities, coddled him, asked his teachers and friends not to overtire him, until William became rebellious.

"But I believe my rebellion was not so much against her as against the kind of person I thought I was going to be." His love for her did not make him her puppet. Stung by the ridicule of schoolmates who made fun of his thin legs, he began to search for ways to improve his physical stature. A boy advised hikes in the mountains to strengthen muscles debilitated by illness. William used the foothills near his home as his gymnasium.

In the meantime he defeated the boys who had made fun of his black-stockinged pipestem legs by being an almost perfect student. At the end of a year of hiking his legs began to fill out. He became a young man of the mountains as well as a scholar.

A boy who was not so fortunate, was Joseph Goebbels, who like William O. Douglas was born healthy and normal. But an operation for osteomyelitis, contracted when he was four, seriously foreshortened one of Joseph's legs and left him limping for life.

Neither the mother nor the boy could accept the deformity. The father turned, halfheartedly, to his normal boys. There was no strong love for learning or warm cohesiveness in the lower-middle-class home.

Even when he grew older and had repudiated religion, Joseph Goebbels was fond of telling how his mother, an extremely pious woman, had once asked her children to join in a prayer circle to beg for the life of the father, who lay dying. His father had miraculously improved. In Joseph's youth he went often with his mother to pray in his own behalf. For many years both mother and son hoped for and expected a miraculous cure.

There was no acceptance of the permanent disability. Joseph withdrew from other children. He spent much time in his own room reading and rereading an old edition of an encyclopedia in the family's library. He was not liked by his classmates or his teachers. His nickname was "the Sly One"; he was known as a boy who sought occasion to be a tattletale.

His bitterness against everyone except his mother, whom he always idolized and idealized, grew with the years. In his diary, which he started at the age of twelve, he described his rejection of mankind. "The more I get to know about the human species, the more I care for my Benno [dog]. . . . As soon as I am with a person for three days, I don't like him any longer, and if I am with him for a whole week I hate him like the plague. . . . I have

learned to despise the human being from the bottom of my soul.
He makes me sick in my stomach. Phooooey!"

In his diary he records set-tos with his father, family quarrels,
arguments, especially about his later espousal of the cause of
Hitler. He tried to enlist in the army in 1914 and was refused,
as he must have known he would be. He wept all night and
spoke to no one for two days.

Like Hitler, Goebbels failed in his early efforts to express himself artistically. His two plays were never published. A novel he
wrote in his youth was embarrassingly emotional and ineptly
written. Like Hitler, he continued to receive the unqualified
admiration and love of his mother, who could see no fault in him.
Like Hitler, he turned to music for comfort and distraction. Like
Hitler, he hated his peers and had ambitions impossible for him
to fulfill. Unlike Hitler, he was attractive and had many affairs
with women, whom he treated badly. The mother was the one
woman whom he loved.

When he decided to commit suicide, however, he did not ask
his mother to die with him. This he required of his wife, Magda,
whom he had treated badly, and of their six beautiful young
children. He could have sent his children with his mother, who
fled the city as the Allied forces moved in. Magda and Joseph
Goebbels were both of the thought that their suicides would
perpetuate their memories, that dying for their cause would make
them historical figures. Magda asked to have her oldest son, a
half-brother to the young children, informed that she died honor-
ably. She asked one of the Nazi doctors to poison the children
hypodermically when the time came for all of them to die. In
the meantime, she and her husband played games with the children and told them stories. As the invading army approached, the
children were told they were to be inoculated, and submitted their
arms willingly. Magda poisoned herself; Joseph shot himself. He
died still not facing reality, wrapped up in the dream world of
Nazi superiority. His mother outlived him many years.

The mother of Toulouse-Lautrec, when her second child died
suddenly and her first was crippled, devoted her whole life to
trying to seize upon the immediate pleasure of helping him to be

happy. Her marriage of expedience dissolved in the face of family calamity, and the father was excluded from companionship with his son.

Gustav Mahler did not limp because he was physically malformed. He presumably limped because his mother was crippled and he wanted to share her pain with her. W. H. Hudson had a crablike gait which set him apart.

In the James family, which produced a novelist and a psychologist of great eminence, there were the "family backaches" and various other disorders which William finally decided were psychosomatic. Yet there was no other family so determinedly cohesive and so given to warm expressions about each other as was the wealthy James family.

At the age of thirteen, Henry James, Sr., lost a leg when he tried to stamp out a fire that he and other schoolboys set inadvertently while playing with a gas-filled balloon. He was an introspective and anxious man. One evening during young manhood Henry James, Sr., had a sudden hallucination as he sat alone at the supper table where his wife had left him while she cared for the two young sons. He was relaxed, comfortable, completely untroubled. He had a sudden awareness of a mysterious shape in the corner, a fetid moving thing capable of sending rays which could kill. It was a ten-second hallucination and he regarded it as such. However, the memory of it unmanned him. For months no doctor could give him relief, but an elderly woman at a spa cured him of his depression by introducing him to Swedenborgianism.

For a long period he had a great lack of faith in mankind and truly believed that the man who wished to perfect his character must first regard himself as "mere rubbish." At the same time he had a bottomless if somewhat ambivalent love for his family. He once told Emerson that he sometimes wished the lightning would strike his wife and children out of existence so that he should suffer no more from loving them. He deplored anxiety, thought it a sin, yet was overanxious.

He played the maternal role in the family, stayed home, kept his children close to him. His wife, a simple but patient woman, played the paternal role. Even the children were likely to scold the father in a paternal fashion. Henry James, Jr., says of his mother, "She was our life, she was the house, the keystone of the arch."

The children were not inclined to move out of the shelter of the family. "Henry," his brother William once said, referring to their travels and internationalism, "was really a native of the James family."

Alice, the brilliant, stoic, affectionate only daughter, broke completely under the strain of the tension-charged household. As a girl she fainted at parties when she was overstimulated. She took to her bed and suffered from an obscure ailment diagnosed variously as "rheumatic gout" or "spinal neurosis" or "nervous hyperaesthesia." Her own insight and that of her brother William as to the probable psychosomatic derivation of her pains did not help her to conquer them.

William James's late youth was clouded by insomnia, digestive disorders, eye troubles, weakness of the back and frequent deep depressions. His discovery that neurotic oppression could have a mental rather than necessarily a physical basis was to be crucial to his own development and his choice of psychology as a career.

All of his life Henry James was miserable with incapacitating spinal problems and digestive problems. He, too, was injured while fighting a fire. Robert James, the youngest boy, became a minor employee of the Milwaukee railroad. He had a certain frail poetic talent; he died alcoholic. Another brother, who died in his thirties, traded on his open, friendly manner but made little use of the real abilities which all the James children shared.

Within this tight, cohesive, affectionate family there were wide spaces of noncommunication. Henry James, Sr., did not think that men of science filled any real function. William James, the scientist, had little respect for his brother's novels. Henry James had no respect for the social group of which he was a member.

William James once wrote to his father, "You live in such mental isolation that I cannot help often feeling bitterly at the thought that you must see in even your own children strangers to what you consider the best part of yourself."[6] Henry James, Jr., the son who best pleased his father and best expressed his father's ambitions, did not choose to marry because he did not respect mankind enough to want to perpetuate it. His crippled back, during a long lifetime in which he rode horseback, hiked and traveled, caused him excruciating agony; but it did not actually incapacitate him or keep him from doing things he really wanted to do.

When Diana Manners, who was to become the wife of Duff Cooper, was almost four, her twelve-year-old brother Haddon died. His death threw his mother into such an agony of grief that she withdrew into a studio in London, "where in her terrible pain she was able to sculpture a recumbent figure of her dead son," the plaster case of which is now in the Tate Gallery. "All her artistic soul," says her daughter, "went into this tomb."[7]

There was no comparable release for Diana in creativity. Already a ridiculously anxious child, she developed a fear and certainty of death at five. Soon she could not raise her arms higher than her shoulders. She could not turn the music page on the piano rack. She tumbled and fell and banged her knees. Visiting doctors (in a day when little girls were trained to be very modest) required her to disrobe, sat in a headshaking, solemn ring while she paraded before them like a naked worm. The diagnosis was progressive paralysis. She would surely die before she was twenty.

A doctor came each day to give the invalid her galvanic treatments. In the meantime her life was to be made as pleasant as possible: "I was never to be gainsaid and spoiling was the order."

The expected death did not come. Instead, she grew into a chubby, healthy girl with a passionate desire to be loved and to be clever. Still, she was always anxious about her mother and fancied her dead or murdered if she was late coming home from a social affair. She continued to have an obsession about death. Her prayers were a nightly insurance policy. She prayed that death might not destroy the Indians and Chinese who were famine stricken, that no member of the family would be ill or have an operation, that the house would not burn, and that neither her father nor her mother would die before she was eighty or ninety. For years she prayed that a dead neighbor whom she had known slightly might be accepted in heaven.

At eleven she fell in love with Fridtjof Nansen, who called her his "Viking." She loved him obsessively and read the two-volume work on his expedition to the North Pole. Adolescence changed the direction of her anxieties. She found a pleasurable excitement in hand-holding and in hidden letters; at fifteen she could run downstairs. Her ugliness discontented her. She disliked the unbecoming clothes which her mother insisted she wear, the peasant shirts and ill-fitting skirts and black stockings. Her schooling, since she was not expected to live, had been pleasant and spasmodic instruction from tutors. Her mother was not concerned for the conventional disciplines, had no respect for timetables, regularity of bedtime, for going out or lessons — she thought them all unnecessary. In late adolescence Diana was beautiful, popular and gregarious.

Ring Lardner wore braces on one misshapen foot and consequently read and studied more often with his mother and played less frequently with other children. Eleanor Roosevelt, Jane Addams and Béla Bartók had spinal problems. Stalin had a withered arm and webbed toes. Orozco, after he lost his left hand, resigned himself to becoming an artist. "Stanislavski" became an actor to overcome his clumsiness. Although Norbert Wiener and David Lloyd George were certainly not crippled they both lacked manual dexterity to a marked degree. Wiener never outgrew the clumsiness that made his childhood days intolerable at times. Lloyd George had difficulty tying his shoes, or closing doors properly. Only four of these children, however, were obviously crippled as youths and as adults.

THE CHILDREN WHO WERE OVERWEIGHT

One overweight child was thought stupid and dull. Another in adolescence was suddenly left out of new social groups based on a boy-girl relationship. The most seriously overweight children, who were said to suffer from glandular difficulties, continued overweight as adults. Other overprotected and inactive children, children who ate because they were neglected and lonely, usually had normal figures when they were grown.

A teacher at St. Paul's Preparatory School in London once said that if anyone were to open Gilbert Chesterton's head, all they would find would be a lump of fat. Gilbert, grossly overweight, as tall as a man at twelve, went around wearing sailor suits as if he were a little boy. He annoyed his teacher by forgetting to do his homework. He perpetually lost his dog-eared books, which had pictures drawn on the text as well as on the margins. He bit his nails; his hands were always dirty. He had colds but no handkerchief.

When his mother took him to the doctor to find out why her son was so overweight and so absent-minded, the doctor told her that the boy would surely be either a genius or an idiot and that she must not be too hard on him. This was an easy assignment for her, since she was by nature a kindly, permissive woman who kept a haphazard house.

The father, who looked like Pickwick with a full head of hair, was a jolly fellow who was always engrossed in some new artistic project. He sold real estate and made a good living, but his real pleasure was in water colors, painting, modeling, photography, stained glass, fretwork, and magic lantern shows. He wrote and directed historical plays, knew English literature backward and forward, and was an argumentative liberal. His sons Gilbert and Cecil were the only boys among their acquaintances who had their own toy theater with inch-high actors and actresses.

In the midst of all this activity, Mrs. Chesterton wandered amiably about, keeping the food warm for their irregular meals by setting the dishes in the ashes in the fireplace. When visiting boys got used to her clothes, which were thrown on haphazardly, and to her protruding black teeth, they were enchanted with the whole house and its occupants. Boys loved being asked to visit the Chestertons and often were.

Gilbert was as friendly as an old sheep, and the boys at school all liked him. If bullied, he never seemed to notice. He never remembered to do his school lessons but he read straight through *Chambers's Encyclopedia* like a cow eating grass — and, his teachers thought, with as little comprehension. No one enjoyed the school debate club more than did Gilbert Chesterton. As an adult, he still counted as his best friends the members of the junior debating society. Gilbert helped to start a chess club and a naturalist club and a sketching club. He was chairman of a committee to produce a magazine called *The Debater*.

One of Gilbert's teachers confessed the boy was too much for him, and this did not apply to his gross overweight. He found the boy unable to originate anything.

Gordon ("Ted") Craig, scenic designer, the illegitimate son of Edward William Gordon, a London architect, and the actress Ellen Terry, was a fat, small boy. When Ellen Terry separated from her lover, she had two children, the dynamic, bossy daughter Edy and the white-haired, fat, lethargic "Ted," who was a glutton. He liked food, lots of it, with plenty of gravy. Vegetables he disliked. He had an extreme distaste for walking, especially with his long-legged, rejecting nurse and his sister, who pulled and pushed him about.

His mother thought men too aggressive and cruel to women, and believed that women were too supine. Therefore, she deliberately trained her daughter to be bold and bossy and her son to be yielding. "Ted" had the additional burden of not understanding his biological origin. He knew from loud whispers among the servants that he was a creature born without a father. As far as he knew he was the only such creature extant.

As an aged man Ted Craig still lamented his role as a neglected child. He writes in his autobiography:

Even a mother can fail to understand [her child] if she has any other occupation which takes more than half her attention from her home and its occupants. Read in her *Memoirs* what she has to say about the "struggle" to get me to do a simple thing. Why struggle? A smile, a laugh about sheep's tails and lamb's tails, and all would have ended happily.

Another rejected boy was Douglas Fairbanks, Jr., whose parents were divorced.* He was plump and unattractive and often heard himself compared unfavorably with his father, the romantic movie actor, and also with his grandfather, Dan Sully, who prior

---

*There are forty-three children among the Four Hundred who describe themselves, or are described, as being rejected by one or both parents.

to his spectacular business failure had been the cotton king of the South. Nothing young Douglas ever did was quite right or quite good enough. He was brought up in hotels and was always underfoot and in the way. He roller-skated through the lobby of the Algonquin Hotel in New York City and once was petrified with fear when he bumped into aged actor John Drew.

Katherine Mansfield, a writer born in New Zealand and brought up in a well-to-do home, had nightmares in the dark of butchers with long knives and daytime nightmares when the Nathan children next door kept calling her "Fatty! Fatty!" Her mother she describes as "Linda Burnell" in a story, "We Are at the Bay," as "a woman whose courage was gone through too much childbearing. . . . And what made it doubly hard to bear was that she did not even love her children. It was useless pretending. Even if she had the strength she would never have nursed and played with the little girls."

"I am ugly, fat, conspicuous and dull; to say nothing of a very bad temper. Oh Lord, please let it be all right and let Paul love me, and don't let me be a fool,"[8] Amy Lowell wrote in her diary as a child. The poetess was not ugly, but she was fat. She would have been pretty if she had not been so heavy. She had delicate fingers, small feet, blue-gray eyes and regular features.

She was apt at learning, opinionated, bookish, critical. Amy was the baby girl in a cultured family which doted on her early intellectual promise. Yet she was not always a satisfactory student, despite her ability. She jumped to conclusions. She was a fearful speller and had her own idea of what French words should mean. She disliked grammar.

While she was in a girls' school, she dominated the other students, talked them down, corrected them, told them more than they wanted to know about her writer brother, who was an authority on Japan and sent her fabulous presents. When she became adolescent and lacked the attention of boys she was miserable. The girls she had antagonized did not help her to make friends with boys, and boys avoided her because of her appearance. She took to having accidents, broken bones and sprained ankles.

She pretended to be reserved and to need solitude, and spent hours in her room with her books and daydreams. The only real happiness she had was at the theater, where she could sit in the dark and identify herself with a slim, beloved heroine on the stage.

Other children to whom being overweight was a problem were Maria Callas, Henry Morton Stanley, and Oscar Wilde. Maria Callas disappointed her mother by not being born a boy who could replace a dead brother. The rejecting mother stuffed the child with starches and would not let her play in the street with other girls who talked of sweethearts or played with dolls. Maria was kept in the house, where she read or played the piano until eleven o'clock at night.

THE SICKLY CHILDREN

The thirty-eight very sickly children among the Four Hundred have a tendency to live long and energetic lives. Among them are such hardy and indefatigable specimens as Joseph Stalin, Clara Barton, William O. Douglas, Thomas Edison, Arturo Toscanini, and Vilhjalmur Stefansson, the explorer who shared the life of the most primitive of Eskimos.

In almost every home where there is a sickly child, there is an overconcerned or driving parent or parental antagonisms. Attitudes are not casual and optimistic in these homes. The child's illness often seems to fill some kind of a need in the child or the parent or both. Sickness and isolation can protect the child against bad, big boys who the parent fears will hurt the child. It can serve to keep the child close to a parent who is unhappy because of a failure in the marital relationship.

The luckiest children are those who rebel as did William O. Douglas, usually in adolescence, against being cast in the role of invalid child. Theodore Roosevelt, who was an invalid as a boy, also became robust in late adolescence. He was asthmatic, as were Marcel Proust and the African-born writer Olive Schreiner, who became a dynamic and dominating woman.

"I have written this at night, being the only time unoccupied with the dear, troublesome little children deserted by their Papa,"[9] wrote a young wife, Martha Bullock Roosevelt, to her husband, who was working for the Northern cause — while she worried about her sixteen-year-old brother, who was a blockade runner for the South.

The recipient of this letter was Theodore Roosevelt, Sr., who was always to be described as the ideal father by his children and as an ideal man by his friends. "My father was the best man I ever knew. He combined strength and courage with gentleness, tenderness and a great unselfishness. He would not tolerate in us children selfishness, or cruelty, idleness, cowardice or untruthfulness,"[10] said his son, the President.

Theodore, the oldest son, was not able to live up to the difficult code of his father. There is no doubt that he was sometimes cruel to his mother, to his aunt, and to his grandmother, whose Southern cause he rejected in favor of his father's espousal of the Lincoln Republicans. His health problems coincided with his father's absence and his own determination to champion his father's cause.

The dear and troublesome children who had been temporarily deserted by their father were the crippled Anna, aged seven; Theodore, aged four; Elliott, who was two; and Corinne, who was one.

Theodore Roosevelt, Sr., a very wealthy man, paid a substitute to fight for him in the actual battles of the war. His peculiar family circumstances did not make him feel free to carry a gun that might kill his wife's closest relatives. He volunteered to do propaganda work, to organize and equip Negro soldiers, and to do extensive social service work for the widows and children of men in service.

His Southern wife, her spinster sister Anna, and their mother lived in perpetual anxiety about their own close relatives in the South. Grandmother Bullock used to say that she hoped she would die before she heard that her sixteen-year-old son Irvine, a blockade runner, had been killed, or before Richmond was taken by the Yankees. Her stepson was an admiral in the Southern navy. Grandmother Bullock wrote her Yankee son-in-law, upon whom she was dependent, telling him about his children, those "pitiful sick things," and advising him that his wife "had her hands full." The Southern in-laws were dependent upon their Northern host.

Six-year-old Theodore felt his responsibilities keenly as the son of a Northern patriot. He used prayers both as a safe propaganda medium and as an expression of hostility to the Southern women. He knelt at his young aunt's knee and prayed that the Southern troops might be ground to powder. He punished his mother, when she scolded him, by threatening to pray for the North.

Until the father went away, Theodore seemed to be in good health. His mother had found him hideous at birth, said he looked like a terrapin, but there is no indication that he was regarded as a sickly boy. His grandmother wrote letters which described his "milk crust" (probably allergy) but his father in 1860 indicated that the "milk crust" was gone and that Theodore was "almost a beauty."

Carleton Putnam says in his Roosevelt biography: "Starting with the fall of 1861 the [family] account of colds, fevers, coughs and stomach upsets is continuous." This is also, significantly, the date of the beginning of the Civil War. It would seem that the very deep emotional tension in the house may have contributed inadvertently to Theodore's asthma.

Martha ("Mittie") Bullock Roosevelt was a sweet and charming but exceedingly immature individual. It was her beauty which made her memorable. Her magnolia complexion and coral cheeks, her dark hair and blue eyes made her one of New York's most beautiful society women. Life was never easy for her; she had no sense of money or time. "Please don't be hard on me," she once wrote to her husband, who was exceedingly capable. She had such distaste for dirt that a sheet had to be spread beside her bed before she could say her prayers, for she wanted no consciousness of dirt to destroy her communication with her Deity.

Along with her husband's absence during the early days of the Civil War, she must have been deeply hurt by Theodore's militant espousal of the North; all of her life she was to be an "unreconstructed rebel."

The Bullock women were sweet, gushing, sentimental. Forthright anger or caustic criticism were inconsistent with their up-bringing and beliefs. Martha's letters are of the "dear-but-trouble-some" variety. Each negative comment must be matched by an equally positive statement. Real feelings are lost in the nebulous mists of propriety and sentiment. She writes to her absent husband to tell him that her oldest son is brimful of mischief and has to be watched all the time. She then assures him that the boy is an affectionate and endearing little fellow.

While she was stroking baby Elliott's ears to put him back to sleep early one morning, Theodore invaded the room and was "jealous." Therefore she felt that he needed discipline. He was described as "hysterical" with glee when he succeeded in getting the younger brother (who was always handsome) to obey him.

There is always this ambivalence and a suggestion of recurrent nagging in the mother's attitude toward her homely first boy. Like Eleanor Roosevelt, who was an unattractive child, this homely child could never quite please its mother. But the father's code permitted no expression of hostility or rebellion toward the mother.

After the father's return, Theodore's asthmatic attacks grew more and more serious. During the ill-fated first trip to Europe, taken when Theodore was eleven, the family letters still record the mother's impatience with him. Theodore, she advised her correspondents, "took nothing in" of the sights of Europe. Instead he looked about with an aristocratic air, then turned to his father with inappropriate questions such as, "Father, why did Texas wish to annex itself to the United States?" Elliott, on the other hand, declared everything to be lovely, "only having taken a hasty glance but taking it all in." The mother resolved to "make" Theodore see the worthwhile sights of Europe. It was she who insisted on the trip. The father had not wanted to go. Theodore frustrated his parents by having a severe asthmatic attack every four or five days. In Venice he was sick and could not sleep until after two. In Trieste he sat up for four hours during the night while his father made him smoke a cigar to stop his wheezing. Black coffee poured into him by his mother and older sister seemed to do the most good. Between attacks he was taken relentlessly to see the sights. They missed nothing. The young children raced through hotels, annoying other guests, and dragged their feet through museums and cathedrals.

Theodore was annoyingly homesick and begged to go home. He wanted his solitude, his nature collections, his books, and his next-door neighbor, whom he designated "Eidieth." Edith Carow, the neighbor, was to be his second wife, and the woman who helped more than any other person to make him a great man.

Theodore never openly disobeyed his mother. When she asked him to do something, he said, "Oh, yes, you pretty sweet thing," and exasperated her by immediately going off to skin a bird or perform some other such task — which must have been nauseating to a person of her temperament and ideas about cleanliness. The children called their mother "Motherling" and never accorded her the status of a mature woman. Crippled Anna, at fourteen, took over the role of housekeeper of the elaborate establishment. (Anna fared better than did most overly responsible older sisters. She grew up into a wonderful and dynamic woman, married at forty and became a mother at forty-three.)

It was Theodore's father who helped him when the boy finally grew rebellious about his own constant illness and weakness. He responded to the father's idea that the boy should "make his body." Theodore began gymnastics at Wood's gymnasium on a side porch where he could exercise his chest on horizontal bars. He went on camping trips, slept on damp ground, forced himself to take hardship. When he was thirteen, he was so shamed by an encounter with some boys who bullied him that he took up boxing. His whole energy and his driving will were centered on this task of "making his own body."

At no time had he been coddled, and between attacks he had always been active. Theodore praised his father in his autobiography for not centering his whole attention on his own sick son. Theodore was never made to feel that his sickeness excused him or his family from a sympathetic interest in other children who were worse off than he. His father was so absorbed in the problems of all sick children that his friends, of whom he had so many, reached for their pocketbooks when they saw him coming. Theodore Roosevelt, Sr., took newsboys off the street and sent them out West to farms. He took his own children with him to visit his Newsboy's Lodging House and the Night School for Little Italians.

His wife, who seemingly took no interest in his projects, was once entertaining some of New York's wealthiest matrons when her husband, who had been currently unsuccessful in getting aid for a proposed hospital for crippled children, invaded her social gathering with several helplessly crippled children from the slums, whom he laid on tables cleared for the purpose. Beside them he placed steel appliances he wanted these underprivileged children to have. His daughter Corinne was pressed into service to explain the devices to the startled guests, who were quickly sympathetic. When Mrs. John Jacob Astor responded by offering money, other women followed suit. The result was the New York Orthopedic Hospital, to which the adult Corinne was to take her little niece, Eleanor Roosevelt, on a memorable visit many years later.

As Theodore grew close to pubescence, his mother found him increasingly rude and crude, yet noted that he was protective as he walked with her and Corinne on the streets and that he purposely placed himself in a protecting position between the women and some street rowdies. At puberty his asthma disappeared.

As a college junior, Theodore had mastered the art of maintaining the effusiveness the feminine family code demanded, but also betrayed his awareness of his widowed mother's continued immaturity. He began a letter: "Darling, beloved, little Motherling, I have just loved your dear, funny, pathetic little letter. . . ."[11]

Eczema covered nearly the whole body of Béla Bartók when he was three months old and he had no relief from the condition until he was five or six. He developed a fear of being near strangers, seldom left the house, and regarded children of his own age as his worst enemies. At five he was misdiagnosed as having curvature of the spine and was not permitted to sit; he took his meals standing, rested by lying flat on the floor. His mother neglected the rest of the family and gave him her almost complete attention. At three he played the drums while she played the piano. He could play forty melodies on the piano when he was four. At nine he was composing. The precocious, mother-tutored boy went to school when he was seven and completed four grades in one year with "firsts" in everything. Dependence upon his mother, or a mother-figure, and a painful inability to relate to other people characterized him all of his life.

Stella Cabrini was fifty-two when her thirteenth child, the premature, delicate Francesca Maria, was born. Since the child was not expected to live, it was christened at once with the names of two children who had not lived. Francesca retained her delicacy throughout childhood and was denied entrance into the Daughters of the Sacred Heart and the Canossian Sisters. No religious order wanted the young girl, who coughed drops of blood during her frequent illnesses. After a grueling apprenticeship in an orphan's home, she formed her own religious order. The world was not big enough for the tireless Sister Cabrini, who founded schools, orphanages and hospitals in far corners of the globe. During the first twenty-five years of her order, one hundred thousand persons were treated in her hospitals. Like Theodore Roosevelt, she was careless of her physical strength, and enjoyed testing her endurance.

Edison, who was a sickly child, slept only five or so hours a day as an adult. Harry Truman, also sickly as a child, walked the legs off his Secret Service men and has a brusque vigor. Jan C. Smuts, Charles Evans Hughes and most of the other thirty-eight sickly children were indefatigable workers and lived a normal life span or are still living.

THE HOMELY BOYS AND GIRLS AND LOVELY MOTHERS

Various investigators, particularly Leta Hollingworth, make much of the attractive appearance of groups of gifted children selected by tests. Among the Four Hundred, however, there is a goodly number of boys and girls who considered themselves homely. Biographers attest to the lack of pulchritude in others.

Women, especially, tend to find themselves unattractive as children. Sheila Kaye-Smith describes herself as a girl whose forehead was half of a hideous gray face. Edith Sitwell, six feet tall, had a rejecting father who tried to mend her looks by putting a painful clamp on her long nose. Sarah Bernhardt was a sharp-featured, scrawny girl. Diana Cooper, who was to be a celebrated beauty, said no one considered her a pretty child except her mother. Jane Addams feared to shame her handsome father by letting people know he had such a homely daughter. Ernestine Schumann-Heink described herself as short and sallow and plain and feared her plainness would keep her from fame as a singer. Eleanor Roosevelt was a gawky girl in braces. Marian Anderson was tall, thin and plain. Santha Rama Rau did not fit her grand-mother's idea of a delicate, petite Indian maiden. "Ouida" was an especially ugly girl. Gertrude Stein and Clara Barton were square chunks of girls, and masculine in appearance.

William Henry Hudson, novelist, had a crablike walk and a hook nose. Laurence Housman was an unattractive boy. Houdini, the magician, was small and bowlegged. Maurice Chevalier was teased because of his big head and small body. Enrico Fermi, Joseph McCarthy, Ivar Kreuger and Charles de Gaulle felt the handicap of an unprepossessing appearance. Tolstoy thought no one would ever be able to love him because of his sunken eyes, low forehead, heavy lips, large bulbous nose and enormous ears. Adolescent Franz Kafka lamented his "inescapable ugliness" which prompted him to wear bady cut clothes, to walk with his back bent, his shoulders crooked and his hands all over the place. A. E. Housman was called "The Mouse" by other boys who trod on him and pretended they could not see him. Henry Ford, John D. Rockefeller, Bertrand Russell and Paul Gauguin were scrawny, irregular-featured boys.

There were also "pretty" boys who were too effeminate to be well accepted by their peers. Scott Fitzgerald had this handicap and was cast as the leading lady in his college shows. Arthur Balfour, delicate of feature, was considered effeminate. The boys who did not experience pubescence were severely handicapped; Alexander Woollcott and Edward Marsh had mumps which made them neuter in gender. Cecil Rhodes always spoke with an un-changed voice and was not known to have an interest in women.

Statesmen were more likely to be handsome. Franklin D. Roosevelt (but not Theodore), Dwight D. Eisenhower, Nehru and Thomas E. Dewey were said to be strikingly handsome as youths and as men. Rupert Brooke was a rarely beautiful young man, as was Hart Crane. Theodore Herzl was an unusually beautiful child. Marie Curie was a delicate, graceful girl with a mop of curls.

Fathers are not often described as being especially handsome, and the mothers who are described as beauties almost always were neglectful or rejecting. Lady Randolph Churchill was a brunette American beauty who was a beautiful but "distant star" to her son. She saw him seldom until he was old enough to be her escort at social functions. Gertrude Atherton describes her rejecting beautiful mother as a woman whose major interest was her own appearance and who had a tremendous ineptness for choosing lovers. Theodore Roosevelt's lovely little mother was, as we have noted, an extremely immature woman.

Arthur Quiller-Couch describes his mother's wonderful wealth of red-auburn hair and her Devon complexion of cream and roses which she kept to the end of her days. "I thought her the most beautiful woman in the world and adored her," he says in his memoirs. She was a wildly generous woman and compassionate, given to nursing her doctor-husband's indigent patients. Her difficulty was her wilful extravagance, which was a terrible burden to her devoted husband. She loved entertaining and fine clothes to such an extent that the family experienced financial insecurity. Her son spent six of his adult years paying off his deceased father's debts.

In the Robinson home, in the village of Head Tide in southern Maine, there were three brilliant sons who came to personal grief: Dean, the brilliant physician who became a drug addict; Herman, the handsome, outgoing boy who went into business, failed and became an alcoholic; and Edwin Arlington Robinson, the homely, odd bachelor who was always being disappointed when his male friends matured and married, and who was driven to nervous collapse when the whole burden of the disintegrating family fell upon his sickly shoulders.

The home seemingly had every virtue. Hermann Hagedorn says of the house and parents:

The house had grace of line. . . . a perfect frame for the idyl of married love which the storekeeper and his wife provided. A tender imaginative strain in her found its complement in his more solid philosophic bent. He treated her like a flower. . . .[12]

The father was always so much in love with his beautiful young wife that the children were seemingly left outside the circle of love which encompassed the parents and shut out the rest of the world. Her son often felt as if his parents did not know he was there when he was with them.

When her third child was born, Mrs. Robinson was very disappointed because she wanted this child to be a little girl. Since the birth was difficult, her husband sent her to a summer resort to regain her health and spirits. When the new baby was six months old, it was still unnamed, and the mother was apathetic over the insistence of the other women at the resort that something be done. When she was uncooperative, the women resolved the matter by each writing a favorite name on a slip which was put into a hat. A woman from Arlington, Massachusetts, who had submitted the name Edwin, had the distinction of calling the child Edwin Arlington Robinson.

Edwin Arlington Robinson was burdened for years with the fragmentation of his distressed family. Women were never to mean anything to him — Isadora Duncan must have frightened him terribly when she asked him to father a child for her.

A vain mother, it seems, can have a negative effect on a daughter with different values. Willa Cather's beautiful mother regarded herself as an authority on high fashion, and never left her bedroom until she was perfectly groomed. She liked to carry a parasol to match her costume and to wear fresh violets when she could. She infringed very little on her children's activities unless they disobeyed her and threatened her comfort. At this point she was likely to whip them with a rawhide whip. She had an immense energy and a corresponding devotion to doing things the right way. She and her daughter Willa patterned their lives to avoid too frequent meetings. Willa and her two oldest brothers had a room of their own in the unfinished attic, where the snow sifted in and there was no heat except from the chimney, and where the rest of the large family left them alone.

The father was a kindly Southern gentleman, refined and delicate, whose business interests were not remunerative enough to keep the large family solvent. His mother-in-law, patient, hardworking and self-effacing, fed the boarders who came at noon, never removed her apron, limped because her hip had been broken wrestling with a gate on a windy night. She did most of the housework and pampered her beautiful daughter. Her granddaughter, Willa, was to write about her with love and compassion.

Willa reacted by becoming William. She cropped her hair, wore a boy's hat and jacket or loud and garish female garments that offended her mother's exquisite taste. Willa's heroes became the "Big Eight," her father's influential friends who were lampooned with him in the county paper when they investigated what they designated as the misuse of funds by the county treasurer. She came to prefer the company of adult men. She made calls with the doctors and once gave chloroform to a boy patient whose leg was being amputated. She dissected frogs and rode horseback through the countryside. The teachers at the high school let her come and go as she pleased because she was so extremely accelerated that school was obviously a bore to her. She read Latin and Greek and did science experiments with Mr. Ducker, the town eccentric and scholar. She was glad she resembled her father, not her mother, in appearance.

In a child's memory book[13] she described herself by filling in blanks. Her favorite amusement was vivisection; her favorite occupation, slicing toads. The trait she admired most in women was "flirting." In men she admired "an original mind." "Passion" was the trait for which she had the most toleration in another individual and "lack of nerve" she could not tolerate in others. She desired a matrimonial partner who had a "lamb-like meekness." Her idea of perfect happiness was to "amputate limbs" and real misery was to do "fancy work." As a traveling companion she would most desire a "cultured gentleman." If shipwrecked on a desolate island she would most desire "pants and a coat." The greatest wonder of the world was a "good-looking woman." The memory book was signed Wm. Cather, M.D. — not Willa Cather.

When this girl decided to be a boy, she was consistent in her re-actions. It was not until she was a junior in college that she gave up her cropped hair and male attire.

It would seem to be more than sheer coincidence that the mothers who are remembered as being particularly beautiful are not among those who influenced their children in the most con-structive ways.

Only two mothers were spoken of as being especially homely: Jack London's mother, who was indifferent to her son, and Leo Tolstoi's devoted mother, who shared her interest in people and ideas with her children.

The physical appearance of fathers is not often mentioned, but horse-faced Woodrow Wilson said bitterly that if he had had his father's good looks he could speak without regard to content.

It is well to remember that the child who has one handicap is by no means necessarily free from other agonies. George Orwell once said, "I had no money, I was weak, I was ugly, I was un-popular, I had a chronic cough, I was cowardly, I smelt."[14] George did not trust his mother, disliked his father and found his board-ing school, described in his *Such Were the Joys*, intolerable.

Thirty-nine of the Four Hundred spoke of themselves as being made miserable because of their appearance. Approximately one-fourth of the Four Hundred have reason to try to compensate for one or more handicaps.

[9]

Early Agonies

> For the most part I do the thing which my
> own nature drives me to do. It is shameful to
> earn so much respect and love for it. Arrows
> of hate have been shot at me, too; but they
> never hit me; because somehow they belong
> to another world, with which I have no
> connection whatsoever.
> I live in that solitude which is painful in
> youth, but delicious in the years of maturity."
> — ALBERT EINSTEIN, *Portraits and Self*
> *Portraits,* edited by Georges Schreiber

THERE IS almost no adverse circumstances of the kind commonly thought to induce mental illness, delinquency or neurosis which some one of the Four Hundred does not experience during his childhood. Some are illegitimate. Others are profoundly affected by the death of a brother or sister. Many are orphaned, half-orphaned, neglected or rejected.

Despite these circumstances there are few of the Four Hundred or their siblings or their parents who withdraw from reality and are hospitalized as mentally ill. They may be depressed, eccentric or neurotic, but they hold fast to a sense of reality. Motivated by a common love for learning and drive for accomplishment, they are seen to be preoccupied, as was Albert Einstein, with self-rewarding activities which gave them their deepest satisfactions.

During the process of working out their very real environmental problems many of the children develop easily recognized neurotic symptoms. They bite their nails, are hyperactive, withdrawn, rebellious or resentful. Although handicapped by environmental circumstances, they are nonetheless persistent in developing individual talents and skills.

THE INTRUDER COMPLEX

Ferenc Molnar related many of the inhibitions that complicated his existence to what he terms "that intruder complex of mine." Although his parents never said so, he was always quite certain that he was an exceedingly poor substitute for the blond, angelic brother who died before Ferenc was born. Molnar's father, who was a physician, kept only the placid, sunny Lacika's picture on his desk. Nothing that dark, active Ferenc ever could accomplish erased his father's longing for the lost Lacika.

At seventeen Ferenc finished high school and brought home a record so excellent that it opened the doors of every university in Europe to him, but Ferenc could see on his father's face the fleeting shadow of a thought, "Why not Lacika?" The identical look was manifest when his second son brought him clippings from the morning paper extolling the production of Ferenc's first play. To this intruder complex Molnar attributed his lifelong shyness, his exaggerated modesty and his uneasy feeling that he did not merit the rights freely given to others.

Emotional disturbance is a frequent aftermath of a death in the family. Children who are bereft of a brother or sister are suddenly aware of the transitory nature of life, and may respond by a powerful urge to achieve quickly before death also strikes them down. The living child is sometimes jealous of a dead child who is always spoken of as perfect. He consequently feels rejected and is determined to excel the lost child in a spectacular fashion. Other children are faced with a bereaved parent whose whole personality is changed by the sudden tragedy in the family. Gloom and despair displace serenity, and the living child feels he must now "live for two" in order to compensate stricken parents for the loss they have sustained. If the family becomes fragmented and noncohesive as a result of the tragedy, the child who is to become eminent may mature quickly, may leave home and seek outside his family or within himself for satisfaction and rewards.

Mary Austin, novelist, had no champion in the family when her father died. It was her understanding lawyer father who had insisted that she have a library card. The mother, whose affections were centered on her favored first-born son, tried to keep Mary from reading books the brother could not also enjoy. Mary's principal joy was in the affection of her little sister Jennie, who tried to comfort the big sister when Mary had a high fever and a sore throat. The doctor was not called until Jennie was near death with diphtheria. Mary recovered from her own diphtheria attack without medical attention, but Jennie died. In her daughter's hearing the mother said, "Why couldn't it have been Mary?"

The precocious oldest daughter in this household invented an imaginary I-Mary to be her companion and punished her rejecting mother by blurting out unpleasant truths when company came; she became agnostic in defiance of her mother's piety. Not even when Mary was an adult and a successful novelist did she develop the ability to experience satisfying personal relationships, and most persons who knew her well found her caustic and unpleasant.

Salvador Dali was a "reborn Salvador." His name was first given to an angelic, perfect Salvador Dali who died when he was seven.* To the parents, the second son, born three years after his brother's death from meningitis, was an exact replica of the dead Salvador. To them he was the deceased child come back to their arms. The second Salvador was grossly unable to compete with their selective memories and soon became hyperactive and even sadistic. He kicked his sister's head as if it were a football. At five he threw another child over a railing and nearly killed him. He bit into a putrescent bat; he broke the doctor's glasses; he trod upon a classmate's violin. By the time he was adolescent he was so eccentric

---

*The living children in these families do not seem to understand that it is customary not to speak evil of the dead and are sincerely convinced that the child they replace was actually never thought troublesome or naughty or stupid.

in his manner and dress that he was stoned when he went to the movies. He had no satisfying relationships with the boys and girls in his immediate neighborhood.

Brooks Adams, the historian, born soon after his most promising and beloved five-year-old brother Arthur died, was also defiant and incomprehensible to his erudite family. By the time that he was old enough to join the nightly family reading circle he was a puzzle to his father and mother, who isolated him on a hassock in the middle of the room, where he wore out his clothes and the rug with his pulling and twisting. He laughed, ranted, twisted and jumped about while his father, Charles Francis Adams, read to the children. At school he performed wretchedly and could neither read nor spell tolerably. His parents took him to the family physician to ask whether a blow on the head by a cricket ball could possibly account for the boy's stupidity, but the doctor assured them that the boy was perfectly normal physically and had suffered no brain damage. Neither parent expected that this problem child would ever be able to go to college. He retained his childhood awareness of rejection as an adult.

Daniel Aaron, who describes him in *Men of Good Hope: Latter-Day Progressives*, pictures the eighty-year-old Brooks Adams as an arrogant, blunt, audacious man who conducted a "one-man mutiny against the whole world." He so exasperated his relatives that his niece called him an "unusable man." His prejudices colored and distorted his very genuine scholarship. He disliked Jews, whom he called "gold bugs," and thought them a secret force behind the League of Nations, which he also mistrusted. To the last he was defensive, mistrustful of himself, apologetic. Aaron quotes him as once moved to protest: "I am not a man with a maggot in my brain — and in all the years when I have been wandering from New York to Jerusalem speculating on the causes which seem to be crushing the world, I have not been morbid, crazy or ill."

In an upper-middle-class family in Guanajuato, Mexico, Diego Rivera became the "intruder" to his mother when he was a year and a half old. The home into which the Portuguese-Jewish-

Negroid-Spanish-Indian twins, Carlos and Diego, were born was a small marble palace in the heart of the city in which the father, Diego Rivera, Sr., was a councilor and man of considerable status and importance. Four previous pregnancies had resulted in miscarriages or stillborn babies, and the full-term twins were the first living children born to the twenty-two-year-old mother.

Carlos died when he was a year and a half old and Maria, his mother, would not be consoled. She spent each night weeping by the side of the grave of the deceased child. Her husband rented a room from the caretaker of the cemetery, in order to be near her. Diego, the living twin, was so rickety and debilitated that his ability to survive was questioned.

The family doctor said that the young mother would lose her sanity unless she could be distracted by becoming a career woman. Maria consented enthusiastically to being enrolled in a course in obstetrics, at which she was so adept that she finished it in half the usual time. Diego, meanwhile, was sent away to the country to be reared by a nurse in a primitive shack in the middle of a wooded area. When he was brought home at the age of four, he was fat and healthy, but neither he nor his mother could ever feel an affection for each other. It was the nurse, Antonia, to whom Diego gave his complete devotion. (Wives and mistresses he always felt he must hurt, even when he loved them.)

Not long after his return from the mountains, his mother told him that he must go to the railway station and wait there until the stationmaster gave him a box in which he would find a new brother or sister. The disgruntled boy went home after several hours of fruitless waiting and was greeted with the news of the arrival of a new baby sister, who was in his mother's bedroom. The angry five-year-old found a pregnant mouse, cut it open to show the embryonic mice inside, and made his mother look at them in an effort to convince her that she had lied to him. She retaliated by crying out that she had whelped a monster when she had given birth to Diego. The father comforted Diego, who was beside himself with anger at having been tricked.

When he was six, Diego shamed his mother again by his behavior in church. The father was an agnostic and freethinker and had forbidden the aunts or mother to take Diego to church;

but a great-aunt disobeyed and took Diego with her so that he might pray for his mother, who was taking her final examinations that day. The priest fled and the congregation was appalled and frightened when the six-year-old boy mounted the pulpit and gave an impassioned anticlerical speech. He had already learned to read so that he might spell out the words in his mother's obstetrics books and prove again that she had lied to him about the birth of his sister. His speech was fluent and convinced the parishioners that the devil had taken possession of the boy's body and spoke through his childish mouth.

The community reaction to Diego's behavior irked the mother so deeply that she sold the family's possessions while the father was away on a business trip and took the children with her to Mexico City. Diego Rivera, Sr., gave up his remunerative position in Guanajuato and followed her. Since he had lost money in mining ventures, they set up housekeeping again in a small apartment in a poor section of town. During a period when the family diet was limited, Diego had scarlet fever and typhoid; and a new baby born into the family lived less than a week. Again Diego was the "intruder." Despite his many difficulties he demonstrated his ability in art and his precocity in language very early and was called "The Boy Wonder of Guanajuato."

The forty-nine individuals who were profoundly affected by the death of one or more brothers and sisters are not all as rejected as were Mary Austin and Brooks Adams. There is however, an immediacy in all their drives which often cuts their childhoods short. Some, like Eleanor Roosevelt, are overanxious to please, and are insecure adolescents. Sigmund Freud, who resented the birth of a brother born when Sigmund was nineteen months old, was filled with guilt eight months later when the "intruder" to whom he had relinquished his mother's breast died. In opposite but related fashion, Alfred Adler could never forgive his mother for smiling too soon after his baby brother died.

Sean O'Casey replaced two brothers of his own name and could never forget his mother's grief. He felt a need to comfort her by his own accomplishments. Adolf Hitler failed miserably to compensate his mother for the three children before him who did not live. Stalin was another of the sickly children who had to make up for his mother's lost babies. Oscar Wilde, Rilke and Vachel Lindsay suffered by having to replace dead sisters.

There was no evidence that the death of a child in the family brings a divided family together in the storybook fashion.

Medical science has lessened but not eliminated the threat of the "intruder complex" in contemporary homes. More research on the relationship between bereavement and rejection is indicated by the severity of the reactions of these fifty-seven bereaved families.

THE ORPHANED AND THE HALF-ORPHANED

When the parent dies, the child is ordinarily able to take the loss without undue emotional upset and the natural grief is eased with the passing of time. The child seems to think of the parental death as a part of the historical process of being born, of living, aging and dying. No personal threat is involved as happens when a brother or sister dies. Among those who lost parents or a parent, a few individuals such as Somerset Maugham and Eleonora Duse felt that the loss of a parent created circumstances which made the rest of their childhood intolerable. In many instances the sudden new responsibility hastened the maturity of the child or enriched his life by making new experiences possible for him.

For generations children's books about orphans or half-orphans have been popular, and David Copperfield, Cosette, Cinderella, Anne of Green Gables, Rebecca of Sunnybrook Farm, Freckles, and whole families of half-orphans like the Careys and the Wiggses and the Moffats have won the hearts of youthful readers. There are doubtless many children who have secretly dreamed of being suddenly orphaned and catapulted into a new and challenging environment.

The orphaned among the Four Hundred are not disappointing to those who hold the storybook concept of the orphan. Among them are several whose lives become more exciting and challenging after they are orphaned. Orphaned Herbert Hoover is nostalgic about the days when he was boarded around with various welcoming aunts and uncles who vied for the pleasure of having him in their homes and would not let him be adopted by a spinster schoolteacher because they believed a boy needed to be reared in a home where there was a father- as well as a mother-figure. His first home, away from home (when half-orphaned), was on an Indian reservation where his uncle was employed as an agent. He and his cousins were the only white children in an Indian school. His last childhood home was with another uncle who was a doctor and helped him prepare for his college entrance examinations at Stanford.

Each of the three children in the Hoover family went to live with a different relative, but their feelings of responsibility for each other were not lessened. When the grandmother who had taken the young sister died, the brothers Herbert and Theodore set up a household and took care of their sister. Theodore gave up his schooling and worked as a linotype operator. Herbert, out of a job at the time, moved into the household and with him came a cousin with whom Herbert had lived on the Indian reservation. She was a sterling young woman who was a good cook and also had a knack of entertaining with Indian dialect stories. The four young people had a jolly time together.

The half-orphaned also have challenges and adventures which give them an opportunity for early maturity and resourcefulness.

When Wanda Gág, who was to be a successful illustrator and the author of popular children's books, was fifteen, her father, a lovable but unsuccessful artist, told her shortly before he died, "What Papa couldn't do, Wanda will have to finish." This meant becoming a famous artist and also helping to rear and support her six younger brothers and sisters.

The friendly neighbors in New Ulm, Minnesota, who gave the family food and money as well as good advice were inclined to believe that Wanda should give up any idea of education beyond the eighth grade and take a job as a clerk in a store. Art, they believed, was unreliable as a source of income.

In the Gág family there had always been parental pleasure in the children's absorption in every kind of creative activity, in painting, modeling and writing. Wanda would not give up her plans for schooling, although the family was on relief. She found it easy to get a full scholarship at an art school in Minneapolis.

Like the Hoover children, Wanda and her sisters and brothers maintained a warm cohesiveness, were cooperative and zealous for each other's welfare. This was also notably true of the Curie, Chamberlain and Flexner children. Widows in this study, of whom there were fifty-eight, seldom remarried. Four of the five who sought new mates separated from their husbands or divorced them.

There were twenty-six widowers among the parents in this survey, fourteen of whom are known to have remarried. Eleven of the fourteen stepmothers were praised by the to-be-eminent child in the family. One reason for the predominance of widows is the rather high incidence of fathers who are much older than their wives.

The fourteen fully orphaned children were commonly reared by grandmothers or uncles or aunts. Sibling relationships are close in these families. The orphaned and half-orphaned are frequently given sympathetic assistance by adults in the community, who do not have the same protective feelings for the children whose living father fails them.

THE ILLEGITIMATE CHILDREN

The man or woman born out of wedlock does not seek to advertise his illegitimacy, and may try to keep the details about his parentage from the press and curious public. The famous man tells of his boyhood delinquencies, and the famous woman tells how she was a homely, unpopular child. They may speak with good grace of being thought dull and describe their adjustment to poverty, physical handicaps or severe or neglectful parents. They do not dwell upon their illegitimacy. The writer born out of wedlock also seems to avoid that topic as a subject in his writings. Nevertheless, there seems to be no evidence that being born out of wedlock is an insurmountable barrier to either success or fame.

Some of the children were brought up with brothers and sisters in homes which were established in open unconventionality. These were Eva Perón, T. E. Lawrence, Toyohiko Kagawa and Paul Cézanne. Each of these knew his father intimately because he lived with the family as the head of the household.

Gordon Craig and Sarah Bernhardt were brought up in homes which were broken before the children were old enough to remember their fathers. Jack London, Booker T. Washington, Ramsay MacDonald and Sir Henry Stanley were not acknowledged by their fathers or supported by them.

Eva Perón, at the height of her popularity as the wife of the Argentinian dictator Juan Perón (who was also illegitimate), destroyed as many records as she could find which related to her birth. Her father, Juan Duarte, a man of modest means, maintained two establishments. Eva was the youngest of the five children in her father's second family. When he died, Eva was two and only the children were invited to the funeral. The mother, left unprovided for, soon found herself another protector. Eva, at fifteen, ran away from her turbulent home with an itinerant musician who abandoned her. She became a third-rate actress, but she had a talent for manipulating people and influencing events. She set up an extramarital establishment with a "mother's boy" whose father had deserted his mother and used her talent for intrigue to help him set up a dictatorship which lasted for many years.

In his late teens, T. E. Lawrence, soldier, writer and adventurer, ran away from his upper-middle-class home and enlisted as a private in the Royal Artillery. His discovery that he and his four brothers were the illegitimate offspring of their parents is thought to have been the reason for his flight from home. His gentleman father, who preferred to live on a very limited income rather than work, had left his wife and four daughters and run away with a governess who bore him five sons.

Despite her irregular status, the ex-governess was exceedingly pious and prim. She developed a distaste for women, who, she said, wasted time chattering, and she seldom permitted women visitors in the home. Her son, T. E. Lawrence, was correspondingly unable to relate to women, but was also rejecting of his parents, declared them both unfit to be parents and found his home intolerable. His oldest brother, a physician, declared their home was quite happy, and this was the appearance it gave to the community, which did not know of its legal status.

Toyohiko Kagawa, the social reformer and evangelist, was another child in a "second" household. His father, Denjiro Kagawa, a wealthy man with driving energy, was secretary to the Privy Council in Japan, was a cabinet member and the owner of a shipping company. Like many other men of his class, he took a mistress. His legal wife, Michi, he left on his farm with his scolding mother-in-law when he set up a second household for gentle and kindly Kame, a Geisha girl from Kobe, whom he purchased.

His first wife was chosen for him by his parents when he was fifteen and she was eight; he chose his mistress for himself and lived with her for twenty-five years. Five children were born to them, of whom Toyohiko was the youngest son.

When both of his parents died, four-year-old Toyohiko and his emotionally disturbed sister Ei were sent to be reared by his father's legal wife and his mother-in-law. Since he had been legally adopted, the women were obliged to give him a home and an education. Both women, especially the older, hated the two children and treated them badly.

Toyohiko, however, was sent to school, where his sympathies for all indigent and rejected persons led him to bring a dirty and diseased beggar into his room to live with him. When he was graduated, he moved into the slums and deliberately lived as the very poorest people lived. His book recounting his adventures made him a wealthy man; but he reserved only forty dollars a month for the use of himself, his wife and five children, and set up schools, hospitals and restaurants with the rest. Although he was affected by an eye disease contracted from the sick people among whom he lived, he retained a childlike gaiety and spontaneity. His wife, who was as interested as he in his work, carried on his institutions while he went to the United States to take a graduate degree at Princeton. He interested himself in world peace and was an internationalist.

Paul Cézanne, the painter, was born to parents who did not get around to making their relationship legal until their third child was born, when Paul was six. Since this was not an unusual circumstance in their community, Paul's illegitimacy does not seem to have affected him too much. The conflict in the home was between the business interests of the father and the great indifference of the son to the practical aspects of life.

Gordon Craig, son of Ellen Terry, resented the devotion of his mother to her career, which impelled her to separate from his father. He married at twenty and had a family which Ellen grumbled about to George Bernard Shaw. He was also the father of Deirdre, Isadora Duncan's daughter, who was tragically drowned with her brother. Professionally, he extended his architect father (whom he never knew), not his mother. Although he was given a chance to act when he was very young, he was never a good actor.

Sarah Bernhardt saw her father only twice and remembered him as a kindly, handsome man. He was Edouard Bernhardt, a well-to-do French law student who picked up the abandoned Dutch mistress of a French consular agent and set up housekeeping with her. When the affair was over, the child, Sarah, was sent to the country to be reared by the father's old nurse. He also settled a small income on his daughter in his will. Since he died while she was still very young, he did not live to protect Sarah from the neglect and abuse of the nurse.

Julie Bernhardt, Sarah's mother, became a famous courtesan of Paris, as did Julie's sister, Rosine. The two women, who were well known in fashionable circles, were kept in luxury by a series of influential and wealthy men. Two other daughters were born to Julie, who had an affection for only one of her offspring, the middle daughter, Jeanne. Sarah she disliked.

Kindly Aunt Rosine visited Sarah and was appalled by the child's unhappiness. Sarah was taken from her father's old nurse and sent to a convent school where she kicked and hit any nun or child who touched her — even inadvertently. When she was expelled for the third time from her school the wealthy Duc de Morny, her mother's patron, sent her to be trained as an actress.

Jack London, American novelist, was never acknowledged by his father (who Irving Stone is convinced was the astrologer W. H. Cheney). It was not Cheney but a San Francisco working-man with a kindly disposition, John London, who assumed the responsibility of being a father to the eight-month-old infant and gave him his name.

When his wife died, John London was forlorn and visited a medium in an attempt to communicate with her. His two young daughters had been temporarily placed in a home, and he was distraught and lonely. He soon found himself married to the medium, Flora Wellman, a homely, wiry woman, a rejecting mother and a problem wife. It was her new stepdaughter, eight-year-old Eliza London, who shooed the flies from the sleeping baby who was her "new brother" and became a mother to him. A friendly Negro woman in the neighborhood was also a mother-figure to Jack. John London, however, was a patient and kindly foster father.

In a letter to Jack London in which he denied paternity, Cheney's writing of the name "Jack London" could not be distinguished from Jack's own signature. Jack London's style of writing was much like that of his father, according to Stone, who has examined the documents. Jack London resembled W. H. Cheney in appearance — and both were distinctive in appearance.

Both Flora Wellman and W. H. Cheney were well educated. Flora left her proper, well-to-do home, when she was twenty-five, to become a medium and a wanderer. The family she deserted always blamed a fever, which took her hair and forced her to wear a wig, for a personality change which made her repudiate her home and parents. Although she paid little attention to her son, it was she who started him writing by suggesting that he enter a writing contest held by a local newspaper.

Ramsay MacDonald, who was to be a prime minister of England, was reared by his grandmother, a woman of rare beauty with a habit of falling into trances during which she experienced heavenly visitations. The boy lived with her in a simple cottage. His mother was a servant girl, his father unknown. MacDonald wrote a moving essay praising his village schoolmaster, who was as close as a father to him and whose teaching methods were truly commendable.

Booker T. Washington, born to a loving and ambitious slave mother, had no special feelings about not knowing who his father was, because the other boys he knew were also likely not to have fathers. The rumor was that his father was a white man on an adjoining plantation, but he did not know. His name he chose for himself when he found the teacher expected him to be more than "Booker."

Sir Henry M. Stanley, when he found Livingstone, may have been making a search for a father-figure. The newspapers were extremely critical and unfair to him when they discovered that he had tried to conceal his illegitimacy and workhouse origins. They also professed to disbelieve his African accounts, and he was accused of having been cruel to the natives.

Illegitimacy, while it may not enhance success, does not seem to inhibit its expression.* What does seem to be inhibited is eminence among the foundlings, or adopted children who are kept unaware of their natural parentage. Because of the higher death rate in the times in which the Four Hundred lived, there were more orphaned children. Many children, unnamed, must have been left on institutional doorsteps. The lack of foundlings or adopted babies among the Four Hundred raises the question as to the reason for the absence of unusual achievement among children who never knew who their parents were.

It seems reasonable to assume that both the parent and child in the foster home would find it safer to stay within conventional boundaries and to keep goals and aspirations sensible and fairly simple. A tendency to be creative or experimental in the home where the child's genetic background is unknown could be threatening and confusing. A deliberate toning down of aspirations may result and would account for the lack of eminence among foundlings and adopted or foster children. Approximately one child in twenty in the United States today is born out of wedlock; and we may be wasting a tremendous potential in many

*Leonardo da Vinci is only one of the famous illegitimate children.

of these children by lowering our expectations from them. Guidance for adoptive parents who are given a child with ability seems especially necessary. The modern Scandinavian attitude which does not stigmatize the illegitimate child and more often leaves him with his mother may make for a better use of talent. A survey of the reactions of adults to having been adopted might be illuminating.

Adoptive parents chosen by professional agencies are likely to be people who are stable economically and emotionally. On this basis many of the eccentric and failure-prone parents under survey would not have been eligible.

The Fearful Boys and Those Who Were Accident-Prone

Charles A. Lindbergh was subject to terrific nightmares about falling off a roof or precipice, but met his fears head-on in daylight. He frightened a playmate by announcing that he intended to jump from a high tree, and only his mother's command deterred him. While he was in high school, he raced his motorcycle along the bank of a stream until the local police, hesitating to bring legal pressure on the son of an eminent politician, plowed up the area so that he could not endanger himself in this particular way.

He had few interests which were not either mechanical or in some way connected with proving his lack of fear. He sat through his classes without speaking unless he was called upon and made mediocre grades. He never wore a white shirt, never dressed up to please the girls. He took no part in sports, never went hunting or fishing or skating with the boys.

His mother, a silent, dour woman, estranged from her husband, never encouraged him to play with other children. To her husband, Senator C. A. Lindbergh, being stoic under danger or pain was the true test of manhood. Senator Lindbergh was proud of his son when he was able to withstand the physical rigors of a thirty-day camping trip in undeveloped country where the mosquitoes and black flies tested their endurance. He told his son about an exhausting thirty-mile walk he had taken with his own father, who was too proud to admit he did not have train fare home from the city after he paid his taxes and debts in full.

When Senator Lindbergh underwent abdominal surgery, he refused an anesthetic, and although the ordeal lasted more than an hour he never gritted his teeth and only once gripped the hand of a friend who sat beside him — during the few seconds when the surgeon's knife pierced the abdominal cavity. During the operation he talked with the friend, a fellow senator, about international banking. The boy who had nightmares about falling and whose father valued the ability to face danger and death so highly was the Charles A. Lindbergh, Jr., who flew the ocean alone in a flimsy plane. His preparation had been a sleepless, roistering night; his food, a few sandwiches.

There were other boys who also had a need to face their fears. The bullfighter Manolete, a widow's only son, was a timid, fearful boy who was teased because he clung to his mother. Although he was famous for facing death so calmly, he was always frightened in the ring and did not enjoy his skirmishes with death. Robert Peary, the explorer, also the only son of a widow, clung to her and stayed in his yard to evade the boys who called him "Skinny" and teased him about his fearfulness.

During his childhood, Vilhjalmur Stefansson was not robust and was called "Softy" by his classmates. He spent hours by himself, sailing a toy boat in a tub of water. Fridtjof Nansen was not a fearful boy, but he was incurably absent-minded and accident-prone. He set himself on fire at three, cut his forehead on the ice at four, caught a fishhook in his lower lip and had to have it cut out with a razor. He peppered his face with gunpowder setting off a homemade cannon, daydreamed and nearly broke his neck on his first ski-jump. He broke both of his skis in a contest in which his brother took first prize. Admiral Richard E. Byrd was also accident-prone, injured his right leg three times, and was invalided out of the Navy.

Gandhi was fearful of snakes and of the dark, and was also fearful that his child-wife, Kasturbai, would discover his weakness. James Joyce was terrified by thunderstorms; he was also afraid of dogs and was bitten twice by them. Hemingway was among the most accident-prone, had a shattered nose and damaged eyesight at fourteen, and later had 227 steel splinters in his right leg, shot wounds in both feet and both hands and both knees, six severe head injuries, six broken ribs, ten brain concussions.

SPEECH PROBLEMS

Emile Zola, Churchill, Proust, and Peary lisped. Somerset Maugham, Arnold Bennett, Aneurin Bevan, Thomas Wolfe, and Marc Chagall were stammerers.

Arshile Gorki experienced an emotional shock which set him talking. The father of Arshile Gorki deserted the family and the five-year-old boy stopped talking. A tutor pretended to leap from a cliff and the boy called out in dismay. The shock restored his speech.

Psychiatrists have noted that an injury to a limb frequently precedes stammering. Arnold Bennett began stammering after he caught his hand in a mangle.

Both Churchill and Bevan conquered their speech problems by dint of practice and patience. Churchill planned talks in which the terminal "s" was eliminated, memorized his speeches and spoke from notes, taking infinite pains with every detail. A specialist whom he visited while he was in Sandhurst told him that only his own determination could help him.

Marc Chagall began to stammer in a secondary school where he was discriminated against by a rejecting teacher.

THE DELINQUENT

Studies of gifted children indicate that the likelihood of their becoming delinquent to the point of being apprehended is very slight. They are commonly law-abiding and have an early sensitivity for the rights and privileges of others. Although this is also true of the Four Hundred, they cannot be categorized as a sedentary, inactive group of boys and girls. A few ran away from home, several were school truants, or were expelled for being rude to the teacher. However, seven found themselves in jail during their adolescence.

Jazz trumpeter Louis Armstrong is the only member of the Four Hundred who was committed to an institution for delinquent boys. This neglected boy, whose father had deserted the family and whose mother was "out on the town," was picked up for firing blank cartridges into the air from his stepfather's revolver. He found life rewarding at the school to which he was sentenced. In his autobiography he says, "The place was more like a health center or a boarding school than a boys' jail. All in all I am very proud of the days I spent at the Colored Waifs Home for Boys" in New Orleans. It was there that he was taught to play an instrument and became a bandleader.

Another boy sent to jail was neither fortunate nor contented. George Robert Gissing, English novelist, served a short prison term for stealing money from the lockers of his well-to-do classmates to buy a sewing machine for a young prostitute who had convinced him she wished to change her occupation. This tenderness for the underprivileged or oppressed is common among exceptionally intelligent children, as Leta Hollingworth has noted in *Children Above 180 I.Q.* Gissing was discovered, disgraced, served his term and never went back to school — which was unfortunate, because he was always a scholar without enough companionship with other scholars. His entire career was stormy and tragic.

David Dubinsky at fifteen was made assistant secretary of his baker's union, despite the fact that he was an employer's son. He was a scholar who could read and write and keep books, while most of the other workers were illiterate. David was arrested and spent two weeks in jail; but his father, still pleased with his son's aggressiveness and his loyalty to his cause, bribed the jailer and got him out. As we have seen, David Ben Gurion was also arrested when he was an adolescent, and his father was also pleased to come to the rescue of the son, who had spoken at a Zionist street meeting in Warsaw.

Brendan Behan, Irish playwright, at age sixteen was discovered in Liverpool near the shipyards carrying a suitcase full of high explosives. He was jailed as an Irish terrorist and sent to an English reform school which he describes in his riotous and memorable *Borstal Boy*. Although his mother worked in Maude Gonne's house and his uncle was an intimate of Yeats, he came from a family of opinionative housepainters. Brendan had been expelled from the Christian Brothers School earlier in his career.

William Osler, on the occasion when he harassed the matron at his school, spent three days in jail.

Manuel Quezon was locked in his school building for fifteen days because he clubbed and injured a corporal of the civil guard who had been molesting young girls but had escaped punishment because his official position gave him immunity. His parents were supportive and Manuel was a local hero.

If William Randolph Hearst, American newspaper editor, had not come from a fabulously wealthy family, he might have been sentenced for a much longer period to a school for delinquent boys than was the ebullient Louis Armstrong. When Hearst shot toy darts into the ceiling of a Paris hotel and tried to pull them out again, the whole ceiling, sculptured cupids and all, fell. "My father," he says casually in his autobiography, "had to buy them a new hotel." He also had a penchant for playing with fire and water in hotels.

The period during which his father was a business failure did not last long. During the panic of 1874, George Hearst suffered financial reverses that forced the family to sell its chalet, its horses, carriages and other movables. The parents were reduced to boarding out with old friends, and the eleven-year-old "Billy Buster" was farmed out on his grandfather's ranch. Within the year, however, the father was a millionaire again.

No boy was more extravagantly indulged. When the lad was to be taken to Europe for a holiday, his farewell party lasted for ten days, but money did not bring him friends. When he was painfully rejected at school, he begged his parents not to be sent to school overdressed and chauffeur-driven, asked for patches to be sewed on his clothes, but they were unmoved by his distress and continued to shower him with gold coins and extravagant toys. The elderly husband and his young wife disliked each other but vied in indulging their only son.

His luxurious quarters at Harvard were the nightly site of beer parties, oyster suppers and bull sessions. He was suspended for six months when he celebrated the Democratic victory of 1884 by hiring several bands to parade through the yard, having fireworks set off in all directions, and buying wagonloads of beer for all the student body. He was expelled permanently in the middle of his senior year for sending his professors chamber pots decorated with their names and photographs.

William Randolph Hearst was not the only member of the Four Hundred who was expelled from school for defiance of his teachers. Salvador Dali was expelled when he refused to allow teachers whom he considered less skilled than he to judge his art work. Erich Kleiber was dismissed for impudence and for showing his lack of respect for his school. Negley Farson was expelled when he helped to throw a tattling teacher into an Andover duck pond.

The world might have lost a great physicist if Enrico Fermi had been expelled when he led a stink-bomb attack on the faculty of his secondary school, the Reale Normale of Pisa. Enrico was a member of the Anti-Neighbor Society, whose purpose was to play pranks on the other students. As a symbol of their membership they carried red or yellow painted padlocks in their pockets. While one member of the society engaged a victim in conversation, the other slipped the shackle through the victim's clothes and locked him in his suit or topcoat. They set pails of water on the tops of doors left ajar. They engaged in make-believe duels defending the honor of girls who were not in the slightest danger of losing it. They had water fights on the roof. They dubbed a homely girl May Queen, much to her embarrassment. These pranks went unheeded, but the stink-bomb attack on the faculty almost brought dismissal. It was only because of the recommendation of a teacher who recognized Fermi's rare ability that he was not expelled. Both he and his best friend, Rasetti, who were the ringleaders in this mischief, were bored and restive because of the inadequate challenge to their ability in the classroom.

Ignace Jan Paderewski was a runaway and a school rebel and

was expelled. Joseph Stalin was expelled for his political activities. Leon Trotsky was suspended for a time from his secondary school when he was falsely accused of being a ringleader when the class "made a concert" for the teacher. A "concert" was a howling noise, made with the lips closed, which marked the teacher's footsteps as he walked. Jealousy of Trotsky's status as top boy in the class made another boy name him as a ringleader when he was merely a participant. William Osler was expelled for rudeness and rebellion.

Huey Long was not suspended when he organized a group of boys into a gang and demanded obedience from the other students. Instead, he succeeded in having a principal fired who tried to curb him. Ivar Kreuger, the Match King and speculator, was a solitary, elfish boy, odd in appearance, who crawled through the school windows, read the teacher's records, and sold the information gained to the other students. His hobby, at which he was unexcelled, was cheating. Mussolini's parents had to send him away from his home town to find a school which could manage him.

Buffalo Bill Cody left school and joined a wagon train because he seriously injured another student who tore up the playhouse Bill was making in the schoolyard with a girl. Young Cody feared the boy's retaliation. Orphaned Ernest Bevin ran away from the farm where he worked, after forcing the farmer to hide in a closet to escape the tool Ernest was brandishing. Jack London was an oyster pirate. Sun Yat-Sen overturned religious shrines in his community after he became a Christian. Chiang Kai-shek was cuffed about by his male relatives for his mischievous ways, at eighteen became abusive to local dignitaries in a restaurant. He cut off his pigtail to show his defiance of the old-fashioned ways when he believed he had gained entrance to a school in Japan. When he was not admitted, he was left short-haired and vulnerable to ridicule.

Noel Coward was a school truant. The Barrymore brothers, Lionel and John, were incorrigible in their behavior at school and were exceedingly poor students. When John was admitted to preparatory school at Seton Hall, New Jersey, a priest asked him to demonstrate his ability as an athlete on bars in the gymnasium.

Liquor, playing cards and a pair of "brass knucks" fell from the boy's pocket.

Ramon Magsaysay, of the Philippines, was often a truant in elementary school and once took his father's gun and went hunting for a week. John R. Mott, founder of the YMCA, was spanked for running down the tracks in front of railroad trains. He and his friends took bolts off freight cars and hubs off farm wagons and buggies. Richard Byrd once went spelunking and found the source of a lost river which was said to run under a cave. He went to sleep there, and was discovered hours later after friends and neighbors had searched the countryside for him. He and his brothers once dug a five-foot trench across a beautiful lawn as part of war games they were playing.

Grover Cleveland, who heard his father preach twice each Sunday, was annoyed when his Latin teacher opened class with a long prayer. While the other students sat with devoutly bowed heads, he and his friend threw their books out the window and stealthily followed them.

Will Rogers was incorrigible at school and ran away from home. Eddie Cantor calls himself a liar, truant, pilferer from pushcarts and a street fighter. He once had his head cracked open in a gang fight, and although an obliging druggist sewed it up, the wound became infected and an operation was performed to save his life. Irvin S. Cobb was known as the naughtiest small boy in Paducah, Kentucky, and in his autobiography professed an inability to pass a pile of shingles without backing up to something — since he had been spanked so often with shingles.

Orville Wright was suspended from his sixth-grade class in Richmond, Indiana, because he was mischievous, but his tolerant parents did not force him to return to school, since they were planning to move in a few months.

Girls were no less troublesome than the boys. Sarah Bernhardt was expelled three times: for imitating a bishop, for throwing stones at the Royal Dragoons and finally for climbing over a wall to stay with a young soldier until long after dark. Gertrude Atherton was an incorrigible child. Ernestine Schumann-Heink was a school truant. Eleonora Duse, Katherine Mansfield, Isadora Duncan and Sarah Bernhardt were in their twenties when they experienced extramarital pregnancies. (One boy, Artur Schnabel, is recorded as having an illegitimate daughter born when Artur was seventeen.)

The concept of the gifted and promising child as a bookworm cloistered in the library is not upheld by the Four Hundred. Although they almost all read omnivorously, they had other strong interests. Among equally talented and promising boys and girls today there are probably many who are being shunted into unproductive and unchallenging careers because they have been involved in similar escapades. It is the mother-smothered and mother-dominated who are the least likely to be involved in serious childhood mischief. A project to visit schools for the delinquent to pick out the hungry readers and children with special talents and a constructive program for such boys and girls should interest some adventurous, inquisitive foundation executive.

PSYCHOSIS IS RARE IN THE HOMES WHICH REAR EMINENT CHILDREN

There are very few men and women reared in the homes which cradle eminence who are institutionalized as a result of mental illness. Nor are there accounts of the home treatment or isolation of deranged persons. Since being psychotic is time consuming and incapacitating, perhaps this is not surprising. However, what seems to be the equally low incidence of mental illness among the parents, brothers and sisters — and possibly even among the offspring — of the Four Hundred is an unexpected finding which bears examination.

Among the parents there were two fathers and two mothers who were institutionalized for disorders not connected with injury or terminal illness. Four men among the Four Hundred were institutionalized and one eminent woman was under professional treatment in an institution for several years. Two brothers and two sisters of the famous were said to be mentally ill.

One in ten persons living in the United States today can expect to be a patient at a mental hospital at some time during his life, according to United States Public Health Service estimates. Half of all hospital beds in the United States are occupied by the mentally ill, most of the younger of whom are diagnosed as schizophrenic. These are patients whose behavior makes it impossible for them to participate in the community or whose communities lack tolerance for their bizarre or withdrawn behavior. The cause of this condition is not understood, but most authorities believe that genetic, biochemical and social factors may all play a significant role. As far as can be determined, schizophrenia is an international phenomenon. The United States and Russia, for example, find about the same percentage of schizophrenics among their populations. If it is true that the families cradling eminence produce less than their share of incapacitating psychotic disorders, speculation as to the reasons for this immunity may be indicated. The limitations of the biographical method, however, make it inadvisable to do more than sort out the psychotics from the larger group.

Maurice Barrymore, popular and successful actor, who was the father of three of the Four Hundred, was discovered sitting on the cast iron steps of the West Thirtieth Street Station in New York City staring into space. A friend saw him there, coaxed him into a taxi and took him to Bellevue. Maurice went docilely, talking all the while about his favorite song, "The Garden of Sleep." He was soon transferred to a private hospital, where he spent several years writing an endless novel which consisted of only one line repeated over and over, "It was a lovely day in June."

"Lily Hawley," Charlie Chaplin's mother, was out of touch with reality for many years and was first hospitalized when her son was eight; but she retained her beauty, her charming manner and a youthful appearance for many years. Max Eastman tells in *Great Companions* of a visit with her at the time when her eminent son brought her from England to an apartment in Hollywood. She had been warned about behaving properly when she went through customs and was repentant when she forgot and hailed the customs officer as "Jesus Christ." She tried to conceal her error by saying quickly, "I mean by that, sir, that when I looked into your eyes, I realized that notwithstanding the blue cap, that you have a gentle and spiritual nature."

When she was brought to the apartment, she put on a phonograph record and danced for Max Eastman, pausing between dips and twirls to sympathize with a caged bird in the room.

In their illness these two parents retained evidences of the love for learning and the striving to achieve which is so much a part of the majority of the parents.

Lafcadio Hearn's mother died in a mental institution in Malta. Her first breakdown came after the birth of her second son in England. She was grimly silent, then wildly violent, in the English home which received her so coldly. When she was sent back to her native country by her rejecting husband, she did not recover.

Elliott Paul was in his teens before his mother felt she could tell him that his father died in an insane asylum before Elliott was four years old. Elliott Paul was twenty-eight when he wrote his first novel. The opening scene described his own father, who was on his knees with other men trying to quiet him. The mother in the story was in tears as a cold, black wagon drove up to the house and strange men in white coats took the sick man away. Strips of torn sheeting were used to bind the father's hands and feet.

When the mother, who had never described the scene to her son, read his description she was shocked and dismayed by its brutal accuracy. She had not thought that a three-year-old could remember so much, not even such a precocious child as Elliott. When the father was taken away, the mother turned to the son for comfort and companionship. Before he was six, she had taught him most of what children were supposed to learn in grammar school. No fear of overtaxing the child's mind deterred her, and Elliott was always grateful to her for her teaching because he was permitted to skip grades. He hated school, found it an "unjust imprisonment for offenses he had not yet committed." Since the father died soon after being admitted to the hospital, it is possible that his insanity was organic rather than functional.

There are other parents whose breakdown was connected with a terminal illness. The father of Friedrich Nietzsche is said by his daughter to have fallen down a flight of stairs and injured his head several months before his suddenly disturbed and painful days were cut short by death. Since the son always feared inheriting his father's illness, the sister's blow-on-the-head theory can be questioned. The Nietzsche family, highly opinionative, is not always in agreement.

Lord Randolph Churchill had a first paralytic attack when he was thirty-two. His speech and gait were affected and he had periods of depression and elation. His son, Winston Churchill, tells of the small brain hemorrhages which preceded his father's death, of the periods of coma, and of the added impairment after each attack. His illness did not bring him closer to his son, who was icily repulsed when he volunteered to be his father's secretary. During his lifetime, Lord Randolph spoke at length with his oldest son only four times. During the fourth conversation the father cautioned the son about not believing all that he heard about his father and spoke pathetically of his "enemies."

The father's untimely death left the son resolved to repeat the life of his father and to do him honor by succeeding where the father had failed because of his illness and early death. He wrote a two-volume biography of Lord Randolph, adopted his father's views, sought out his father's friends, rejected his father's opponents, memorized his father's speeches and told his friends that he expected to die at forty-six as his father had done.

When he abandoned some of his father's political beliefs, he was not able to work on the biography for a considerable period and resorted to various rationalizations to justify himself in his own eyes. As he matured, he was able to think of himself as a separate and whole individual apart from his father. To his own children he was a willing and delightful companion.

There are many parents who are eccentric, neurotic, or are incapacitated by psychosomatic disorders. The mothers of Fritz Kreisler and Arthur Koestler had painful illnesses which were observed but not treated by Freud. Thomas Beecham's wealthy mother used to leave home periodically because of her "nerves." Sir Thomas Beecham and his sister Emily as young adults successfully championed their mother's cause when her unfaithful husband tried to have her hospitalized for mental illness. Hart Crane's mother suffered a nervous collapse during a period of conflict with her husband. David Daiches's mother had a post-partum breakdown but recovered.

Some of the fathers also display neurosis or eccentricity. There are fathers who are too engrossed in self-initiated, unprofitable learning projects to make a living for their families and who are regarded as exceptionally "odd" by their contemporaries. There are fathers who cannot keep their waistcoats buttoned straight, fathers who are perpetually on a soapbox, fathers who walk at night to avoid having to speak to their neighbors. Among the Four Hundred, fathers tend to be ebullient, grandiose, imaginative and failure-prone, but they are not often sent to mental institutions.

The children in the homes under survey can perhaps be emotionally comfortable among their own misadventures because nothing they do will be worse than something their fathers have already done. Or if the father is stable and a pillar in the community, then the mother may provide the neighbors with cause to speak of her inexplicable behavior. One very real characteristic of the families under survey is that they are unconcerned about their public image.

Vaslav Nijinsky, the dancer, was rejected so severely by his classmates who were also training for the Russian Imperial Ballet that the student displaced as the top boy, Ronzai, felt free to play a trick on Vaslav that nearly killed him. The boys were prone to play sadistic tricks on each other after hours at the boarding school. They lashed at each other with whips, tried to tear off each other's clothes with buttonhooks. Ronzai was angry at Vaslav because when he dared the Polish boy to hit him with a big India rubber ball at thirty paces, Vaslav did so, knocked out four of Ronzai's teeth and bloodied his nose.

Ronzai retaliated by raising the standard on a heavy music stand, over which the boys were jumping, several inches above Vaslav's known limit and then spreading soap flakes on the floor. Vaslav fell heavily and was not expected to live. His head was terribly injured, his chest was crushed. The incident shocked the adult ballet dancers of Moscow, who filled the young student's room with flowers. Vaslav's mother wept by his bedside alone. Vaslav's father, an unreliable fellow who appeared infrequently with fine presents and little money for food, was with his own dance troupe.

After months of convalescence Vaslav had to learn to walk again, as if he were an infant. During this period one of the boys in his class, a wealthy boy from an aristocratic family, felt impelled to make friends with the persecuted Polish boy with whom the other boys had not been willing to sit in class, and whom they had excluded from all their games. It was he who helped Vaslav prepare a party, a real feast with sausages and sweets, upon which the affectionate mother spent her last coin. Although every boy in the class had accepted the invitation, even the offending Ronzai, no one came. Vaslav and his mother both wept bitterly. Vaslav, according to his wife, was always a mother's boy, her most tender, affectionate, faithful child.

Vaslav had little companionship from his father, himself a ballet dancer who had not succeeded in accordance with his ability on account of his Polish origin. Vaslav did not receive the whole attention of his mother because she was preoccupied with his oldest brother, who was mentally ill, and had given up her own dancing career to look after him. At the height of his own career Vaslav Nijinsky became schizophrenic and was hospitalized for many years.

Rudolph Hess, Nazi leader who fled to England, puzzled the psychiatrists who examined him because they had reason to suspect that his loss of memory and fear of being poisoned might be feigned. His life-pattern, regardless of diagnosis, resembled that of other mother-smothered, father-hating boys. The Hess children dared not play in the house when their irascible father was at home. As an adult, Hess continued to identify with his mother, adopted her unusual ideas about food, the occult, and the efficacy of nature cures. Brutal men frightened him, controversy dismayed him; he was kind to insects, animals and older women. The didactic, punctilious man was called the "Brown Mouse" by his associates, and is said to have married in order to quell rumors concerning his tendencies to inversion.

The exception among those who were hospitalized is Van Wyck Brooks, whose home life as a child is described as relatively untroubled and whose parents were not seen by him as over-possessive. Brooks describes himself as a hyperesthetic, accelerated boy who was closer to adults than to his peers. He says little about his classroom experiences until he reached Harvard, which met many of his needs. He says much more about a year spent abroad when he was thirteen with a tutor whom he liked. Like Clara Barton, who was also hospitalized, the work which brought him the widest fame was done after his hospitalization. In 1931, after four years passed in mental hospitals, he came out into a new era dazed, with a feeling of youth, and with a hard ball of panic in his stomach which was never entirely to disappear. Prior to his period of incapacitating depression he was deeply concerned with what he considered the failure of the United States to provide a background for genius. During his hospitalization he wrote articles for magazines and for a weekly newspaper.

The lack of functional illness among the Four Hundred cannot be attributed to the absence of early symptoms thought to indicate the onset of mental illness. Albert Schweitzer used to laugh aloud in the classroom without apparent cause. Albert Einstein went about chanting to himself hymns he dedicated to his self-created deity. Edison set fire to a barn and smashed eggs by sitting on them to hatch them. Eleanor Roosevelt lived in fantasy as the mistress of her dead father's household. Stanley Baldwin nursed a grudge against his headmaster to such an extent that he spoiled his secondary-school and college years for himself. He resented being flogged before the student body for being caught with ordinary schoolboy pornography in his possession. Salvador Dali waited until his classmates, with whom he had no satisfying contacts, were watching, then leaped from the top of the stairs to attract their attention. Nasser tried to kill himself when he was six; Maxim Gorky almost did so at nineteen. Among the Four Hundred there are dozens of withdrawn, hyperactive, overaggressive, moody, easily depressed children.

Nor do the Four Hundred escape being erratic or neurotic as adults. They seem to be subject to depression, especially in middle life. Many have periods of prolonged depression and "nervous exhaustion" which take them from their work at times. Paderewski turned to farming at one period in his life because he could not bear to play the piano. Chevalier, another boy who was extremely close to his mother and could not relate to women with any depth of affection, suddenly found himself unable to memorize his lines and required a prolonged rest cure and treatment. He married the girl who helped him recover, but found her overpossessive when he was well again. Rachmaninoff required hypnotic treatment periodically to pull him out of his depressions.

Gustav Regler, while a young soldier in the German army, was overcome by carbon monoxide poisoning while recuperating in a field hospital. Thought incurably ill, he was sent back to Germany to a mental hospital, where for a time he was unable to speak. During periods of acute disturbance, however, he spoke freely and recovered with the help of a Dr. Schomberg, who had similar attitudes to those held by Gustav's pacifist father. During his hospitalization Gustav, still in late adolescence, spent his recuperative period reorganizing his beliefs about religion and society. The doctor let him go reluctantly, saying, "Only one part of you despises war. I have read your diary [Regler had read Rilke on the battlefield]. You will volunteer for other wars as senseless as this one."[1]

Once the effects of being gassed had passed, Regler did not break down again, despite repeated involvements in various traumatic situations.

Maurice Ravel died in surgery during a brain operation calculated to cure the aphasia which made him unable to work. There were also those who died mentally ill as a result of being syphilitic: Toulouse-Lautrec and Nietzsche. While institutionalized Nietzsche continued his writing.

The small number of psychotics among the families cannot be easily attributed to willful concealment. When an individual becomes interesting enough to the public to be the subject of a book-length biography, such concealment is improbable. Mental deficiency is also an undesirable condition, and there are several references to mental deficiency among the family members. Since individuals thought deficient are frequently found to be mentally ill rather than mentally retarded, there may be family members who should have been regarded as psychotic instead of deficient. The references to them as deficient, however, indicates a certain honesty in reporting and suggests that psychotic behavior is also honestly reported.

Pearl Buck has contributed a valuable account of her own adjustment to a mentally deficient daughter. Mary Austin, another woman novelist, had a mentally deficient daughter. William Beveridge, Wilfred Grenfell, and William Dean Howells had small brothers who became retarded and uncontrollable after illnesses. Sigmund Freud had a cousin who was a hydrocephalic imbecile, two other cousins who became insane, and another who was epileptic. Gertrude Stein had two defective siblings.

It is the whole family, rather than the one child who becomes eminent, who seem to share a freedom from psychosis.* Ony five of the brothers and sisters in these prolific families are described as mentally ill: the brother of Vaslav Nijinsky, the sisters of Kagawa and of Olive Schreiner, and Dr. Dean Robinson, brilliant brother of the poet Edwin Arlington Robinson. In the last instance drug addiction was a contributing factor in the mental illness. Jean, spinster schoolteacher, sister of Robert Frost, became mentally ill, according to her brother, as a reaction to the outbreak of war.

The primary function of this survey, after all, is not to interpret behavior but to catalogue types of behavior. The families in which eminent persons of the twentieth century were reared, as we have said, have a great love for learning, strong physical and achievement drives, and are highly opinionative. They are also observed to have few psychotics among them.

It can therefore be suggested — but by no means proved — that these factors may have some role in producing a climate which

---

*Among descendents of the Four Hundred three instances of mental illness were noted: Lucia, daughter of James Joyce; Albert Einstein, Jr.; and a child born to Sigrid Undset, whose stepchild was also mentally ill.

helps to keep the family members from losing touch with reality and from a withdrawal from society which takes them to the mental hospital. Perhaps they simply do not have time to be mentally ill. The intensity of the drive toward a goal may be too compelling to leave time for the individual to nurse his anxieties to the breaking point.

There are comparatively few mental breakdowns in a country which is being invaded. Catatonics in stuporous withdrawal on a hospital ship have been known to come into quick touch with reality and try to save themselves in an intelligent fashion when the ship is bombed. Milton H. Erikson, psychiatrist, tells of a fire in a hospital where a patient who had been catatonic for years took the keys from a frightened attendant and efficiently engineered the evacuation of the ward. After the fire he returned the keys to the attendant and went back into his stupor. Can it be possible that becoming famous may be comparable to being in a perpetual crisis?

Suicide and depression are seen to be more of a threat to the eminent than is psychosis. That this is not irrelevant or accidental is evidenced by the findings of the Terman study that the fifteen suicides among the one thousand intellectually gifted men and women now in middle life is a slightly higher rate than is found in the general population.

Among the Four Hundred there have been, to date, eight suicides: Jack London, Virginia Woolf, Stefan Zweig, Paul Goebbels, Vachel Lindsay, Arshile Gorki, Ivar Kreuger, and Robert La Follette, Jr. The manner of the violent deaths of Jan Masaryk, Hart Crane, Ernest Hemingway, and Adolf Hitler are not fully agreed upon. There are already more suicides than instances of psychosis among the Four Hundred, which is the reverse of the relationship of suicide to psychosis in populations generally. There are many references to periods of acute depression in the biographies and autobiographies of eminent men and women.

There is no way of determining whether the Four Hundred had fewer or more environmental handicaps than did most persons in their times and communities. It is fairly evident, however, that almost any conceivable handicap has been successfully overcome by some eminent person. In many instances the handicaps are considered by those who experience them to have been motivating factors in their achievements. This does not mean that other individuals may not "break" under similar stress. Both parents and children in the families of the Four Hundred are seemingly protected from incapacitating mental illness. This protection may possibly be associated with their physical resilience and an all-consuming concentration on a chosen task.

[10]

Dislike of School and Schoolteachers

> . . . his back
> Slumped to the old half-cringe, his hands fell slack,
> A big boy's arm went around him — and a twist,
> Sent shattering pain along his tortured wrist.
> As a voice cried, a bloated voice and fat,
> "Why it's Miss Nancy. Come along you rat!"
> — STEPHEN VINCENT BENÉT,
> *Going Back to School*

THREE OUT OF FIVE of the Four Hundred had serious school problems. In order of importance, their dissatisfactions were: with the curriculum; with dull, irrational or cruel teachers; with other students who bullied, ignored, or bored them; and with school failure. In general, it is the totality of the school situation with which they are concerned, and they seldom have one clear-cut, isolated complaint.

Tutors are accepted with better grace than is the classroom teacher, for the tutor has good personal communication with the student and can adapt to his varying levels of attainment in a more realistic fashion. Boys and girls who are tutored by parents are usually grateful and responsive. Grandparents, friends of the family, and literate men and women of the community who develop a special interest in an inquiring youngster are well accepted. Librarians often fill a useful function. The school paper, the debating society, the peer group of intellectuals with whom the late adolescent frequently consorts, the theater, the printing shop, books which are self-discovered, the parental dinner table with its highly articulate guests, the parental library or studio are all given precedence over the classroom as a source of learning and insight.

Rejection of the classroom is an international phenomenon and has little to do with whether the schools are public or private, secular or clerical, or with the philosophy of teaching employed in the various schools.

Rabindranath Tagore, of India, whose parents were wealthy and literate and highly opinionative, says that it was fortunate that he ended his school life at thirteen, because he could not have endured the unbearable torture of school for a longer period. In an autobiographical sketch he declares:

According to the school, life is perfect when it allows itself to be treated as dead, to be cut into symmetrical conveniences. And this was the cause of my suffering in school. . . . I was fortunate enough to extricate myself before insensibility set in.[1]

Thomas Mann, who also came from a well-to-do and literate home, described in his memoirs a school experience which was "stagnating and unsatisfactory."

Ernest Jones, of England, a beloved only son reared in a supportive, comfortable, upper-class home, found his secondary school a preparation for helping him to understand the abuses in Nazi concentration camps. Victims in his school were lowered headfirst into latrines. A favorite sport was to lay a boy on his back, lie across him face downward and get six or seven others to add to the weight by doing the same. The only way the victim could escape was to hurt one of his tormentors in a vital part.

Leon Trotsky, of Russia, says in his autobiography, "The percentage of freaks among people in general is high, but it is especially high among teachers." He proceeds to prove the point by describing in minute detail several of his instructors.

A teacher shook thirteen-year-old Edward Grieg and shouted at him when he found him completing his *Opus 1, Variation of a German Melody for the Piano* in class. Grieg was so resistant to school that he used to stand under the rain spout in order to get so wet that the teacher would send him home to change clothes. When the teacher discovered this stratagem, Grieg had to invent others. Henry T. Finck quotes him as saying:

The only excuse I will make for myself is that school was in the last degree unsympathetic to me; its materialism, its coarseness, its coldness were so abhorrent to my nature that I thought of the most incredible ways of escaping from it, if only for a short time. . . . I have not the least doubt that school developed in me nothing but what was evil and left the good untouched.[2]

Pope John XXIII, when an Italian schoolboy, was once sent home from school with a note to his village priest "begging him to reprove the boy for not being conscientious about his studies and always coming to class unprepared." The boy, however, suspected the contents of the note and did not deliver it.

An American schoolboy of Armenian ancestry, a poor widow's son who had spent a period in an orphanage, was not grateful for his schooling. In his autobiography, William Saroyan says:

I must remember also the peculiar smell of the school, and of every classroom; warm oil on the wood floor, chalk dust, desks, old books, paper, pencils, pencil shavings, ink, the teacher herself. The wretched smell of school. Every school has it. Emerson school had it bad. . . . I resented school, but I never resented learning.[3]

At the same time that he was being a school problem, he read nearly every book in the Fresno, California, public library.

Although girls in general are often less resistant to school than are boys, American girls among the Four Hundred — Susan B. Anthony, Pearl Buck, Mary Austin, Gertrude Atherton, Isadora Duncan, and Willa Cather — did not like school. A Norwegian girl, Sigrid Undset, shared their feelings:

I hated school so intensely. It interfered with my freedom. I avoided the discipline by an elaborate technique of being absent-minded during classes. But my schoolmates found me out from the very beginning . . . and they set about to make me see how unpleasant life ought to be made for anyone who is different from other people.[4]

In England, Vera Brittain was bullied by two unpleasant schoolgirls, older than she, who twisted her arm to make her listen to sexual information told in revolting terms.

These burgeoning, exploding, often highly verbal boys and girls were undoubtedly problems in their classrooms. They were too eager to get at the truth of things to be satisfied with lip wisdom. A voracity for new ideas and a relish for reading irked students who were indifferent to learning or failed to rival them in the classroom. So they were sometimes suspended over fires or over sword points, doused with water until they were half drowned, mimicked, snickered at, or nicknamed derisively. They were often isolated and ignored and frequently asked to keep still. Sometimes they were even feared as children who were supernaturally endowed.

Three out of five of the Four Hundred disliked school, yet four out of five of the Four Hundred boys and girls showed evidences of being unusually intelligent or exceptionally talented.

Prokofiev, at five, composed a galloping horse song and at seven composed an opera, "The Giant" (ignoring the black keys). Yehudi Menuhin was studying the violin seriously at the age of three and a half and was admitted to the Vienna Conservatory at seven. At three, Paderewski picked out melodies with one finger, and at four used all his fingers. (This did not prevent a teacher from telling him he could never expect to be a good pianist because his third fingers were too short). Sousa organized his first band when he was eleven. Schweitzer played the organ for church services when he was nine. Norman Angell was editor of a newspaper at fifteen.

Marconi began working on his idea for a radio when he was fourteen, sent his first message when he was twenty-one. Reginald Fessenden was ready for college at fourteen. At five, Steinmetz could do multiplication and division with fractions. Norbert Wiener received his doctorate from Harvard at eighteen. Sigmund Freud was top boy in his class for six years and was seldom called upon to recite because he knew all the answers. After finishing a book on mathematical physics, schoolboy Enrico Fermi remarked to his sister that he had not noticed it was written in Latin. When Fermi was in elementary school he also designed electric motors which worked.

At four, Marie Curie was memorizing the names of the intricate objects her father, a physics teacher, used; and in elementary school she was at least two years ahead of her classmates in every subject. As a child she spoke German, French, and Russian with equal ease. At eleven, Albert Einstein was reading philosophy and also textbooks on science and mathematics. For recreation he played the music of the great composers on his violin. Although he usually took seven courses instead of the required four, J. Robert Oppenheimer, who had given a scientific lecture before a learned society at eleven, was graduated from Harvard summa cum laude with the highest honors ever given an undergraduate.

At ten George Gissing was reading Shakespeare and Dickens. Vera Brittain wrote novels, on scrap paper from her father's pottery factory, while she was in elementary school. At ten, Arthur Koestler had a passion for mathematics, physics, and the construction of mechanical toys, and had a facility for learning languages.

Politicians from disadvantaged homes must have exceptional drive and ability to get to positions of power. Joseph McCarthy and Huey Long were the sons of poor farmers. McCarthy, a homely, "mother-smothered" boy who disliked his father, skipped a grade in grammar school and when he was nineteen completed four years of high school work in one year. Huey Long completed a three-year law course in eight months. David Lloyd George, a widow's fifteen-year-old son, prepared for the Preliminary Law Examination with only his fifty-year-old uncle, a shoemaker by trade, to help him. They worked in secret to avoid ridicule. At the age of twelve Jan Christiaan Smuts was a skilled ranch hand but could neither read nor write. After his brother, who was the son being prepared for the pulpit of the Dutch Reformed Church, died, Jan was sent to school. On the veld he had run from approaching strangers. At school he behaved "like a wild bird." However, he was soon memorizing a book after a single reading. In a week he learned enough Greek to make the highest mark in a class which had been in session for many months.

Among the Four Hundred the boys who seemed to show the most extreme intellectual precocity were Jan Christiaan Smuts, Norbert Wiener, J. Robert Oppenheimer, Arthur Koestler, Norman Angell, J. Middleton Murry, and Bertrand Russell. Mary Ellen Chase was "put in" the fifth reader on the first day of school. Unfortunately, she had to continue reading from the same "highest" reader for seven years. Helen Keller, who dictated a letter in colloquial French at the age of ten, was the most brilliant girl. Isadora Duncan started teaching her unique form of modern dancing professionally at seven, and at ten, with her mother's permission, gave up school to give her full time to teaching.

The least recognized, and often the most unhappy, children are those who have an early empathy that other children do not have. Their sensitivity to injustice and inequalities, their easily aroused guilt feelings frequently bring them into disfavor with adults and cause them to be ridiculed by other children. Adults praised Albert Schweitzer when he could substitute for the church organist at nine, yet he was punished or ridiculed when he refused to wear the proper clothes his parents so painfully provided for him, when he would not join in robbing the nests of birds, when he insisted on being as poorly clad as were the village boys. Early evidences of altruism are often not well received from children, especially from boys.

Lord Robert Cecil, despite the encouragement of his father and the help of his brother, tried in vain to reform the conditions at Eton which made the study of the great classical authors a farce. Father Dominique Piré, who won the Nobel Peace Prize in 1958 for his work with displaced persons, was deeply affected by being a displaced person at four and a half years of age. Gandhi was guilt-stricken over what he felt was neglect of his father, ate forbidden meat because he believed the Hindu practice of vegetarianism might account for India's subservience to England. Jane Addams observed the shabby homes of working people and asked pointed questions. Pearl Buck identified with the Chinese children she knew. Altruism and sympathy are qualities which are often undervalued or unnoticed when displayed by gifted children.

THE CHILDREN WHO WERE THOUGHT DULL — OR FAILED

Intellectually capable children who fail often do so because they limit their interests to a particular academic subject and neglect their other lessons. The originality of their presentations also sometimes antagonizes the teacher. The student who feels very strongly about his work may be embarrassed when other students laugh at his attempts to be creative, or at his unusual response to stimuli, and may seek safety in withdrawal and non-participation. Some students fail because they are not neat or punctual. Others are boring because they want to talk about matters that interest no one but themselves. Children who have odd mannerisms or are unusual in appearance, as was G. K. Chesterton, may also be wrongly classified as dull because they look stupid. Others are emotionally disturbed children, like Adolf Hitler, whose hostile, hyperactive, or withdrawn behavior causes them to be thought dull.

Proust wrote on and on and his teachers thought his compositions disorganized. Hugh Walpole wrote long historical novels when he was a schoolboy, but no one wanted to read them.

A student often fails in a school where form rather than content is stressed but will do well in another kind of school where the teachers have different standards. Emile Zola got a zero in literature at the Lycée St. Louis in France and also failed in German, and rhetoric. He passed, however, in algebra, mathematics, physics, and chemistry. Sent to another lycée in Marsailles, he also failed. He then proceeded to place second in written examinations at the Sorbonne although these tests were supposed to be much more difficult.

Stephen Crane, Eugene O'Neill, William Faulkner, and F. Scott Fitzgerald experienced failure in college because they did not enjoy the content of the courses they took. D. H. Lawrence stood thirteenth in a class of twenty-one pupils enrolled in composition in the Nottingham High School. The Beaux Arts rejected Cézanne when he applied for entrance.

Among the military men and politicians there are those who were always slow students and evidenced little interest in cultural matters as adults. Gamal Abdel Nasser spent two years in grade two, failed to pass grade three, and was twelve years old before he finally passed his primary-school examinations. He was finally admitted to a secondary school where the principal, aware of Nasser's role as a student agitator and of his popularity, passed him. When he failed law school, he went into the army.

Special skills in oratory, a dogged persistence, a high tolerance for frustration and social adaptation are the most frequently observed characteristics of the slow and average students who succeed in making themselves well known. A drive for power and attention can sometimes substitute for ability.

The stubborn boys who fail because they will not scatter their energies seem especially important because it is often they who make the giant steps forward which change life significantly for the total population. They included Edison, the Wright brothers, Henry Ford and Einstein.

Thomas Edison said of school, "I remember that I was never able to get along at school. I was always at the foot of the class. I used to feel that the teachers did not sympathize with me, and that my father thought I was stupid."[5]

Albert Einstein was considered dull by his teachers and by his parents. His son Albert, Jr., while a professor of agriculture at the University of California in Berkeley, told Bela Kornitzer, who interviewed him while gathering data for his book *American Fathers and Sons*: "Actually, I understand my father was a very well-behaved child. He was shy, lonely and withdrawn from the world even then. He was even considered backward by his teachers. He told me that his teachers reported to his father that he was mentally slow, unsociable and adrift forever in his foolish dreams." It was for this reason that the father, when Albert was sixteen, urged him to forget his "philosophical nonsense" and apply himself to the "sensible trade" of electrical engineering. A slowness of speech had predisposed his parents to think him dull.

Among the students who show strong evidence of ability and still fail there is usually more than one inhibiting factor. Having a broken home and an unsatisfactory teacher, however, do not necessarily mean that there is no chance for fulfillment for the child. A total of twenty-six were thought dull.

When Sergei Rachmaninoff made poor grades at the Conservatory of St. Petersburg, he turned his 1's into 4's on his report card and forestalled his mother's discovery that he was an unsatisfactory student. After one of his teachers dropped in to commiserate with her about her son's failures, his mother withdrew him from school and sent him to Moscow to live in the household of an exceptionally famous teacher, several of whose pupils had become widely known. No one doubted the lazy, hyperactive boy's talents, but his mother could not manage him.

Sergei was not close to his mother, whom he found stern and depressing. He missed his kind and expansive father, who had once sat at the piano for hours improvising and told the children fantastic tales to entertain them. The father, Vasily Rachmaninoff, lost the fifth and last estate which his wife had purchased for him. When the family was bankrupt, the parents separated and the mother and six children moved into an uncomfortable, crowded flat. Sergei was also distressed by the death of his favorite sister, Yelena, who died at a time when she had been selected to be coached for an operatic role. He neglected his practicing, played truant, and wept bitterly when he left home at eleven to live in a strange household under strict discipline.

The musical instruction he received was superior, but the four years spent in his teacher's turbulent, demanding household changed him from a heedless boy to a youth who had the looks and mannerisms of an old man. He had a look of perpetual disappointment, his face was lined, his manners were shy and awkward. After four years he had a violent quarrel with his teacher, who shouted at him and threw objects in the room at him, presumably because Sergei had asked for a room of his own with a piano in it. The enraged music master called Sergei's Moscow relatives to a conference from which the boy was excluded, and let them know that he could no longer have the boy as a student-resident.

Victor I. Seroff, Rachmaninoff's biographer, quotes Yury Sakhnovsky, a Moscow critic and old friend of the composer, to the effect that it was the teacher's known homosexuality which caused the quarrel and Sergei's leaving the house.

If this was the real reason, Sergei did not advance it to shield himself from the wrath of his relatives. Only one person among them, his father's sister, who was personally aware of his teacher's autocratic and unpleasant ways, defended the boy. This aunt welcomed him into her own home and gave him a room of his own with a piano in it. He delighted in the companionship of her four young children and was warmly received by the three servants, who accepted him as someone for whom they expected to have lifelong responsibility. It was in this understanding household that he entered into a period of rich, independent composition.

There were several possible causes for Rachmaninoff's failure in school. For Pablo Picasso there was only the excuse of his devotion to one form of expression. He stubbornly refused to do anything but paint. Since he did learn to read and write and count, he may have learned more in school than he pretended.

When Pablo was ten, his father, Don José Ruiz Blasco, a fun-loving young artist previously subsidized by his family, had to admit his inadequacy to provide for his wife and three children and take a mediocre post as an art master at the Institutio de Guardia, a school for secondary education in Corunna. Don José, the ninth professional painter in his family, proudly accepted the talent of his son Pablo as a matter of course, as did his patient wife, whose maiden name, Picasso, the artist used professionally because he thought it more distinctive.

José's inability to make his talent profitable prompted him to want Pablo to have an education other than that the boy could receive by simply setting his easel beside his father's and painting all day long, but Pablo resisted school stubbornly and seemed completely unable to learn to read or write. The other students grew used to seeing him come late with his pet pigeon — and with the paintbrush he always carried as if it were an extension of his own body.

His father used pigeons as models, and Pablo, who was so much his father's boy, needed his own pigeon for companionship at school and tried to make school an extension of his father's studio. His worst days were those when his father failed to come for him at one o'clock as he had promised because he became so engrossed in his own painting that he forgot to call for his lonesome son.

The teacher of the little private school, an old friend of the family, did not harass the gentle, affectionate child who was given to getting up and leaving the classroom without permission. Pablo followed the wife of his teacher about like a small puppy and spent much of his time with her in her kitchen quarters. If he had to sit among the other boys, he watched the clock and recited in a singsong to himself, "One o'clock, one o'clock!" If asked to pay attention, he obediently tried so hard that all he could think of was paying attention; the words of the teacher flowed over and about him and he understood nothing.

Picasso's biographer, Jaime Sabartes, tells how the father, affectionate but concerned for the boy's future, took him out of school when he was ten (the year José, too, took a job against his will) and hired a tutor to prepare the reluctant Pablo for the entrance examinations for secondary school. The tutor gave up in despair when he simply could not teach Pablo arithmetic.

During this time Pablo's talent in art became increasingly obvious and hopeful relatives helped Don José send his son to Madrid to the Academia de Bellas Artes. There was a flurry of excitement in the family when Pablo not only passed the entrance examinations but passed them with ease, accomplishing in a day tests devised to last a month. Relatives and friends confidently expected the talented youth to win scholarships and prizes and to bring them honor, if not wealth, from the little shares they had bought in him by donating money for his tuition.

In the meantime Pablo was completely happy in Madrid, but he saw no reason to study with teachers who obviously had nothing to teach him. So he wandered about the city, enjoying the street scenes, sketching, painting as he pleased. His relatives were disappointed, but the sympathetic Don José kept sending him as much money as he could. Pablo soon had to come back home to set up his own little studio in the entranceway of an umbrella shop. He gave his first one-man show before he began to shave.

When Albert Einstein was fifteen, his father, Hermann Einstein, who operated a small electrochemical factory in Munich, Germany, failed in business and left for Milan, where he fancied business might be better. Hermann was a jovial, hopeful man, fond of beer and good food, of Schiller and Heine. Albert's mother was an amateur musician, and the engineers from the factory often dropped in to hear his mother play Beethoven. Hermann's brother, another engineer, who lived with them, was an intellectual who was interested in politics.

In this home, which did not lack a love for learning and books and music, the boy they thought so dull was playing for hours on his own violin. He was reading Kant and other philosophers at eleven or twelve and such books as Buchner's *Force and Matter*. His speech was always hesitant; learning languages was difficult for him.

The family went to Milan when Einstein was fifteen, and he was left behind to complete his work at the Gymnasium in Munich; but he found school so intolerable that he asked the school doctor to give him a certificate saying he had a nervous breakdown and must spend at least six months with his parents in Italy.

It was at the formative age of sixteen that Einstein had a "time-out," a period of freedom from the classroom and scheduled activities. The warmth and beauty of Italy gave him complete satisfaction. He wandered through churches and hiked through the Apennines. It was at this time that he began to ponder what would happen if a ray of light were to be imprisoned — a query important to his later intellectual development.

In his upper-middle-class Jewish family there could be no tolerance for an idle boy who did not do well in school. Other relatives did better than Hermann Einstein, whose business in Milan was also unsuccessful; and it was they who gave a hundred Swiss francs a month to subsidize Albert, not out of faith but out of family charity, so that he might attend the Polytechnic Institute in Zurich, which took expatriate students. Albert had given up his German citizenship.

When he failed to pass his entrance examinations in zoology, botany and languages, there was nothing to do but go back to the secondary school and remedy his deficiencies. Einstein enrolled in an ordinary canton school in Arau, Switzerland, and after a year was admitted to the Polytechnic Institute in Zurich.

He once replied to a girl who wrote him a personal letter complaining about her teacher's not appreciating her: "I, too, was once treated so by my professors who did not like my spirit of independence and although they needed an assistant, refused to appoint me as one."[6]

None of his schoolmates boasted of his friendship, and his teachers, when approached in later years, did not remember having had him in class. When he was graduated, he had difficulty in finding a position. He wanted to be a secondary-school teacher, but could not find a post. He answered newspaper advertisements, to no avail. He was a temporary assistant in a technical school for a few months; then he took a job tutoring slow students in a boarding school and was discharged because he insisted on teaching in his own way. He took a job in the patent office but kept on studying and publishing. As early as 1907 he presented material which was the main support for his theory of relativity, but it made not the slightest impression on the learned world.

In his autobiographical notes written at the age of sixty-seven Einstein said:

It is, in fact, nothing short of a miracle that the modern methods of instruction have not yet entirely strangled the holy curiosity of inquiry; for this delicate little plant, aside from stimulation, stands mostly in need of freedom; without this it goes to wreck and ruin without fail. It is a very grave mistake to think that the enjoyment of seeing and searching can be promoted by means of coercion and a sense of duty.[7]

He disliked any artificial show of knowledge or learning of facts that cluttered up the mind. When asked about the speed of sound, he said that he did not know the answer to that question, but he knew where to find the fact in a reference book if and when he needed it. The important thing was to react delicately, and to have a perpetual sense of wonder.

The examination was the part of traditional schooling that he most disliked. Its elimination, he believed, would do away with painful dulling of the memory, and it would no longer be necessary to take years to hammer facts into students' heads which they would be certain to forget in a few months.

He never forgot the strain of preparation for the examination he had to take before he could enter the school at Zurich. "The constraint was so terrifying that after I passed the final examination I found myself unable to think of a scientific problem for almost a year," his friend and biographer Antonina Vallentin quotes him as saying.

There were other students who could not, or would not, take examinations with ease or competence. Gertrude Stein refused to take her final examination in William James's class. He admired her for her spirit, said he understood — and gave her the highest mark in his class. Anatole France, during an oral examination, was tricked into agreeing with a didactic professor who ironically stated that the River Rhone flowed into Lake Michigan. Puccini consistently failed examinations. The bacteriologist Paul Ehrlich hated examinations of any kind, and all his life he profoundly pitied anybody who had to pass one. His complete ineptness at composition led his teachers to excuse him from this requirement. His speech, copied from that of his father, was hasty, full of interjections and frequent gesticulations. At college he barely passed his assigned work. Someone once pointed him out to Robert Koch saying, "That is little Ehrlich. He is very good at staining [microscopic slides], but he will never pass his examinations."[8]

THE IMPORTANCE OF A TIME-OUT

There are frequent references to a "time-out," a period when the normal activities of life are suspended and the boy or girl has a free period in which to think, to plan, to read unrestrainedly, or to meet an entirely new group of people under novel circumstances. Winston Churchill had two such periods. John Kennedy, in late adolescence, contracted jaundice while in school in England and had a free period of traveling about Europe with a friend. H. G. Wells had such a period when he broke his leg at the age of eight. The habit of reading he formed then kept him from becoming a draper's assistant. An illness in young manhood set him writing. Matisse started painting during a convalescence.

As a youth of nineteen, Havelock Ellis took a job teaching school in the Australian bush. His duties were light and he had his evenings entirely to himself in an isolated little hut where he read stacks of books in English, French, German and Latin. It was to this year that he attributed his later exceptional development.

Charles Evans Hughes was graduated from high school twice before he was twelve and could not enter college because of his youth. At the Newark High School he had lost two front teeth when larger boys flung him against the wall while playing a whipcracker game. For six months he wandered the streets of New York, benefiting from the enrichment the city offered, enjoying his freedom and getting used to his changed appearance. He felt better prepared to enter college after this interval. William Randolph Hearst and John La Farge also had profitable "time-out" periods during which they wandered in New York City. Richard Byrd went around the world alone at thirteen. Norman Angell, at seventeen, went off to America to be a cowboy. Louis Brandeis never forgot the free summer when he tramped about Europe with his father and brother. Marie Curie had a free year in the country at fifteen.

Edna St. Vincent Millay was given a grade of C by her eighth-grade English teacher, for whom she had consistently done A work. The teacher resented Edna's criticism of the book report assignment on *The Last of the Mohicans* and would not accept the six other books Edna had recently read as a substitute. Her mother — an independent woman who had sent her husband away because he gambled — quarreled with the principal over the incident and took her daughter out of school. Edna, who had been a popular straight-A student, was chagrined and unhappy and lonely at home alone. Her sisters were properly in school, her mother was away all day, and often at night, working as a nurse. The ensuing period of isolation, during which she prepared herself most adequately for high school and improvised at the piano which one of her mother's patients provided for her, was formative — if unhappy.

Ten per cent of the Four Hundred describe a "time-out" period which significantly influenced their later development.

THE MINORITY WHO DID NOT COMPLAIN

Two in five of the Four Hundred either say they did not have school problems or fail to describe any. To a few of them public education came as a tremendous advantage because the child had no other place in which to read and learn and to meet adults who also read books. George Washington Carver was uncomplaining about the intellectual poverty of the early schools he attended, but at no time was he ever so happy as when he was a graduate student at Iowa State College, where young Henry Wallace was privileged to know and learn from him.

The other students who do not complain about school are those who, recognized by teachers as having unusual abilities, were given special guidance and encouragement and were accelerated. Ernest Rutherford, later a world-renowned physicist, was born on a flax farm near Brightwater, New Zealand. His father, James Rutherford, a wheelwright who had to change his occupation after a severe accident handicapped him, harnessed water power to drive his new flax mill, experimented with different methods of soaking the flax, and developed a special labor-saving device for scraping flax fiber. The mother, who liked to sing and read, had been a teacher. Although the father made a good living, the seven sons (two of whom were drowned while sailing) and five daughters had no reason to expect that their parents could give them much except an education.

In Rutherford's primary school at Havelock, New Zealand, a teacher with more than the usual interest in ability, a Mr. Reynolds, taught the brighter children for an hour each morning before the regular classes began. In the community-sponsored secondary school, named Nelson College, science was optional; and Ernest was often the only boy in his class. His scholarship he had won by right of answering 580 out of 600 test items. The teacher, Dr. W. S. Littlejohn, and his enthusiastic student were often seen walking and talking together, stopping to draw diagrams in the dust, completely oblivious of passers-by. When Ernest was absorbed in a book, he could be hit on the head and not be disturbed, his classmates found. Ernest was not only a good science student but also won prizes in history, English literature, French and Latin.

When the news came that he had been awarded a scholarship

to the University of New Zealand, he tossed his spade aside with the remark, "That's the last potato I'll ever dig," and left his father's farm. Although the university had less science equipment than many an ordinary high school, he became deeply interested in experiments with magnetization of iron, which led to his invention of a magnetic detector of radio waves, and spent hours doing ingenious experiments in a miserable, cold, drafty, concrete-floored cellar ordinarily used for a storeroom. He became engaged to his landlady's daughter, Mary Newton, who had to wait several years before he could support her as his wife. Another scholarship sent him to Cambridge. When he chose his first job, it was a research chair at McGill University which attracted him, although he could have earned much more in his native New Zealand. The laboratory at McGill, financed by a tobacco millionaire, was one of the best equipped in the world. School, for this "well-rounded" scholar, is not described as an unpleasant experience.

Carlos Romulo was another all-around good student who is not described as a boy who disliked school. He won a medal for oratory in high school, was editor of his high-school annual, and a cub reporter for the Manila *Times*. It was his gift for oratory which resulted in his being sent to Columbia University, where he majored in English literature.

TUTORS ARE LIKED

There is an acute need in the Four Hundred for direct and frequent communication with intelligent adults. When this need is met to a reasonable degree in the school, the school rebellion is much lessened. The tutor, who is after all a teacher, does not draw upon himself the venom which the classroom teacher often elicits from the Four Hundred. Although the tutor often lacks the proper qualifications for teaching in a well-accredited school, he is valued by his pupil with whom he can work in a one-to-one relationship.

Benjamin Cardozo was prepared for Columbia by a funny, roly-poly little man who had a deep desire to be a great poet. He wrote a book-length satirical poem, in criticism of the government, which did not win acclaim. At the same time, his pot-boilers, his children's books, which he pretty obviously wrote with tongue in cheek, made Horatio Alger renowned as the author of books about poor boys who became rich by dint of hard work, frugality and good character. Horatio Alger had been recommended to the Cardozos by Joseph Seligman, the banker, whose children he taught for twelve years. Under Alger's direction, Benjamin Cardozo was able to pass his entrance examinations for Columbia when he was thirteen.

Lincoln Steffens, who was acutely unhappy in his military school and was awarded twenty days in solitary confinement for drunkenness, was transferred by his sympathetic father to the care of a tutor, an English expatriate in San Francisco, who introduced the boy to conversation the like of which he had never heard before. The tutor's room was a center for several Oxford men, who gathered there to talk endlessly and well of cultural matters. To the boy it was an exhilarating experience. In the days of his solitary confinement he had profited by doing vast amounts of reading, so that he was prepared for the baptism of ideas he received from his tutor and his tutor's friends.

There is no parent-tutored boy or girl among the Four Hundred who was not grateful for the experience. Elizabeth Kenny, the Australian nurse who developed her own way of treating infantile paralysis, in her autobiography says of her mother's teaching:

The memory of those quiet evenings with my mother has lived with me down through the years, and I have always found it hard to understand why teaching should be thought so irksome to him who imparts the knowledge, as well as to the young mind that balks at receiving it.[9]

During the day, Elizabeth was left to her own devices. By the age of six she was practically living on horseback, riding to the village for the mail, helping to round up stock, racing her cousin Douglas to the home of her grandparents ten miles away

When her younger brother seemed frail, she improvised a gymnasium for him and exercised him until he was as strong and sturdy as the other children. When her father needed help in marketing his agricultural products, she helped him and the entire community by undertaking to find markets — in which she was overwhelmingly successful. But her foray into business brought upon her the condemnation of many of the men and most of the women in the community, who thought business was not a young girl's concern — not even when it saved the community from bankruptcy. Her mother was Elizabeth's only teacher until the young girl entered nurse's training.

The problems in home tutoring occur when the parent cannot relinquish the role of teacher and constant companion when the child becomes adult. Dmitri Shostakovitch was one of the three musically talented children of a Russian widow, Sonya Shostakovitch, who after the Revolution was a typist in the office of Weights and Measures, where her husband worked before his death. When Dmitri, whose inability in arithmetic made his schoolwork a nightmare to himself and his teachers, wanted to stay home and study only music his mother consented. He also read omnivorously, as did his two sisters. Although they were poor, they managed to have two grand pianos in the house. Marusia, two years older than her brother, graduated from the high school and planned to continue her music studies at the conservatory. When Marusia and Dmitri made their first appearance at a concert, Marusia wore a dress made of an old bedspread. There was never enough money for all their needs; and the youngest daughter, Zoya, who had to give up her dancing lessons, became bitter and alienated from her mother because she felt all the special advantages went to the two older children.

The scanty fare, driving hours of practice, and constant pressure took their toll and Dmitri developed a glandular infection in his throat. When the twenty-year-old Marusia and the seventeen-year-old Dmitri went away for a rest cure to the Crimea, they both wept bitterly; for they had not been away from their mother before.

The children's maturity, their marriages, and their engrossment in their families and careers hurt the mother terribly. She resented her son's marriage to a lovely young wife — whom he loved and with whom she could find no fault. On New Year's Eve in 1932 she sat alone and wrote a most unhappy letter to her sister in the

United States begging her to come live with her and be a companion to her. Dmitri and Nina had gone to see their friends. Marusia and her husband were celebrating at the University. Zoya, still unreconciled and alienated, was far away in Moscow. The mother hated staying with Zoya and her husband; she felt that she played the role of a useless servant in her son's apartment. She slept on the couch in the living room and resented their going out, their big parties, their automobiles, the expensive restaurants they frequented.

"We are modest people," she wrote to her sister, "we love work. . . . How will I live . . . not waiting for his wakening in the morning . . . not opening the door for him when he comes home. If they move to a new apartment they may not want me. . . . The nest is destroyed."[10]

Although it was doubtless the mother's decision to let Dmitri stay home from school, together with her early tutoring of him, that made the round-faced, bespectacled, immature boy an early success in his musical career, the cost to both of them was terrific when the mother was not able to let him grow away from her and live the life of a normal adult. Although she tried to destroy his marriage, and not even the birth of grandchildren made her happy, he had the strength to resist her influence.

William Cooper Howells and his wife Mary throughout their thirty-seven years of marriage shared a common philosophy and were happy despite periods of tension and misfortune.

The husband was a printer, and in the early days of their marriage he wandered from job to job. The husband and wife took long walks in the country together, talking and enjoying the landscape. William Dean Howells, the second of eight children, was embarrassingly small for his age, but his big brother Joe, four years older and aggressive, was on hand to protect him. None of the children attended school with any regularity, since they found their father's newspaper office, the family library and their father's teaching better suited to their learning needs. A total of sixteen or eighteen months, in random periods, was all the formal schooling the future novelist received. He could set type at six, began to write verses at seven or eight, at eleven could do a man's work in the print shop.

Howells was profoundly influenced by his father. All of his life he believed, like his father, that work and good works saved, and that self-concern damned. Other boys found they could tease him by working on his early-developed sense of justice. Their insensitivity pained him. He found it hard, however, to be apart from his father as he began to grow up.

During one period of the family life, when there were seven young children in the family, the father lost his printing business as a result of his idealism about slavery. He had previously gone bankrupt when he published an opinionative book on the nature of aristocracy. The family moved into a tiny, dilapidated cabin in a remote area. Here the father, encouraged by his brothers, was determined to start a utopia, a community in which he and the settlers he hoped to attract could live apart from the world. The community's economic basis was an existing gristmill, which was to be turned into a paper mill. The venture was not successful, and the mother, Mary Dean Howells, was unhappy and frightened. She drew apart from her husband, with her oldest son, Joe, as her champion. William was close to his father, with whom he read and walked and talked during the crisp autumn days. This was his "time-out" period — a waiting time and a thinking time. He was deeply sensitive to the family tension, which, however, did not go deep enough to disturb the love the family members bore each other.

William's close family ties made it hard for him to leave home and his own creativity seemed to depend on his knowing that his family was happy and secure. When he was asked to go to Xenia, Ohio, to work for a week, he was so emotionally upset by being away from home that he begged to return on the night of his arrival. He went on to Dayton on a similar job and lived there with his favorite uncle Isaac. The fifteen-year-old boy was so homesick for his parents that he sobbed at the table while he ate. His mother, when he returned home, let him know that she felt satisfaction in his inability to stay away, although she knew she was wrong and the family needed his wages.

When William Cooper Howells's brothers withdrew their financial support for the utopia that did not materialize, the entire family moved to Columbus, where abolitionists were better tolerated. There the father took a job with the *Ohio State Journal* and was eventually made clerk of the Ohio House of Representatives. It was then that Howells had his creative spurt, began to write, had his first poem published and found remunerative employment.

In the family of Winston Churchill, about which so much has been written, there are multiple examples of the qualities in parents and other relatives which seem to be related to the production of an eminent man. There was respect for learning, an experimental attitude, failure-proneness, a plentitude of opinionative relatives, a lack of dependence on the opinions of others, and turbulence in the family life as a result of the erratic behavior of his irrepressible uncle and father.

During the time that Winston was thought dull, he was, like other such boys, evidencing qualities which presaged ability. Rejected by his father and neglected by his mother, he experienced a "smothering" relationship with his mother-figure, Mrs. Everest, and developed the love for martial poetry, the enthusiasm for battle, and the disregard for personal safety which other such boys evidence. He was hyperactive, prone to constant colds, had poor peer relationships. He had the handicap of a speech defect.

On both sides of the family, American and English, there was strong drive, both physical and intellectual. Aurora Murray Jerome, Winston's maternal great-grandmother, who lived with her husband Isaac and nine children in Massachusetts, was a woman of such energy and resourcefulness that there are still legends about her in her native Berkshire hills. Her son, Leonard Jerome, Winston's American grandfather, was a diplomat, a newspaper man, a financier, and a Wall Street stock-market gambler whose spectacular failure came at the time of the marriage of his daughter, Jennie Jerome, to Lord Randolph Churchill. Aurora Murray Jerome produced more than one energetic, erratic, experimental son. The oldest of her sons, Aaron, while still a theology student at Princeton, made $40,000 on a mulberry tree speculation and used his gains to house needy fellow students. Addison Jerome, another son, was known as a wit and the leader of an international social set. Lawrence Jerome was, with his brother Leonard, one of the founders of the Rochester *Daily American*.

Clarissa Jerome, Winston's American grandmother, was a strong and positive woman with ideas about diet, good hygiene and fashionable attire. She reintroduced the fichu as an item of flattering neckwear and turned her daughter over to Ward McAllister, the self-styled "snob of snobs," to teach her the secrets of fashion, perfect manners and good eating.

Lord Randolph Churchill, Winston's father, was an idler and a playboy until he became an enthusiastic and tireless politician. He failed his Oxford examinations on the first try and was a problem student at Eton. His brother, the Marquess of Blandford, established a chemical laboratory on the ground floor of Blenheim Castle. Their mother, Winston's paternal grandmother, the Duchess of Marlborough, was an overmasterful, high-handed, but fundamentally kind woman who kept the erratic Churchills together during a period when the failing family fortunes were being mended by marriages to rich American women.

There is failure-proneness among the family members. Lord Randolph, Winston's father, was out of politics by the time he was thirty-seven. His wife, after his death, bankrupted herself by the publication of eleven issues of the *Anglo-Saxon Review*, which did not sell well enough at the price of five dollars per issue to warrant further publication. "Jeanette had lost her last penny on the glorious enterprise. She laughed. It had, indeed, been a wonderful time while it lasted."[11]

This dynamic mother of Winston Churchill had tremendous physical stamina. She was an enthusiastic horsewoman and a tireless traveler. A favorite sport was fishing for huge eel in the stagnant water of a bog near Blenheim Castle. She was a passionate eel-fisherwoman. "No one," says Kraus, "understood this strange proclivity. She actually laughed at the eel's ferocious fight to the end. . . . Dying, and even after skinning, the eel still wriggles in a horrible fashion."

In 1912, shortly before her divorce from George Cornwallis-West, she was described in the *Literary Digest* as the organizer of the great spectacle, *Shakespeare's Day*, which she staged almost singlehanded at Earls Court. She is described as a strong-chinned woman with the manners of a born organizer. Great crowds came to see the tournaments, the plays presented in a replica of the Globe Theatre, the authentic dances, and the queen of the beauty contest.

During a period of family turbulence, while his parents were not being accepted in British society because of a quarrel with the Prince of Wales and were deeply involved in controversial political issues as well, Winston was in the nursery or elementary school. During this period he had the whole, undivided, uncritical attention of his nurse, Mrs. Everest. In his autobiography he says, "My nurse was my confidante. . . . At her death she was my dearest and most intimate friend during the twenty years I had lived . . . innocent and loving . . . of simple faith."[12]

It was this nurse who taught him to read and count and do simple arithmetic and who introduced him to his hobby of playing with toy soldiers. She was quite helpless in controlling his hyperactivity, and she worried over his constant colds and his double pneumonia. He won his way with her sometimes by threatening to worship idols which frightened the fond woman, for she feared for the soul of the obstreperous boy to whom she was so devoted. He once displayed great moral courage by inviting his fat, commonplace nurse to Harrow to visit him and by kissing her unashamedly before the other boys.

As we have seen, his mother was a star whom he worshipped — but at a distance — and his father, with whom he had only three or four long conversations, was hostile and indifferent. Any approach by the son to the father was met with icy withdrawal.

Winston's first school was chosen by his mother for its good reputation and social prestige; but Winston resisted the sadistic headmaster's behavior stoutly, kicked the man's hat to pieces, and was withdrawn by his mother and sent to a school in Brighton run by two kindly old ladies. In this benign atmosphere, Winston was called the naughtiest small boy in England by his dancing teacher. He was frequently permitted to leave the classroom and run about in the schoolyard to release his exuberant energies. He did not want to study Latin or Greek there, or mathematics, and he was not coerced.

Eton, which his father had attended, was in a swamp, Harrow was on a hill. The latter school was selected because the family thought Winston might be healthier there. Since his father was at that time Chancellor of the Exchequer, Winston's malingering and his other obvious deficiencies as a student were ignored. Once he was admitted, the school felt no obligation to give him any honors he did not win. He remained in the lowest form all during his days in Harrow, a period he described in manhood as a wasted time and a miserable interlude.

While still a young man, Churchill discussed with Frank Harris his poor relationship with Lord Randolph. Harris asked him if he had liked his father and Churchill replied: "How could I? . . . I was ready enough to as a boy, but he wouldn't let me. He treated me as if I had been a fool; barked at me whenever I questioned him. I owe everything to my mother, to my father nothing."[13]

At Harrow, of which Winston Churchill had only bitter memories, he tried to talk of politics on his first day at school, but the teacher was not responsive. His only prizes were for fencing and for reciting martial poetry. He refused to study mathematics, Greek, or Latin and was placed in the lowest form — in what would today be termed the remedial reading class, where slow boys were taught English. His English, however, was not poor; his knowledge of Shakespeare was unusual and self-motivated. He had no intimate friends and was "cheeky" at school at the time that his father, who was much in the press, was being vituperative in Parliament. The boy who did not know his rejecting father well nonetheless kept a scrapbook of his father's exploits as they were described in the press and was unfriendly to boys whose fathers disagreed with Lord Randolph on political issues. In a very determined way, he was imitating his father while he was in preparatory school, but this devotion was unrewarded.

His father, ashamed of his son's seeming dullness, was sure Winston would never be able to earn a living in England and contemplated sending him to one of the colonies, possibly to

Africa, when he was a young adult. Winston was taken from Harrow and put in the care of a tutor who was well known for his success in getting boys into Sandhurst. This exasperated man concluded that Winston had not gone through Harrow but over it or under it.

It was during this period that Lord Randolph, perturbed by his increasing illness and lack of funds, sold twenty letters (in advance of writing) to a sensational paper, the *Daily Graphic*, and went off to Africa to hunt and send the news of his exploits to the paper. The two thousand pounds he earned he invested well in African mines. He lived outdoors, went unshaven, enjoyed his exploits and came back in better health. In the meantime, his wife had fled to the Continent to escape the ribbing other papers were giving her husband, and Winston failed his examinations for Sandhurst the second time.

Lord Randolph came home less tense, and his wife thought they might enjoy an interlude of quiet, close family life during the Christmas holidays. Lady Wimbourne, Jennie's sister, loaned them the use of a house in Bournemouth, but Randolph went away to attend one of the famous parties of the wild Lord Fitzgibbon of Ireland.

During these years Winston had lacked close friends of his own age but had enjoyed playing with his younger brother and his younger cousins. His mother's sisters had had reason to fear for the physical welfare of their children when Winston was about; and his cousins found him fascinatingly dangerous. He organized them into battle with the village children during holidays, built forts and initiated intricate strategy. Each morning the servants held an agitated counsel to determine what to do with Winston today. His own nurse was helpless to check him. However, not the younger children but Winston was injured in an accident that was to end his childhood. He was eighteen, his brother twelve and his cousin was fourteen when a game of fox and hare brought Winston to a bridge with the other boys in hot pursuit. Behind him was certain capture, below was the top of a welcoming fir tree. He leaped, missed, fell thirty feet to hard ground. He did not regain consciousness for three days and was bedridden for three months.

During his convalescence from the operation on a kidney ruptured in the fall, he found himself intellectually. He spent much time in London and at Parliament, where various relatives were politically influential. He met Balfour, Chamberlain, Rosebery, Asquith, and other men of consequence who were to be important to him in the future. He listened to sessions of Parliament. He was also able to do the work that enabled him to barely pass the Sandhurst examinations on the third try.

While enumerating their complaints about the classroom, Churchill and others among the Four Hundred also indicate preferences and appreciations. They best liked teachers who let them go ahead at their own pace and who gave them permission to work unimpeded in the area of their special interest. They remember affectionately all adults and classmates who challenged their thinking, introduced them to exciting books, or supplied them with materials for work. They especially liked the "time-out" periods which give them time for self-evaluation. They sought out places where ideas were being bandied about: the debate club, the school newspaper, the discussion group. They liked to be needed and to be used and to have early responsibility. They responded warmly to people who took time to listen to them and to those who had faith in them. Intelligent appreciation of their special interests was most highly valued.

Any attempt to equate their degree of education with eminence only serves to indicate that the public demands certification for professional workers. It is the lawyers, teachers, doctors, engineers who have the most formal training. The writers, artists, actors and inventors have the least academic training and also are prone to dislike the classroom intensely. Politicians run the gamut in amount of schooling.

But who can say that the informally educated Wright brothers, Edison, Marconi, Noel Coward, Pablo Picasso, Pablo Casals and Sam Clemens gave less or more to society than the more formally schooled Schweitzer, Einstein, Gandhi, Freud, Fessenden, Fermi, Cushing and Brandeis? What is happening to children who are the contemporary counterparts of those who were informally educated, in these days of compulsory education, is more to the point.

In the past it has been the family itself which has given the motivation for formal training for specialized services; and often it has also supplied needed encouragement to those young people who do the more individual and self-initiated tasks or seek their training in the theater, pressroom, political or labor organization, or studio.

Three hundred and fifty-eight of the Four Hundred came from business or professional homes, and nearly all of their homes had a love for learning and achievement. Horace Mann Bond, dean of the school of education at Atlanta University, says:

If we could give to every child in the land the same opportunities for intellectual stimulation now enjoyed by the children of the professional, technical and kindred workers, we would increase our "talent pool" five fold.[14]

His conclusion is supported by the extensive studies which have indicated that it is still largely the sons and daughters of professional workers or business executives who are encouraged by their parents to train for the professions.

There is, however, an increasing awareness that something has gone wrong in the homes which were once the source of high achievers and the highly creative. Students coming from such homes are too frequently uninterested and unimaginative. These children from professional or learning-centered homes can pass tests, do competent papers, make the grades of C or B required of them and yet remain totally uninvolved in the learning process during or outside of class hours. The college diploma is valued for the social and economic benefits it brings. The young graduates plan to make a good living, enjoy leisure hours, and to be financially secure in their old age.

This attitude is prevalent among students who come from schools which are expensively staffed and where the competition to gain admittance to prestige colleges is high. The parents have long since been discouraged by these schools from participating in the learning process as it involves the child. They are told that it is the duty of the teacher to teach; the duty of the parent is to provide financial and emotional security.

Intellectually able children are not often taught by their parents to read as they were in many homes among the Four Hundred, for the parent who does so nowadays is subject to sharp criticism and is accused of trying to "push" his child in order to bolster his own presumably weak ego. The school does not want children in the first grade who can already read, because such a child does not fit into the organized activities. At all levels of learning throughout the early years this lock step is maintained.

Peer pressures are used to make the child feel that deviating from this pattern makes him socially undesirable. In what anthropologists tell us is the most peer-oriented culture in the world, the child becomes almost afraid to think until he learns what his classmates are thinking. Creative thinking is at its peak in about the second grade. The child is still eager to learn, excited by the wonders of the world, perceptive to a degree that he may never attain again. The high school is a particularly barren period for any expression of intellectual vigor or originality. Often it is not until he is in college, and sometimes not even then, that the student regains the drive for self-initiated learning, the originality and intuitiveness, the seeking for truth and beauty. The highly achieving adult — Einstein is a good example — often has a great joy in his work and retains a childish pleasure in learning which may make him seem naïve to the public.

The famed and intellectually sophisticated adult can withstand the pressures against him for conformity; the third-grade child often cannot. E. Paul Torrance of the Bureau of Educational Research at the University of Minnesota says, "Unusual or original ideas are common targets of peer pressures to conformity."

The phenomenon of indifference in students who come to college well prepared and with good scores on tests has led to various experiments and to deliberation about the lack of a love for learning in the students. Harvard University has recently been offering a dozen scholarships a year to young men with culturally and socially disadvantaged backgrounds. Most of these men were valedictorians of high schools which do not ordinarily send students to prestige colleges. Some of the schools are not even accredited. Each student accepted in this experimental program comes to Harvard because some high-school teacher recognized in him an insatiable desire for knowledge. In his high school he was self-motivated and set the pace for other students. These are students from "risky" backgrounds, and their performance to date has been about what might be expected. Some are doing well, some are failing; but both Harvard and the foundation which supplies the scholarship funds are pleased with the results thus far. Some students who had the most glaring deficiencies in their backgrounds have been sent to preparatory schools, such as Andover, for remedial work.

The Harvard experiment is one of several on various levels which recognizes the compelling need to make good use of all students, anywhere and everywhere, who have marked ability. The school rebellions of so many of the Four Hundred highlight the need to do something more for eager and inquiring students than the sheer physical expansion of school plant in which children of the same chronological age but with widely varying abilities and interests are required to perform essentially identical tasks.

[11]

"Out of the Cradle Endlessly Rocking"

> What is needed is . . . a readiness for bold-
> ness or even extravagance — a capacity for
> informed and serious guessing as to the poten-
> tialities utterly different from those that a
> different epoch can directly suggest. We can
> often be wrong. In all such efforts, to be
> wrong fifty times is far more forgivable than
> to be timid once.
>
> — GARDNER MURPHY,
> *Human Potentialities*

THERE IS A DANGER in trying too hard to be conclusive and of being drawn into tidying data to give easy answers to difficult problems. Such efforts too often lead to putting the right saddle on the wrong horse.

An uncritical adoption of new ideas has already caused many abrupt reversals in methods of child-rearing. Parents reared on strict schedules are convinced of a need for demand feeding for their own infants. Fathers and mothers reared permissively are attracted to the idea that setting limits makes for emotional security in their own children.

There are no easy answers as to how to rear capable, creative children who will happily make effective use of their talents and skills. However, an over-all view of the experiences of the Four Hundred may stimulate us to some informed and serious guessing as to the best way to initiate a new level of creativeness and flowering of excellence.

RECONNOITERING AMONG THE FINDINGS

Most of the eminent are not born in the great metropolitan centers but drift in to the larger centers from the farms, villages, and smaller cities. Stage celebrities more often come from the cities than do persons of other occupations.

In almost all the homes there is a love for learning in one or both parents, often accompanied by a physical exuberance and a persistent drive toward goals. Fewer than ten per cent of the parents failed to show a strong love for learning.

Three-fourths of the children are troubled — by poverty; by a broken home; by rejecting, overpossessive, estranged, or dominating parents; by financial ups and downs; by physical handicaps; or by parental dissatisfaction over the children's school failures or vocational choices.

One-half of the parents were opinionative about a controversial subject which set them apart in their own time but is accepted with little or no animus today. Opinionative parents reared nearly all the statesmen, the humanitarians and the reformers.

None of the twenty poets among the Four Hundred is the son or daughter of a poet.

Seventy-four of eighty-five writers of fiction or drama and sixteen of twenty poets come from homes where, as children, they saw tense psychological dramas played out by their parents.

Twenty-one of thirty-two physicians, lawyers and scientists come from family backgrounds which give them opportunities for outdoor explorations, considerable personal freedom, and early responsibility. They are often physically active, make collections, and are mischievous.

Nearly half the fathers were subject to traumatic vicissitudes in their business or professional careers.

One-fourth of the mothers are described as dominating, but only one-twentieth of the fathers warrant this description.

Wealth is much more frequent than is abject poverty. One family had public assistance; one subject was reared in a work-house; two were in orphanages. Five others experience extreme deprivation. There are twenty-one families which lived on inherited income or were known to be very wealthy. Three hundred and fifty-eight families (some wealthy) can be classified as representing the business or professional classes.

Handicaps such as blindness; deafness; being crippled, sickly, homely, undersized, or overweight; or having a speech defect occur in the childhoods of over one-fourth of the sample. In many of these individuals, the need to compensate for such handicaps is seen by them as a determining factor in their drive for achievement.

Among explorers and adventurers, there is almost always a history of accident-proneness.

Dictators, military men and poets have the highest percentage of dominating or overpossessive (smothering) mothers. An over-possessive parent of a peer-rejected child (especially a mother who dislikes her husband) is the most likely to rear a dictator or a military hero who enjoys the carnage of battle.

The loss by death of a brother or sister is described as extremely traumatic by fifty-seven persons.

Stepmothers, of whom there were fourteen, played a helpful role to eleven stepsons or stepdaughters, and are not appreciated by three stepsons.

Among the children of twenty-three alcoholic fathers, there are fourteen who are humorous writers, actors or actresses, or singers.

The homes of the Four Hundred were exceptionally free of mental illnesses requiring hospitalization.

The children enjoyed being tutored, whether by professional tutors or by their parents.

The secondary school was the most frequently disliked, and the prestige college was the best accepted.

Three-fifths of the Four Hundred expressed dissatisfaction with schools and schoolteachers, although four-fifths showed exceptional talent.

COMPARISON WITH RECENT STUDIES

While sifting raw data from our notes and making observations derived from scanning or reading in their entirety some five thousand volumes we have been uneasily aware that we may inadvertently have reflected some personal bias. We are reassured, however, by recent studies made by psychological and social scientists which tend to corroborate the observations we made on the Four Hundred and which raise similar questions.

The troubled home has been the subject of recent inquiry by others, some of whom share our anxieties as to the interpretation of findings concerning this relationship between troubled homes and creativity. In the July, 1961, *Quarterly* published by the Carnegie Corporation, which has given financial support to various studies of creativity, the editor says:

It must be reported that creative people claim more than others do that their childhoods were not entirely happy. (They may be telling the objective truth, or it may be that this is simply another sign of their often-noted ability to see accurately and accept what others may repress.) At any rate, the finding should not be interpreted by parents as meaning that they should make their children miserable in the hope of making them creative.

This article advocates less emphasis on "togetherness" and on producing "well-rounded children" and encourages the provision of maximum opportunities for the able student to work out his own interests under the supervision of creative teachers.

Dislike of school, the troubled home, the dominating mother and the ability to risk failure are all found again in a study of top-flight architects done at the University of California Institute of Personality Assessment and Research, the director of which, Dr. Donald W. MacKinnon, says:

> not all of them [top-flight architects] had the kind of happy homes . . . generally thought to be conducive to sound psychological development.[1]

Almost without exception one or both of the parents showed considerable skill in drawing or painting. Often it was the mother who, in the architect's early years, fostered his artistic potentialities by her own example and by teaching him herself. There were a few among these architects who had experienced the most brutal treatment from sadistic fathers with no impairment of their architectural ability; however, they were less successful businessmen than the architects who had more kindly fathers.

The outstanding architects tended to be superior in intellect, but not necessarily "highly gifted." In a test of concept mastery, they were slightly superior to undergraduate students but slightly below research scientists also studied at the Institute. In college they did as little work as possible in courses which did not interest them, and made A's in courses which pleased them. One of the presently most creative men was once advised by the dean of his college to quit because he had no talent. Another failed his design dissertation when he attacked the stylism of the faculty, and he was obliged to take his degree in art. Similar circumstances were observed among research scientists who made good grades in high school (and were unhappy both at home and at school) but dropped to the minimum passing level when they were in college and their self-initiated interests deflected their attention.

The quality most often noted by MacKinnon among the architects was perceptiveness. He says in the same study:

> [They] were characterized by an unusual openness to experience, a wide perceptiveness of what exists within as well as what goes on outside. They had the capacity to admit complexity and disorder into

their perceptions without being made anxious by the chaos, and the ability to form a new order out of the richness thus permitted.

They were found to have persistent intensity, relative independence and a high level of energy effectively channeled; and were able to risk failure and override periods of depression, from which they were found not to be immune. They were not "easy to take" in the classroom.

SEX IDENTIFICATION AND SEXUAL ADJUSTMENT

Biographers, sometimes openly, sometimes hesitantly, indicate that certain gifted men are regarded as being somewhat effeminate and certain gifted women overly masculine. Among the parents, the dominating mother is the woman with the long, firm stride and independent ways and the father is often the dreamer of dreams.

E. Paul Torrance, director of the Bureau of Educational Research of the University of Minnesota and a perceptive observer of the creative, finds that creative girls often seem masculine and creative boys often seem effeminate. He believes that this merely reflects the nature of creativity itself, which demands both sensitivity and independence in the same person. Indifferent observers do not notice that the effeminate boys are also independent and the independent girls are sensitive. Their contemporaries and the biographers of the Four Hundred may have been equally unobservant on this score.

MacKinnon strengthens this observation by citing the fact that the architects he studied were masculine in appearance and in overt behavior, and reported no problems in sex identification in interviews, yet they were made to appear effeminate by tests which equate a breadth of interests, a sensitive intellect, self-awareness, and openness to one's own inner feelings as being effeminate. It would seem advisable to try to change the cultural stereotypes of "male" and "female" traits. The result might well be a flowering of excellence in a climate where both independence and sensitivity are valued in any one human being.

An unusual degree of intelligence is in itself a social handicap in a society geared to conformity. Terman and Oden found that, although most of their subjects married, the spinsters and bachelors were those who scored highest on the Concept Mastery Test — the best "brains" in the group.

THE HIGHLY CREATIVE CHILD OF TODAY ALSO PROVES TO BE A SCHOOL PROBLEM

Highly creative elementary-school children observed by Torrance[2] are younger editions of some of the more teacher-harassing of the Four Hundred. They seem to be playing around when they should be working at assigned tasks. They engage in manipulative and/or exploratory activities, many of which are discouraged or even forbidden. They enjoy learning, and this looks to the teacher like play rather than work. They are intuitive and imaginative; enjoy fantasy; see unusual uses in ordinary objects; are flexible, inventive, original, perceptive, and sensitive to problems. They respond readily to such questions as "What could be done to make this toy more fun to play with?" They have vital energy.

Torrance finds that seventy per cent of the children rated high in creativity would not be selected to be members of a special class for intellectually gifted children. He finds some children who are intellectually gifted and are also highly creative. He finds other children of average or superior intelligence who are highly creative. But he finds still other children with extremely high intelligence quotients who are not at all creative.

Teachers, he finds, are partial to the child of high intelligence and low creativity. This child is not a rebel and does the school assignments with dispatch and perfection. The creative child is often thought to have wild or silly ideas or to be naughty. He is not thought of as being serious, or dependable, or even promising — although he is likely to do as well on a standardized achievement test as does the highly intelligent child who is not creative. This annoys the teacher who deduces from this that he could do his classroom work better if he would only try. He makes discipline hard for her, as for instance when he gives a unique answer to a prosaic question and sets the class laughing.

"In a number of studies of highly creative children," Torrance says, "it is evident that many of them bring upon themselves many of their woes. Obviously, one task of education is to aid such children to become less obnoxious without sacrificing their creativity."

Throughout the generations such children have been distracting influences in the classroom. Harold L. Ickes was graduated from the eighth grade one year late because a peppery teacher set him back a year for laughing uproariously in class at the wrong time. Claude Monet was turbulent and irreverent in school, especially in drawing class, and played truant at will; yet he did his school-work as well as the other children when he chose to. He set his classmates laughing with his caricatures, for which their parents soon insisted on paying him very well. While still a schoolboy he was earning a substantial income as a caricaturist. Neither his parents nor his teacher could manage him.

The mothers of highly creative children are different from the mothers of the highly intelligent children who are not creative, according to Jacob W. Getzels and Philip W. Jackson of the University of Chicago.[3] It is the mothers of the highly creative children who most nearly resemble the mothers of the Four Hundred. The "high creativity" mothers want their children to have friends who are interested in ideas, who are not easily bored, who have an openness and a fine sense of values. They are rela-tively indifferent to monetary values and are themselves liberal in their political views.

The mothers of adolescents who are intellectually gifted but lack creative ability are much more concerned with financial problems, although their husbands are better educated and better employed than are the husbands of the less materialistic mothers of the highly creative students. The high-I.Q. mothers are more bent on having companions for their children who are clean-mouthed, well-behaved, and from good families.

From the total group of the highly intelligent and the highly creative children, Getzels and Jackson isolated two sub-groups: one composed of highly intelligent children without marked creative ability whose median I.Q. is about 150, and another con-sisting of highly creative children whose median intelligence quotient — about 127 — places them in the category of superior but not highly gifted children.

Of the two extreme groups, one not intellectually gifted, and the other not creatively gifted, Getzels and Jackson say:

The essence of the performance of our Creative adolescents lay in their ability to produce new forms, to risk conjoining elements that are customarily thought of as independent and dissimilar, to go off in new directions. . . . The High I. Q. adolescent seemed to possess to a high degree the ability and the need to focus on the usual, to be channelled and controlled in the direction of the right answer.

The high-I.Q. students were likely to choose the conventional occupations: doctor, lawyer, engineer. Over half of the "high creatives" planned unconventional careers: adventurer, writer, inventor.

We have seen that both the Chicago and Minnesota researchers found that the teacher is likely to prefer the child who has a high intelligence and low creative ability. Such children are regarded as being serious, ambitious and promising.

The life histories of the largely teacher-nominated Terman group of gifted children gives further support to the contention that teachers prefer the highly intelligent child who is not particularly creative. The teacher was asked for the names of the three brightest children and that of the youngest child in her room. She was also asked for the name of the brightest child she had taught the year before. As Terman expected, it was the youngest child who most often proved to be the most intellectually superior. Since the 1920's, when these children were selected, the lock step in education has made acceleration less popular, and selecting the youngest child is not now likely to uncover the brightest child in the room. The teacher's ability to choose the child in her class who subsequently scored highest on the Stanford-Binet intelligence test was less than chance.

If a potential Edison or Einstein or Picasso or Churchill or Clemens had been in school in California in those days, he would surely not have been chosen to be screened for inclusion in the Stanford study of genius.

Teachers, then as now, value conformity and clerical skills. Careful and definitive studies on these gifted individuals which have been continued at intervals during their adult lives show that the largest single group (9.53 per cent) of the men in the Terman study still resident in California in 1940 were lawyers. The second largest group (8.97 per cent) were classified as "higher clerical workers" — junior accountants, statistical clerks, bookkeepers, and the like. However, as a total group, they did well from the standpoint of "professional and business accomplishment as measured by responsibility, and importance, prestige and income." Four per cent are in *Who's Who*.

The childhood background of these competent and conforming men and women included in the Stanford study resembles that of the children of high I.Q. and low creativity studied by Getzels and Jackson. Only a few came from "inferior or very inferior families." Most of the fathers were professional or business men and there were books in the homes. In marked contrast to the Four Hundred only one child in a hundred showed a sharp dislike for the classroom and only seven per cent showed even a mild dislike. The childhood traits of conformity and competence continue into adult life.

Politically they are near center; over half are Republican. They are good community members, are Gray Ladies, Scout leaders, school trustees, Civil Defense leaders, church workers, and belong to sports clubs, mountain-climbing clubs and choral societies. They take responsibilities in civic, political and professional organizations.

The Terman group has a mental hospitalization rate approaching that of the general population. Their suicide rate is at the norm for men and slightly above the norm for women. Two women killed themselves shortly before they were to have obtained their Ph.D. degrees. Most of the mentally ill were not schizophrenic, but were alcoholic or were manic depressive.

Although they were, as a total group, extremely successful and valuable citizens, there is little evidence of the quality that advances rather than enhances the status quo. Terman and Oden say of them:

There are, however, a few fields, all dependent on special talent in which there has been a lack of outstanding accomplishment. These are the fine arts, music, and to a lesser extent, literature. The group has produced no great musical composer and no great creative artist.[4]

TODAY'S COUNTERPARTS OF THE FOUR HUNDRED

The following excerpts from life histories of children in elementary school are given to emphasize the continuity of problems peculiar to the creative child. Although these are children from comfortable suburbs in the United States, there is no reason, from the professional literature, to assume that these are isolated cases, or that they do not have their thousands of counterparts in all nations.

The eleven-year-old boy whom we shall call "Boy A" has a Stanford-Binet I.Q. of 151. In examination he shows even performance in all areas, except that he is not as good in routine clerical work as he is in other areas. His highest achievements are in vocabulary and mathematics. His appearance is attractive; he has no unusual mannerisms, shows no signs of immaturity or emotional disturbance, is friendly and cooperative, has an assured manner and a droll sense of humor. His mother is employed in research, is Phi Beta Kappa, holds a graduate degree, and attended a prestige college. His father, although an engineer, has a hobby of learning languages, can read a newspaper in twenty languages, can speak several of them well enough to communicate. The home is learning-centered, opinionative, non-rejecting. There are other children, also capable. Boy A is descended from an important figure in American history, a man of daring and imagination.

The parents play conventional roles in suburbia. The home is well-kept and attractive; the parents make themselves useful in the church and in Boy Scouts, and they are warm and friendly neighbors. They read with their children, take them on trips and supply them with educational toys. They subscribe to children's book clubs.

An early interest in electricity absorbed the attention of Boy A. The family basement is a tangle of old TV sets, radios, lamps, irons, and the like, which he assembles and reassembles. At eight he was searching for needed information in the encyclopedia with dispatch and efficiency. At eleven he draws, for fun, a diagram of the working of a transistor radio with delicately shaded drawing and typed commentary. He sings in the church choir and has composed a *Boy's Hymn* which is pleasing and melodious. His interest in music may eclipse his enthusiasm for electricity and science. His wide reading is mostly in the areas of biography, science, and music. He has a record collection. His talent in organization was demonstrated when he secured his friends' cooperation in his "Inventor's Fair," which was actually a rummage sale to raise money to pay for things he needs for his inventions. He seeks children who share his interests and usually has a "best" girl friend. He is independent, seems happy outside of school. He has the quality which made Schweitzer's life complicated at school — a sensitivity and deep empathy which make him the champion of right and justice. When other children engage in their habitual pastime of bullying a child in the neighborhood who is handicapped, he flies to the rescue with shouts and imprecations and flailing fists. (Schweitzer also was prone to sudden rages when his feelings were touched.) Boy A is habitually concerned with anyone in trouble, a child, an old person, an animal. This may be an extension of his mother's warmth, for she is the person on her block who is most responsive to the needs of others.

His teacher in kindergarten found him unlike other children and retarded him on the basis of "emotional immaturity." He had no doubt been more interested in the electrical outlets than in making paper chains. Over the years, his resistance to school has not lessened. Although his achievement and high I.Q. are known, the school feels that he must be made to conform, that he must go through the curriculum as it is planned. In a primary class he once tore an arithmetic workbook to shreds and was sent home with a new one and a warning that if he did not fill in all the blanks properly, he could not be promoted. Motivated by a desire to please a friend of the family who convinced him that the teacher really had no choice but to try to make him conform, he finished the semester's work in three or four after-school sessions, pausing frequently for conversation, consolation — and cookies. The assigned task obviously had no relevance to his learning needs.

The school principal, when interviewed at that time, thought it wise to try to take his interest away from electricity and focus it on baseball, in order to make him more like other children. There was no thought of putting him ahead instead of retarding him academically. The school demands that the routine set up for all children be followed — otherwise the authority of the school is challenged. This school has a class for academically talented children, but apparently no one has thought of putting Boy A in this group.

The resiliency of creative, intelligent Boy A has kept him emotionally stable despite his reputation for eccentricity and instability at school. He is teased and derided in the school atmosphere, but not among children who do not know him at school. Those teachers who are aware of his real needs are not able to make things right for him in a situation basically wrong. He has maintained an achievement score commensurate with his ability, but his grades in school are low — not good enough for college entrance, unless they improve.

In Boy A, and also in Boy B, who is about to be described, there are qualities which appear frequently among the Four Hundred and are ordinarily evaluated as harbingers of excellence. These boys are sensitive to the feelings and emotions of others and also seem more responsive to touch, sight, smell, and sound than are most other children.

In several of the Four Hundred can be found an exceptionally keen response to sensory stimuli which set them apart from others. First memories are of jewels, landscapes, or the varicolored stripes on a nurse's dress. Albert Schweitzer almost fainted when he first heard brass instruments played in harmony. Jean Sibelius, fearing ridicule, tried to conceal from his classmates the mysterious connection which sound and color had for him. His acute perceptiveness always made him appear as if he were someone dropped from a distant planet. Salvador Dali painstakingly describes himself as a person reacting to sensations rather than ideas or words. Frank Lloyd Wright was grateful for the colored papers and cubes of wood his mother gave him as first playthings. Shouts and blows and rejections which other children can take in their stride are often devastating and traumatic to those children. They are also often acutely aware of the unhappiness and the miseries of other children and of adults. As children they evidence an empathy which is never experienced by some adults.

Boy B is another creative child whose scores place him among the gifted group in intelligence. His parents also are bookish, have a love for learning, and are opinionative. This boy is also self-assured, attractive, and perpetually engaged in his own ingenious inventions and self-initiated studies. The following life history, written by his mother, is reprinted with her permission:

"The year is 1954. Our son Jimmie was born on an eventful day. Even at that time, the nurses told me he didn't act like a new born baby. They thought because he wasn't hungry immediately that he was in some way different. Of course, he changed when we took him home from the hospital; he demanded formula every two hours around the clock. He continued this pattern of eating and growing rapidly all throughout infancy. Other than this I had no indication that he was different. Since he was a non-aggressive, shy, dreamy-eyed baby, I thought he was average in intelligence. What was even more confusing, was the fact that he did not even say words when the books said he was supposed to. When he finally did, at the age of two and one half, he spoke in sentences, both clearly and accurately. He taught himself to walk one week before his first birthday and then he walked like a two year old child. This pattern stayed with him in everything he undertook later on. Whenever Jimmie decided to do anything, he never gave up until the task was completed to his satisfaction. . . .

"When we bought Jimmie his first Christmas toys, we were confused when we found out he showed no interest in playing with them. They were made specifically for his age, which was one year at the time. He had even tried them out briefly in the store and seemed to like them. Little did we know that toys were never going to interest Jimmie very much, and once he played with a game and mastered it, he was through with it.

"At fourteen months, he pointed to the little pictures on the back of one of some hard cover story books, and asked me (in pantomime) the name of each picture.

"He 'drilled' me for a few weeks, and then when I asked him to point to the fireman, taxi, bear, etc. he could do it perfectly. He was fifteen months old. When I realized how advanced he was, I was both joyous and panic-stricken. Even at that time, I could foresee the eventual problems he would have with children and school. I had heard of all the dangers of pushing and I was actually afraid to answer his questions, knowing this would certainly put him that much ahead of his age group. But I soon realized that with a truly gifted child, he is the one who does all the pushing of those around him in his search for answers. It was interesting for me to observe how differently the gifted child learns. All Jimmie needed was somebody to answer his questions; learning was always his choice as to subject and method. For instance, when he was two, I took him to the children's section of our town library. In one corner, there was a huge globe of the world. He ran over to it, and instead of just spinning the globe in typical two year old fashion, he asked what the names of several of the countries were. We then bought him a map of the world, and for some time he would repeat his original pattern of learning, by asking the names of countries and islands, until he had mastered it himself.

"The first time Jimmie got excited about any toys was when my husband brought home some advanced wooden puzzles. He was two at the time and when he saw the puzzles and started to do them, we noticed how quickly he moved and how stimulated he appeared. Needless to say, puzzles were the order of the day from that time on.

"Around the age of two and one half, I began to worry about playmates for him. Being an only child, his first experience with another child was almost disastrous. This child was aggressive to the point that Jimmie never knew when he was going to get socked in the head or pushed. Jimmie was peace-loving and not aggressive and could not understand why the other child even wanted to strike him. Here again, as new parents, we were determined to follow the trend and see to it that Jimmie learned 'how to get along with all kinds of children'; so we let him associate with this other child frequently, hoping Jimmie would 'adjust.' The reverse happened and Jimmie withdrew into his little shell, so that when any strange child approached him, he would cringe. We were terribly worried. After all, we were trying to do the right thing, weren't we? Hadn't we written to a psychiatrist who had done extensive work with gifted children and explained our dilemma with Jimmie? We had told her of

Jimmie's preoccupation with maps, puzzles, encyclopedias, etc., at the age of two and one half. She in turn was very concerned about his social and emotional adjustment and felt Jimmie didn't really need all this enrichment, that perhaps it was confusing to him. We also realized that the average two year old could be expected to at least play side by side with other two year olds, and that they did resort to hitting, biting, scratching, etc. But Jimmie wasn't average and how was he ever going to have any pleasant play experience with other children? I thought surely there must be other bright preschool children in our area; so out of desperation, I called our local newspaper and inserted some publicity to the effect that I was anxious to meet mothers who had children with similar problems. I was able to find five children who appeared to be bright. They met once a week at our home for a preschool workshop session. After consultations with the mothers we agreed on a program, which I originated. It included simple science experiments, Lotto and puzzles, story telling and outdoor games. It was here that Jimmie found himself and other children, who because of their brightness were also more mature socially and better able to participate in group play.

"Jimmie was very happy those days and we noticed he was beginning to show rather an intense interest in the world around him. At two years and nine months he asked the names of letters and by three was picking out small words. When he was three, he started on a range of interests far beyond his years. I can remember how he used to cry for flower and vegetable seeds every time he saw them in a store. When we finally gave in and bought them for him, he would proceed to plant them on his 'farm.' By summer, we were eating Jimmie's corn, string beans, watermelons, tomatoes, radishes, and potatoes. He wasn't nearly so excited about planting these seeds as he was about watching the plants grow. It is interesting to note that neither my husband nor I have green thumbs and never exhibited any interest in growing things before Jimmie did. In fact, our lawn probably had the most crabgrass in the neighborhood.

"Around the age of three and one half, Jimmie became interested in rocks. He noticed their difference and wanted us to tell him their names. After exhausting his search in our yard, we took him for a walk near a mountain. We could see how motivated and happy he was collecting rocks of all shapes and colors. It was difficult for his father and me to identify these for him, but with the aid of some rock manuals, we survived. Of course, Jimmie never forgot those names.

"At four his planetarium projector was his favorite toy and a secondary interest in stamp collecting started at this time and has continued. At his present age of six years and eight months he has five completed albums of stamps.

"The philosophical aspects of science often absorb him and result in such statements as 'The moon is the machine of the ocean because it controls the tides,' or 'If we shoot rockets into space and they all bounce back from the same place, that would be the end of space.' He likes to talk about ideas and to speculate about the unknown.

"All went well with Jimmie until his first day in kindergarten. One might say he was ready for school, but school was not ready for him. His first teacher didn't know what to do with him during those first beginning weeks. Jimmie showed a reluctance to attending and finally became ill. Upon questioning him, he said all he did those early weeks was just sit by himself and stare at the teacher. The toys held no interest for him. Needless to say, the time came for our first parent-teacher conference, which took place on the sidewalk outside the school. She said she was worried about him. Her biggest complaint was that he didn't act like other children, he was too good, not aggressive enough and too serious. She would like to experiment with him so that she could prevent him from becoming a hermit. This teacher made it quite clear that she had had experience with one other gifted child and it was not pleasant.

"It was in this class that Jimmie was exposed to intolerance by both the teacher and the children. When she made it plain to Jimmie that she wanted him to act silly like the other children, he obeyed. In fact, he soon discovered the sillier he acted the more approval he got from his teacher and the children. Her experiment was a success. He became the class clown, not only in school, but in our home. I complained to the principal, who recommended that he be tested by their own school psychologist.

However, she wanted to know if we would like to withdraw him from school. Of course, we were horrified at such a thought. Wasn't he entitled to an education; did it have to be the same education every child had? We decided to let him be tested and perhaps on the basis of this evaluation, they would place him in first grade in January. At the age of five, he was tested for two and one half hours. The results showed that he was a highly gifted child, but they felt he was socially maladjusted and should be placed in a next-to-slow kindergarten, so he could 'catch up'! They were afraid if they put him in first grade he would become bored and second grade would be too much for him physically. Obviously, they hadn't read Terman's studies of how a gifted child is also advanced socially and that there is a correlation between mental age and social age.

"Rather than expose him to any more of this intolerance which had already manifested itself in psychosomatic disturbances during his sleeping and eating behavior, we did finally withdraw him from public school.

"This was the darkest hour. We had hit rock bottom. What is just as sad as a man without a country is a child without a school. Naturally we felt bitter; was this the equal opportunity in education we had heard so much about? We soon discovered that equality meant sameness to some educators.

"For the remaining part of the year, we enrolled Jimmie in a private school we could hardly afford. The school was overly permissive and allowed the children to wrestle and fight in the classroom. Academically it offered little for Jimmie, and coupled with the chaotic atmosphere of the classroom, he found the whole thing distasteful. By this time, he had developed a neurosis about having children hit him, even accidentally. He felt this showed that they disliked him. He would strike back, but he soon discovered this still did not stop them. Being children, they did not understand Jimmie, so being fearful of what they did not comprehend, they would hit him. Today, in dealing with parents of other gifted children, I find most of the children to not like fighting and would rather avoid physical contact. Perhaps it's because they have other more adult methods of settling arguments. Whatever it is, I should think society would be more concerned with children who enjoy hurting other human beings. We certainly need more peace-loving individuals in this war-tense world we live in today.

"By the end of his first school year, Jimmie was very upset and it took all summer to get him in condition for school again next year. This time we enrolled him in another private school which taught the children love and tolerance and did not permit hitting in the classroom. In a few weeks he was fine again, since it was here he finally felt accepted. Here again, the teacher was unaware of his giftedness, because he was interested in materials instead of just books. The gifted children she has known have done nothing but read. Since he was always the first one through with his work, he found enough time on his hands to become a behavior problem. We then decided to have him tested again. The results this time made more sense to us since they were closely correlated with his performance at home. The Director of Education at his new school took his I.Q. evaluation into account and has agreed to accelerate him to the third grade next year and to enrich him in subject matter. Only the next chapter can tell us how Jimmie will prosper.

"Jimmie is six years and eight months as of this writing and this year he has shown a deep interest in paleontology, meteorology (he has his own weather station) and electronics. He builds his own radio and transmitter sets with hardly any assistance. He has forged ahead with his inventions, too. Jimmie has always had the ability to use ordinary materials in new and unusual ways with a definite purpose in mind. This year, when he heard about the airplane disasters at Idlewild and La Guardia airfields, he felt quite dismayed and decided to do something about it. Using a cardboard shoe box, two strips of paper and two magnets, he invented a device which the pilot could use in the cockpit of his plane which would tell him when a plane was 'off course' or 'approaching.' Needless to say, Thomas Edison is his idol.

"Jimmie knows he is a gifted child and he knows why some people resent him. But he also knows that this is a God given gift and that He too had a purpose in mind; and that was so that one day Jimmie could use his gifts to better the world and serve humanity. In this way, he can be helping all the people.

"No one can accuse Jimmie of not trying to adjust to the average or slow child. When he has invited them to our house, it was always Jimmie who would play their way, no matter how uncomfortable for him. Is it too much to ask to have other children try to learn to adjust to gifted children? To use a shopworn phrase, they too 'have to learn how to get along with all kinds of people,' even gifted people.

"As parents of a gifted child, we have felt so alone in trying to find the solution to the best way of nurturing our child to his fullest potential. I can remember saying to my husband a few years ago, God sent us a gifted one, but He forgot to enclose a book of instructions."

Teachers are sometimes parents of creative and intelligent children; and, as teachers who are also parents, they are made all the more uncomfortable by the plights of the children who cannot fit into the classroom. Gifted teachers, like gifted students, often have difficulties in the lock-step classroom. Sometimes their rebellions, as parents or as teachers, make them newsworthy. A New Jersey scientist and his wife were brought into court by their suburban school system when they kept their three musically and academically advanced children at home and taught them themselves. Another teacher went to court to try to establish his right not to turn in lesson plans, since he wanted to be free to follow the lead of his pupil's curiosities. Another teacher in a well-to-do suburb made the headlines for a whole summer because the parents of his pupils resented the dismissal of this man who had communicated his own love for learning to their children but had not been loyal to the curriculum. In defense of teachers, it must be said that a volume could be written on the creative and intelligent approaches that are currently being made by classroom teachers here and there to the problem of how to deal with gifted and talented children — approaches which reach, however, only a small minority of such children.

The following description by a high-school teacher of the experiences of his five-year-old daughter in kindergarten during 1960-1961 is reprinted with the permission of E. Paul Torrance of the Bureau of Educational Research, University of Minnesota:

"As I watched my oldest child develop, I was impressed by her interest in the world about her. She was so different from the high school students I was accustomed to working with. She seemed so eager to learn and to explore. Then when she started talking in sentences at 14 months, I was surprised how quickly she learned nursery rhymes we had been reading to her. . . .

"As she grew older, her curiosity and interest in the world around her seemed to grow rapidly. She asked endless questions — everything from where babies come from to what makes the leaves turn color in the fall. I determined to answer all these questions as they came up, never putting her off with 'I don't know' or 'I'll tell you later.' I gave fairly complete explanations to her questions and showed her how we could look up answers in books to questions I didn't know. All the time I felt she was just nodding her head and accepting what I said without understanding. Soon, however, I was startled to find her asking more questions based on these first answers I had given.

"Before long we began to accumulate such things as a telescope, microscope, plastic skeleton, butterfly and insect collection, baby mice, bird eggs and a number of fossil trilobites and crinoids which she found in the rock driveway. All of these areas we pursued as long as she showed interest in them, with the whole procedure treated as a game and no attempt made to consciously learn anything.

"After seeing her first ballet at age three, she decided to become a ballerina and took great pleasure in spending hours creating new dance steps to the music of Tchaikovsky and others. This interest in ballet was dulled for a period by an authoritarian teacher who insisted that she conform to the forward rolls the rest of the class was learning. However, the interest was renewed with a change in teachers and a more advanced class. . . .

"Then this year she started kindergarten. She had been anxious all summer, even though I kept reminding her that she would not be allowed to read until a year later in the first grade. . . . The first few weeks of kindergarten she was delirious with excitement.

Every day she was eager for school. Show-and-Tell time was her favorite. She collected leaves from 22 different varieties of trees in the yard. Then she pasted them in a book, printed their names underneath and took them to Show-and-Tell with an explanation of what makes leaves change color. Next she took her pet turtle with her book illustrating the life cycles of fishes, reptiles and amphibians.

"About November she began to complain that all the other kids were bringing their toys and dolls for Show-and-Tell or telling what they saw on TV. Her interest dropped further as she found that the teacher did all of the reading instead of letting the kids read. The end came when the teacher refused to let her use the Teach-a-Time clock to show the other kids how to tell time and made her paste paper instead.

"Her interests then began to move in the direction of what she wore that was different from the other children. She began to quote more and more what the teacher said and accepted it as law over anything else.

"Interest was revived briefly when the teacher said she could bring her telescope and book on astronomy during the week they were to talk about outer space. However, the teacher didn't understand her explanation of how the reflecting type telescope works and pointed the wrong end at the sun during an observation attempt. By this time, she accepted the teacher's word to the point where she was afraid to correct the teacher and turn the telescope around. From that day on she has refused to bring another thing for Show-and-Tell and began talking only of when the next school vacation would begin."

These three gifted children are reminiscent of many of the intellectually gifted among the Four Hundred, but they are also from a segment which is better accepted because of the current respect for talent in science. They are children from homes where there is a love for learning; they are enrolled in schools generally considered to be superior in quality. In the past it has been the family which has been the prime influence in developing such children's potentials. The parents of the Four Hundred had strong intellectual and physical drives, were open to new experiences and kept their own love for learning intact even into old age. Today's parents of gifted children are subject to stronger pressure to have the child conform to mediocrity than were the parents of the Four Hundred.

Now as in the days of the Four Hundred, the child who is both intelligent and creative remains society's most valuable resource. When we learn to work with him instead of against him, his talents may reward us in ways beyond our ability to imagine.

Reference Notes

CHAPTER 1: Homes which respected learning and achievement

1. John F. Fulton, *Harvey Cushing, a Biography* (Springfield, Ill.: Thomas, 1946), p. 18.
2. Anne Roe, *The Making of a Scientist* (New York: Dodd, Mead, 1953).
3. *One Hundred Gifted Children* (Lawrence, Kan.: Kansas University Publications, 1930).
4. *The Gifted Student* (New York: Harcourt, Brace, 1955).
5. *America's Resources of Specialized Talent* (New York: Harper, 1954).
6. Karl Flesch, *Memoirs* (London: Rockliff, 1957), p. 7.
7. *Dance to the Piper* (Boston: Little, Brown, 1951), p. 25.
8. José María Corredor, *Conversations With Casals* (London: Hutchinson, 1956), pp. 21-22.
9. *Ibid.*, p. 40.
10. *Ibid.*, p. 46.
11. Brian Connell, *Knight Errant: A Biography of Douglas Fairbanks, Jr.* (Garden City, N. Y.: Doubleday, 1955), p. 24.
12. *Ibid.*, p. 48.
13. César Saerchinger, *Artur Schnabel, a Biography* (New York: Dodd, Mead, 1957), p. 22.
14. Hesketh Pearson, *Gilbert: His Life and Strife* (London: Methuen, 1957).
15. John Cowper Powys, *Autobiography* (New York: Simon, 1934).
16. William Beveridge, *India Called Them* (London: Allen, 1947).
17. David C. McClelland, *et. al.*, *Talent and Society* (Princeton, N.J.: Van Nostrand, 1958).

CHAPTER 2: Opinionative parents

1. Jane Addams, *Twenty Years at Hull House, with Autobiographical Notes* (New York: Macmillan, 1910), p. 15.

2. *Days of Our Years* (New York: Hillman-Curl, 1939), pp. 5-6.
3. *The Autobiography of William Allen White* (New York: Macmillan, 1946).
4. Barnet Litvinoff, *Ben Gurion of Israel* (New York: Praeger, 1954).
5. Patricia Strauss, *Cripps, Advocate Extraordinary* (New York: Duell, 1942), pp. 27, 30.
6. Lawrence Hanson, *Noble Savage* (New York: Random House, 1954).
7. *Who's Who in America, 1921-1922* (Chicago: A. N. Marquis, 1921).
8. Robert H. Knapp and H. B. Goodrich, *Origins of American Scientists* (Middletown, Conn.: Wesleyan University Press, 1952).
9. *The Making of a Scientist* (New York: Dodd, Mead, 1953).

CHAPTER 3: Failure-prone fathers

1. Harold H. Anderson (ed.), *Creativity and Its Cultivation* (New York: Harper, 1959).
2. *Arrow in the Blue, an Autobiography* (New York: Macmillan, 1952), p. 18.
3. *Land Without Justice* (New York: Harcourt, Brace, 1958), p. 23.
4. Sylvia Sprigge, *Berenson; a Biography* (Boston: Houghton Mifflin, 1960).
5. D. Horton, "The Function of Alcohol in Primitive Societies: A Cross-Cultural Study." *Quart. J. Stud. Alcohol.*, 4:199, 1943.
6. Hesketh Pearson, *G. B. S. A Full Length Portrait* (New York: Harper, 1942), p. 6.
7. Maurice Chevalier, *With Love* (Boston: Little, Brown, 1960).
8. Eleanor Roosevelt, *This Is My Story* (New York: Harper, 1937), p. 21.

CHAPTER 4: Dominating mothers, but few dominating fathers

1. Robert Magidoff, *Yehudi Menuhin: The Story of the Man and the Musician* (New York: Doubleday, 1955), p. 237.

2. James Roosevelt and Sidney Shalett, *Affectionately, F. D. R. A Son's Story of a Lonely Man* (New York: Harcourt, Brace, 1959), p. 49.

3. John Gunther, *Roosevelt in Retrospect, a Profile in History* (New York: Harper, 1950), p. 172.

4. Roosevelt and Shalett, *op. cit.*, p. 22.

5. John Gunther, *op. cit.*

6. Roosevelt and Shalett, *op. cit.*, p. 32.

7. Siao-Yu, *Mao Tse-tung and I Were Beggars* (Syracuse, New York: Syracuse University Press, 1959), p. 216.

CHAPTER 5: "Smothering" mothers

1. *Sex and Personality* (New York: McGraw-Hill, 1936).

2. Anthony R. E. Rhodes, *D'Annunzio, the Poet as Superman* (New York: McDowell, 1959).

3. Tommaso Antongini, *D'Annunzio* (London: Hinemann, 1938), pp. 484, 486.

4. Christine Garnier, *Salazar, an Intimate Portrait* (New York: Farrar, 1954).

5. *Maternal Overprotection* (New York: Columbia University Press, 1945).

6. *Old Men Forget; the Autobiography of Duff Cooper* (London: Hart-Davis, 1953), p. 29.

7. Lawrence and Elizabeth Hanson, *The Tragic Life of Toulouse-Lautrec* (New York: Random House, 1956), p. 24.

8. *Syngman Rhee, the Man Behind the Myth* (New York: Dodd, Mead, 1954), p. 15.

9. Boris Souvarine, *Stalin* (New York: Alliance, 1939), p. 5.

10. Blanche E. C. Dugdale, *Arthur James Balfour, First Earl of Balfour* (New York: Putnam, 1937).

11. John Berryman, *Stephen Crane* (New York: Sloane, 1950).

12. *Mrs. Eddy, the Biography of a Virginal Mind* (New York: Scribner's, 1929).

CHAPTER 6: Troubled homes

1. New York *Times*, May 12, 1961.

2. Samuel C. Webster (ed.), *Mark Twain Business Man* (Boston: Little, Brown, 1946), pp. 43, 44.

3. *Ibid.*, p. 40.

4. John DeLancey Ferguson, *Mark Twain: Man and Legend* (Indianapolis: Bobbs-Merrill, 1943).

CHAPTER 7: Not-so-troubled homes

1. Alpheus T. Mason, *Brandeis: A Free Man's Life* (New York: Viking, 1946), p. 28.

2. In Kenneth E. Anderson (ed.), *Research on the Academically Talented Student* (Washington, D.C.: National Education Association, 1961), p. 47.

3. *The Autobiography of William Carlos Williams* (New York: Random House, 1951), pp. 11, 12.

4. Helen B. Clapesattle, *The Doctors Mayo* (Minneapolis: University of Minnesota Press, 1941), p. 180.

CHAPTER 8: Children who had handicaps

1. Sean O'Casey, *Mirror in My House* (New York, Macmillan, 1956), p. 164.

2. Rudyard Kipling, *Something of Myself* (New York: Doubleday, 1937), p. 8.

3. Jonathan Daniels, *The Man of Independence* (Philadelphia: Lippincott, 1950).

4. Arthur William Mann, *LaGuardia* (Philadelphia: Lippincott, 1959), p. 28.

5. Arthur Koestler, *Arrow in the Blue: An Autobiography* (New York: Macmillan, 1952).

6. Francis O. Matthiessen, *The James Family* (New York: Knopf, 1947), p. 116.

7. Diana Cooper, *The Rainbow Comes and Goes* (Boston: Houghton Mifflin, 1958).

8. Samuel Foster Damon, *Amy Lowell: A Chronicle* (Boston: Houghton Mifflin, 1935), p. 92.

9. Carleton Putnam, *Theodore Roosevelt, Vol. I: The Formative Years* (New York: Scribner's, 1958).

10. *Theodore Roosevelt: An Autobiography* (New York: Macmillan, 1913).

11. Corinne Roosevelt Robinson, *My Brother, Theodore Roosevelt* (New York: Scribner's, 1921).

12. *Edwin Arlington Robinson* (New York: Macmillan, 1938), p. 10.

13. Reproduced in part in Mildred R. Bennett, *World of Willa Cather* (New York: Dodd, Mead, 1951).

14. John Alfred Atkins, *George Orwell* (London: Calder, 1954).

CHAPTER 9: Early agonies

1. *The Owl of Minerva; the Autobiography of Gustav Regler* (New York: Farrar, 1959), p. 56.

CHAPTER 10: Dislike of school and schoolteachers

1. Amiya Chakravarty (ed.), *A Tagore Reader* (New York: Macmillan, 1961).

2. Henry T. Fink, *Grieg and His Music* (London: John Lane, 1929), p. 8.

3. *The Bicycle Rider in Beverly Hills* (New York: Scribner's, 1952), p. 36.

4. Stanley J. Kunitz and Howard Haycraft (eds.), *Twentieth Century Authors* (New York, Wilson, 1942), p. 1432.

5. Matthew Josephson, *Edison: A Biography* (New York: McGraw-Hill, 1959), p. 20.

6. Antonina Vallentin, *The Drama of Albert Einstein* (New York: Doubleday, 1954), p. 34.

7. Paul A. Schlipp (ed.), *Albert Einstein: Philosopher-Scientist* (New York: Tudor, 1951), p. 17.

8. Martha Marquardt, *Paul Ehrlich* (New York: Schuman, 1951).

9. *And They Shall Walk: The Life Story of Sister Elizabeth Kenny* (New York: Dodd, Mead, 1943), p. 14.

10. Victor I. Seroff, in collaboration with Nadejda Galli-Shohat, *Dmitri Shostakovich* (New York: Knopf, 1943).

11. René Kraus, *Young Lady Randolph* (New York: Putnam, 1943), p. 352.

12. *My Early Years* (London: Odham's Press, 1930).

13. Frank Harris, *Contemporary Portraits, Third Series* (New York: The author, 1920), p. 92.

14. Eli Ginsberg (ed.), *The Nation's Children*, published for the Golden Anniversary of the White House Conference (New York: Columbia University Press, 1960).

CHAPTER 11: "Out of the cradle endlessly rocking"

1. Donald W. MacKinnon, "Genvs Architectvs Creator Varietas Americanvs," *Journal Amer. Institute Architects*, Sept., 1960.

2. E. Paul Torrance, *Status of Knowledge Concerning Education and Creative Scientific Talent* (Salt Lake City: University of Utah Press, 1961).

3. "Family Environment and Cognitive Style: A Study of the Sources of Highly Intelligent and Creative Adolescents," *Amer. Sociological Review*, 26:3, 1961.

4. Lewis M. Terman and Melita H. Oden, *The Gifted Group at Midlife* (Stanford University, Calif.: Stanford University Press, 1959).

Bibliography and Biographical Notes

T HIS SECTION identifies the subjects included in the survey and gives some biographical information about each subject. It lists enough of the books used as source material to serve as a guide to readers interested in further information about particular men or women. When a book speaks strongly to a given point, or if in the opinion of the authors it has unusual merit, it is starred.

Illustrative materials were selected with the purpose of presenting families who reared children who became eminent in various occupations: writers, artists, scientists, military leaders, and so forth. The method of selection of subjects (biographies in the public library) resulted in an overwhelming number of writers being included but very few scientists, financiers or inventors. Consequently, some of the most interesting of the writers' families could not be described. The family which is not described in detail is not necessarily less eminent or less interesting than are other families treated at length. The book could be rewritten several times with different but equally powerful examples.

The number of books listed does not reflect the number of books published about a subject or his importance in the eyes of the authors. An attempt was made to include as many books as necessary to describe the significant childhood influences in the life of each subject. Sometimes one book does this adequately, sometimes several are required. In every case the qualification for inclusion in this survey is demonstrated by including at least one book for foreign-born and two for American-born subjects.

The notes in parentheses are intended to indicate to which section of our discussion the individual would probably have been assigned had it been possible to use an anecdote from each person's life.

The following information is given for each subject:
field of eminence, b = *birthplace*, f = *father's occupation*, m =

mother's occupation. The subject's *educational level* is coded: c+ = education beyond college, c = graduated from college, c — = some college, s = secondary school, g = grade school, M = military training, S = special training (e.g. art or music).

ADAMS, BROOKS, historian b Quincy, Mass., f historian, c+.
  Anderson, Thornton, *Brooks Adams, constructive conservative,* Cornell U.P., 1951 (thought dull by his family).
  Beringause, Arthur F., *Brooks Adams: a biography,* Knopf, 1955.

ADAMS, HENRY, historian, b Boston, f historian, c+.
  *Adams, Henry, *The education of Henry Adams,* Houghton Mifflin, 1935 (a classic on school rejection).
  Stevenson, Elizabeth, *Henry Adams: a biography,* Macmillan, 1955.

ADAMS, MAUDE, actress b Salt Lake City, f businessman, m actress, g (was child actress).
  Robbins, Phyllis, *Maude Adams: an intimate portrait,* Chapman, 1956.
  ———, *Young Maude Adams,* Jones, Marshall, 1959.

ADDAMS, JANE, Nobel Peace Prize winner, founder of Hull House, b Cedarville, Illinois, f wealthy mill owner, c.
  Addams, Jane, *Twenty years at Hull House with autobiographical notes,* Macmillan, 1916 (opinionative family).
  Linn, J. W., *Jane Addams: a biography,* Appleton-Century, 1935.

ADENAUER, KONRAD, statesman, b Cologne, f civil servant, c.
  Weymar, Paul, *Adenauer: his authorized biography,* Dutton, 1957.

ADLER, ALFRED, psychiatrist, b Vienna (reared in small town), f grain merchant, c+.
  Bottome, Phyllis, *Alfred Adler: a biography,* Vanguard, 1957 (excellent study in sibling rivalry).

ALEICHEM, SHOLEM (Rabinowitz), writer, b Pereyaslev, Russia, f kept general store, ran inn, s.
  *Aleichem, Sholem, *The great fair: scenes from my childhood,* Noonday, 1958 (sensitive study of failure-prone father).

ALLEN, FRED, actor, b Cambridge, Mass., f bookbinder, s.
  Allen, Fred, *Much ado about me,* Little, Brown, 1956.
  ———, *Treadmill to oblivion,* Little, Brown, 1954 (an impoverished home).

ALLENBY, EDMUND, military leader, b Suffolk, England, f inherited wealth, M.
  Wavell, Sir Archibald, *Allenby: a study in greatness,* Oxford, 1941 (thought dull).

ANDERSON, MARIAN, singer, b Philadelphia, f worked in refrigerator room, sold coal and ice, m housemaid, s & S.

Anderson, Marian, *My Lord, what a morning*, Viking, 1956.

Vehanen, Kosti, *Marian Anderson: a portrait*, McGraw-Hill, 1941.

ANDERSON, SHERWOOD, poet, novelist, story writer, b Camden, Ohio, f harness maker, odd jobs, m washerwoman, c.

Howe, Irving, *Sherwood Anderson*, Sloane, 1951.

Schevill, James, *Sherwood Anderson: his life and his work*, U. Denver P., 1951.

ANGELL, NORMAN, author, lecturer, b Holbeach, England, f department store owner, s.

*Angell, Norman, *After all: the autobiography of Norman Angell*, Farrar, Straus & Young, 1952.

ANTHONY, SUSAN B., woman suffrage advocate, b Adams, Mass., f textile mill owner; after reverses, innkeeper, c.

Anthony, Katherine Susan, *Susan B. Anthony: her personal history and her era*, Doubleday, 1954.

Dorr, Rheta L., *Susan B. Anthony: the woman who changed the mind of a nation*, Stokes, 1928 (opinionative family).

Lutz, Alma, *Susan B. Anthony: rebel, crusader, humanitarian*, Beacon, 1959.

ARMSTRONG, LOUIS, jazz musician, b New Orleans, f laborer, g.

Armstrong, Louis, *Satchmo: My life in New Orleans*, Prentice-Hall, 1954.

Eaton, Jeanette, *Trumpeter's tale: the story of Louis Armstrong*, Morrow, 1955.

McCarthy, Albert J., *Louis Armstrong*, Cassell, 1960.

ATHERTON, GERTRUDE, novelist, b San Francisco, f wealthy business-man, grandfather secretary of Bank of America, s—.

Atherton, Gertrude, *My San Francisco: a wayward autobiography*, Bobbs-Merrill, 1946 (rejected, precocious girl).

———, *Adventures of a novelist*, Liveright, 1932.

ATTLEE, CLEMENT, labor leader, politician, b Putney, England, f wealthy solicitor, c.

Attlee, Clement, *As it happened*, Viking, 1954 (liked school).

Clemens, Cyril, *The man from Limehouse: Clement Richard Attlee*, J. P. Didier, 1946.

AUSTIN, MARY, novelist, b Carlinville, Ill., f lawyer (died young), m nurse (as widow), c.

*Austin, Mary, *Earth horizon: autobiography*, Literary Guild, 1932 (precocious child—rejecting mother).

Doyle, Helen, *Mary Austin, woman of genius*, Gotham House, 1939.

BADEN-POWELL, ROBERT STEPHENSON, military leader, founder of Boy Scouts, b Paddington, England, f mathematics professor, writer, lecturer, m artist, clubwoman, s & M.

Baden-Powell, Robert, *Lessons of a lifetime*, Holt, 1933.
Reynolds, Ernest E., *Baden-Powell: a biography*, Oxford, 1957 (study in extension of parental interests).

BALDWIN, STANLEY, politician, b Bewdley, England, f industrialist, c.
Baldwin, Arthur Windham, *My father: the true story*, Allen & Unwin, 1955 (strong school rejection).
Young, George M., *Stanley Baldwin*, Hart-Davis, 1952.

BALFOUR, ARTHUR J., philosopher, politician, b East Lothian, England, f inherited income, c.
Dugdale, Blanche E. C., *Arthur James Balfour, first earl of Balfour*, Putnam, 1937.

BARKLEY, ALBEN W., politician, b Graves County, Ky., f sharecropper, c.
Barkley, Alben W., *That reminds me*, Doubleday, 1954 (exceptionally supportive home).
Barkley, Jane Hadley, *I married the Veep*, Vanguard, 1958.

BARRIE, JAMES MATTHEW, novelist, dramatist, b Kirriemuir, Scotland, f weaver, c+.
Barrie, James Matthew, *Margaret Ogilvy, by her son*, Scribner's, 1897 (intruder complex).
Mackail, Denis George, *Barrie: the story of J.M.B.*, Scribner's, 1941.

BARRYMORE, ETHEL, actress, b Philadelphia, f actor, m actress, s.

BARRYMORE, JOHN, actor, b. Philadelphia, f. actor, m actress, s—.

BARRYMORE, LIONEL, actor, b Philadelphia, f actor, m actress, s—.
Barrymore, Ethel, *Memories: an autobiography*, Harper, 1955 (neglected girl).
Barrymore, John, *Confessions of an actor*, Bobbs-Merrill, 1926.
Fowler, Gene, *Good-night, sweet prince*, Viking, 1944.
Barrymore, Lionel, *We Barrymores*, Appleton-Century-Crofts, 1951.

BARTOK, BELA, composer, pianist, b Nagyszentmiklos, Hungary, f director of agricultural school, pianist, cellist, m teacher, s & S.
*Fassett, Agatha, *The naked face of genius*, Houghton Mifflin, 1958.
Stevens, Halsey, *The life and music of Béla Bartók*, Oxford, 1953.

BARTON, CLARA, founder American Red Cross, b North Oxford, Mass., f farmer-soldier, c—.
Barton, William Eleazer, *Life of Clara Barton*, Houghton Mifflin, 1922.
Ross, Ishbel, *Angel of the battlefield*, Harper, 1956.
Williams, Blanche C., *Clara Barton, daughter of destiny*, Lippincott, 1941.

BARUCH, BERNARD M., businessman, statesman, b Camden, S. C., f physician, agricultural expert, c.
*Baruch, Bernard M., *Baruch, my own story*, Holt, 1957 (supportive, learning-centered home).
Coit, Margaret Louise, *Mr. Baruch*, Houghton Mifflin, 1957.

BEECHAM, THOMAS, conductor, impresario, b St. Helens, England, f wealthy manufacturer, c & S.
Beecham, Thomas, A *mingled chime: an autobiography*, Putnam, 1943.
Reid, Charles, *Thomas Beecham*, Dutton, 1962.

BEHAN, BRENDAN F., writer, b Dublin, Ireland, f housepainter, s—.
Behan, Brendan, *Borstal boy*, Knopf, 1959 (revolutionary-opinionative family).
Behan, Dominic, *Tell Dublin I miss her*, Putnam, 1962.

BEHAVE, VINOBE, reformer, b Baroda, India, f textile merchant, c.
Tennyson, Hallam, *India's walking saint: the story of Vinobe Behave*, Doubleday, 1955.

BELL, ALEXANDER GRAHAM, inventor, b Edinburgh, Scotland, f speech teacher, s.
Costain, Thomas Bertram, *The cord of steel*, Doubleday, 1960.
Mackenzie, Catherine D., *Alexander Graham Bell, the man who contracted space*, Houghton Mifflin, 1928.

BELL, GERTRUDE, traveler, administrator, b Yorkshire, England, f inherited wealth, c.
Bell, Gertrude, *The letters of Gertrude Bell*, Boni & Liveright, 1927.
Kamm, Josephine, *Gertrude Bell: daughter of the desert*, Bodley Head, 1956 (talented girl encouraged by stepmother).

BELLOC, HILAIRE, author, b La Celle, St. Cloud, France, f barrister, c.
Lowndes, Marie A., *The young Hilaire Belloc*, Kenedy, 1956 (product of international, intercultural marriage).
Speaight, Robert, *The life of Hilaire Belloc*, Farrar, Straus & Cudahy, 1957.

BELLOWS, GEORGE, artist, b Columbus, Ohio, f architect & builder, c.
Boswell, Peyton, *George Bellows*, Crown, 1942 (supportive, middle-class home).
Eggers, George William, *George Bellows*, Whitney Museum of American Art, 1931.

BEN GURION, DAVID (GREEN), politician, b Polnsk, Poland, f lawyer, c—.
Litvinoff, Barnet, *Ben Gurion of Israel*, Praeger, 1954.
St. John, Robert, *Ben Gurion: the biography of an extraordinary man*, Doubleday, 1959.

BENNETT, ARNOLD, novelist & dramatist, b Hanley, Staffordshire, England, f pawnbroker, lawyer, m draper's asst., s.
Allen, Walter Ernest, *Arnold Bennett*, Hone & Van Thal, 1948 (highly opinionative, intellectually striving father).
Pound, Reginald, *Arnold Bennett: a biography*, Harcourt, Brace, 1953.

BERCOVICI, KONRAD, novelist, short-story writer, b Braila, Rumania, f cattle breeder, trader, s—.

*Bercovici, Konrad, *It's the gypsy in me*, Prentice-Hall, 1941 (opinionative, multilingual family).

BERENSON, BERNARD, art critic, author, b Butremans, Lithuania, f peddler, c.

Berenson, Bernard, *Rumor and reflection*, Simon & Schuster, 1952.

Sprigge, Sylvia, *Berenson: a biography*, Houghton Mifflin, 1960.

BERNADOTTE, COUNT FOLKE, diplomat, b Stockholm, f inherited wealth, M.

Bernadotte, Count Folke, *Instead of arms: autobiographical notes*, Bonniers, 1948.

Hewins, Ralph, *Count Folke Bernadotte: his life and work*, Denison, 1950 (sternly fundamentalist upbringing).

BERNHARDT, SARAH, actress, b Paris, f law student, S.

Bernhardt, Sarah, *Memories of my life*, Appleton, 1907.

Berton, Mme. Thérèse, *The real Sarah Bernhardt, whom her audiences never knew*, Boni & Liveright, 1924.

Verneuil, Louis, *The fabulous life of Sarah Bernhardt*, Harper, 1942.

BESANT, ANNIE, theosophist, political leader, b London, f unsuccessful businessman, privately educated.

Nethercot, Arthur Hobart, *The first five lives of Annie Besant*, U. Chicago, 1960 (story of a girl reared by wealthy spinster with ideas about teaching gifted children).

Williams, Gertrude L., *The passionate pilgrim*, Coward-McCann, 1931 (failure-prone, intellectual father; ineffectual mother).

BEVAN, ANEURIN, politician, b Tredegar, England, f coal miner, g—.

Brome, Vincent, *Aneurin Bevan*, Longmans, Green, 1953.

Bevan, Aneurin, *In place of fear*, Simon & Schuster, 1952 (stammering son of widow).

BEVERIDGE, WILLIAM, social reformer, b Rangpur, India, f British administrator in India, c+.

*Beveridge, William, *India called them*, Allen & Unwin, 1947.

BEVIN, ERNEST, labor leader, b Winsford, Somerset, England, f agricultural laborer, g.

Evans, Trevor, *Bevin of Britain*, Norton, 1946.

Williams, Francis, *Ernest Bevin: portrait of a great Englishman*, Hutchinson, 1952.

BLACK, HUGO L., politician, jurist, b Harlan, Alabama, f farmer & general storekeeper, c+.

Frank, John Paul, *Mr. Justice Black: the man and his opinions*, Knopf, 1949 (strong dominating mother—supportive home).

Williams, Charlotte, *Hugo L. Black: a study in the judicial process*, Johns Hopkins, 1950.

BOK, EDWARD, editor, b Den Helder, Holland, f translator, g.
Bok, Edward, *The Americanization of Edward Bok*, Scribner's, 1924 (school rebel, aided by father, wins battle over penmanship).
——, *Twice thirty: some short and simple annals of the road*, Scribner's, 1925.

BOTTOME, PHYLLIS, novelist, short-story writer, b Rochester, Kent, England, f minister, privately educated.
*Bottome, Phyllis, *Search for a soul*, Reynal, 1948 (excellent study in sibling rivalry).
*——, *The challenge*, Harcourt, Brace, 1953 (a divided family).

BRANDEIS, LOUIS D., jurist, b Louisville, Ky., f businessman, c+.
Mason, Alpheus Thomas, *The Brandeis way*, Princeton U.P., 1938.
——, *Brandeis: a free man's life*, Viking, 1946.

BRISCOE, ROBERT, politician, b Dublin, f owner furniture business, c.
Briscoe, Robert, and Alden Hatch, *For the life of me*, Little, Brown, 1958.

BRITTAIN, VERA, journalist, lecturer, b Newcastle, Staffordshire, England, f wealthy pottery manufacturer, c—.
*Brittain, Vera, *Testament of youth: an autobiographical study of the years 1900-1925*, Macmillan, 1933 (interesting description of lack of sex education).
——, *Testament of experience: an autobiographical story of the years 1925-1950*, Macmillan, 1950.

BROMFIELD, LOUIS, writer, b Mansfield, Ohio, f poor dirt farmer, c—.
*Bromfield, Louis, *From my experience*, Harper, 1955.
——, *Pleasant Valley*, Harper, 1945.
Brown, Morrison, *Louis Bromfield and his books*, Cassell, 1956.

BROOKE, RUPERT, poet, b Rugby, England, f schoolmaster, c.
Stringer, Arthur J. A., *Red wine of youth*, Bobbs-Merrill, 1948 (sickly boy with extremely dominating mother).

BROOKS, VAN WYCK, essayist, critic, translator, b Plainfield, N. J., f Wall St. broker, c.
Brooks, Van Wyck, *Scenes and portraits: memories of childhood and youth*, Dutton, 1954.
*——, *Days of the phoenix: the nineteen-twenties I remember*, Dutton, 1957 (details mental illness).
——, *From the shadow of the mountain*, Dutton, 1961.

BUCK, PEARL, novelist, b Hillsboro, W.Va., f missionary, c+.
*Buck, Pearl, *Fighting angel: portrait of a soul*, Reynal & Hitchcock, 1936 (account of a rejecting father with strong drives for achievement).
*——, *The exile*, Reynald & Hitchcock, 1936 (account of a mother who tutored her own children).
*——, *My several worlds*, Day, 1954.

BURBANK, LUTHER, horticulturist, b Lancaster township, Mass., f farmer (friend of Agassiz), s.

Beeson, Emma B. (sister), *Early life and letters of Luther Burbank*, Wagner, 1927 (a study in evasion—omits relevant details).

Burbank, Luther, and Wilbur Hall, *The harvest of the years*, Houghton Mifflin, 1927.

Howard, W. L., *Luther Burbank*, Ronald, 1946 (effect of dominating mother on marriages of son is told).

Williams, Henry Smith, *Luther Burbank: his life and work*, Hearst, 1915.

BYRD, RICHARD E., polar explorer, b Winchester, Va., f editor of Winchester *Star*, s & M.

Byrd, Richard E., *Skyward*, Putnam, 1928.

———, *Alone*, Putnam, 1938.

Steinberg, Alfred, *Admiral Richard E. Byrd*, Putnam, 1960.

CABRINI, SISTER FRANCES XAVIER, social worker, b St. Angelo, Lombardy, Italy, f prosperous farmer, older sister spinster schoolteacher, g.

Borden, Lucille, *Francesca Cabrini: without staff or scrip*, Macmillan, 1945.

Mayard, Theodore, *Too small a world*, Bruce, 1945 (sister-dominated, sickly girl is tireless adult).

CANTOR, EDDIE, comedian, b New York City, f unsuccessful violinist, grandmother ran illegal employment agency for immigrant girls, g—.

*Cantor, Eddie, *My life is in your hands*, Harper, 1928 (the bitter story of a disadvantaged childhood).

———, *Take my life*, Doubleday, 1957 (an unusual grandmother, tireless and imaginative).

———, *The way I see it*, Prentice-Hall, 1959.

CALLAS, MARIA, singer, b New York City, f druggist, g & S.

Callas, Evangelia, *My daughter Maria Callas*, Fleet, 1960 (mother describes her rejection of daughter).

Jellinek, George, *Callas: portrait of a prima donna*, Ziff-Davis, 1960.

CARDENAS, LAZARO, soldier, politician, b Jiquilpan, Mexico, f weaver, proprietor of pool hall, g.

Townsend, William C., *Lázaro Cárdenas, Mexican democrat*, Wahr, 1952.

Weyl, Nathaniel, *The reconquest of Mexico*, Oxford, 1939.

CARDOZO, BENJAMIN N., jurist, b New York City, f jurist, lawyer after forced resignation, c+.

Hellman, George Sidney, *Benjamin N. Cardozo, American judge*, McGraw-Hill, 1940.

Pollard, Joseph Percival, *Mr. Justice Cardozo: a liberal mind in action*, Yorktown, 1935 (son spends lifetime "making up" for father's failure).

CARNEGIE, ANDREW, industrialist & philanthropist, b Dumfermline, Scotland, f unemployed weaver, m kept grocery store, g—.

Alderson, Bernard, *Andrew Carnegie, the man and his work*, Doubleday, Page, 1902.

Carnegie, Andrew, *Autobiography*, Houghton Mifflin, 1920.

Hendrick, Burton J., and Henderson D. MacIntyre, *Louise Whitfield Carnegie: the life of Mrs. Andrew Carnegie*, Hastings House, 1951 (effect of dominating mother).

CARUSO, ENRICO, operatic tenor, b Naples, Italy, f skilled mechanic, S.

Caruso, Dorothy, *Enrico Caruso: his life and death*, Simon & Schuster, 1945 (one of the three living children of twenty-one).

Ybarra, Thomas R., *Caruso: the man of Naples and the voice of gold*, Harcourt, Brace, 1953 (a rejecting father—helped by stepmother).

CARVER, GEORGE WASHINGTON, botanist, b near Diamond Grove, Mo., f slave, foster f prosperous farmer, c+.

Holt, Rackham, *George Washington Carver*, Doubleday, 1943.

Means, Florence C., *Carver's George*, Houghton Mifflin, 1952.

CASALS, PABLO, cellist, composer, conductor, b Vendrell, Spain, f village organist, g & S.

*Corredor, J. M., *Conversations with Casals*, Dutton, 1957.

Littlehales, Lillian, *Pablo Casals*, Norton, 1948.

CASELLA, ALFREDO, pianist, composer, b Turin, Italy, f music teacher, m private income, tutored & S.

Casella, Alfredo, *Music in my time*, U. Oklahoma, 1955 (mother was his only teacher until he went to conservatory).

CATHER, WILLA, novelist, b Winchester, Va., f real estate, loans, c.

*Bennett, Mildred R., *World of Willa Cather*, Dodd, 1951 (detailed account of Willa as "William" Cather).

Brown, Edward K., *Willa Cather: a critical biography*, Knopf, 1953.

Lewis, Edith, *Willa Cather living: a personal record*, Knopf, 1953.

CECIL, EDGAR, politician, b Stamford, Lincolnshire, England, f inherited wealth, c.

Cecil, Edgar, *A great experiment, an autobiography by Viscount Cecil*, Oxford, 1941 (permissive, supportive home).

CEZANNE, PAUL, painter, b Aix-en-Provence, France, f well-to-do hat dealer who became a banker, s & S.

Rewald, John, *Paul Cézanne: a biography*, Simon & Schuster, 1948.

CHAGALL, MARC, painter, b Vitebsk, Russia, f worker in herring factory, c— & S.

*Chagall, Marc, *My life*, Orion, 1960 (an opinionative, warm, imaginative family).

Venturi, Lionello, *Chagall: biographical and critical study*, Skira, 1956.

CHAMBERLAIN, AUSTEN, politician, b Birmingham, f screw manufacturer, politician, c.

CHAMBERLAIN, JOSEPH, politician, b London, f manufacturer, s.

CHAMBERLAIN, NEVILLE, politician, b Birmingham, f screw manufacturer, politician, c.
Hodgson, Stuart, *The man who made the peace*, Dutton, 1938.
Petrie, Sir Charles A., *The Chamberlain tradition*, Stokes, 1938 (excellent account of cohesiveness in home maintained despite death of two young mothers).

CHAPLIN, CHARLES, actor, producer, b London, f popular ballad singer, m actress, g—.
Chaplin, Charles, Jr., *My father, Charlie Chaplin*, Random House, 1960.
Cotes, Peter, and Thelma Niklaus, *The little fellow*, Philosophical Library, 1951.
Payne, Pierre S. R., *The great god Pan*, Hermitage, 1952.
Tyler, Parker, *Chaplin, last of the clowns*, Vanguard, 1948.

CHASE, ILKA, writer, b New York City, m editor of *Vogue*, s.
Chase, Ilka, *Past imperfect*, Doubleday, 1942 (amusing description of lack of sex education in home).
————, *Free admission*, Doubleday, 1948.
Chase, Edna Woolman, and Ilka Chase, *Always in Vogue*, Doubleday, 1954 (broken homes in three successive generations).

CHASE, MARY ELLEN, educator, b Blue Hill, Maine, f municipal court judge, state legislator, farmer, m ex-schoolteacher, c+.
Chase, Mary Ellen, *A goodly heritage*, Holt, 1932.
————, *A goodly fellowship*, Macmillan, 1939.
————, *Recipe for a magic childhood*, Macmillan, 1952.
*————, *White gate*, Norton, 1954.

CHEKHOV, ANTON, playwright, fiction writer, b Taganrog, Russia, f small storekeeper, warehouse employee, c+.
Magarshack, David, *Chekhov the dramatist*, Grove Press, 1952.
Saunders, Beatrice, *Tchekov, the man*, Dufour, 1961.

CHESTERTON, GILBERT K., journalist, writer, b Kensington, England, f house agent in own father's business, s & S.
Chesterton, Gilbert K., *The autobiography of G. K. Chesterton*, Sheed & Ward, 1936.
Ward, Maisie, *Return to Chesterton*, Sheed & Ward, 1952.
Wills, Garry, *Chesterton: man and mask*, Sheed & Ward, 1961.

CHEVALIER, MAURICE, actor, singer, b Paris, f housepainter, m lacemaker, g.
Chevalier, Maurice, *Man in the straw hat: my story*, Crowell, 1949.
*————, *With love*, Little, Brown, 1960 (mother's boy).

CHIANG KAI-SHEK, general, politician, b near Ningpo, China, f owner of salt house, m did needlework as widow, s & M.

Chang, Hsin-hai, *Chiang Kai-shek, Asia's man of destiny*, Doubleday, 1944.
*Hahn, Emily, *Chiang Kai-shek*, Doubleday, 1955.

CHURCH, RICHARD, writer, b London, f post-office employee, m elementary-school teacher.
*Church, Richard, *Over the bridge*, Dutton, 1956 (literary classic on the possessive mother and son with psychomatic problems).
*Church, Richard, *Golden Sovereign*, Dutton, 1957.

CHURCHILL, JENNIE JEROME, writer, b New York City, f journalist, Wall Street speculator, ¼ owner New York *Times*, tutored.
Cornwallis-West, Mrs. George, *The reminiscences of Lady Randolph Churchill*, Century, 1909 (does not describe herself as a mother).
Kraus, René, *Young Lady Randolph*, Putnam, 1943 (home tutored).

CHURCHILL, WINSTON, politician, author, b Blenheim Castle, England, f inherited income, politician, s & M.
Bocca, Geoffrey, *Adventurous life of Winston Churchill*, Julian Messner, 1958 (school experiences).
*Churchill, Winston, *My early life*, Odham, 1930 (school rebel).
————, *Lord Randolph Churchill*, Macmillan, 1906 (account of father's illness).
Cowles, Virginia, *Winston Churchill: the era and the man*, Harper, 1953.
Eade, Charles (ed.), *Churchill by his contemporaries*, Simon & Schuster, 1954 (experiences at Harrow).
Leslie, Anita, *The remarkable Mr. Jerome*, Holt, 1954 (American family background).
Rowse, A. L., *The Churchills: from the death of Marlborough to the present*, Harper, 1958 (traumatic family background).

CLEMENS, SAMUEL, writer, b Florida, Missouri, f justice of peace, merchant, land speculator, g——.
Clemens, Clara, *My father Mark Twain*, Harper, 1931.
Clemens, Samuel, *The autobiography of Mark Twain*, Harper, 1959.
Meltzer, Milton, *Mark Twain himself*, Crowell, 1960.
*Webster, Samuel C. (ed.), *Mark Twain business man*, Little, Brown, 1946 (anecdotes about family).

CLEVELAND, GROVER, politician, b Caldwell, New Jersey, f minister, s.
Lynch, Denis Tilden, *Grover Cleveland: a man four square*, Liveright, 1932.
McElroy, Robert McNutt, *Grover Cleveland: the man and the statesman*, Harper, 1923.
Nevins, Allan, *Grover Cleveland: a study in courage*, Dodd, Mead, 1923.

COBB, IRVIN S., humorist, journalist, b Paducah, Ky., f employee of steamboat company, s.
Cobb, Elizabeth, *My wayward parent*, Bobbs-Merrill, 1945.
*Cobb, Irvin S., *Exit laughing*, Bobbs-Merrill, 1941.

CODY, BILL (Wm. Frederick), scout & showman, b Scott County, Iowa, f farmer-politician, organizer of emigrant societies, g—.

Croft-Cooke, Rupert, and William Meadmore, *Buffalo Bill: the legend, the man of action, the showman*, Sidgwick & Jackson, 1952.

*Russell, Donald, *The lives and legends of Buffalo Bill*, U. of Oklahoma, 1960.

Muller, Dan, *My life with Buffalo Bill*, Reilly & Lee, 1948.

CONRAD, JOSEPH (Teodor Josef Konrad Korzeniowski), novelist, b Berdichev, Ukraine, f land agent, unpublished poet, s.

Aubry, Jean, *Sea dreamer*, Doubleday, 1957.

Conrad, Jessie, *Joseph Conrad as I knew him*, Doubleday, Page, 1926.

Allen, Jerry, *The thunder and the sunshine*, Putnam, 1958.

Retinger, J. H., *Conrad and his contemporaries*, Minerva, 1941.

COOPER, DIANA, actress, b London, f inherited wealth, m artist, tutored.

COOPER, DUFF, politician, b London, f successful surgeon, c.

Cooper, Diana, *Trumpets from the steep*, Houghton Mifflin, 1960.

*———, *The light of common day*, Houghton Mifflin, 1959.

*———, *The rainbow comes and goes*, Houghton Mifflin, 1958.

*Cooper, Duff, *Old men forget: the autobiography of Duff Cooper*, Dutton, 1954.

COPLAND, AARON, composer, b Brooklyn, N.Y., f department store owner, m partner to father in store, s.

Copland, Aaron, *Our new music*, McGraw-Hill, 1941.

Smith, Julia, *Aaron Copland: his work and contribution to American music*, Dutton, 1955.

COWARD, NOEL, actor, playwright, b Teddington, England, f traveler for piano firm, m ran boarding house, g—.

*Coward, Noel, *Present indicative: autobiography*, Doubleday, 1937.

———, *Future indefinite*, Doubleday, 1954.

CRAIG, EDWARD GORDON, actor, stage designer, b Bristol, England, f architect, m actress, g.

Craig, Edward Gordon, *Index to the story of days: some memoirs of Edward Gordon Craig*, Viking, 1957 (neglected, overweight child).

CRANE, HART, poet, b Garrettsville, Ohio, f chocolate manufacturer, s—.

Weber, Brom, *Hart Crane*, Hermitage House, 1948 (division between parents distresses son).

———, (ed.), *Letters of Hart Crane*, Hermitage House, 1952.

CRANE, STEPHEN, writer, b Newark, N.J., f Methodist minister, m freelance journalist, c—.

Beer, Thomas, *Stephen Crane*, Knopf, 1923.

Berryman, John, *Stephen Crane*, Sloane, 1950.

CRIPPS, STAFFORD, lawyer & Socialist leader, b High Wycombe, Buckinghamshire, England, f wealthy lawyer, c+.

Cooke, Colin, *Richard Stafford Cripps*, Holder & Stoughton, 1957.

Estorick, Eric, *Stafford Cripps, master statesman*, Day, 1949.

Strauss, Mrs. Patricia, *Cripps, advocate extraordinary*, Duell, 1942.

CRONIN, ARCHIBALD JOSEPH, writer, b Cardross, Scotland, f businessman, c+.

Cronin, A. J., *Adventures in two worlds*, McGraw-Hill, 1952.

CUNNINGHAM, ANDREW, British admiral, b Dublin, Ireland, f professor of anatomy at Dublin and Edinburgh, s & M.

Cunningham, Andrew, *A sailor's odyssey: the autobiography of the Admiral of the Fleet*, Hutchinson, 1951 (a mother's boy who feared his father for reasons poorly defined).

CURIE, MARIE, physical chemist, b Warsaw, Poland, f science teacher in secondary school, m headmistress in own girls' school, c+.

*Curie, Eve, *Madame Curie*, Doubleday, 1939 (supportive but troubled home, good sibling relationships).

CUSHING, HARVEY, surgeon, b Cleveland, Ohio, f, grandfather, and great-grandfather physicians, c+.

Fulton, John F., *Harvey Cushing*, Thomas, 1946.

Thompson, Elizabeth H., *Harvey Cushing*, Schuman, 1950.

DAICHES, DAVID, critic, b Northern England, f rabbi, c+.

*Daiches, David, *Two worlds: an Edinburgh Jewish childhood*, Harcourt, Brace, 1956 (exceptionally sensitive account of revolt of youth against father's religious ideology—love for learning and opinionativeness in family—sibling rivalry).

DALI, SALVADOR, painter, b Figueras, f lawyer, g & S.

*Dali, Salvador, *The secret life of Salvador Dali*, Dial, 1942 (description of sensitivity of artist to sensory stimuli).

Cowles, Fleur, *The case of Salvador Dali*, Little, Brown, 1960 (account of emotionally disturbed boy).

D'ANNUNZIO, GABRIELE, author, soldier, b Pescara, Italy, f Mayor of Pescara, unsuccessful businessman, c.

Antongini, Tommaso, *D'Annunzio*, Little, Brown, 1938.

Rhodes, Anthony R. E., *D'Annunzio: the poet as superman*, McDowell-Obolensky, 1960.

Winwar, Frances, *Wingless victory*, Harper, 1956.

DARROW, CLARENCE, lawyer, b Kinsman, Ohio, f minister (resigned), then carpenter & furniture maker, c+.

*Darrow, Clarence, *The story of my life*, Scribner's, 1932 (opinionative, intellectual, failure-prone father).

Stone, Irving, *Clarence Darrow for the defense*, Doubleday, 1941.

DAY LEWIS, CECIL, poet, b Ballintogher, Ireland, f Anglican curate, c.
*Day Lewis, Cecil, *The buried day*, Chatto & Windus, 1960 (precocious child in conflict with overpossessive widower-father).

DEBS, EUGENE, socialist leader, b Terre Haute, Ind., f kept grocery store, g.
*Ginger, Ray, *The bending cross*, Rutgers U.P., 1949 (strongly supportive family, good sibling relationships).
Morais, Herbert M., *Gene Debs: the story of a fighting American*, International, 1948.

DEBUSSY, CLAUDE, composer, b St. Germain-en-Laye, France, f kept china shop, s.
Harvey, Harry B., *Claude of France*, Allen, Towne & Heath, 1948.
*Seroff, Victor, *Debussy, musician of France*, Putnam, 1956 (neglected, rejected boy, probably illegitimate, spent holidays in luxurious, stimulating surroundings, his winters in poverty and intellectual isolation).

DE GAULLE, CHARLES, soldier, politician, b Lille, France, f professor of philosophy & literature, s & M.
Barres, Philippe, *Charles de Gaulle*, Doubleday, 1941.
Clark, Stanley F., *The man who is France*, Dodd, Mead, 1960.
Hatch, Alden, *The de Gaulle nobody knows*, Hawthorne, 1960.

DE LA RAMEE, MARY LOUISE (OUIDA), novelist, b Bury St. Edmunds, England, f French teacher in England, thought to be a spy, g.
Bigland, Eileen, *Ouida, the passionate Victorian*, Duell, Sloan & Pearce, 1951 (mother, English girl from small town, was deserted by mysterious French intellectual).
ffrench, Yvonne, *Ouida, a study in ostentation*, Cobden-Sandreson, 1938.
Stirling, Monica, *The fine and the wicked*, Coward-McCann, 1958.

DELIUS, FREDERICK, composer, b Bradford, England, f export merchant, c—.
Beecham, Sir Thomas, *Frederick Delius*, Hutchinson, 1959.
*Delius, Clare, *Frederick Delius: memories of my brother*, Nicholson & Watson, 1935 (dominating father—indefatigable mother).

DE MILLE, AGNES, dancer, b New York City, f Hollywood producer, c.

DE MILLE, CECIL, movie producer, b Ashfield, Mass., f playwright, m teacher, c.
de Mille, Agnes, *And promenade home*, Little, Brown, 1958.
*———, *Dance to the piper*, Little, Brown, 1952 (opinionative family).
Koury, Phil A., *Yes, Mr. De Mille*, Putnam, 1959.

DE VALERA, EAMON, politician, b New York City (left at 2), f artist, Spanish immigrant to U.S., uncle (father figure) farmer, County Limerick, Ireland, c+.
MacManus, M. J., *Eamon de Valera*, Ziff-Davis, 1946 (opinionative uncle reared boy).

DEWEY, JOHN, philosopher, educator, b Burlington, Vt., f general store-keeper, c+.
*Eastman, Max, *Great companions*, Farrar, 1942.
Edman, Irwin (ed.), *John Dewey, his contribution to the American tradition*, Bobbs-Merrill, 1955.
Geiger, John R., *John Dewey in perspective*, Oxford, 1958.
*Huff, Warren and Edna (eds.), *Famous Americans*, Webb, 1941 (store-keeper father had strong literary tastes; son, small, frail, was omnivorous reader. Mother, from family more distinguished than father's family, was twenty years her husband's junior).

DEWEY, THOMAS E., lawyer, politician, b Owosso, Michigan, f publisher Owosso *Times*, postmaster of Owosso, c+.
Hughes, Rupert, *Attorney for the people: the story of Thomas E. Dewey*, Houghton Mifflin, 1940.
Walker, Stanley, *Dewey, an American of this century*, McGraw-Hill, 1944.

DJILAS, MILOVAN, writer, former Yugoslav Communist party official, b near Kolasin, Montenegro, f farm owner, c.
*Djilas, Milovan, *Land without justice*, Harcourt, Brace, 1958 (unusual, detailed, valuable account of literary and psychological merit; opinionative family; criticism of teacher).

DOUGLAS, WILLIAM O., jurist, b Maine, Minn., f Presbyterian minister, c+.
*Douglas, William O., *Of men and mountains*, Harper, 1950.
———, *Strange lands and friendly people*, Harper, 1951.

DOYLE, ARTHUR CONAN, dectective-story writer, b Edinburgh, f clerk, architect, builder, c+.
Carr, John Dickson, *The life of Sir Arthur Conan Doyle*, Harper, 1949 (failure-prone father whose father and brothers were successful).
Doyle, Adrian Conan, *The true Conan Doyle*, Coward-McCann, 1946.

DREISER, THEODORE, editor, writer, b Terre Haute, Ind., f mill-owner, then day laborer after business failure, c—.
Dreiser, Helen, *My life with Dreiser*, World, 1951.
Dreiser, Theodore, *Dawn: a history of my life*, Liveright, 1931.
Kazin, Alfred, *The stature of Theodore Dreiser*, Indiana U.P., 1955.
Matthiessen, Francis, *Theodore Dreiser*, Sloane, 1951.

DUBINSKY, DAVID, labor leader, b Brest-Litovsk, Russian Poland, f baker, owner of small shop, g.
Danish, Max D., *World of David Dubinsky*, World, 1957.
Dewey, John, *David Dubinsky*, Inter-Allied, 1951 (father failure—good stepmother).

DUNCAN, ISADORA, dancer, b San Francisco, f businessman, g—.
Duncan, Isadora, *My life*, Boni & Liveright, 1927 (father wealthy but failure-prone business man, separated from family).

Desti, Mary, *The untold story: the life of Isadora Duncan*, Liveright, 1929 (exceptionally permissive mother).

DUSE, ELEONORA, actress, b Vigevano, Italy, f actor, m actress.
Harding, Bertita, *Age cannot wither*, Lippincott, 1947.

DUVEEN, JOSEPH, art connoisseur & dealer, b Hull, England, f art dealer, g—.
Behrman, Samuel, *Duveen*, Random House, 1952 (grandmother collects Delft).
Duveen, James, *The rise of the House of Duveen*, Knopf, 1957 (family shares interest in collecting for three generations).

DVORAK, ANTONIN, composer, director, b Muhlhousen, Bohemia, f butcher, s & S.
Robertson, Alec, *Dvořák*, Dutton, 1945 (supportive, but nonintellectual, nonmusical home).
Stefan-Gruenfeldt, *Antonin Dvořák*, Greystone, 1941.

EARHART, AMELIA, aviatrix, b Atchison, Kan., f lawyer, s.
Briand, Paul L., *Daughter of the sky*, Duell, Sloan & Pearce, 1960.
Putnam, George P., *Soaring wings: a biography of Amelia Earhart*, Harcourt, Brace, 1939.

EDDY, MARY BAKER, founder of Christian Science Church, b Bow, N.H., f prosperous farmer, s—.
*Dakin, Edwin F., *Mrs. Eddy: the biography of a virginal mind*, Scribner's, 1929.
d'Humy, Fernand, *Mary Baker in a new light*, Library Publishers, 1952.
Johnston, Julia M., *Mary Baker Eddy, her mission and triumph*, Boston Science Pub., 1946.
Powell, Lyman P., *Mary Baker Eddy, a life size portrait*, Macmillan, 1930.

EDEN, ANTHONY, politician, b Windlestone Hall, Durham, England, f inherited wealth, avocation painting, c+.
Campbell-Johnson, Alan, *Eden: the making of a statesman*, Washburn, 1955.
Eden, Anthony, *Full circle: memoirs of Anthony Eden*, Houghton Mifflin, 1960.
Churchill, Randolph S., *The rise and fall of Sir Anthony Eden*, Putnam, 1959.

EDISON, THOMAS A., inventor, b Milan, Ohio, f innkeeper, grain business, m ex-schoolteacher, g—.
Edison, Thomas Alva, *The diary and sundry observations of Thomas Alva Edison*, Philosophical Library, 1948.
*Josephson, Matthew, *Edison: a biography*, McGraw-Hill, 1959.

EHRLICH, PAUL, bacteriologist, b Silesia, Germany, f innkeeper, c+.
Marquardt, Martha, *Paul Ehrlich*, Schuman, 1951.

EINSTEIN, ALBERT, theoretical physicist, b Ulm, Germany, f electrical engineer, set up small factory, c+.
Frank, Phillip, *Einstein: his life and times*, Knopf, 1953.
Schlipp, Paul A., *Albert Einstein: philosopher-scientist*, Tudor, 1951.
Vallentin, Antonina, *Drama of Albert Einstein*, Doubleday, 1954.

EISENHOWER, DWIGHT D., military leader, politician, b Denison, Tex., f storekeeper, mechanic, plant manager, s & M.
Childs, Marquis W., *Eisenhower, captive hero: a critical study of the general and the President*, Harcourt, Brace, 1958.
Davis, Kenneth S., *Soldier of democracy: a biography of Dwight Eisenhower*, Doubleday, 1945.
Gunther, John, *Eisenhower: the man and the symbol*, Harper, 1952.
*Kornitzer, Bela, *Great American heritage: story of the five Eisenhower brothers*, Farrar, Straus, 1955.
Kunigunde, Duncan, *Earning the right to do fancy work*, U. Kansas, 1957.

EISENSTEIN, SERGEI, motion picture producer, b Riga, Latvia, f prosperous shipbuilder, m inherited wealth, c.
Seton, Maria, *Sergei M. Eisenstein*, Wyn, 1952 (separated parents—rejected child).

ELGAR, EDWARD, composer, b Broadheath, England, f organist, s.
McVeagh, Diana M., *Edward Elgar: his life and music*, Dent, 1955.
Newman, Ernest, *Elgar*, Lane, 1922.
*Young, Percy, *Elgar*, Collins, 1955 (mother opinionative).

ELLIS, HAVELOCK, scientist, man of letters, b Croydon, England, f sea captain, c.
Calder-Marshall, Arthur, *The sage of sex: a life of Havelock Ellis*, Putnam, 1960.
Collis, John Stewart, *Havelock Ellis: artist of life*, Sloan, 1959.
Ellis, Havelock, *My life*, Houghton Mifflin, 1939.

FAIRBANKS, DOUGLAS, Jr., actor, b New York City, f successful actor, s.

FAIRBANKS, DOUGLAS, Sr., actor, b Denver, Colorado, f lawyer, speculator in silver, m kept boarding house, s.
Connell, Brian, *Knight errant*, Doubleday, 1955.
Hancock, Ralph, *Douglas Fairbanks, the fourth musketeer*, Holt, 1953.

FARSON, NEGLEY, writer, b Plainfield, N.J., grandfather adopted him at age 2, unsuccessful speculator, c—.
Farson, Negley, *The way of a transgressor*, Harcourt, Brace, 1936 (accident-prone boy).
———, *A mirror for Narcissus*, Doubleday, 1956.

FAULKNER, WILLIAM, novelist, b New Albany, Miss., f ran livery stable, also treasurer of University of Miss., c—.

Coughlan, Robert, *Private world of William Faulkner*, Harper, 1954.
Howe, Irving, *William Faulkner: a critical study*, Random House, 1952.
Miner, Ward L., *The world of William Faulkner*, Cooper, 1959.

FERMI, ENRICO, physicist, b Rome, f division head on railway, m ex-elementary schoolteacher, c+.
*Fermi, Laura, *Atoms in the family*, U. Chicago, 1954 (rejected child of dominating mother).

FERRIER, KATHLEEN, singer, b Higher Walton, England, f village schoolmaster, s & S.
Ferrier, Winifred, *Life of Kathleen Ferrier*, Hamilton, 1955.
Rigby, Charles A., *Kathleen Ferrier: a biography*, Hale, 1956 (an all-around student).

FESSENDEN, REGINALD, physicist, b Milton, Canada, f minister, c+.
Fessenden, Mrs. Helen May, *Fessenden, builder of tomorrows*, Coward McCann, 1940 (all-around student).

FITZGERALD, F. SCOTT, fiction writer, b St. Paul, Minn., f wholesale grocery salesman (unsuccessful), c—.
Kazin, Alfred, *F. Scott Fitzgerald: the man and his work*, World, 1951 (marked influence of father failure).
Mizener, Arthur M., *The far side of paradise*, Houghton Mifflin, 1951.
Turnbull, Andrew, *Scott Fitzgerald*, Scribner's, 1962.

FLAGSTAD, KIRSTEN, operatic soprano, b Hamar, Norway, f court stenographer by day, conductor evenings, m vocal coach at Oslo Opera, c.
Biancolli, Louis, *The Flagstad manuscript*, Putnam, 1952 (failure-prone father, dominating mother).

FLEMING, ALEXANDER, bacteriologist, b Lochfield, Ayrshire, f farmer, m managed farm with help of stepson after f's death, c+.
Ludovici, Laurence J., *Fleming, discoverer of penicillin*, Dakers, 1952 (supportive family, good sibling relationship).
Maurois, André, *Life of Sir Alexander Fleming*, Dutton, 1959.

FLESCH, KARL, violinist, teacher, b Wieselburg, Hungary, f surgeon, s & S.
Flesch, Karl, *Memoirs*, Rockliff, 1957 (a record of congenial parents).

FLEXNER, ABRAHAM, lawyer, educator, b Louisville, Ky., f wholesale merchant to peddlers, c+.
Flexner, Abraham, *Abraham Flexner: an autobiography*, Simon & Schuster, 1960 (record of good sibling relationship).
Flexner, Abraham, *I remember*, Simon & Schuster, 1940 (a strong mother —father's business failed).

FORD, FORD MADOX, writer, teacher, b Merton, England, f (a German citizen) musical editor of London *Times*, c.
Goldring, Douglas, *Trained for genius*, Dutton, 1949 (a most opinionative family background).

FORD, HENRY, automobile manufacturer, b Greenfield, Mich., f farmer, g.
Garrett, Garet, *The wild wheel*, Pantheon, 1952.
Nevins, Allan, *Ford: the times, the man, the company*, Scribner's, 1954
(boy thought dull by father).
Richards, William C., *The last billionaire*, Scribner's, 1948.

FORSTER, EDWARD MORGAN, novelist, b London, f architect, c.
Forster, E. M., *Hill of Devi*, Harcourt, Bruce, 1953 (woman "smothered"
sickly boy).
————, *Marianne Thornton: a domestic biography, 1797–1887*, Harcourt,
Brace, 1956 (biography of great-aunt in whose home he lived).
Trilling, Lionel, *E. M. Forster*, New Directions, 1943.

FRANCE, ANATOLE, novelist, critic, poet, b Paris, f bookseller, c.
Axelrad, Jacob, *Anatole France: a life without illusions*, Harper, 1944.
Cerf, Barry, *Anatole France: the degeneration of a great artist*, Dial, 1926.

FRANCO, FRANCISCO, soldier, dictator, b El Ferrol, Spain, f naval officer
(paymaster), s & M.
Arrarás, Joaquín, *Francisco Franco: the times and the man*, Bruce, 1938 (a
rejected child, unhappy childhood).
Coles, Sydney F. A., *Franco of Spain*, Spearman, 1955 (account of unhappy
childhood).

FRANK, ANNE, writer, b Frankfurt, Germany, f businessman s.
Frank, Anne, *Diary of a young girl*, Doubleday, 1952.
Schnabel, Ernst, *Anne Frank: portrait in courage*, Harcourt, Brace, 1958
(record of a child thought less capable than brilliant sister).

FREUD, SIGMUND, founder of psychoanalysis, b Freiburg, Moravia, f
owner of small textile mill, c+.
Freud, Martin, *Glory reflected: Sigmund Freud, man and father*, Vanguard,
1958 (extremely dominating mother; son rejects elderly father).
*Fromm, Erich, *Sigmund Freud's mission*, Harper, 1959 (provocative analysis of son's relationship with parents).
Jones, Ernest, *Life and work of Sigmund Freud* (vol. I), Basic, 1953.

FROST, ROBERT, poet, b San Francisco, f editor the S.F. *Bulletin*, m
teacher, c—.
Cook, Reginald L., *Dimensions of Robert Frost*, Rinehart, 1958.
Cox, Sidney H., *Swinger of birches*, New York U.P., 1957.
Sergeant, Elizabeth S., *The trial by existence*, Holt, 1960 (rebellious, ineffectual father; opinionative mother).

GAG, WANDA, painter, author, b New Ulm, Minn., f artist (woodcarver in
Bohemia prior to emigration), s & S.
*Gág, Wanda, *Growing pains: diaries and drawings for the years 1908–
1914*, Coward-McCann, 1940.

Scott, Alma D., *Wanda Gág, the story of an artist,* U. Minn., 1949 (adaptation to being orphaned).

GALSWORTHY, JOHN, novelist, playwright, b Coombe, Surrey, f lawyer, c.
Marrot, Harold V., *The life and letters of John Galsworthy,* Scribner's, 1936 (son rejects mother, favors opinionative father).

GANDHI, MOHANDAS K., political leader, b Porbandar, India, f prime minister of Porbandar, c+.
Fischer, Louis, *The life of Mahatma Gandhi,* Harper, 1950.
*Gandhi, Mohandas K., *Gandhi's autobiography: the story of my experiments with truth,* Public Affairs, 1948 (mother's boy).
Stern, Elizabeth G., *The women in Gandhi's life,* Dodd, Mead, 1953 (dependent on women for most satisfying relationships).

GARLAND, HAMLIN, writer, b West Salem, Wis., f farmer (poor), c.
Garland, Hamlin, *A son of the middle border,* Macmillan, 1917 (son rejects farmer-father, favors mother).
Halloway, Jean, *Hamlin Garland,* U. Texas, 1960.

GAUGUIN, PAUL, painter, b Paris, f journalist (unsuccessful), s.
Estienne, Charles, *Gauguin,* Skira, 1953.
*Hanson, Lawrence and Elizabeth, *Noble savage,* Random House, 1954 (boy-in-manhood reenacts happiest days of boyhood as lived in tropical Peru with native nurse).
*Gauguin, Pola, *My father, Paul Gauguin,* Knopf, 1937.

GERSHWIN, GEORGE, composer, b Brooklyn, N.Y., f various small businesses, s—.
Armitage, Merle, *George Gershwin: man and legend,* Duell, Sloan & Pearce, 1958 (close sibling relationship).
Ewen, David, *Journey to greatness,* Holt, 1946.
Jablonski, Edward, *Gershwin years,* Doubleday, 1958.

GIBRAN, KAHLIL, poet, painter, b Bechari, Lebanon, f small business, s.
Naimy, Mikhail, *Kahlil Gibran,* Philosophical Library, 1950 (record of mother-smothered, eccentric youth).
Young, Barbara, *A study of Kahlil Gibran, this man from Lebanon,* Knopf, 1945.

GIDE, ANDRE, writer, b Paris, f wealthy law professor, c.
Ames, Van Meter, *André Gide,* New Directions, 1947.
Gide, André, *The journals of André Gide,* Knopf, 1947.
Guérard, Albert Joseph, *André Gide,* Harvard U.P., 1951.

GILBERT, WILLIAM S., playwright, b London, f naval surgeon (also novelist), c.
*Pearson, Hesketh, *Gilbert: his life and strife,* Methuen, 1957 (separated parents—son had father's personality problems).

GISSING, GEORGE R., novelist, b Wakefield, England, f shopkeeper and chemist, c—.
Donnelly, Mabel C., *George Gissing, grave comedian*, Harvard U.P., 1954.
Ward, A. C., *Gissing*, Longmans, Green, 1959 (a delinquent boy).

GLASGOW, ELLEN, novelist, b Richmond, Virginia, f businessman, g—.
*Glasgow, Ellen, *The woman within*, Harcourt, Brace, 1954 (description of psychosomatic symptoms in mother and daughter).
———, *Letters*, Harcourt, Brace, 1958.

GOEBBELS, JOSEPH PAUL, politician, b Rheydt, Germany, f plant manager, c+.
Goebbels, Joseph, *Goebbels' Diaries, 1942–43*, Doubleday, 1948.
Riess, Curt, *Joseph Goebbels*, Doubleday, 1948.

GOMPERS, SAMUEL, labor leader, b London, f cigarmaker, g—.
Gompers, Samuel, *Seventy years of life and labor*, Dutton, 1957.
Harvey, Rowland Hill, *Samuel Gompers: champion of the toiling masses*, Stanford U.P., 1935.

GORKI, ARSHILE (born Vosdanig Adoian), artist, b Khorkom Vari, Hayotz Dzore, Turkish Armenia, f trader, carpenter, c.
Schwabacher, Ethel, *Arshile Gorki*, Macmillan, 1957.

GORKY, MAXIM (born Alexei Peshkov), writer, b Nizhni Novgorod, Russia, f dyemaker in father-in-law's establishment, g—.
Gorky, Maxim, *Reminiscences*, Dover, 1946.
*———, *Autobiography*, Citadel, 1949.
Roskin, Aleksandr I., *From the banks of the Volga*, Philosophical Library, 1946.

GRAHAME, KENNETH, writer, b Edinburgh, f lawyer, s.
Green, Peter, *Kenneth Grahame*, World, 1959.

GRENFELL, WILFRED, physician & missionary, b Moslyn House School, Parkgate, England, f headmaster, missionary, c+.
Grenfell, Wilfred, *A Labrador doctor*, Houghton Mifflin, 1919.
———, *Forty years for Labrador*, Houghton Mifflin, 1932.
Kerr, James L., *Wilfred Grenfell: his life and work*, Dodd, Mead, 1959 (an exceedingly permissive family).

GRIEG, EDVARD, composer, b Bergen, Norway, f British consul, s—.
Johansen, David M., *Edvard Grieg*, Am.-Scan. Foundation, 1938.

HARDY, THOMAS, novelist, b Upper Bockhampton, Dorsetshire, England, f stone mason, s & S.
Hardy, Evelyn, *Thomas Hardy*, St. Martin's Press, 1955 (sickly boy; dominating mother).
*Hardy, Florence Emily, *Early life of Thomas Hardy*, Macmillan, 1928.
Weber, Carl J., *Hardy of Wessex*, Columbia U.P., 1940.

322 / CRADLES OF EMINENCE

HEARN, LAFCADIO, writer, b Santa Maura (Greek island), f army officer, s—.
McWilliams, Vera S., *Lafcadio Hearn*, Houghton Mifflin, 1946 (severely rejected, handicapped child).

HEARST, WILLIAM RANDOLPH, newspaper publisher, b San Francisco, f mining magnate, c—.
Hearst, William Randolph, *William Randolph Hearst: a portrait in his own words*, Simon & Schuster, 1952 (overindulged only son).
Swanberg, W. A., *Citizen Hearst*, Scribner's, 1961 (parents who did not agree).
Tebbel, John W., *The life and good times of William Randolph Hearst*, Dutton, 1952.
Winkler, John K., *William Randolph Hearst: a new appraisal*, Hastings House, 1955.

HEMINGWAY, ERNEST, writer, b Oak Park, Illinois, f physician, s.
Hemingway, Leicester, *My brother, Ernest Hemingway*, World, 1962.
Fenton, Charles A., *The apprenticeship of Ernest Hemingway*, Farrar, Straus & Young, 1954 (parents with different goals for son).
Lania, Leo, *Hemingway*, Viking, 1961.
McCaffery, John K. M., *Ernest Hemingway: the man and his work*, World, 1950.
*Sanford, Marcelline Hemingway, *At the Hemingways*, Little, Brown, 1962 (mother had unusual musical talent, not fulfilled; father demanding, highly opinionative).

HERZL, THEODOR, politician, b Budapest, f wealthy businessman, c.
Herzl, Theodor, *Theodor Herzl: a portrait for this age*, World, 1955.
Patai, József, *Star over Jordan*, Philosophical Library, 1946.

HESS, RUDOLPH, politician, b Alexandria, Egypt, f merchant, c.
Rees, John R. (ed.), *The case of Rudolph Hess*, Norton, 1948.

HEWART, GORDON, jurist, b Bury, Lancashire, f draper, c+.
Jackson, Robert, *The Chief: the biography of Gordon Hewart, Lord Chief Justice of England*, Harrap, 1959 (supportive home).

HILLMAN, SIDNEY, labor leader, b Zagare, Lithuania, f unsuccessful grain and flour merchant, m small shopkeeper, g+.
Josephson, Matthew, *Sidney Hillman, statesman of American labor*, Doubleday, 1952 (son rebels against parental dogmatism in religion).
Soule, George Henry, *Sidney Hillman, labor statesman*, Macmillan, 1939.

HITLER, ADOLF, politician, b Braunau, Austria, f customs official, s—.
Hitler, Adolf, *Mein Kampf*, Stackpole, 1939.
*Kubizek, August, *The young Hitler I knew*, Houghton Mifflin, 1955 (valuable documentary on a mother-smothered, emotionally disturbed boy).

HOLMES, OLIVER WENDELL, jurist, b Boston, f physician, poet, c+.
Biddle, Francis B., *Mr. Justice Holmes*, Scribner's, 1952.
Howe, Mark de Wolfe, *Justice Oliver Wendell Holmes*, Harvard U.P., 1957 (strong father-son conflict in personal philosophy).

HOOVER, HERBERT, engineer, politician, b West Branch, Iowa, f blacksmith, c.
Hinshaw, David, *Herbert Hoover, American Quaker*, Farrar, Straus, 1950 (family cohesiveness—opinionative mother goes on speaking tours).
Hoover, Herbert, *Memoirs*, Macmillan, 1951 (self-sufficient orphan).

HOUDINI, HARRY, magician, b Appleton, Wis., f rabbi, g—.
Gresham, William L., *Houdini, the man who walked through walls*, Holt, 1959.
Kellock, Harold, *Houdini: his life story*, Harcourt, Brace, 1928 (a mother's boy).

HOUSMAN, ALFRED EDWARD, poet, b Fockbury, England, f solicitor, unsuccessful inventor, c—.

HOUSMAN, LAURENCE, writer, illustrator, b Bromsgrave, England, f solicitor, unsuccessful inventor, s & S.
Hawkins, Maude M., *A. E. Housman: man behind a mask*, Regnery, 1958.
Symons, Katharine, & others, *Recollections*, Holt, 1937.
*Housman, Laurence, *My brother, A. E. Housman*, Scribner's, 1939 (examination failure).
——, *The unexpected years*, Bobbs-Merrill, 1936.

HOWELLS, WILLIAM DEAN, writer, b Martin's Ferry, Ohio, f newspaper editor, printer, g—.
Cady, Edwin Harrison, *The road to realism*, Syracuse U.P., 1956.
Howells, Mildred (ed.), *William Dean Howells*, Doubleday, 1928.
Howells, Wm. Dean, *Years of my youth*, Harper, 1916.
Brooks, Van Wyck, *Howells: his life and world*, Dutton, 1959.

HUDSON, WILLIAM HENRY, naturalist, author, b Quilnes, Argentina, f farmer, brewery worker, tutored.
*Hudson, William Henry, *Far away and long ago*, Dutton, 1928 (handicapped boy).
Tomalin, Ruth, *W. H. Hudson*, Philosophical Library, 1954.

HUGHES, CHARLES EVANS, jurist, b Glens Falls, New York, f Baptist minister, c+.
Perkins, Dexter, *Charles Evans Hughes*, Little, Brown, 1956.
Pusey, Merlo John, *Charles Evans Hughes*, Macmillan, 1951 (extremely precocious only child).

HUGHES, LANGSTON, writer, b Joplin, Mo., f businessman (successful) & rancher in Mexico, c—.

*Hughes, Langston, *The big sea: an autobiography*, Knopf, 1940 (sensitive description of a divided family).

——, *I wonder as I wander: an autobiographical journey*, Rinehart, 1956.

HUXLEY, ALDOUS, novelist, critic, b Godalming, England, f editor, biographer, historian, c.

Atkins, John, *Aldous Huxley*, Calder, 1956.

Brooke, Jocelyn, *Aldous Huxley*, Longmans, 1954.

IBSEN, HENRIK, poet, dramatist, b Skien, Norway, f merchant (unsuccessful), s.

Koht, Halvdan, *The life of Ibsen*, Norton, 1931.

Zuker, Adolph E., *Ibsen the master builder*, Holt, 1929 (rejected religious beliefs of family).

ICKES, HAROLD L., political reformer, b Frankstown township, Pa., f proprietor of notions store, c+.

Ickes, Harold L., *Autobiography of a curmudgeon*, Reynal & Hitchcock, 1943.

——, *Secret diary of Harold L. Ickes*, Simon & Schuster, 1933 (rejected his failure-prone father).

JAMES, HENRY, novelist, b New York City, f lifelong student of religion, inherited income, c+.

JAMES, WILLIAM, psychologist, philosopher, b New York City, c+.

Edel, Leon, *Henry James: the untried years, 1843–1870*, Lippincott, 1953.

James, Henry, *A small boy and others*, Scribner's 1913.

Le Clair, Robert C., *Young Henry James*, Bookman, 1955.

*Matthiessen, Francis O., *The James family*, Knopf, 1947.

Perry, Ralph B., *The thought and character of William James*, Harvard U.P., 1948.

JOHN XXIII, POPE (ANGELLO RONCALLI), b Sotto il Monte, Italy, f farmer, s & S.

Perrotta, Paul Christopher, *Pope John XXIII: his life and work*, Nelson, 1959.

Aradi, Zsolt and others, *Pope John XXIII*, Farrar, Straus, 1959.

JONES, ERNEST, psychiatrist, b Rhosfelyn-Llwchwr, Wales, f colliery engineer, secretary of steel works, c+.

*Jones, Ernest, *Free associations: memoires of a psycho-analyst*, Basic Books, 1959 (a candid story of his own childhood by Freud's biographer— strong rejection of school).

JONES, RUFUS, Quaker philosopher, b South China, Me., f farmer, c.

Hinshaw, David, *Rufus Jones, master Quaker*, Putnam, 1951.

Jones, Rufus M., *A small town boy*, Macmillan, 1941.
Vining, Elizabeth, *Friend of life*, Lippincott, 1958.

JOYCE, JAMES, writer, b Dublin, f doctor, actor, singer, commercial secretary, political secretary (unsuccessful), c.
*Ellmann, Richard, *James Joyce*, Oxford, 1959.
Joyce, Stanislaus, *My brother's keeper: James Joyce's early years*, Viking, 1958.

KAFKA, FRANZ, poet, writer, b Prague, f wholesale drygoods, c+.
Eisner, Paul, *Franz Kafka and Prague*, Arts Inc., 1950.
Janouch, Gustav, *Conversations with Kafka*, Praeger, 1953.
Kafka, Franz, *The diaries of Franz Kafka*, Schocken Books, 1948.
*———, *Dearest father: stories and other writings*, Schocken Books, 1954 (extreme expression of dislike for father).

KAGAWA, TOYOHIKO, social reformer, evangelist, b Kobe, Japan, f diplomat and merchant, c+.
Axling, William, *Kagawa*, Harper, 1932.
Davey, Cyril, *Kagawa of Japan*, Abington, 1961.

KAYE-SMITH, SHEILA, novelist, b St. Leonards-on-Sea, England, f surgeon, tutored.
Kaye-Smith, Sheila, *Three ways home: an experiment in autobiography*, Harper, 1937.

KEITH, ARTHUR, physical anthropologist, b Quarry Farm, near Aberdeen, Scotland, f farmer, c+.
Keith, Arthur, *Autobiography*, Philosophical Library, 1950 (driving, encouraging mother).

KELLER, HELEN, author, lecturer, b Tuscumbia, Ala., f editor, c.
*Brooks, Van Wyck, *Helen Keller: sketch for a portrait*, Dutton, 1956.
Keller, Helen, *The story of my life*, Doubleday, 1903.
———, *Teacher: Anne Sullivan Macy*, Doubleday, 1955.

KENNEDY, JOHN F., politician, b Boston, f politician, c+.
Burns, James M., *John Kennedy, a political profile*, Harcourt, Brace, 1960.
*Dinneen, Joseph F., *The Kennedy family*, Little, Brown, 1959.

KENNY, ELIZABETH, nurse, b Warrialda, New South Wales, Australia, f potato & onion rancher, tutored & S.
Kenny, Elizabeth, *And they shall walk*, Dodd, Mead, 1943.

KENT, ROCKWELL, artist, b Westchester County, N.Y., f lawyer, c—.
Kent, Rockwell, *This is my own*, Duell, Sloan & Pearce, 1940.
———, *It's me, oh Lord*, Dodd, Mead, 1955 (widow's son).

KERN, JEROME, composer, b New York City, f president of streetcar association, c & S.

Ewen, David, *The story of Jerome Kern*, Holt, 1953 (permissive, wealthy parents, musical mother).

————, *The world of Jerome Kern, a biography*, Holt, 1960.

KHRUSHCHEV, NIKITA, politician, b Kalinovka, Ukraine, Russia, f blacksmith, g.

Alexandrov, Victor, *Khrushchev of the Ukraine*, Philosophical Library, 1957.

Paloczi-Horvath, George, *Khrushchev*, Little, Brown, 1960.

KING, MARTIN LUTHER, minister, social reformer, b Atlanta, Ga., f Baptist minister, c+.

King, Martin Luther, *Stride toward freedom: the Montgomery story*, Harper, 1959 (supportive family; all-around good student).

Reddick, Lawrence D., *Crusader without violence*, Harper, 1959.

KING, WILLIAM L. MACKENZIE, politician, b Kitchener, Ontario, Canada, f unsuccessful lawyer, c+.

Dawson, Robert MacG., *William Lyon Mackenzie King* vol. I, U. Toronto P., 1958.

Hardy, Henry R., *Mackenzie King of Canada*, Oxford, 1949.

*Hutchinson, Bruce, *The incredible Canadian*, Longmans, Green, 1952.

KIPLING, RUDYARD, writer, b Bombay, India, f teacher of art, s.

Beresford, George C., *Schooldays with Kipling*, Putnam, 1936.

Carrington, Charles Edward, *The life of Rudyard Kipling*, Doubleday, 1955.

*Kipling, Rudyard, *Something of myself, for my friends known and unknown*, Doubleday, 1937.

KITCHENER, HORATIO HERBERT, soldier, b Ballylongford, Ireland, f army officer, Irish administrator, s & M.

Ballard, General C. R., *Kitchener*, Dodd, Mead, 1930.

Magnus, Philip M., *Kitchener: portrait of an imperialist*, Murray, 1958.

KLEE, PAUL, painter, b Berne, Switzerland, f teacher, s & S.

Grohmann, Will, *Paul Klee*, Abrams, 1954.

Ponente, Nello, *Paul Klee: biographical and critical study*, Skira, 1960.

San Lazzarro, Gualtieri di, *Klee: a study of his life and work*, Praeger, 1957.

KLEIBER, ERICH, conductor, b Vienna, Austria, f teacher of Greek, Latin and German, s & S— (expelled Prague Conservatoire).

Russell, John, *Erich Kleiber: a memoir*, Deutsch, 1957.

KOESTLER, ARTHUR, writer, b Budapest, f manufacturer, c—.

Atkins, John Alfred, *Arthur Koestler*, Spearman, 1956.

*Koestler, Arthur, *Arrow in the blue*, Macmillan, 1952 (illuminating description of the development of guilt and fear in small son of speculative father and anxious mother).

KREISLER, FRITZ, violinist, b Vienna, Austria, f physician and ichthyologist, c.

Lochner, Louis Paul, *Fritz Kreisler*, Macmillan, 1950.

KREUGER, IVAR, financier, b Kalmar, Sweden, f match-factory owner, c.
  Shaplen, Robert, *Kreuger, genius and swindler*, Knopf, 1960 (a rejected child).

LaFARGE, JOHN, priest, editor, b Newport, Me., f artist, s & S.
  *LaFarge, John, *The manner is ordinary*, Harcourt, Brace, 1954 (famous father is unable to endure tensions of family life).
  ———, *An American amen*, Farrar, Straus, 1958.

LA FOLLETTE, ROBERT, JR., politician, b Madison, Wis., f politician, c.

LA FOLLETTE, ROBERT, SR., politician, b Primrose, Wis., f farmer, c+.
  Doan, Edward N., *The La Follettes and the Wisconsin idea*, Rinehart, 1947.
  La Follette, Belle and Fola, *Robert M. La Follette*, vol I., Macmillan, 1953.

LA GUARDIA, FIORELLO, politician, b New York City, f army musician, c+.
  Cuneo, Ernest, *Life with Fiorello*, Macmillan, 1955.
  Mann, Arthur William, *La Guardia*, Lippincott, 1959.

LARDNER, RING, humorist, writer, b Niles, Mich., f businessman, s.
  Elder, Donald, *Ring Lardner*, Doubleday, 1956 (handicapped boy—dominating mother—failure-prone father).
  Lardner, Ring, *The story of a wonder man*, Scribner's, 1927.

LASKI, HAROLD J., political scientist, b Manchester, England, f cotton shipper, philanthropist, c+.
  Martin, Kingsley, *Harold Laski*, Viking, 1953 (small, precocious boy).

LAUDER, HARRY, singer, b Portobello, Scotland, f laborer, g—.
  Lauder, Harry, *Roamin' in the gloamin'*, Lippincott, 1928 (poverty—dominating, driving widow).
  Malvern, Gladys, *Valiant minstrel*, Messner, 1943.

LAWRENCE, D. H., novelist, b Nottingham, England, f collier, m teacher, s.
  Aldington, Richard, *D. H. Lawrence: portrait of a genius but . . .*, Duell, Sloan & Pearce, 1950 (an exceptionally maladjusted youth—mother-smothered).
  Bynner, Witter, *Journey with genius*, Day, 1951.
  Fay, Eliot G., *Lorenzo in search of the sun*, Bookman Associates, 1953.
  Moore, Harry Thornton, *The intelligent heart*, Farrar, Straus, 1954.

LAWRENCE, GERTRUDE, actress, b London, f actor, g—.
  Aldrich, Richard S., *Gertrude Lawrence as Mrs. A.*, Greyston, 1954.
  Lawrence, Gertrude, *A star danced*, Doubleday, 1945 (child actress from a divided home).

LAWRENCE, MARJORIE, dramatic soprano, b Dean's Marsh, Victoria, Australia, f prosperous farmer, s & S.

Lawrence, Majorie, *Interrupted melody: the story of my life*, Appleton-Century-Crofts, 1949 (a runaway girl—persistent toward goal).

LAWRENCE, THOMAS E., archaeologist, soldier, writer, b Tremadoc, Caernarvonshire, Wales, f inherited income, c+.

Armitage, Flora, *The desert and the stars*, Faber, 1956 (withdrawn, emotionally maladjusted youth).

Carrington, Charles E., *T. E. Lawrence (of Arabia)*, Appleton-Century, 1936.

Lawrence, Thomas E., *The home letters of T. E. Lawrence and his brothers*, Blackwell, 1954.

LEACOCK, STEPHEN B., humorist, economist, b Swanmoor, Hampshire, England, f farmer, c+.

*Leacock, Stephen B., *The boy I left behind me*, Doubleday, 1946.

LEHMANN, LOTTE, singer, b Perleberg, Germany, f small town official, s & S— (sent home from music school, unsuccessful).

Lehmann, Lotte, *My many lives*, Boosey & Hawkes, 1948 (parents did not wish her to be a singer).

LENIN, NIKOLAI, Communist leader, b Simbirsk, Russia, f superintendent of rural schools, c.

Wolfe, Bertram D., *Three who made a revolution*, Dial, 1948.

Trotsky, Leon, *Nikolai Lenin*, Doubleday, 1955 (opinionative brother is executed).

LEWIS, JOHN L., labor leader, b Lucas, Iowa, f coal miner, s.

Alinsky, Saul David, *John L. Lewis: an unauthorized biography*, Putnam, 1949.

Sulzberger, Cyrus Leo, *Sit down with John L. Lewis*, Random House, 1938.

Wechsler, James A., *Labor baron*, Morrow, 1944.

LEWIS, SINCLAIR, novelist, b Sauk Center, Minn., f physician, c.

Lewis, Grace H., *With love from Gracie*, Harcourt, Brace, 1956.

*Schorer, Mark, *Sinclair Lewis: an American life*, McGraw-Hill, 1961 (peer-rejected, pimply-faced object of derision).

Smith, Harrison (ed.), *From Main Street to Stockholm: letters of Sinclair Lewis*, Harcourt, Brace, 1952.

LINDBERGH, CHARLES A., aviator, b Detroit, Mich., f politician, c—.

Davis, Kenneth S., *The hero*, Doubleday, 1959 (social isolate in adolescence).

Haines, Lynn and Dora B., *The Lindberghs*, Vanguard, 1931 (detailed information about father's stoicism under pain and reference to his belief in the superiority of the white races).

LINDSAY, VACHEL, poet, b Springfield, Ill., f physician, c—.

Masters, Edgar L., *Vachel Lindsay: a poet in America*, Scribner's, 1935.

Ruggles, Eleanor, *West-going heart*, Norton, 1959.

LITVINOV, MAXIM, diplomat, b Belostok, Russia, f produce merchant, c.
Pope, Arthur U., *Maxim Litvinoff*, Fischer, 1943 (learning-centered, liberal household).

LLOYD GEORGE, DAVID, politician, b Chorlton-on-Medlock, Manchester, England, f headmaster in National School; after father's death, uncle was father figure (Church of the Disciples minister), s & law study.
George, William, *My brother and I*, Eyre & Spottiswoode, 1958.
Jones, Thomas, *Lloyd-George*, Harvard U.P., 1951.
Lloyd-George, Richard, *My father, Lloyd George*, Crown, 1961.
*Owen, Frank, *Tempestuous journey*, McGraw-Hill, 1955 (extreme drive toward goals).

LONDON, JACK, writer, b San Francisco, foster-father common laborer, f itinerant astrologer, m professional medium, s—.
London, Joan, *Jack London and his times*, Doubleday, 1939.
*Stone, Irving, *Sailor on horseback: the biography of Jack London*, Houghton Mifflin, 1938.

LONG, HUEY P., politician, b Winfield, La., f farmer, s— & c—.
Kane, Harnett T., *Louisiana hayride: the American rehearsal for dictatorship 1928–1940*, Morrow, 1941.
Martin, James, *Dynasty*, Putnam, 1960 (there was money for the older children's college expenses, none for Huey's).
Opotowsky, Stan, *The Longs of Louisiana*, Dutton, 1960 (best account of youthful exploits—rejected by siblings).
Smith, Webster, *The Kingfish: a biography of Huey P. Long*, Putnam, 1933.

LOWELL, AMY, poet, critic, b Brookline, Mass., f wealthy mill-owner, s.
Damon, S. Foster, *Amy Lowell*, Houghton Mifflin, 1935 (account of reaction to overweight).
Gregory, Horace, *Amy Lowell: a portrait of the poet in her time*, Nelson, 1958 (rich, neglected girl; turned to coachman and elder brother).

MAGSAYSAY, RAMON, politician, b Iba, Philippines, f teacher, c.
Romulo, Carlos, *The Magsaysay story*, Day, 1956 (opinionative father).

MAHLER, GUSTAV, composer, conductor, b Kalischt, Bohemia, f proprietor of small vegetable store, g & S.
Mahler, Alma Maria, *Gustav Mahler: memories and letters*, Viking, 1946.
*Mitchell, Donald, *Gustav Mahler: the early years*, Macmillan, 1958 (unhappy home—mother hated father).

MANN, ERIKA, author, actress, b Munich, Germany, f successful author, s & S.

MANN, KLAUS, author, b Munich, Germany, f successful writer, s.

MANN, THOMAS, author, b Lübeck, Germany, f wealthy grain merchant who went bankrupt, c—.

Brennan, Joseph G., *Thomas Mann's world*, Columbia U.P., 1942.

Mann, Erika, *The last year of Thomas Mann*, Farrar, Straus & Cudahy, 1958.

Mann, Klaus, *The turning point*, Fischer, 1942.

*Mann, Monika, *Past and present*, St. Martin's, 1960 (permissive home—much love of learning).

*Mann, Thomas, *A sketch of my life*, Knopf, 1960 (strongly influenced by unconventional, foreign mother).

MANOLETE, MANUEL, matador, b Cordoba, Spain, f butcher.
Conrad, Barnaby, *Death of Manolete*, Houghton Mifflin, 1958 (fearful mother's boy).

MANSFIELD, KATHERINE, writer, b Wellington, New Zealand, f chairman of Bank of New Zealand, c—.
Alpers, Antony, *Katherine Mansfield*, Knopf, 1953.
Berkman, Sylvia, *Katherine Mansfield: a critical study*, Yale U.P., 1951.
Mansfield, Katherine, *Journal of Katherine Mansfield*, Knopf, 1927.

MAO TSE-TUNG, communist leader, b Shao-Shan, China, f rice merchant (hired labor), c.
Payne, Pierre, *Mao Tse-tung, ruler of Red China*, Schuman, 1950.
*Siao-Yu, *Mao Tse-tung and I were beggars*, Syracuse U.P., 1957 (boys take time-out).
Stevenson, William, *Yellow wind*, Houghton Mifflin, 1959.

MARSH, EDWARD, sec'y to Churchill, b London, f surgeon, c.
*Hassall, Christopher, *Edward Marsh: a biography*, Harcourt, Brace, 1959 (handicapped boy with restrictive, religious mother).

MARCONI, GUGLIELMO, inventor, electrical engineer, b Bologna, Italy, f wealthy silkworm farmer, s—.
Dunlap, Orrin E., *Marconi: the man and his wireless*, Macmillan, 1937 (shy boy).
Jacot de Boinod, Bernard L., *Marconi—master of space*, Hutchinson, 1935.
Marconi, Degna, *My father, Marconi*, McGraw-Hill, 1962 (rejecting father destroyed boy's experiments; accepting Irish mother assisted boy to fulfill talent).

MARSHALL, GEORGE C., soldier, politician, b Uniontown, Pa., f wealthy coal operator, s & M.
Frye, William, *Marshall, citizen soldier*, Bobbs-Merrill, 1947 (a father's boy).
Marshall, Katherine, *Together: annals of an army wife*, Tupper, 1946.
Payne, Pierre S. R., *The Marshall story*, Prentice-Hall, 1951.

MASARYK, JAN, diplomat, b Prague, f philosopher, politician, c.

MASARYK, THOMAS, philosopher, politician, b Hodonin, Moravia, f coachman, m cook, c+.

*Capek, Karel, *President Masaryk tells his story*, Putnam, 1935 (gifted boy from disadvantaged home).

Lockhart, Robert, *Jan Masaryk: a personal memoir*, Philosophical Library, 1951 (international family).

MATISSE, HENRI, painter, b Le Cateau, France, f grain merchant, c.

Escholier, Raymond, *Matisse: a portrait of the artist and the man*, Praeger, 1960 (started painting during time-out period due to illness).

Lassaigne, Jacques, *Matisse: biographical and critical study*, Skira, 1959.

MAUGHAM, W. SOMERSET, novelist, playwright, b Paris, f diplomat, c+.

Cordell, Richard A., *Somerset Maugham: a biographical and critical study*, Indiana U.P., 1961.

Maugham, W. Somerset, *Mr. Maugham himself*, Doubleday, 1954.

Pfeiffer, Karl G., *W. Somerset Maugham*, Norton, 1959 (school rejection —trauma over mother's death).

MAULDIN, WILLIAM H., cartoonist, b Mountain Park, N.M., f farmer, businessman, miner, s.

Mauldin, William H., *Back home*, Sloan, 1947.

*————, *A sort of saga*, Sloan, 1949 (father-failure is central theme of this whimsical narrative).

MAUROIS, ANDRE (b. Emile Herzog), writer, b Elbeuf, Alsace, f textile manufacturer, c+.

Maurois, André, *I remember, I remember*, Harper, 1942 (father made bitter by failure).

MAYO, CHARLES HORACE, surgeon, b Rochester, Minn., f physician, c+.

MAYO, WILLIAM JAMES, surgeon, b Le Sueur, Minn., f physician, c+.

*Clapesattle, Helen B., *The doctors Mayo*, U.Minn.P., 1941.

Hammontree, Marie, *Will and Charlie Mayo*, Bobbs-Merrill, 1954.

MEHTA, VED, writer, b Delhi, India, f municipal health officer, c.

*Mehta, Ved, *Face to face*, Little, Brown, 1957 (parents differ on proper attitude to take to blind son).

Mehta, Ved, *Walking the Indian streets*, Little, Brown, 1959.

MENCKEN, HENRY LOUIS, editor, satirist, b Baltimore, Md., f tobacco merchant, s.

Angoff, Charles, *H. L. Mencken*, Yoseloff, Thomas, 1956.

Kemler, Edgar, *The irreverent Mr. Mencken*, Little, Brown, 1950.

Manchester, William, *Disturber of the peace*, Harper, 1950.

Mencken, Henry L., *Minority report*, Knopf, 1956.

MENDES-FRANCE, PIERRE, politician, b Paris, f wealthy dress-manufacturer, c+.

Werth, Alexander, *Lost statesman: the strange story of Pierre Mendes-France*, Schuman, 1958 (precocious youth, received doctorate in law at 18; highly supportive, cohesive home).

MENNINGER, KARL, psychiatrist, writer, b Topeka, Kan., f physician, c+.

MENNINGER, WILLIAM, psychiatrist, b Topeka, Kan., f physician, c+.
*Menninger, Flo V., *Days of my life: memories of a Kansas mother and teacher*, Smith, 1939.
Winslow, Walker, *The Menninger story*, Doubleday, 1956.

MENUHIN, YEHUDI, violinist, b New York City, f teacher, tutored & S.
Gavoty, Bernard, *Yehudi Menuhin and Georges Enesco*, Kister, 1955.
*Magidoff, Robert, *Yehudi Menuhin: the story of the man and the musician*, Doubleday, 1955 (mother interpreted any disobedience as rejection of her).

MILLAY, EDNA ST. VINCENT, poet, b Rockport, Me., f school superintendent, m nurse, c.
Millay, Edna, *Letters, edited by Allan Ross Macdougall*, Harper, 1952.
Shafter, Toby, *Edna St. Vincent Millay: America's best beloved poet*, Messner, 1957 (conflict between parents over father's gambling described; also mother's conflict with school authorities).

MILNE, A. A., poet, playwright, b London, f teacher, c.
*Milne, Alan A., *Autobiography*, Dutton, 1939 (exceptionally cohesive and permissive home, father made learning pleasurable).

MODIGLIANI, AMEDEO, painter, sculptor, b Livorno, Italy, f banker, s— & S.
Modigliani, Amedeo, *Modigliani: a memoir*, Putnam, 1961.
*Modigliani, Jeanne, *Modigliani: man and myth*, Crown, 1958 (intellectual, opinionative mother).

MOLNAR, FERENC, playwright, novelist, b Budapest, f physician, c+.
Molnar, Ferenc, *Companion in exile*, Gaar, 1950.

MONET, CLAUDE, painter, b LeHavre, France, f grocer (unsuccessful), g— & S.
Rouart, Denis, *Claude Monet*, Skira, 1958.
Weekes, C. P., *The Invincible Monet*, Appleton-Century-Crofts, 1960 (school truant).

MONTESSORI, MARIA, physician, educator, b Chiaravalle, Italy, f military man, c+.
Standing, E. Mortimer, *Maria Montessori: her life and work*, Hollis & Carter, 1957 (a precocious child who fulfilled mother's ambitions for her).

MONTGOMERY, BERNARD LAW, soldier, b Donegal, England, f Episcopalian minister, s & M.
*Montgomery, Bernard L., *Memories of Field-Marshal the Viscount Montgomery of Alemein*, World, 1958 (home tensions, school problems, intense mother-rejection).
Moorhead, Alan, *Montgomery, a biography*, Hamilton, 1946 (mother seen as indefatigable adult).

MOORE, GEORGE, novelist, b Moore Hall, County Mayo, Ireland, f country gentleman, politician, s & S.
Brown, Malcolm J., *George Moore: a reconsideration*, U. Wash. P., 1955.
Hone, Joseph M., *The life of George Moore*, Macmillan, 1936 (appallingly ugly son of opinionative father who suffered for his ideas).

MOTT, JOHN R., YMCA leader, b Livingston Manor, N.Y., f lumber merchant, c.
Fisher, Galen M., *John R. Mott, architect of cooperation and unity*, Association Press, 1952.
Matthews, Basil J., *John R. Mott, world citizen*, Harper, 1934.

MURRY, JOHN MIDDLETON, writer, b London, f civil servant, c.
Lea, Frank Alfred, *The Life of John Middleton Murry*, Oxford, 1960 (driving, dominating father).

MUSSOLINI, BENITO, politician, b Dovia, Forli, Italy, f blacksmith, m teacher, c.
*Hibbert, Christopher, *Il Duce: the life of Benito Mussolini*, Little, Brown, 1962.
Monell, Pavlo, *The intimate life of a demagogue*, Vanguard.
Megaro, Gaudens, *Mussolini in the making*, Houghton Mifflin, 1938.
*Mussolini, Rachele, *My life with Mussolini*, Hale, 1959 (description of mother's complaining in her classroom of her loss of income because of husband's political views).
Seldes, George, *Sawdust Caesar*, Harper, 1935 (describes his youthful delinquencies, his grandiose ways, his love of martial poetry).

MacARTHUR, DOUGLAS, army officer, b Little Rock, Ark., f general, s & M.
*Gunther, John, *The riddle of MacArthur*, Harper, 1951.
Hunt, Frazier, *The untold story of Douglas MacArthur*, Devin-Adair, 1954.

McCARTHY, JOSEPH, politician, b farm near Grande Chute, Wis., f farmer, c+.
Anderson, Jack, and Ronald W. May, *McCarthy: the man, the Senator, the "ism,"* Beacon, 1952 (three mother figures, mother and two landladies —disliked father).
Rovere, Richard H., *Senator Joe McCarthy*, Harcourt, Brace, 1959.

MacDONALD, BETTY, humorist, b Boulder, Colo., f mining engineer, m dress designer, c—.
MacDonald, Betty, *The plague and I*, Lippincott, 1948.
———, *Anybody can do anything*, Lippincott, 1950.
———, *Who, me?*, Lippincott, 1959.

MacDONALD, JAMES RAMSAY, politician, b Lossiemouth, Scotland, f laborer, m servant girl, g.
Hamilton, Mary Agnes, *J. Ramsay MacDonald*, Cape, 1929.

MacDonald, James R., *Wanderings and excursions*, Cape, 1925 (finest tribute to gifted teacher).

MacDonald, Ramsay, *Margaret Ethel MacDonald*, Seltzer, 1924.

Weir, L. MacNeill, *Tragedy of Ramsay MacDonald*, Stokes, 1929.

NANSEN, FRIDTJOF, explorer, zoologist, humanitarian, b Froen, Norway, f lawyer, c—.

Hall, Anna Gertrude, *Nansen*, Viking, 1940.

Shackleton, Edward, *Nansen, the explorer*, Witherby, 1959.

NASSER, GAMEL ABDEL, politician, b Alexandria, Egypt, f postmaster, s & M.

*St. John, Robert, *The boss: the story of Gamel Abdel Nasser*, McGraw-Hill, 1960 (father-rejection—a mother's boy).

NEHRU, JAWAHARLAL, politician, b Allahabad, India, f statesman, c.

Morales, Francis Robert, *Jawaharlal Nehru: a biography*, Macmillan, 1956.

Nehru, Jawaharlal, *Toward freedom: autobiography*, Day, 1941.

NIEBUHR, REINHOLD, theologian, b Wright City, Mo., f minister, c+.

Davies, David R., *Reinhold Niebuhr, prophet from America*, Macmillan, 1948 (supportive home).

Harland, Gordon, *The thoughts of Reinhold Niebuhr*, Oxford, 1960.

NIEMOLLER, MARTIN, theologian, b Westphalia, Germany, f Lutheran minister, c.

Davidson, Clarissa S., *God's man: the story of Pastor Niemöller*, Washburn, 1959 (relatively untroubled home).

NIETZSCHE, FRIEDRICH W., philosopher, poet, b Rocken, Saxony, f Lutheran pastor, c+.

Förster-Nietzsche, Elisabeth, *The life of Nietzsche*, Sturgis & Walton, 1912 (tense, woman-dominated household).

Nietzsche, Friedrich W., *My sister and I*, Boar's Head, 1959 (bitter attack on mother, sister and sweetheart written in mental hospital).

Reyburn, Hugh Adam, *Nietzsche: the story of a human philosopher*, Macmillan, 1948.

NIJINSKY, VASLAV, dancer, b Kiev, Russia, f & m dancers, S.

Bourman, Anatole, *The tragedy of Nijinsky*, McGraw-Hill, 1936 (father, mother and only sister talented ballet dancers; only brother mentally ill).

Nijinsky, Romola, *Nijinsky*, Simon & Schuster, 1934.

———, *The last years of Nijinsky*, Simon & Schuster, 1952 (love for dancing helps in recovery from mental illness).

NIXON, RICHARD M., politician, b Yorba Linda, Calif., f laboring man and storekeeper, c+.

De Toledano, Ralph, *Nixon*, Duell, Sloan & Pearce, 1960 (good all-around student, excelled in debating).

Costello, William, *The facts about Nixon: an unauthorized biography*, Viking, 1960.

Kornitzer, Bela, *The real Nixon: an intimate biography*, Rand, 1960.

NKRUMAH, KWAME, politician, b Ankroful, Nzima, Gold Coast, f gold miner, c+.

Nkrumah, Kwame, *Ghana: the autobiography of Kwame Nkrumah*, Nelson, 1957 (happily functioning polygamous household).

NORRIS, GEORGE W., politician, b Sandusky County, Ohio, f farmer, c.

Neuberger, Richard Lewis, and Stephen Kahn, *Integrity: the life of George W. Norris*, Vanguard, 1937 (mother divorces second husband, who is unkind to her children).

O'CASEY, SEAN, playwright, b Dublin, f Protestant church official, g—.

Krause, David, *Sean O'Casey: the man and his work*, Macmillan, 1960.

*O'Casey, Sean, *Mirror in my house: the autobiographies of Sean O'Casey*, vol. 1, Macmillan, 1956.

O'NEILL, EUGENE, playwright, b New York City, f actor, c—.

Boulton, Agnes, *Part of a long story*, Doubleday, 1958.

Bowen, Croswell (with the assistance of Shane O'Neill), *Curse of the misbegotten*, McGraw-Hill, 1959 (childhood resentment of being born as replacement for deceased brother, and of being told that it was the pain of his birth which was the reason for his mother's becoming a drug addict).

OPPENHEIM, E. PHILLIPS, novelist, b Leicester, England, f merchant, s—.

Oppenheim, E. Phillips, *The pool of memory*, Little, Brown, 1945 (school rejection—supportive, congenial parents).

OPPENHEIMER, J. ROBERT, physicist, b New York City, f textile manufacturer (wealthy), c+.

Alsop, Joseph and Stewart, *We accuse!*, Simon & Schuster, 1954.

Kugelmass, J. Alvin, *J. Robert Oppenheimer and the atomic story*, Messner, 1953.

OROZCO, JOSE CLEMENTE, painter, b Zapotlán, Mexico, f editor, c.

Helm, MacKinley, *Man of fire*, Harcourt, Brace, 1953.

ORWELL, GEORGE, writer, b Motihari, India, f British civil servant, s.

Atkins, John Alfred, *George Orwell*, Ungar, 1955.

*Orwell, George, *Such were the joys*, Harcourt, Brace, 1953 (strong denunciation of his boarding school—brutal bed-wetting cure described).

OSLER, WILLIAM, physician, humanitarian, author, bibliophile, b Bondhead, Ontario, Canada, f minister, c+.

Cushing, Harvey W., *The life of Sir William Osler*, Clarendon, 1925.

Reid, Edith, *The great physician*, Oxford, 1931.

PADEREWSKI, IGNACE JAN, pianist, politician, b Kurylowaka, Poland, f manager of estates, g & S.

Paderewski, Ignace Jan, and Mary Lawton, *The Paderewski memoirs*, Scribner's, 1938.

Phillips, Charles J. M., *Paderewski: the story of a modern immortal*, Macmillan, 1934 (school rebel).

PASTERNAK, BORIS, writer, b Moscow, f painter, m musician, c+ & S.

Pasternak, Boris, *Safe conduct: an autobiography*, New Directions, 1958 (supportive, intellectual parents).

————, *I remember: sketch for an autobiography*, Pantheon, 1959 (Strong school rejection; love for home).

Ruge, Gerd, *Pasternak: a pictorial biography*, McGraw-Hill, 1959.

PATTON, GEORGE S., soldier, b San Gabriel, Calif., f lawyer, s & M.

Mellor, William B., *Patton, the fighting man*, Putnam, 1946.

Semmes, Harry H., *Portrait of Patton*, Appleton, 1955.

Wellard, James H., *General George S. Patton, Jr., man under Mars*, Dodd, Mead, 1946.

PAUL, ELLIOT, writer, b Malden, Mass., f farmer, c——.

Paul, Elliot, *Linden on the Saugus Branch*, Random House, 1947 (exercise in total recall by precocious, mother-tutored boy—never one to praise the classroom).

————, *A ghost town on the Yellowstone*, Random House, 1948 (anecdotal boyhood memories, ribald, nostalgic).

————, *My old Kentucky home*, Random House, 1949 (at age 18—one in series of autobiographical books; whole series called *Items on the grand account*).

PAVLOV, IVAN P., physiologist, b Ryazan, Russia, f Greek Orth. priest, c+.

Babkin, Boris P., *Pavlov*, U. Chicago, 1949 (time-out period established him as scholar).

PEARY, ROBERT E., arctic explorer, b Cresson, Pa., f lumberman, c.

*Stafford, Marie (Peary), *Discoverer of the North Pole*, Morrow, 1959 (widowed mother tried to make resistant boy effeminate, made him wear sunbonnets; accompanied him to college).

Weems, John Edward, *Race for the pole*, Holt, 1960.

Peary, Robert Edwin, *Letters to mother*, Channel, 1959.

PERON, EVA T., dictator's wife, b Los Toldas, Argentina, f business, g——.

Flores, María, *The woman with the whip*, Doubleday, 1952 (a rejected girl).

Perón, Eva, *My mission in life*, Vantage, 1953.

PICASSO, PABLO, painter, sculptor, b Malaga, Spain, f art teacher, g——.

Penrose, Roland, *Picasso: his life and work*, Harper, 1959.

Raynal, Maurice, *Picasso: biographical and critical studies*, Skira, 1953.

*Sabartés, Jaime, *Picasso: an intimate portrait*, Prentice-Hall, 1948.

PIRE, FATHER DOMINIQUE, humanitarian, b Dinant, Belgium, f small-town official, c+.
Vehenne, Hughes, *Story of Father Dominique Piré*, Dutton, 1961.

PIUS XII, POPE (EUGENIO PACELLI), b Rome, f specialist in church law, s & S.
Doyle, Charles H., *Life of Pope Pius XII*, Didier, 1945.
Halecki, Oscar, *Eugenio Pacelli, pope of peace*, Creative Age, 1951 (scholarly, supportive family).
Hatch, Alden, and Seamus Walshe, *Crown of glory*, Hawthorne, 1957.
Smit, Jan Olav, *Angelic shepherd*, Dodd, Mead, 1950.

POWYS, JOHN COWPER, writer, poet, critic, b Shirley, Derbyshire, England, f clergyman, s—.
Coombes, H., *T. F. Powys*, Barrie & Coombes, 1960 (concise and reasoned account of a tense household which produced four novelists).
*Powys, John Cowper, *Autobiography*, New Directions, 1960.
Powys, Littleton, *Still the joy of it*, Macdonald, 1956.

PROKOFIEV, SERGEI, composer, b Sontzovka, Exaterinoslav, Russia, f agronomist, estate manager, S.
Nestyev, Israel V., *Prokofiev*, Stanford U.P., 1960 (mother left home with boy to seek training; parents separated).

PROUST, MARCEL, novelist, b Paris, f professor of medicine, s.
March, Harold, *The two worlds of Marcel Proust*, U. Penn., 1948.
Mauroise, André, *Proust: portrait of a genius*, Harper, 1950.
*Painter, George D., *Proust, the early years*, Little, Brown, 1959 (asthmatic boy, smothering mother, rejecting father).

PUCCINI, GIACOMO, operatic composer, b Lucca, Italy, f musician, village organist as were paternal ancestors for 4 generations, g & S.
Carner, Mosco, *Puccini: a critical biography*, Knopf, 1958.
Marek, George R., *Puccini: a biography*, Simon & Schuster, 1951.
Specht, Ricard, *Giacomo Puccini: the man, his life, his work*, Knopf, 1933.

PYLE, ERNIE, newspaperman, b farm near Dana, Indiana, f farmer, c—.
Miller, Lee Graham, *An Ernie Pyle album*, Sloan, 1946.
———, *Story of Ernie Pyle*, Viking, 1950 (supportive home—good peer relationships—mediocre school record).

QUEZON, MANUEL, politician, b Baler, Philippines, f schoolteacher, c+.
Quirino, Carlos, *Quezon, man of destiny*, McCullough, 1935.
Quezon, Manuel, *Good fight*, Appleton-Century, 1946.

QUILLER-COUCH, ARTHUR T., man of letters, b Polperro, Cornwall, f physician, c+.
Brittain, Fred, *Arthur Quiller-Couch*, Macmillan, 1948.
*Quiller-Couch, Arthur T., *Memories and opinions*, Macmillan, 1945 (opinionative, affectionate family).

RACHMANINOFF, SERGEI, pianist, composer, b Novgorod, Russia, f estate manager (unsuccessful), tutored & S (conservatory at 9).
Bertensson, Sergei, and Leyda Jay, *Sergei Rachmaninoff*, N.Y. Univ., 1956.
Seroff, Victor, *Rachmaninoff*, Simon & Schuster, 1950.

RAMA RAU, SANTHA, writer, b Madras, India, f diplomat, c+.
*Rama Rau, *Remember the house*, Harper, 1956 (a girl reared in many countries; participant in world cultures, an intellectual mother with organizing abilities).
———, *Gifts of passage*, Harper, 1961.

RASPUTIN, GRIGORI E., politician, b Pokrovskoye, Siberia, f farmer, g—.
Liepman, Heinz, *Rasputin—a new judgment*, Muller, 1959.
Rasputin, Maria, *My father*, Cassell, 1934.

RAVEL, MAURICE, composer, b Ciboure, France, f mining engineer, S.
Myers, Rollo H., *Ravel: life and works*, Yoseloff, 1960.
Seroff, Victor I., *Maurice Ravel*, Holt, 1953.

REGLER, GUSTAV, author, b Merzig, Germany, f bookseller, c+.
*Regler, Gustav, *The owl of Minerva*, Straus & Cudahy, 1960 (a dreaming, opinionative father; gentle, fearful mother).

REUTHER, WALTER, labor leader, b Wheeling, W.Va., f factory worker. union official, c—.
Dayton, Eldorous L., *Walter Reuther: the autocrat of the bargaining table*, Devin-Adair, 1958.
Howe, Irving, and B. J. Widick, *The UAW and Walter Reuther*, Random House, 1949.

RHEE, SYNGMAN, politician, b Nung-an-go, Korea, f inherited wealth, c+.
Oliver, Robert T., *Syngman Rhee, the man behind the myth*, Dodd, Mead, 1954 (sickly child of elderly smothering mother and rejecting father).

RHODES, CECIL, administrator, financier, b Bishop Stortford, England, f curate, s—.
Gross, Felix, *Rhodes of Africa*, Cassell, 1956 (poor sibling relationships—irritable, eccentric father).
Maurois, André, *Cecil Rhodes*, Collins, 1953.
Millin, Sarah G., *Cecil Rhodes*, Harper, 1933.

RIBBENTROP, JOACHIM von, diplomat, b Wessel-am-Rhine, f business, s & S.
Schwarz, Paul, *This man Ribbentrop*, Messner, 1943.

RILKE, RAINER MARIA, poet, writer, b Prague, f railway official, c—.
Peters, H. Frederick, *Rainer Maria Rilke: masks and the man*, U.Wash., 1960.
Rilke, Rainer Maria, *Letters*, Norton, 1945.
———, *Selected letters*, Macmillan, 1946.

RIVERA, DIEGO, painter, b Guanajuato, Mexico, f town official, public health officer, s & S.
*March, Gladys (ed.), *My art, my life: an autobiography*, Citadel, 1960.
Wolfe, Bertram D., *Diego Rivera: his life and times*, Knopf, 1939.

ROBINSON, EDWIN ARLINGTON, poet, b Head Tide, Maine, f ship's carpenter, storekeeper, c—.
Hagedorn, Hermann, *Edwin Arlington Robinson*, Macmillan, 1938.
Neff, Emery E., *Edwin Arlington Robinson*, Sloane, 1948.

ROBINSON, JACKIE, baseball player, b Cairo, Ga., f farmer, city laborer, m domestic worker, c.
*Robinson, Jackie, *Jackie Robinson: my own story*, Greenberg, 1948.
Rowan, Carl Thomas, *Wait till next year*, Random House, 1960.

ROCKEFELLER, JOHN D., oil magnate, b Richford, N.Y., f cancer-cure salesman, s & S.

ROCKEFELLER, JOHN D., JR., philanthropist, b Cleveland, Ohio, f financier, c.

ROCKEFELLER, NELSON, politician, b Bar Harbor, Me., f philanthropist, c.
*Chase, Mary Ellen, *Abby Aldrich Rockefeller*, Macmillan, 1950 (child-centered home well described).
Flynn, John Thomas, *God's gold: the story of Rockefeller and his times*, Harcourt, Brace, 1932.
Fosdick, Raymond, *John D. Rockefeller, Jr.*, Harper, 1956.
*Manchester, William, *A Rockefeller family portrait*, Little, Brown, 1959 (author describes a physical vitality persisting through three generations).
Morris, Joe Alex, *Those Rockefeller brothers: an informal biography of five extraordinary young men*, Harper, 1953.
Morris, Joe Alex, *Nelson Rockefeller: a biography*, Harper, 1960.
Nevins, Allan, *Study in power*, Scribner's, 1953.
Poling, James, *The Rockefeller record*, Crowell, 1960.

RODIN, AUGUSTE, sculptor, b Paris, f police inspector, s—.
Cladel, Judith, *Rodin: the man and his art*, Century, 1917.
Lawton, Frederick, *The life and work of Auguste Rodin*, Unwin, 1906.
Ludovici, Anthony, *Personal reminiscences of Auguste Rodin*, Lippincott, 1926.

ROGERS, WILL, actor, humorist, b Oologah, Indian Territory, s—.
Croy, Homer, *Our Will Rogers*, Duell, Sloan & Pearce, 1953 (incorrigible son of well-to-do widower).
Rogers, Will, *Autobiography*, Houghton Mifflin, 1949.

ROLLAND, ROMAIN, man of letters, lecturer, b Clamecy, France, f notary, c+.

Rolland, Romain, *Journey within*, Philosophical Library, 1947 (a most over-possessive mother—disliked father).

Zweig, Stefan, *Romain Rolland: the man and his work*, Seltzer, 1921.

ROMULO, CARLOS, statesman, author, b Camiling, Philippines, f mayor, governor, c+.

Romulo, Carlos, *I saw the fall of the Philippines*, Doubleday, 1942.

———, *I walked with heroes*, Holt, 1961.

Spencer, Cornelia, *Romulo, voice of freedom*, Day, 1953.

ROOSEVELT, ELEANOR, lecturer, writer, leader in social and international affairs, b New York City, f businessman, s.

ROOSEVELT, FRANKLIN D., politician, b Hyde Park, N.Y., f financier (often unsuccessful), c+.

Burns, James M., *The lion and the fox*, Harcourt, Brace, 1956.

Gunther, John, *Roosevelt in retrospect: a profile in history*, Harper, 1950.

*Roosevelt, Eleanor, *This is my story*, Harper, 1937.

———, *This I remember*, Harper, 1949.

*Roosevelt, James, *Affectionally, F.D.R.: a son's story of a lonely man*, Harcourt, Brace, 1959.

Schriftgiesser, Karl, *The amazing Roosevelt family*, Funk, 1942.

Steinberg, Alfred, *Mrs. R.: the life of Eleanor Roosevelt*, Putnam, 1958.

ROOSEVELT, THEODORE, politician, b New York City, f glass importer, volunteer social worker, c.

*Putnam, Carleton, *Theodore Roosevelt, vol. 1: the formative years*, Scribner's, 1958.

Riis, Jacob A., *Theodore Roosevelt, the citizen*, Outlook, 1904.

Robinson, Corinne Roosevelt, *My brother, Theodore Roosevelt*, Scribner's, 1921.

Roosevelt, Theodore, *Theodore Roosevelt: an autobiography*, Macmillan, 1913.

RUSSELL, BERTRAND, mathematician, philosopher, social reformer, b Trelleck, England, f politician, inherited wealth, c+.

Leggett, H. W., *Bertrand Russell, O.M.*, Philosophical Library, 1950.

*Wood, Alan, *Bertrand Russell, the passionate skeptic*, Simon & Schuster, 1957.

RUTHERFORD, ERNEST, physicist, b Nelson, New Zealand, f farmer, c+.

Rowland, John, *Ernest Rutherford, atom pioneer*, Philosophical Library, 1957.

SALAZAR, ANTONIO DE OLIVEIRA, politician, b Santo Comba-Dao, Portugal, f bailiff, innkeeper, c+.

Ferro, Antonio, *Salazar: Portugal and her leader*, Faber & Faber, 1939.

Garnier, Christine, *Salazar: an intimate portrait*, Farrar, Straus, 1954.

SANDBURG, CARL, author, b Galesburg, Ill., f railroad laborer, c.
Detzer, Karl W., *Carl Sandburg: a study in personality and background*, Harcourt, Brace, 1941.
*Sandburg, Carl, *Always the young strangers*, Harcourt, Brace, 1953.
————, *Prairie-town boy*, Harcourt, Brace, 1955.

SANGER, MARGARET, social reformer, b Corning, N.Y., f stonecutter, s & S.
Lader, Lawrence, *Margaret Sanger story*, Doubleday, 1955.
Sanger, Margaret, *Margaret Sanger: an autobiography*, Norton, 1938.

SANTAYANA, GEORGE, philosopher, poet, b Madrid, f lawyer, c+.
Howgate, George W., *George Santayana*, Oxford, 1938 (a rejected boy).
Santayana, George, *Persons and places: the background of my life*, Scribner's, 1944.

SAROYAN, WILLIAM, fiction writer, playwright, b Fresno, Calif., f Protestant minister, grape grower, m day worker as widow, s—.
Saroyan, William, *The twin adventures*, Harcourt, Brace, 1950.
*————, *The bicycle rider in Beverly Hills*, Scribner's, 1952 (source for description of school rejection and of feelings of rejection because of nationality).

SCHNABEL, ARTUR, pianist, b Lipnick, Austria, f wool merchant, g & S.
Saerchinger, César, *Artur Schnabel*, Dodd, Mead, 1957.

SCHREINER, OLIVE, writer, b Wittebergen Mission Station, Basutoland, South Africa, f Methodist missionary, tutored.
Cronwright-Schreiner, S. C. (ed.), *Letters of Olive Schreiner*, Little, Brown, 1924.
Gregg, Lyndall, *Memories of Olive Schreiner*, Chambers, 1957.
Hobman, Daisy L., *Olive Schreiner: her friends and times*, Watts, 1955 (failure-prone father who loved his wife and children with infinite tenderness).

SCHUMANN-HEINK, ERNESTINE, operatic contralto, b Lieberri, Bohemia, f Austrian army officer, g.
Lawton, Mary (ed.), *Schumann-Heink, the last of the Titans*, Macmillan, 1928.

SCHWEITZER, ALBERT, philosopher, physician, musician, b Kayersburg, Alsace, f Lutheran minister, c+.
Cousins, Norman, *Dr. Schweitzer of Lambaréné*, Harper, 1960.
Langley, Nina, *Dr. Schweitzer, O.M.*, Harrap, 1956.
Payne, Pierre, *Three worlds of Albert Schweitzer*, Nelson, 1957.
Schweitzer, Albert, *Out of my life and thought*, Holt, 1933.
*————, *Memoirs of childhood and youth*, Macmillan, 1950.

SHAW, GEORGE BERNARD, playwright, novelist, critic, b Dublin, f manufacturer (unsuccessful), m music teacher, s.

Harris, Frank, *Bernard Shaw*, Simon & Schuster, 1931.
Irvine, William, *The Universe of G.B.S.*, Whittlesey House, 1949.
Pearson, Hesketh, *G.B.S.: a full length portrait*, Harper, 1942.

SHOSTAKOVICH, DMITRI, composer, b St. Petersburg, f worked in patent office, m as widow worked in patent office, s— & S.
Martynov, Ivan I., *Dmitri Shostakovich: the man and his work*, Philosophical Library, 1947.
*Seroff, Victor I., *Dmitri Shostakovich: the life and background of a Soviet composer*, Knopf, 1943 (written in collaboration with sister of subject's mother; an account of a smothering and dominating mother who could not be happy when her son persisted in his attempts to free himself from her).

SIBELIUS, JEAN, composer, b Hameenlinna, Finland, f physician, s & S.
Ekman, Karl, *Jean Sibelius: his life and personality*, Knopf, 1938.
*Johnson, Harold E., *Jean Sibelius*, Knopf, 1959 (describes Sibelius as a naïve, shy, dreaming boy with keen perceptions of both eye and ear. As a student he disliked all forms of discipline. Supportive home).
Ringbom, Nils E., *Jean Sibelius: a master and his work*, U.Okla., 1954.

SITWELL, EDITH, poet, critic, novelist, b Scarborough, England, f inherited income, unsuccessful (at times) financier, tutored.

SITWELL, OSBERT, poet, playwright, novelist, b Scarborough, England, f inherited wealth, S.

SITWELL, SACHEVERELL, poet, critic, b Scarborough, England, f inherited income, c.
*Sitwell, Osbert, *Scarlet tree*, Little, Brown, 1946 (cutting commentary on schools; a family album of uncommon interest, skillfully told).
———, *Great morning!*, Little, Brown, 1947.
*———, *Left hand, right hand!*, Little, Brown, 1944 (a delightful, eccentric, but very dominating father—three talented, highly individual youngsters).
———, *Laughter in the next room*, Little, Brown, 1948.
———, *Noble essences: a book of characters*, Little, Brown, 1950.

SMITH, ALFRED E., politician, b New York City, f trucker, g—.
Handlin, Oscar, *Al Smith and his America*, Little, Brown, 1958.
Warner, Emily (Smith), *Happy Warrior: a biography of my father, Alfred E. Smith*, Doubleday, 1956.

SMITH, LILLIAN, writer, b Jasper, Fla., f manufacturer, c— & S.
*Smith, Lillian, *Killers of the dream*, Norton, 1949.
*———, *The journey*, World, 1954.

SMUTS, JAN CHRISTIAAN, soldier, politician, b Riebeck West, South Africa, f prosperous farmer, legislator, c.

Kraus, René, *Old master*, Dutton, 1944.

Millin, Sarah G., *General Smuts*, Little, Brown, 1936.

SOUSA, JOHN PHILIP, bandleader, composer, b Washington, D.C., f band-master, cabinetmaker, g— & S.

Berger, Kenneth W., *The march king and his band*, Exposition, 1957.

Lingg, Ann M., *John Philip Sousa*, Holt, 1954.

SPENDER, STEPHEN, poet, critic, b London, f journalist, novelist, c—.

*Spender, Stephen, *World within world*, Harcourt, Brace, 1951.

STALIN, JOSEPH, politician, b near Tiflis, Georgia, U.S.S.R., f shoe-maker, s—.

Fischer, Louis, *Life and death of Stalin*, Harper, 1952.

Svanidze, Budu, *My uncle, Joseph Stalin*, Putnam, 1953.

STANISLAVSKI, (born Constantine Alexeev), actor, producer, b Moscow, f inherited wealth, mill owner, tutored.

Gorchakov, Nikolai M., *Stanislavski directs*, Funk, 1954.

Stanislavski, Constantin, *My life in art*, Little, Brown, 1924.

STANLEY, HENRY MORTON, explorer, b near Denbigh, Wales, adopted, g—.

Anstruther, Ian, *I presume: Stanley's triumph and disaster*, Bles, 1956.

Stanley, Dorothy (ed.), *The autobiography of Sir Henry Morton Stanley*, Houghton Mifflin, 1909.

STEFANSSON, VILHJALMUR, arctic explorer, b Arnes, Manitoba, Canada, f farmer, c+.

Hanson, Earl P., *Stefansson, prophet of the North*, Harper, 1941.

STEFFENS, LINCOLN, journalist, f prosperous merchant, c+.

*Steffens, Lincoln, *Autobiography of Lincoln Steffens*, Harcourt, Brace, 1931 (congenial parents; supporting, permissive, stimulating home).

———, *The letters of Lincoln Steffens*, Harcourt, Brace, 1938.

STEIN, GERTRUDE, writer, b Allegheny Pa., f vice-president streetcar co. (unsuccessful), c—.

Brinnin, John M., *The third rose*, Little, Brown, 1959.

Rogers, William G., *When this you see, remember me: Gertrude Stein in person*, Rinehart, 1948.

Sprigge, Elizabeth, *Gertrude Stein: her life and work*, Harper, 1957.

Stein, Gertrude, *Everybody's autobiography*, Random House, 1937.

STEINMETZ, CHARLES P., electrical engineer, b Breslau, Germany, f engi-neer, c.

Hammond, John W., *Charles Proteus Steinmetz: a biography*, Century, 1924.

Lavine, Sigmund A., *Steinmetz, maker of lightning*, Dodd, Mead, 1955.

Leonard, J. N., *Loki: the life of Charles Proteus Steinmetz*, Doubleday, 1929.

STEVENSON, ADLAI E., politician, b Los Angeles, f farm manager, c.
Busch, Noel F., *Adlai E. Stevenson of Illinois*, Farrar, Straus, 1952.
Davis, Kenneth S., *Prophet in his own country*, Doubleday, 1957.
Ives, Elizabeth, *My brother Adlai*, Morrow, 1956.
Martin, John B., *Adlai Stevenson*, Harper, 1952.

STRAVINSKY, IGOR, composer, b Oranienbaum, Russia, f singer, c & S.
Stravinsky, Igor, *Stravinsky: an autobiography*, Simon & Schuster, 1936.
Strobel, Heinrich, *Stravinsky: a classic humanist*, Merlin, 1955.
Tansman, Alexander, *Igor Stravinksy: the man and his music*, Putnam, 1949.

STUART, JESSE, writer, b Cedar Riffles, Ky., f farmer, c+.
Stuart, Jesse, *Beyond dark hills: a personal story*, Dutton, 1938.
———, *Thread that runs so true*, Scribner's, 1949.
*———, *God's oddling: story of Mick Stuart, my father*, McGraw-Hill,
1960 (an energetic father who wanted schooling for his children).

SULLIVAN, ARTHUR S., composer, b London, f army bandmaster, S.
Darlington, William A., *The world of Gilbert and Sullivan*, Crowell, 1950.
Power-Waters, Alma, *The melody maker*, Dutton, 1959 (school truant—
home tutored).
Sullivan, Herbert, *Sir Arthur Sullivan: his life, letters and diaries*, Doran,
1927 (parents were in love to the end of their days; encouraged son's
early evidenced talent).

SUN YAT-SEN, politician, b Chou-Hung, Macao, f rice farmer, c+.
Chen, Stephen, *Sun Yat-sen: a portrait*, Day, 1946.
Hahn, Emily, *The Soong Sisters*, Doubleday, 1941.

TAFT, ROBERT A., politician, b Cincinnati, Ohio, f politician, c+.
Harnsberger, Charles T., *A man of courage: Robert A. Taft*, Wilcox &
Follett, 1952.
Taft, Helen, *Recollections of full years*, Dodd, Mead, 1914.
White, William S., *The Taft story*, Harper, 1954.

TAGORE, RABINDRANATH, poet, artist, composer, b Calcutta, India, f
wealthy merchant, c—.
Chakravarty, Amiya (ed.), *A Tagore reader*, Macmillan, 1961.
Tagore, Rabindranath, *My reminiscences*, Macmillan, 1917.
Thompson, Edward John, *Rabindranath Tagore: poet and dramatist*, (2nd
edition), Oxford, 1948.

THOMAS, DYLAN, poet, b Carmarthenshire, Wales, f teacher, s.
Brinnin, John M., *Dylan Thomas in America*, Little, Brown, 1955.
Thomas, Caitlin, *Leftover life to kill*, Little, Brown, 1957.

TITO (JOSEPH BROZ), politician, b Kumrovec, Croatia, f horsetrader, s—.
Dedijer, Vladimir, *Tito*, Simon & Schuster, 1952.
Maclean, Fitzroy, *The heretic: the life and times of Joseph Broz-Tito*,
Harper, 1957.

TOLSTOI, LEO N., novelist, philosopher, b Yasnaya Polyana, Russia, f estate
    manager, c—.
Dole, Nathan Haskell, *The life of Count Tolstoi*, Crowell, 1911.
Simmons, Ernest J., *Leo Tolstoy*, Little, Brown, 1946.
*Tolstoi, Alexandra, *Tolstoy: a life of my father*, Harper, 1953.
Tolstoi, Count Ilya, *Reminiscences of Tolstoy*, Century, 1914.

TOSCANINI, ARTURO, conductor, b Oleorrente, Italy, f tailor, S.
Chotzinoff, Samuel, *Toscanini: an intimate portrait*, Knopf, 1956.
Ewen, David, *Story of Arturo Toscanini*, Holt, 1951.
Haggin, Bernard H., *Conversations with Toscanini*, Doubleday, 1959.
Taubman, Hyman H., *The maestro*, Simon & Schuster, 1951.

TOULOUSE-LAUTREC, HENRI, painter, b Albi, France, f in-
    herited wealth, c.
Gauzi, François, *My friend: Toulouse-Lautrec*, Spearman, 1957.
Hanson, Lawrence, *Tragic life of Toulouse-Lautrec*, Random House, 1956.
Lassaigne, Jacques, *Lautrec*, Skira, 1953.
Perruchot, Henri, *Toulouse-Lautrec*, World, 1960.

TROTSKY, LEON, Communist leader, b Yanovka, Russia, f well-to-do
    farmer, c.
*Trotsky, Leon, *My life: an attempt at an autobiography*, Scribner's, 1930.
———, *Diary in exile*, Harvard U.P., 1958.

TRUJILLO MOLINA, RAFAEL, army officer, politician, b San Cristobal,
    Dominican Republic, f laborer, g—.
Besault, Laurence de, *President Trujillo: his work and the Dominican Re-
    public*, Washington, 1936 (neglected boy).
Hicks, Albert C., *Blood in the streets: the life and rule of Trujillo*, Creative
    Age, 1946.
Ornes, Germán E., *Trujillo: little Caesar of the Caribbean*, Nelson, 1958.

TRUMAN, HARRY, politician, b Lamar, Mo., f farmer, s.
Daniels, Jonathan, *The Man of Independence*, Lippincott, 1950.
Hillman, William, *Mr. President*, Farrar, Straus, 1952 (early reader—read
    Bible through twice before he was twelve—an upwardly mobile home
    —parents were community leaders—father had strong physical drive,
    worked from daylight to dark).
McNaughton, Frank, and Walter Hehmeyer, *This man Truman*, McGraw-
    Hill, 1945.

UNDSET, SIGRID, novelist, b Kalundborg, Denmark, f archaeologist, s.
Larsen, H. A., "Sigrid Undset," *Am.-Scandinavian Review*, 1929.
Winsnes, Andreas H., *Sigrid Undset*, Sheed & Ward, 1953.

VAN PAASSEN, PIERRE, journalist, author, b Gorcum, Holland, f business,
    c+.

*Van Paassen, Pierre, *Days of our years*, Hillman-Curl, 1939.
———, *Visions rise and change*, Dial, 1955.

VERNE, JULES, writer, b Nantes, France, f lawyer, c+.
Allotte de la Fuye, M., *Jules Verne*, Macmillan, 1941.
Waltz, George H., *Jules Verne: the biography of an imagination*, Holt, 1943.

WAKSMAN, SELMAN, bacteriologist, b Novaia-Priluka, Ukraine, f carpenter, landlord, m storekeeper, c+.
*Waksman, Selman, *My life with the microbes*, Simon & Schuster, 1954.

WALLACE, HENRY A., agriculturalist, politician, b Adair County, Iowa, f editor, *Wallace's Farm Journal*, Sec'y of Agric., c.
Kingdon, Frank, *An uncommon man: Henry Wallace and 60 million jobs*, Readers Press, 1945.
Lord, Russell, *The Wallaces of Iowa*, Houghton Mifflin, 1947.
Macdonald, Dwight, *Henry Wallace: the man and the myth*, Vanguard, 1948.

WALPOLE, HUGH, novelist, b Auckland, New Zealand, f Episcopal minister, c.
Hart-Davis, Rupert, *Hugh Walpole*, Macmillan, 1952.
Walpole, Hugh, *Roman fountain*, Doubleday, 1940.

WASHINGTON, BOOKER T., educator, b Franklin County, Va., f unknown, m did housework, c.
Mathews, Basil J., *Booker T. Washington: educator and interracial interpreter*, Harvard U.P., 1948.
Spencer, Samuel R., *Booker T. Washington and the Negro's place in American life*, Little, Brown, 1955.
Washington, Booker T., *Up from slavery*, Page, 1909.

WEBB, BEATRICE, writer, b Standish House, Gloucester, England, f wealthy manufacturer (prone to reverses), s— & tutored.
Cole, Margaret I., *Beatrice Webb*, Longmans, 1945.
Webb, Beatrice, *Our partnership*, Longmans, 1948.

WELLS, H. G., writer, b Bromley, Kent, f gardner, shopkeeper, m housekeeper, c+.
Brome, Vincent, *H. G. Wells: a biography*, Longmans, 1951.
Vallentin, Antonina, *H. G. Wells: prophet of our day*, Day, 1950.
*Wells, H. G., *Experiments in autobiography: discoveries and conclusions of a very ordinary brain*, Macmillan, 1934.

WEIZMANN, CHAIM, chemist, politician, b Motol, Russia, f lumber business (dramatic ups and downs), c+.
Berlin, Isaiah, *Chaim Weizmann*, Farrar, Straus, 1958.
Weizmann, Chaim, *Trial and error: an autobiography*, Harper, 1949.

WHARTON, EDITH NEWBOLD, novelist, b New York City, f engineer, also inherited wealth, tutored at home.
Lubbock, Percy, *Portrait of Edith Wharton*, Appleton-Century, 1947.
Wharton, Edith, *A backward glance*, Appleton-Century, 1934.

WHISTLER, JAMES A. McNEILL, painter, etcher, b Lowell, Mass., f engineer (failure-prone, personality problems), s & M (expelled).
Mumford, Elizabeth, *Whistler's mother*, Little, Brown, 1939 ("Jamie" was perpetually tardy, unable to submit to routine, as child or as adult).
Parry, Albert, *Whistler's father*, Bobbs-Merrill, 1939 (mother described as a woman who was obnoxious in her dominating).
Pearson, Hesketh, *The man Whistler*, Harper, 1952.

WHITE, WALTER FRANCIS, author, sec'y NAACP, b Atlanta, Ga., f postman, c.
Cannon, Poppy, *Gentle knight: my husband, Walter White*, Rinehart, 1956.
White, Walter Francis, *Man called White: the autobiography of Walter White*, Viking, 1948 (race riot turned boy's mind to becoming champion of the Negro).

WHITE, WILLIAM ALLEN, editor, writer, b Emporia, Kan., f doctor (without degree), hotelkeeper, c—.
Hinshaw, David, *A man from Kansas: the story of William Allen White*, Putnam, 1945.
*White, William Allen, *Autobiography of William Allen White*, Macmillan, 1946.

WIENER, NORBERT, mathematician, writer, b Columbia, Mo., f professor, c+.
*Wiener, Norbert, *Ex-prodigy: my childhood and youth*, Simon & Schuster, 1953 (parents differed in sense of values).
———, *I am a mathematician: the later life of a prodigy*, Doubleday, 1956.

WILDE, OSCAR, poet, wit, dramatist, b Dublin, f physician, c+.
Byrne, Patrick, *The Wildes of Merrion Square*, Staples Press, 1953.
Harris, Frank, *Oscar Wilde*, Michigan State U.P., 1959.
Holland, Vyvyan, *Son of Oscar Wilde*, Dutton, 1954.
Pearson, Hesketh, *Oscar Wilde: his life and wit*, Harper, 1946.

WILLIAMS, WILLIAM CARLOS, physician, writer, b Rutherford, N.J., f engineer, c+.
Williams, William Carlos, *Yes, Mrs. Williams: a personal record of my mother*, McDowell, Obolensky, 1959.
*———, *The autobiography of William Carlos Williams*, Random House, 1951 (love for learning—unconventional home).

WILLKIE, WENDELL, politician, b Elwood, Ind., f lawyer, m lawyer, c+.
Barnes, Joseph, *Willkie*, Simon & Schuster, 1952.

Dillon, Mary, *Wendell Willkie*, Lippincott, 1952.
Hatch, Alden, *Young Willkie*, Harcourt, Brace, 1944.

WILSON, WOODROW, professor, politician, b Staunton, Va., f minister, c+.
Baker, Ray Stannard, *Woodrow Wilson: life and letters*, Doubleday, 1927.
Day, Donald (ed.), *Woodrow Wilson's own story*, Little, Brown, 1952.
McAdoo, Eleanor Wilson, *The Woodrow Wilsons*, Macmillan, 1937.

WOLFE, THOMAS, writer, b Asheville, N.C., f stonecutter, c+.
Holman, Clarence Hugh, *Thomas Wolfe*, U.Minn., 1960 (an all-around student).
Nowell, Elizabeth, *Thomas Wolfe: a biography*, Doubleday, 1960.
Wheaton, Mabel Wolfe, and LeGette Blythe, *Thomas Wolfe and his family*, Doubleday, 1961 (father described as an irritable man with a gift for narrative, a man who loved his children, liked to set an extravagant table—resented wife's real estate deals; mother was a driving, "needling" woman).

WOOLF, VIRGINIA, writer, b London, f editor of *Dictionary of National Biographys*, home-tutored.
Woolf, Leonard, (ed.), *A writer's diary*, Harcourt, Brace, 1954.
*Pippett, Aileen, *The moth and the star*, Little, Brown, 1955 (delicate, home-tutored girl).

WOOLLCOTT, ALEXANDER, journalist, writer, b The Phalanx, N.J., f unsuccessful expatriated lawyer, c.
Adams, Samuel Hopkins, *A. Woollcott: his life and his world*, Reynal & Hitchcock, 1945.
Kaufman, Beatrice, and Joseph Hennessey, (eds.), *The letters of Alexander Woollcott*, Viking, 1944.

WRIGHT, FRANK LLOYD, architect, b Richland Center, Wis., f minister, m teacher, c—.
*Wright, Frank Lloyd, *An autobiography*, Duell, Sloan & Pearce, 1943.
———, *A testament*, Horizon, 1957.
Wright, John Lloyd, *My father who is on earth*, Putnam, 1946.
Wright, Olgivanna Lloyd, *Our house*, Horizon, 1959.

WRIGHT, ORVILLE, aviation pioneer, b Dayton, Ohio, f minister, s—.

WRIGHT, WILBUR, aviation pioneer, b Millville, Ind., f minister, s—.
Kelly, Fred C., *The Wright brothers*, Harcourt, Brace, 1943.
Wright, Wilbur and Orville, *Miracle at Kitty Hawk: the letters of Wilbur and Orville Wright*, Farrar, Straus, 1951.

WRIGHT, RICHARD, writer, b near Natchez, Miss., f mill worker, s—.
Wright, Richard, *Black Boy*, Harper, 1945 (strong opinions about religion and learning in the family).
———, *Black power*, Harper, 1954.

YEATS, WILLIAM BUTLER, poet, dramatist, b near Dublin, f artist, s & S.
Ellmann, Richard, *Yeats—the man and the masks*, Macmillan, 1948.
Yeats, William Butler, *Autobiographies: Reveries over childhood and youth*,
   Macmillan, 1927 (his aunts and uncles thought him dull, his teachers
   found him slow and annoying, only his father enjoyed him).
———, *J. B. Yeats: letters to his son*, Dutton, 1946.

ZINSSER, HANS, bacteriologist, b New York City, f chemist, c—.
Wagenknecht, Charles, (ed.), *When I was a child*, Dutton, 1946.
*Zinsser, Hans, *As I remember him*, Little, Brown, 1940.

ZOLA, EMILE, novelist, b Paris, f engineer, s.
Hemmings, Frederick W., *Emile Zola*, Clarendon Press, 1953.

ZWEIG, STEFAN, writer, b Vienna, f businessman (successful), c+.
Zweig, Friderike M. W., *Stefan Zweig*, Crowell, 1946.
Zweig, Stefan, *World of yesterday*, Viking, 1943.

COLLECTIVE BIOGRAPHIES

Bolton, Sarah K., *Famous American authors*, Crowell, 1954.

Bradford, Gamaliel, *American portraits*, Houghton Mifflin, 1922.

Churchill, Winston, *Great contemporaries*, Putnam, 1937.

Cooper, A. C., and Charles A. Palmer, *Twenty modern Americans*, Harcourt, Brace, 1954.

Eastman, Max, *Great companions*, Farrar, Straus, 1959.

Huff, Warren, and Edna L. W. Huff, *Famous Americans*, Charles Webb, 1941.

Kornitzer, Bela, *Famous fathers and sons*, Hermitage, 1952.

Kunitz, Stanley J., *Twentieth century authors*, H. W. Wilson, 1942.

Law, Frederick H., *Modern great Americans*, Century, 1926.

Ludwig, Emil, *Three portraits: Hitler, Mussolini, Stalin*, Alliance, 1940.

Madison, Charles A., *Critics and crusaders: a century of American protest*, Holt, 1947.

Riedman, Sarah R., *Men and women behind the atom*, Abelard-Schuman, 1958.

Untermeyer, Louis, *Makers of the modern world*, Simon & Schuster, 1955.

Wolfe, Bertram D., *Three who made a revolution*, Dial, 1948.

Wilson, H. W. (publisher), *Current Biography*, 1940–1961.

PROFESSIONAL REFERENCES CITED

Anderson, Harold H., (ed.), *Creativity and its cultivation*, Harper, 1959.

Anderson, Kenneth E., (ed.), *Research on the academically talented student*, National Education Assoc., 1961.

Brandewein, P. F., *The gifted student as future scientist*, Harcourt, Brace, 1955.

Getzels, Jacob W., and Phillip W. Jackson, "Family environment and cognitive style: a study of the sources of highly intelligent and creative adolescents," *American Sociological Review*, v. 26, No. 2, 1961.

Ginsberg, Eli, *The nation's children*, Teachers Coll., Columbia U., 1961.

Hollingworth, Leta S., *Children above 180 I.Q.*, World Book Co., 1942.

Knapp, R. H., and H. B. Goodrich, *Origins of American scientists*, U.Chicago P., 1952.

Levy, David M., *Maternal overprotection*, Columbia U.P., 1945.

McClelland, David C., Alfred L. Baldwin, Urie Bronfenbrenner, and Fred L. Strodtbeck, *Talent and Society*, Van Nostrand, 1958.

MacKinnon, Donald W., "Genvs Architectvs: creator varietas Americanvs," *J. Amer. Institute Architects*, Sept. 1960.

Murphy, Gardner, *Human potentialities*, Basic Books, 1958.

Roe, Anne, *Making of a scientist*, Dodd, Mead, 1953.

Rubin, Louis J., (ed.), *Nurturing classroom creativity*, Ventura County (Calif.) Secondary Schools, 1960.

Taylor, Calvin W., (ed.), *Research conference on the identification of creative scientific talent*, U. Utah P., 1959.

Terman, Lewis M., and C. C. Miles, *Sex and personality*, McGraw-Hill, 1936.

Terman, Lewis M., and Melita H. Oden, *The gifted group at mid-life*, Stanford U.P., 1959.

Torrance, E. Paul, *Status of knowledge concerning education and creative scientific talent*, Bureau of Educational Research, U.Minn., June 1961.

Wolfle, Dael, *America's resources of specialized talent*, Harper, 1954.

Witty, Paul, *One hundred gifted children*, Kansas U. Publications, 1930.

Index

355